Designing Wildlife Habitats

Dumbarton Oaks Colloquium on the History of Landscape Architecture XXXIV

Designing Wildlife Habitats

JOHN BEARDSLEY

Editor

DUMBARTON OAKS RESEARCH LIBRARY AND COLLECTION

WASHINGTON, D.C.

Library of Congress Cataloging-in-Publication Data

Dumbarton Oaks Colloquium on the History of Landscape Architecture (34th: 2010)
Designing wildlife habitats / John Beardsley, editor.
    p. cm.
Includes bibliographical references and index.
ISBN 978-0-88402-385-2 (pbk. : alk. paper)
1. Habitat (Ecology)—Congresses. 2. Biodiversity—Congresses.
3. Ecosystem health—Congresses. I. Beardsley, John. II. Title.
QH540.D86 2013
577—dc23

2012022087

General editor: John Beardsley
Art director: Kathleen Sparkes
Design and composition: Melissa Tandysh
Managing editor: Sara Taylor

Volume based on papers presented at the symposium "Designing Wildlife Habitats,"
held at the Dumbarton Oaks Research Library and Collection, Washington, D.C., on
May 14–15, 2010.

www.doaks.org/publications

Contents

View of the
stream and
falls in the
"wild garden"
at Dumbarton
Oaks, 1930s.

CHAPTER 1

Introduction

Cultivating Wildlife

JOHN BEARDSLEY

IN 2010, WHEN THE SYMPOSIUM WAS HELD FOR which this publication is the record, Dumbarton Oaks was observing its seventieth year as a research institution for the humanities affiliated with Harvard University. At the same time, Garden and Landscape Studies was approaching its fortieth anniversary. Its first symposium was held in 1971, and the program of Studies in Landscape Architecture, the forerunner to today's Garden and Landscape Studies, was established in 1972. In the program's early years, under Director Elisabeth MacDougall, symposia generally took chronological or regional foci: Italian, French, English, Dutch, Islamic, Mughal, ancient Roman, medieval, baroque. In the last two decades, however, under the leadership of John Dixon Hunt, Joachim Wolschke-Bulmahn, and Michel Conan, the program's foci and its colloquia have diversified considerably. Symposia have been held on such topics as vernacular and regional landscapes, theme parks, nature and ideology, places of commemoration, and sacred and profane rituals in gardens and landscapes.

But only once before has a Garden and Landscape Studies symposium at Dumbarton Oaks addressed the intersection of landscape design with the broad practices of environmental management and ethics generally signified by the term "environmentalism." In 1998, Dumbarton Oaks hosted "Environmentalism in Landscape Architecture," which included a presentation on changing paradigms in ecology by Robert Cook, then Arnold Professor and director of the Arnold Arboretum at Harvard, along with an analysis of the works of the Tennessee Valley Authority, Ian L. McHarg, and a younger generation of artists and landscape architects. And only once before has Dumbarton Oaks looked specifically at the intersection of design and science, at a session in 2004 titled "Botanical Progress, Horticultural Innovation, and Cultural Change," jointly organized by Michel Conan and scientist John Kress of the Smithsonian Institution's Department of Botany. This symposium examined the linkages among botany, horticulture, and cultural change as seen through practices as distinct as gardening, religion, literature, politics, and economics. The symposium documented in this volume builds on the environmental focus of the one and the scientific content of the other to look at a subject new to Dumbarton Oaks: the role of design in the protection, management, restoration, and even wholesale re-creation of habitat for wildlife.

These are the institutional contexts for this publication. But it also charts some disciplinary changes. In recent years, there has been a pronounced shift in the rhetoric of design, from a concern with how landscapes look to a concern with how they function: programmatically, socially, economically, and ecologically. Put in shorthand, the shift has been from appearance to performance. This is the most recent expression of a decades-long conflict between those who see design first and foremost as an art and those who regard it more as a science, and especially as an expression of ecological principles. If we look back over the recent history of landscape architecture, we can identify people associated with one camp or the other—say Pete Walker, Martha Schwartz, George Hargreaves, or Ken Smith with art; Ian McHarg, Andropogon, or the interdisciplinary firm Applied Ecological Services with ecology. Such polarizations are misleading, as there have always been people who straddle art and science: Frederick Law Olmsted in his day, Leberecht Migge among early European modernists, Lawrence Halprin among later American modernists, and Michael Van Valkenburgh Associates today.[1] Moreover, there is often plenty of ecology in the art-minded, plenty of artfulness in the ecology-minded—although, as symposium co-organizer Alexander J. Felson argues in this volume, some of the ecological principles that landscape architects have been applying are outdated or misconstrued, and landscape architects and ecologists can have substantially different environmental agendas.

Given the increasing attention paid to landscape performance—especially ecological performance—we should not be surprised by the recent emergence of a group of practitioners who are determined to generate productive collaborations between design and science, either by working closely with scientists or by themselves becoming scientists. There are now people in the profession with Master of Landscape Architecture degrees along with doctoral degrees in fields such as botany, ecology, or biology. Part of the agenda of this publication is to chart this disciplinary shift, to introduce and to interrogate designers more mindful of science. At the same time, it is to suggest the challenges that designers face in sustaining the full range of biodiversity. While landscape architecture can be said to have addressed botanical diversity quite successfully, it has been far less consistent in reckoning with the requirements of mammals, birds, reptiles, amphibians, and even insects.

There is some irony to the lack of attention paid by designers to the nonhuman inhabitants of landscape. The vision of a garden shared peacefully by humans and animals is one of the oldest and most familiar landscape tropes—but also one of the most elusive. Whether threatened by habitat destruction or climate change, displaced by urbanization or invasive species, poisoned by industrial toxins, or hunted to extinction, many animal species have failed to thrive in the company of people. There is growing scientific consensus, as reported in an essay by Elizabeth Kolbert in the *New Yorker*, that we are in the midst of the sixth great extinction in earth history—and the first caused by human activities.[2] By some estimates, as many as half of the earth's species will be gone by the end of this century. Humans are altering the planet in profound ways, with extensive implications for biodiversity. Hardly a day goes by that we do not hear of some new threats to individual species or reports of whole ecosystems on the brink of collapse, from the Arctic to the Amazon. It is not necessary to dwell on this, especially in a publication addressed to landscape scholars and practitioners. It might suffice for our purposes to invoke the notions of the Nobel Prize–winning atmospheric chemist Paul Crutzen, who proposed in the year 2000 that we use the term "Anthropocene" to designate the current epoch of earth history, in order to emphasize the central role of humanity in the dramatic transformations of ecosystems and climates.[3]

These are the global contexts for this publication. But what agency can landscape professionals have in conserving, managing, or re-creating wildlife diversity? Established conservation practices within ecology have already begun to shape the practice of landscape architecture, including reserve design for focal species and biodiversity more generally; the sizing and spacing of habitat patches, corridors, and edge conditions; and the analysis of food webs and predator-prey dynamics. Current initiatives suggest a still larger role for landscape architecture in the creation of productive habitats, especially as the practice engages

JOHN BEARDSLEY

with ecosystem services and restoration ecology and generates designer-led ecological experiments. Design is increasingly perceived as instrumental to the appearance and the ecological function of landscapes and to the opportunities for environmental remediation.

This publication aims to move beyond historic arguments about conservation versus preservation, as well as beyond more recent debates about preservation versus restoration.[4] Most people in the landscape disciplines would doubtless agree that it is much more efficient—and far less costly—to preserve intact ecosystems than to restore or re-create them. So we should pursue preservation where possible. But as there are fewer and fewer intact ecosystems to preserve—especially in the context of changing climates—it becomes increasingly apparent that maintaining biodiversity will require the restoration, even the complete reinvention, of habitats. We cannot replicate damaged or lost ecosystems exactly, but we might attempt to establish systems that resemble, act like, and provide many of the same services as the originals—however those originals are defined, whether wild or cultivated. While we might have reservations about assuming so commanding a position in ecosystem restoration, environmental historians like William Cronon have recently been reminding us that humans have always shaped their landscapes, for better and for worse.[5] The important question is how we do it. As an art historian, I am inclined to curatorial metaphors: I am concerned with the criteria by which we select species or systems for study and collection, how we research and interpret them, and how we present them. Others, notably William Jordan III and Frederick Turner, have suggested that gardening provides the right metaphors for the stewardship responsibilities we have for other species.[6] While gardening in its narrowest sense might be regarded as an imposition of human will on a landscape, in its larger sense it implies the intelligent and creative management of communities of species to create healthy and self-sustaining relationships among all its parts. Again, in design at least, those communities of species are typically thought of in terms of plants; the requirements of wildlife are less well understood. Indeed, because they are incompletely understood even among scientists,

these requirements are rarely integrated in rigorous ways into design.

To speak of natural systems and wildlife through metaphors of curating and gardening might seem counter to ideas of wild nature as the antithesis of culture. In an influential 1995 essay, "The Trouble with Wilderness," William Cronon sought to put this dualistic argument to rest. He argued that such polarities left us "little hope of discovering what an ethical, sustainable, honorable human place in nature might actually look like"; he also suggested that conceptualizing culture as entirely separate from wild nature allowed us to "evade responsibility for the lives we actually lead."[7] Cronon was talking about wilderness, but his argument also applies to wildness. As long as we see wildlife as something distinct from culture, existing in some pristine condition apart from us, separate from ideas of curating, gardening, management, or stewardship, we have little hope of achieving an ethical and sustainable relationship with animals and little hope of assuming responsibility for the impact of our lives on other species. We can extrapolate from Cronon's argument that wildness in animals, like the wilderness they are said to inhabit, is a cultural construct, a point that Harriet Ritvo develops in this volume. Wildness is the expression of subtle and protracted negotiations between humans and nonhuman species.

While the contemporary focus on habitat restoration might seem like a new initiative, landscape architects have a long history of engagement with environmental repair. Most famously, perhaps, Frederick Law Olmsted persuaded George Vanderbilt to restore thousands of acres of forest at Biltmore, his estate near Asheville, North Carolina, in the early 1890s. In roughly the same years, in the Boston Fens, Olmsted oversaw the re-creation of a functioning marsh on tidal flats fouled by industrial discharge and sewage; this constructed wetland was designed to cleanse water and control flooding. Both projects were done in cooperation with scientists: Olmsted engaged Gifford Pinchot, later the first director of the U.S. Forest Service, to help devise the management plan at Biltmore, while Charles Sprague Sargent, director of the Arnold Arboretum, advised him on plant selections for the Fens.[8] But there are many other examples of designer-scientist collaborations in the protection and enhancement of biodiversity. Jens Jensen's knowledge of plant communities and succession was honed by his friendship with University of Chicago botanist Henry C. Cowles—both were members of a hiking and conservation group called the Prairie Club. Jensen would use this knowledge in restoring native prairie and woodland communities, as at the Lincoln Memorial Garden in Springfield, Illinois. There, plants and seeds collected by schoolchildren, scouting groups, and garden clubs from disturbed sites around the state were planted on sixty-three acres of former farmland beginning in 1936, creating a mixed forest of oaks, hickories, and maples with an understory of indigenous flowering trees, woody shrubs, and herbaceous plants, all interspersed with meadows of tall prairie flowers.[9] A former Cowles student, ecologist Edith Roberts collaborated with landscape designer Elsa Rehmann on an arboretum and botanical garden for Vassar College in New York, begun in 1924; in a 1933 issue of *Ecology*, Roberts wrote that the project "was to establish, on less than four acres of rough land, the plants native to Dutchess County, NY, in their correct associations, with the appropriate environmental factors of each association in this region." The two also coauthored a popular manual, *American Plants for American Gardens* (1929).[10]

In roughly the same years, and again quite familiarly, the forester and wildlife ecologist Aldo Leopold was a prime force behind one of the most important landscape designs of the twentieth century, if viewed from the perspective of environmental restoration and conservation: the University of Wisconsin Arboretum. Anticipated in landscape architect John Nolen's 1911 plan for Madison and inaugurated in 1934 under the direction of horticulture professor G. William Longenecker, the arboretum was created on derelict farmland and represented an effort to reintroduce historic communities of both plants and animals indigenous to the local Wisconsin landscape. As Leopold said at the dedication, "our idea . . . is to re-construct . . . a sample of original Wisconsin—a sample of what Dane County looked like when our ancestors arrived here during the 1840s."[11] Although we might quarrel with his evocation of an "original" presettlement landscape, we can admire the breadth of his vision,

which included habitat for both plants and animals—he titled his remarks "What is the University of Wisconsin Arboretum, Wild Life Refuge, and Forest Experiment Preserve?" Moreover, we can still be inspired by his observation that conservation and restoration are both ethical and aesthetic matters. As he wrote in *A Sand County Almanac* in 1949, "a thing is right when it tends to preserve the integrity, stability, and beauty of the biotic community. It is wrong when it tends otherwise." Contemporary designers still struggle to reconcile the ethical and the aesthetic.[12]

Indeed, if we reflect upon the many exchanges among scientists and environmental designers and planners during the early twentieth century—a period when landscape architecture, ecology, and nature conservation were all relatively young fields of inquiry and practice—we are left wondering what happened to so sunder these disciplines, such that a century later the intersection of landscape architecture with ecology and conservation biology appears novel, even unprecedented.[13] The mid-twentieth-century schism between ecology and design is especially puzzling given the extent to which backyard-scale wildlife habitats were then beginning to penetrate popular culture: the idea has been heavily promoted for many years by the National Audubon Society, and the National Wildlife Federation offers a "Certified Wildlife Habitat" designation for homeowners, schools, and churches, a program they pioneered in 1973.[14] We might blame the split on an increased emphasis on disciplinary specialization in the modern era. We might blame the vagueness of landscape architecture's identity—in the academic context, it is sometimes housed in departments of fine arts or architecture, sometimes in programs of forestry or agriculture, sometimes in colleges of social and behavioral sciences. But we might also point to the great complexities of the contemporary effort to integrate functional ecologies into design, which to some degree have required a reinvention of both. To begin with, as Marcus Hall observes, there are regional differences in approaches to ecological restoration. Are we restoring cultural landscapes, as is often the case in places like Europe with long histories of human modification, or are we aiming for the kind of naturalized wilderness that seems to be favored in the United States? Do we restore according to nature's methods or culture's methods? That is, do we "seed" a site with plants and animals and let the outcomes be what they may, or do we take a more interventionist and managed approach? How do we measure success? That is to say, when is an ecosystem deemed sufficiently restored? And in a context of limited resources, how do we decide which landscapes to restore? Should all damaged landscapes even be repaired, or should some number of them be left as memorials to the power of human intervention?[15]

With specific respect to design, how should ecology be embodied in form? Many ecological functions are hidden and hard to manifest in design. Indeed, aesthetics may continue to be of secondary concern—or of no concern at all—within particular ecological contexts or environmental restoration opportunities. Where design and science might be reconciled, there is, on the one hand, a danger that science might become so artful that it departs from functional principles. On the other, there is a risk that design might become so captivated with science that it overestimates how much information and certainty the latter can provide. One of the common criticisms of Ian McHarg's method today is that he was overly reliant on a model of ecology that was deterministic: successional, predictable, and trending toward stability in climax conditions. While the model of ecology that prevails in design today is more dynamic, complex, and adaptable, there is still a sense among many designers that science should be able to provide a set of parameters within which they can act with a reasonable degree of confidence. This may or may not be true going forward—we face a time of increasing change and uncertainty in the operations of ecological systems, as in so much else. Will we really be able to predict the rise in sea levels, or flood rates and sediment loads in rivers, or the distribution of species in warmer climates? Design in this context becomes a form of research into the possibilities and limitations of both science and art.

Reflections on past intersections of design and science and on changes in ecological paradigms remind us of the many histories at issue here. There are cultural histories, notably the histories of human interactions with other species. What species have we "gardened" in the past and why? What species have we abhorred and why? There are economic histories, especially global histories of translocation and trade in animals and animal parts. There are histories of science: changes in the ways we catalogue species and changes in the ways we understand the operations of ecosystems. There are the natural histories of ecosystems themselves, especially the ways they are transformed by human and natural forces. And there are evolving histories in our understanding of ecosystem functions: it is well known that efforts to restore native prairies in the American Midwest were facilitated by the recognition that fire plays a crucial role in their management. Only some of these histories are addressed in this publication, but all are important for the light they might shed on the current and critical cause of biodiversity protection and restoration.

At the same time as we acknowledge the role of history in understanding our current situations, we need to focus as much, if not more, on the troubling prospects before us. Climate change is surely among the defining ecological and political challenges of this century; it is bound to cause as much social and economic as ecological disturbance. It is also a global concern, which confounds the more commonly local perspectives on preservation and restoration. In many hearts and minds, climate change demands immediate and vigorous response, especially in coastal, urban areas where disturbances are expected to be particularly pronounced. Design has the potential to be an agent of change as we rethink our infrastructures for energy, flood control, and transportation—to name just a few—for the coming century. Again, design in these contexts could be conceptualized as a form of research, as a way of raising questions and testing hypotheses about habitat function and species adaptability in changing environmental conditions—although, if design is going to assume the character of research, we have to be prepared at times to see it fail. The challenge will be to use the frameworks of design and planning to make the most of the opportunities for biodiversity conservation, habitat restoration, and mitigation of past, present, and anticipated environmental damage—for human and nonhuman species alike.

While readers of this volume might all agree that it is a worthy goal to promote biodiversity through design, there are bound to be philosophical differences among us about why we do this. In what must surely be among the most depressing meditations on the subject, an essay called "Why Look at Animals?," the English critic and novelist John Berger tells us that our fascination with nature is a function of our alienation from it. Every tradition that has mediated the direct relationship between humans and nature has been sundered, he says, whether economic and productive or magical, oracular, even sacrificial. Our pets are mementos of these sundered relationships; meanwhile, we see wild animals as through the glass of an aquarium. Zoos are monuments to the impossibility of real encounters with animals and to the disappearance of animals from daily life. Like other institutions in which we collect, study, and present nature, they only underscore how marginalized other species have become in our lives—they are memory theaters of connections we have lost.[16] But there are surely more positive ways to interrogate the matter of human relations to animals and to nurturing nature more generally. Do we promote biodiversity for educational reasons? Is our goal, for instance, to educate new generations of people who we hope will be better stewards than we have been? Or do we protect biodiversity for ecosystem services? As ecologist Shahid Naeem details in this volume, species richness characterizes most healthy ecosystems; these ecosystems manifest multiple benefits, from stormwater infiltration and flood control to decomposition of wastes, restoration of degraded lands, and absorption of carbon dioxide. Or do we save species as a current or potential resource? With respect to animals, this might be for food or for hunting and tourist development, as in the case Jane Carruthers presents here of the Pilanesberg National Park in South Africa. In this event, are we rationalizing biodiversity protection for the good it can do us, or rationing it on behalf of those species that we now know to be of benefit to us at the expense of others whose services we do not yet recognize? Or do we value diversity for its own sake, for what we might describe as its inherent values? Are we motivated, for instance, by what Edward O. Wilson and others have termed "biophilia," the possibly inherent affinity we feel for other forms of life? Wilson suggests that biophilia is rooted in biology, and countering Berger's argument about alienation, he describes

it as "the connections that human beings subconsciously seek with the rest of life."[17]

In addition to raising these various historical, scientific, and philosophical issues, this volume suggests questions of political economy as well. Who decides, for example, what species or ecosystems to save, where, and how? Do we aim for target species and focal landscapes, or do we take an approach based in whole systems, as many of the authors in this volume argue? Are we willing to pursue biodiversity preservation notwithstanding the economic costs? And what of the inevitable conflicts between human and nonhuman needs? These conflicts are nearly universal, but they are driven home with special force in squatter communities around the world. In Rio de Janeiro, for instance, squatters are invading Tijuca National Park, accelerating deforestation and consequent flooding and landslides—with catastrophic human and environmental consequences. Are these issues—of social equity and environmental justice—included in the province of design? And if so, how are they to be addressed in the context of biodiversity protection and enhancement?

As an initial foray into the field of design for wildlife, this volume cannot hope to answer all of these questions. Instead, it presents a range of disciplinary, geographical, and historical approaches. The first section, "Frameworks," includes essays by an environmental historian, an art historian, a field biologist turned conservation officer, an ecologist, and an anthropologist. Environmental historian Harriet Ritvo offers a meditation on degrees of wildness in animals, using Charles Darwin's analogies between natural and artificial selection as a point of departure to suggest ever-greater slippages between the wild and the domesticated, with evident implications for management of wildlife. Art historian B. Deniz Çalış evokes the long history of collecting animals in menageries and hunting preserves by looking at the various conceptions of wildness and wilderness in the sixteenth- and seventeenth-century Ottoman court. Conservation officer Joshua R. Ginsberg brings the matter of animal management squarely into the present, revealing how wildlife organizations now operate across a range of scales and with multiple objectives, from zoo display and endangered-species breeding facilities to managed reserves and even regional plans. He notes that conservation strategies change dramatically from context to context, based both on the analysis of proximate and ultimate threats at each scale and on the social ecologies of particular species of concern. Ecologist Shahid Naeem explains the correlations between species richness and ecosystem services; he notes that most ecosystems are composed of many individuals of a few species and few individuals of far more numerous species, and raises the provocative question of how to protect what he terms these rare or "poor" species. Discounting—like Harriet Ritvo—the opposition between the wild or natural and the tame or managed, he expresses a preference for the unmanaged over the managed landscape but acknowledges that restored landscapes might display greater biodiversity than unmanaged ones. Anthropologist Shepard Krech III concludes the "Frameworks" section with a look at the ambiguous histories of indigenous peoples with respect to birds in neotropical forests. Drawing distinctions in the degrees of environmental knowledge and concern between truly local peoples and those who have migrated into an area of conservation concern, he suggests the importance of locally inflected strategies to combat avian habitat loss, including corridors to link forest fragments, a matrix of forest and agricultural lands, living fences, and complex agroforestry woodlots.

The balance of the book, "Sites, Scales, Systems," presents specific case studies of design in the context of biodiversity protection and restoration—again, from a variety of disciplinary perspectives. Environmental historian Jane Carruthers looks at the creation of Pilanesberg National Park in the 1970s, the first national park in South Africa to take shape on a designer's drafting table specifically as a tourist destination and for local economic development. Despite an inauspicious political start, it was one of the first instances of community conservation in Africa in which indigenous people participated in the creation and management of the park; it also involved both environmental restoration and the reintroduction of wildlife. Designer Stuart Green compares two of his projects, Alice Springs Desert Park in Australia and Cambodia Wildlife Sanctuary in Cambodia, for the rewards and challenges they offer to designers and conservationists. Steven N.

Handel and Kristina Hill take us into what might seem like surprising territory for wildlife habitat— the city. Handel, an ecologist, looks at several projects in which he has been involved, revealing how degraded urban lands might be made fit for wildlife and how wildlife can aid in biodiversity restoration. Hill, both a landscape architect and ecologist, looks at current efforts to protect and restore urban biodiversity, especially in Europe; she suggests how cities might paradoxically serve as refuges for wildlife in the context of changing climates. Another landscape architect and ecologist, Alexander J. Felson, develops a number of the theoretical and methodological questions that have motivated his experiments in wildlife habitat design. Returning to some of the questions of scale raised by Joshua R. Ginsberg, Chinese planner and designer Kongjian Yu presents the work of his firm, Turenscape, across a range of scales, from national initiatives for biodiversity protection in China, to metropolitan plans for Beijing, to project-scale designs for parks that include provisions for wildlife habitat. These essays are interspersed with portfolios of projects by Nelson Byrd Woltz Landscape Architects and Michael Van Valkenburgh Associates. The former have been working on a project to reconcile biodiversity protection with productive agriculture on a sheep and fruit farm in New Zealand; principal designer Thomas Woltz presented this project at the symposium and elaborates on it here. The latter have recently won a competition to design a new generation of wildlife crossings for interstate highways in the American West, a competition organized with the help of Canadian planner Nina-Marie Lister, who also spoke at the symposium.

To some readers, wildlife and wilderness might seem a long way from the historical concerns of Dumbarton Oaks. But both have been part of the story of the institution from its inception. When its patrons, Mildred and Robert Woods Bliss, retained Beatrix Farrand to help them convert a fifty-seven-acre farm into an urban garden in the 1920s, one of the first things Farrand expressed was a hope that "a part of the grounds could be developed as a 'Wilderness' where hollies, yews, ivies, and spring flowering Magnolias and winter flowering shrubs would make an attractive walk to be followed in winter." The passage appears in a 1922 report from

FIGURE 1.1
The "Wilderness Walk" in the gardens at Dumbarton Oaks,
Summer 1932.

© Dumbarton Oaks Research Library and Collection, Rare Book Collection,
Washington, D.C.

FIGURE 1.2
Streamside planting in the "wild garden" at Dumbarton Oaks,
ca. 1935.

© Dumbarton Oaks Research Library and Collection, Rare Book Collection,
Washington, D.C.

Farrand to Mildred Bliss; it comes in the context of a discussion of the north slopes of the property, so she may have been envisioning a managed woodland where old fields shaded into forest at the far northwest edge of the estate. The term "wilderness" recurs in Farrand's "Plant Book," which was composed in the 1940s to aid in the management of the portion of the gardens conveyed—along with the house and its collections—to Harvard University. There, writing of a walk that circles the East Lawn and separates the gardens from R Street, she recalled: "When the walk was first spoken of, it was called the 'Wilderness Walk,' as it was like many a path in old southern places where a wilderness was an essential part of the seventeenth- or eighteenth-century design" (Figure 1.1).[18] There was still another kind of wildness in Farrand's scheme

for the gardens: in a stream valley that divided distant fields and forest from the more intensively cultivated spaces closer to the house, she developed plans for naturalistic plantings evocative of the Irish gardener and author William Robinson's ideas of the "wild garden," where azaleas, hemlocks, and naturalized bulbs would be reflected in series of pools created by damming the stream.[19] Remnants of these plantings can still be seen along the stream edge, now part of Dumbarton Oaks Park, the portion of the estate given by the Blisses to and now administered by the National Park Service (Figure 1.2).

With respect to gardens, "wilderness" in Farrand's day had developed several connotations. The term can be traced back to seventeenth- and eighteenth-century English usages, where it referred to planned arrangements of trees and shrubs planted in remote sections of a garden, featuring a variety of walks and vistas. English wildernesses often featured American plants, in an evocation of "real" wilderness. Initially, wilderness walks were bounded by hedges, but, by the middle of the eighteenth century, these had given way to shrubs underplanted with flowers. The term had passed into American usage by then—especially in the South, as Farrand recognized: George Washington described planning several "walks, groves, and wildernesses" for his Mount Vernon estate, while Thomas Jefferson wrote of a wilderness at Monticello "to be improved for winter walking or riding."[20] Later nineteenth-century usages of "wilderness" suggest a modified, primeval forest rather than the designed plantations of the eighteenth century; it seems to be the earlier tradition to which Farrand was referring when she wrote of wilderness at Dumbarton Oaks—a designed and managed forest, but evocative of unspoiled nature and native biodiversity. Indeed, Farrand suggested that the "Wilderness Walk" at Dumbarton Oaks be abundantly planted with hemlocks, hollies, maples, and oaks, with an understory of yew and boxwood.

There is still another kind of wildness at Dumbarton Oaks, which is a function of its proximity to Rock Creek Park, a vast urban forest that reaches from the city limits to the Potomac River. Both Dumbarton Oaks and Dumbarton Oaks Park are contiguous with Rock Creek Park and are part of its extensive ecosystem. The stream in Dumbarton Oaks Park drains into Rock Creek and, like the creek itself, serves as a conduit for wildlife. There are significant populations of large and small mammals in the park, some of whom—foxes and raccoons, for instance—cross the fence into Dumbarton Oaks. And the variety of habitats in the gardens provides food and shelter to migratory and nesting birds— a three-year-long survey conducted by Garden and Landscape Studies staff with volunteers from the Wilderness Society recorded eighty-six species of birds, including a broad array of neotropical migrants such as Scarlet Tanager and Baltimore Oriole as well as numerous species of thrushes, flycatchers, vireos, and warblers; raptors such as Barred Owl, Cooper's Hawk, and Red-shouldered Hawk; and breeding populations of more than a dozen species, including Red-bellied Woodpecker, Great Crested Flycatcher,

FIGURE 1.3
Aquatic habitat in the Ellipse fountain at Dumbarton Oaks, summer 2010.

Photograph by Jane Padelford.

FIGURE 1.4
Beatrix Farrand's
plan for a pool,
featuring tall
grasses and lilies,
at Dumbarton
Oaks, ca. 1930.

© Dumbarton Oaks
Research Library
and Collection, Rare
Book Collection,
Washington, D.C.

and Song Sparrow. Some of the more unusual visitors during the survey period included Peregrine Falcon and Mourning Warbler (see Appendix 1). In cooperation with the garden staff, the Garden and Landscape Studies program has also been working to make the gardens hospitable to a still larger range of species through the creation of an aquatic habitat in the Ellipse fountain (Figure 1.3). Evocative of a Beatrix Farrand drawing for the pool terrace (Figure 1.4), the habitat has introduced new kinds of plant life, along with fish, crawfish, turtles, and various amphibians to the gardens, which in turn has drawn additional bird species, such as the Green Heron. While this habitat is hardly a wilderness, it represents a continuing effort to manage the Dumbarton Oaks Gardens for greater biodiversity.

Indeed, whether conceptualized as wilderness, wild garden, or managed ecosystem, Dumbarton Oaks and the larger landscape of which it is a part have long exemplified the kind of curated biodiversity that now characterizes many, if not most, conservation areas around the globe. Dumbarton Oaks is an instance of a managed landscape that shades into a still wilder system; as such, it might be seen as part of a larger and more significant effort to escape the polarities of wild nature and culture, which William Cronon theorized were part of the reason for human failure to achieve ethical and sustainable relationships with other species. Both the academic program in Garden and Landscape Studies and the gardens at Dumbarton Oaks have a role to play in managing and—where possible—restoring biodiversity, as well as cultivating wildness and wildlife in both local and global landscapes. This publication and the symposium it records were intended to advance this tradition.

Notes

1 For a nuanced look at the relationship between artistic and ecological ambitions in recent landscape architecture, see Elizabeth K. Meyer, "The Post-Earth Day Conundrum: Translating Environmental Values into Landscape Design," in *Environmentalism in Landscape Architecture*, ed. Michel Conan (Washington, D.C.: Dumbarton Oaks Research Library and Collection, 2000), 187–244.

2 Elizabeth Kolbert, "The Sixth Extinction?," *New Yorker*, May 25, 2009, 53–63.

3 Apparently coined by the ecologist Eugene Stoermer, the term "Anthropocene" first appeared in print in an essay by Crutzen in 2000. See "The Anthropocene: A Man-Made World," *The Economist*, May 26, 2011, http://www.economist.com/node/18741749.

4 An excellent examination of the preservation-restoration debate, and restoration's surprisingly long history, can be found in Marcus Hall, *Earth Repair: A Transatlantic History of Environmental Restoration* (Charlottesville: University of Virginia Press, 2005).

5 See William Cronon, *Changes in the Land: Indians, Colonists, and the Ecology of New England*, rev. ed. (New York: Hill and Wang, 2003).

6 See the essays by William Jordan III and Frederick Turner in *Beyond Preservation: Restoring and Inventing Landscapes*, ed. A. Dwight Baldwin Jr., Judith De Luce, and Carl Pletsch (Minneapolis: University of Minnesota Press, 1994), 17–66.

7 William Cronon, "The Trouble with Wilderness; or, Getting Back to the Wrong Nature," in *Uncommon Ground: Toward Reinventing Nature*, ed. William Cronon (New York: W. W. Norton, 1995), 69–90. Cronon's argument receives an intriguing update with particular reference to the history of aesthetics in Timothy Morton, *Ecology without Nature: Rethinking Environmental Aesthetics* (Cambridge, Mass.: Harvard University Press, 2007).

8 On Olmsted's efforts at environmental repair, see Anne Whiston Spirn, "Constructing Nature: The Legacy of Frederick Law Olmsted," in Cronon, *Uncommon Ground*, 91–113.

9 For more on Jensen and the Lincoln Memorial Garden, see Robert E. Grese, *Jens Jensen: Maker of Natural Parks and Gardens* (Baltimore: Johns Hopkins University Press, 1992), 113–20.

10 The works of Roberts and Rehmann are discussed in Hall, *Earth Repair*, 173–74.

11 Dave Egan, "Historic Initiatives in Ecological Restoration," *Restoration and Management Notes* 8, no. 2 (1990): 89.

12 Aldo Leopold, *A Sand County Almanac* (1949; repr., New York: Oxford University Press, 1989), 225. On the continuing effort to reconcile environmental ethics and aesthetics, see Elizabeth Meyer, "Sustaining Beauty: The Performance of Appearance," *Journal of Landscape Architecture* (Spring 2008): 6–23, which was reprinted in *Landscape Architecture* (October 2008): 92–131.

13 I am grateful to Eric MacDonald of the University of Georgia for prompting me to ask this question.

14 "History of the Backyard Wildlife Habitat," National Wildlife Federation, accessed August 15, 2011, http://www.nwf.org/Get-Outside/Outdoor-Activities/Garden-for-Wildlife/Gardening-Tips/History-of-the-Backyard-Wildlife-Habitat-Program.aspx?CFID=21438960&CFTOKEN=1133e38ffc3427fd-CF4E3BFF-5056-A84B-C3991AB27E4D315A.

15 Hall, *Earth Repair*, 195–204.

16 John Berger, "Why Look at Animals?," in *About Looking* (1977; New York: Vintage International, 1991), 3–28.

17 See Edward O. Wilson, *Biophilia* (Cambridge, Mass.: Harvard University Press, 1984); and Stephen R. Kellert and Edward O. Wilson, eds., *The Biophilia Hypothesis* (Washington, D.C.: Island Press, 1993).

18 Beatrix Farrand to Mildred Bliss, report, June 24 and 25, 1922, Dumbarton Oaks Research Library and Collection, Rare Book Collection, Washington, D.C.; and Diane Kostial McGuire, ed., *Beatrix Farrand's Plant Book for Dumbarton Oaks* (Washington, D.C.: Dumbarton Oaks, Trustees for Harvard University, 1980), 30.

19 Robinson's ideas were developed in his 1870 book, *The Wild Garden*.

20 For a detailed analysis of the use of the term "wilderness" in landscape design, see Therese O'Malley, *Keywords in American Landscape Design* (Washington, D.C.: National Gallery of Art, 2010), 669–74. Quotations from Washington and Jefferson can be found on page 671.

Appendix 1: Dumbarton Oaks Bird Survey

Observers: Kevin Mack (KM), David Moulton (DM), Michael Lee (ML), Don Mehlman (DME),
Walter Howell (WH), and Melissa Brizer (MB)

Period: September 1, 2009, through June 30, 2012

Dates are given for species with single sightings during the survey period.

▲ Mallard		
Wild Turkey	March 30, 2012	MB, WH
Great Blue Heron		
Green Heron		
Black Vulture		
Turkey Vulture		
Osprey	April 29, 2010	ML
Bald Eagle	December 9, 2011	WH, ML, DME (one adult)
Sharp-shinned Hawk		
Cooper's Hawk		
◇ Red-shouldered Hawk		
Red-tailed Hawk		
Peregrine Falcon	April 14, 2010	ML
▲ Mourning Dove		
Barred Owl		
◇ Chimney Swift		
◇ Ruby-throated Hummingbird		
▲ Red-bellied Woodpecker		
Yellow-bellied Sapsucker		
◇ Downy Woodpecker		
Hairy Woodpecker		
▲ Northern Flicker		
Pileated Woodpecker		
◇ Eastern Wood-Pewee		
Acadian Flycatcher		
Least Flycatcher	October 8, 2010	ML
Eastern Phoebe		
▲ Great Crested Flycatcher		
Eastern Kingbird	May 22, 2010	DM
Blue-headed Vireo		
Philadelphia Vireo		
Red-eyed Vireo		
◇ Blue Jay		
American Crow		
Fish Crow		
Northern Rough-winged Swallow		
◇ Carolina Chickadee		
◇ Tufted Titmouse		
▲ White-breasted Nuthatch		
Brown Creeper	October 8, 2010	ML
▲ Carolina Wren		

House Wren		
Golden-crowned Kinglet		
Ruby-crowned Kinglet		
◇ Blue-gray Gnatcatcher		
Veery	May 7, 2010	DM
Swainson's Thrush	May 22, 2010	DM
Hermit Thrush	April 13, 2011	ML
◇ Wood Thrush		
▲ American Robin		
▲ Gray Catbird		
▲ Northern Mockingbird		
Brown Thrasher		
European Starling		
Cedar Waxwing		
Tennessee Warbler	October 4–5, 2011	ML, DME
Northern Parula		
Chestnut-sided Warbler	May 17, 2010	ML
Magnolia Warbler		
Black-throated Blue Warbler	May 1, 2010	DM, KM
Yellow-rumped Warbler		
Black-throated Green Warbler	October 6, 2011	ML
Yellow-throated Warbler	May 10, 2011	ML
Prairie Warbler	April 22, 2010	ML
Blackpoll Warbler		
Black-and-white Warbler	May 7, 2010	DM
American Redstart	May 17, 2010	ML
Mourning Warbler	October 7, 2011	ML
Common Yellowthroat		
Scarlet Tanager		
◇ Eastern Towhee		
Chipping Sparrow		
Field Sparrow	April 25, 2011	ML
▲ Song Sparrow		
Lincoln's Sparrow	December 16, 2009	ML
White-throated Sparrow		
White-crowned Sparrow	October 8, 2010	ML
Dark-eyed Junco		
▲ Northern Cardinal		
Rose-breasted Grosbeak	October 4–5, 2011	ML
◇ Common Grackle		
▲ Brown-headed Cowbird		
Baltimore Oriole		
House Finch		
▲ American Goldfinch		
◇ House Sparrow		

Eighty-six species
▲ Breeding confirmed
◇ Observed regularly during the breeding season

CHAPTER 2

Edging into the Wild

HARRIET RITVO

IN *THE VARIATION OF ANIMALS AND PLANTS under Domestication*, which appeared first in 1868 and later in a revised edition in 1875, Charles Darwin developed a theme to which he accorded great rhetorical and evidentiary significance. The first chapter of *On the Origin of Species*, published in 1859, had included a description of artificial selection as practiced by farmers, stockbreeders, and pet fanciers. Domesticated animals and plants were numerous, familiar, and exposed to constant observation; they provided a readily available body of evidence. Darwin thus used a reassuringly homely example, one that was accessible by the general public as well as by members of the scientific community, to introduce the most innovative component of his evolutionary theory—that is, the idea of natural selection as the engine of evolutionary change.

Reassuring as it was, the analogy between natural and artificial selection was far from perfect. The point of Darwin's analogy was to make the idea of natural selection seem plausible by characterizing its efficiency and shaping power. He devoted special attention to domesticated pigeons in *Variation*, allotting two entire chapters to them, while pigs, cattle, sheep, and goats had to share a single chapter, as

did ducks, geese, peacocks, turkeys, guinea fowls, canaries, goldfish, bees, and silk moths.[1] He noted, for example, that some of the prize birds bred by London pigeon fanciers diverged so strikingly in size, plumage, beak shape, flying technique, vocalizations, bone structure, and many other attributes that if they had been presented to an ornithologist as wild specimens, they would unquestionably have been considered to represent distinct species, perhaps even distinct genera (Figure 2.1). Darwin argued that if the relatively brief and constrained selective efforts of human breeders had produced such impressive results, it was likely that the more protracted and thoroughgoing efforts of nature would work still more efficaciously.

But as Darwin acknowledged, there were some fairly obvious reasons why the two processes might diverge. The superior power of natural selection— "Man can act only on external and visible characters: nature . . . can act on . . . the whole machinery of life. Man selects only for his own good; Nature only for that of the being which she tends"[2]—might constitute a difference of kind rather than of degree, as might the much greater stretches of time available for natural selection. Further, although the

FIGURE 2.1

"English Barb," a fancy pigeon
breed admired by Charles Darwin.

Reprinted from Charles Darwin, *The
Variation of Animals and Plants under
Domestication* (New York: Orange Judd,
1868), 1:180.

FIGURE 2.2

Shorthorns were the prestige
cattle breed of the early
nineteenth century.

Reprinted from David Low, *On the
Domesticated Animals of the British
Islands* (London: Longman, Brown,
Green, and Longmans, 1845), 206.

FIGURE 2.3

An elite product of
the Victorian dog fancy.

Reprinted from J. H. Walsh, *The Dog
in Health and Disease*, 3rd ed. (London:
Longmans, Green, 1879), 198.

mechanism of the two processes appeared superficially similar, their outcomes tended to be rather different. Natural selection produced a constantly increasing and diversifying variety of forms; it never reversed or exactly repeated itself. At first it might seem that the constant development of new breeds of domesticated animals echoed the natural proliferation of wild species. But anyone familiar with artificial selection would have realized that, although improved varieties of wheat and cattle showed little tendency to revert to the condition of their aboriginal wild ancestors, the strains produced by human selection were neither as prolific nor as durable as those produced by nature (Figure 2.2). Indeed, the animals and plants celebrated as the noblest achievements of the breeder's art were especially liable to delicacy and infertility. This tendency produced a predictable and paradoxical dilemma. Highly bred strains, long isolated from others of their species to preserve their genealogical purity, far from serving as a springboard for future variation, often had to be revivified with infusions of less-rarefied blood (Figure 2.3). Yet any relaxation of reproductive boundaries threatened subsidence into the common run of conspecifics.

At least in part, the disjunction between these two versions of selection reflects a dichotomy between the wild and the domesticated that has operated powerfully within both scientific and general culture, although it has not normally been the subject of much reflection. With regard to animals especially (as opposed to plants), it has tended to be taken for granted.

When Lord Byron wrote that "the Assyrian came down like the wolf on the fold" ("The Destruction of Sennacherib," 1815), his audience had no trouble understanding the simile or feeling its force, even though wolves had not threatened most British flocks since the Wars of the Roses (Figure 2.4). Almost two centuries later, expressions such as "the wolf is at the door" remain evocative, although the Anglophone

FIGURE 2.4
The wolf was exterminated in Britain by medieval hunters.

Reprinted from James Edmund Harting, *British Animals Extinct within Historic Times* (London: Trübner, 1880), 151.

FIGURE 2.5
Wolf Hollow assistant director Z. Soffron with Weeble, one of the resident wolves.

© Bourbon Street Photography.

experience of wolves has diminished still further. For most of us, they are only to be encountered (if at all) in zoos, or in establishments like Wolf Hollow, which is located in Ipswich, just north of Boston, where a pack of gray wolves lives a sheltered suburban existence behind a high chain-link fence.[3] Their captivity in Massachusetts has produced some modification of their nomadic habits and their fierce independent dispositions. (The pack was established twenty years ago with pups, so that only inherent inclinations, not confirmed behaviors, needed to be modified.) Their relationship with their caretakers seems affectionate and playful, sometimes even engagingly doglike—so much so that visitors need to be warned that it would be very dangerous for strangers to presume on this superficial affability (Figure 2.5). The animals themselves give occasional indications that they retain the capacities of their free-roaming relatives—that though apparently reconciled to confinement, they are far from tame. When large loud vehicles rumble past on nearby Route 133, the wolves tend to howl. And despite their secure enclosure within the built-up landscape of North American sprawl, their calls evoke the eerie menace that has immemorially echoed through the wild woods of fairy tale and fable. At least within the controlled setting of Wolf Hollow, this frisson of fear is clearly attractive. The website howls when you open it, and visitors are invited to howl with the wolves before they leave the sanctuary.

The symbolic resonance of large, ferocious, wild animals—the traditional representatives of what seems most threatening about the natural world—has thus proved much more durable than their physical presence. Indeed, their absence has often had equal and opposite figurative force. Thus, the extermination of wolves in Great Britain, along with such other unruly creatures as bears and wild boars, was routinely adduced as evidence of the triumph of insular (as opposed to continental) civilization in the early modern period (Figure 2.6). As they dispersed around the globe, British settlers and colonizers set themselves parallel physical and metaphorical challenges, conflating the elimination of dangerous animals with the imposition of political and military order. In North America, hunters could claim bounties for killing wolves from the seventeenth century into the twentieth century, although by the latter period wolves had abandoned most of their historic range, persisting only in remote mountains, forests, and tundras. In Africa and (especially) Asia, imperial officials such as Edward Lockwood, a magistrate in the Bengal Civil Service, celebrated the "extermination of wild beasts" as one of "the undoubted advantages . . . derived from British rule."[4]

Very occasionally, large and aggressive predators could symbolize help rather than hindrance. They served as totems for people whose own inclinations were conventionally wolfish or leonine. And alongside the legendary and historical accounts of big bad wolves existed a minority tradition that emphasized cooperation rather than competition. From this perspective, the similarities of wolf society to that of humans implicitly opened

the possibility of individual exchange and adoption. A slender line of imagined lupine nurturers ran from the foster mother of Romulus and Remus to Akela, who protects and mentors Mowgli in *The Jungle Book* (1894). But in this way, as in others, Rudyard Kipling's animal polity looked toward the past rather than the future. By the late nineteenth century, human opinions of wolves and their ilk had indeed become noticeably mixed. The cause of this amelioration, however, was not an altered understanding of lupine character or an increased appreciation of the possibilities of anthropo-lupine cooperation, but rather a revised estimation of the very qualities that had made wolves traditional objects of fear and loathing.

The shift in European aesthetic sensibility that transformed rugged mountains into objects of admiration rather than disgust is a commonplace of the history of art. For example, in the early eighteenth century, even the relatively modest heights of what was to become known as the English Lake District impressed Daniel Defoe as "eminent only for being the wildest, most barren and frightful of any that I have passed over in England, or even in Wales itself."⁵ The increasingly romantic tourists who followed him gradually learned to appreciate this harsh dramatic landscape, so that a century later the noted literary opium-eater Thomas De Quincey could characterize the vistas that had horrified Defoe as a "paradise of virgin beauty."⁶ Of course, this altered perception had complex roots, but it is suggestive that it coincided with improvements in transportation and other aspects of tourist infrastructure. As economic and technological developments made the world seem safer and more comfortable, it became possible to experience some of its extremes as thrilling rather than terrifying. Or, to put it another way, as nature began to seem a less overwhelming opponent, the valence of its traditional symbols began to change. Ultimately (much later, after their population numbers and geographic ranges had been radically reduced), even wild predators began to benefit from this reevaluation. The ferocity and danger associated with wolves and their figurative ilk became a source of glamour, evoking admiration and sympathy from a wide range of people who were unlikely to ever encounter them. As representatives of the unsettled landscapes in which

they had managed to survive, they inspired nostalgia rather than antagonism.

Symbolic shifts were supplemented by shifts in scientific understanding, which redefined high-end predators as a necessary element of many natural ecosystems. Late nineteenth-century attempts at wild animal protection were modeled on the hunting preserves of European and Asian elites. Thus, the immediate antecedents of modern wildlife sanctuaries and national parks were designed to protect individual species that were identified as both desirable (either intrinsically or as game) and in danger of extinction, such as the bison in North America or the giraffe in Africa (Figure 2.7). They were much less concerned with preserving the surrounding web of life. Indeed, in most cases, early wildlife management policies had the opposite effect, continuing, for example, to encourage the persecution of predators such as lions, hyenas, and wild dogs. Although not all of the species targeted for protection provided conventional hunting trophies—for example, by the end of the nineteenth century, many great ape populations received some form of protection—all were herbivores. Further, none offered significant

FIGURE 2.7
American bison, one of the first endangered species to receive protection.

Reprinted from Richard Lydekker, *The Royal Natural History*, vol. 2, *Mammals* (London and New York: Frederick Warne, 1894), 192.

resistance to human domination of their territory. (If they did, policies could be reversed. For example, hippopotamuses, which enjoyed protection in some parts of southern Africa, were slaughtered with official encouragement in Uganda, where their belligerent attitude toward river traffic interfered with trade.[7]) Predators inclined to kill the species designated for protection received no protection themselves, either physical or legal. On the contrary, in many settings people simply replaced large predators at the top of the food chain and showed no mercy to their supplanted rivals.

Deep ancient roots can be unearthed for holistic or ecological thinking. Although most of the British pioneers of game preservation had enjoyed the classical education prescribed for privileged Victorian boys, the works of Charles Darwin may have offered more readily accessible arguments for understanding biological assemblages as interconnected wholes. Darwin provided many illustrations of the subtle and complex relationships among the organisms that shared a given territory. For example, in *On the Origin of Species*, he explained the frequency of several species of wildflowers in southern England as a function of the number of domestic cats kept in nearby villages. The cats had no direct interest in the flowers, but more cats meant fewer field mice to prey on beehives—therefore, fewer mice meant more bees to fertilize the flowers.[8] Nevertheless, it was not until the last half of the twentieth century that individual species were routinely considered as components of larger systems by wildlife managers and that the standard unit of management became the ecosystem rather than the species. In consequence, large predators were redefined as essential components (even indicators) of a healthy environment rather than as blots on the landscape. They often began to receive legal protection, however belated and ineffective. And there has been a movement to reintroduce them to areas that have been ostensibly preserved in their wild form or that are in process of restoration. Thus, in recent decades wolves have reoccupied several of their former habitats in the western United States, both as a result of carefully coordinated reintroduction by humans, as in Yellowstone National Park, and as a result of independent (but unimpeded) migration from Canada. It is interesting that the reemergence or even the

prospective reemergence of the wolf has inspired a parallel reemergence of traditional fear and hostility among neighboring human populations.

I have been using several terms as if their meanings were clear and definite, when in fact they are contested and ambiguous. As has often been repeated, the cultural critic Raymond Williams characterized "nature" as "perhaps the most complex word in the English language."[9] The term "wilderness" is similarly problematic. In the context of preservation or restoration, it often collocates with words like "pristine" and "untouched," and therefore connotes a condition at once primeval and static. This connotation suggests that the first task of landscape stewards is to identify this ur-condition, but even a moderately long chronological perspective demonstrates that any such effort is bound to be quixotic. The environment in which modern animals have evolved has never been stable. Less than twenty thousand years ago, much of North America and Eurasia was covered by glaciers. After their gradual release from the burden of ice and water, most northern lands continued to experience significant shifts in topography and climate and, therefore, in flora and fauna. These natural changes have been supplemented for thousands of years by the impact of human activities. The theoretical and political problems presented by "wilderness" are knottier still. In a groundbreaking essay published more than a decade ago, William Cronon argued that wilderness and civilization (or "garden") were not mutually exclusive opposites, but rather formed part of a single continuum. Far from being absolute, "the one place on earth that stands apart from humanity," wilderness was itself "a quite profoundly human creation."[10] Cronon's formulation sparked (and continues to spark) agonized resistance on the part of environmentalists who base their commitment on the notion of untouched nature.

If wildness in landscape has been effectively (if controversially) problematized, the same cannot be said for wildness in animals. The *Oxford English Dictionary* (OED) defines the adjective "wild" unambiguously and emphasizes its zoological application. The first sense refers to animals: "Living in a state of nature; not tame, not domesticated: opp. to TAME." In a standard lexicographical ploy, "tame"

FIGURE 2.8
Semiwild; reintroducing the wolf to Yellowstone National Park. Park officials, including Bruce Babbitt, secretary of the interior, carry the first crate to the Crystal Bench pen, January 12, 1995.

National Park Service photograph no. 15032; photograph by Jim Peaco.

is defined with equal confidence and complete circularity as (also the first sense) "Reclaimed from the wild state; brought under the control and care of man; domestic; domesticated. (Opp. to *wild*.)."[11] But outside the dictionary, these terms are harder to pin down and their interrelationships are more complex. Like Cronon's wilderness and garden, the wild and the tame or domesticated exist along a continuum. In a world where human environmental influence extends to the highest latitudes and the deepest seas, few animal lives remain untouched by it. At least in this sense, therefore, few can said to be completely wild—for example, it would be difficult to so characterize the wolves that were captured, sedated, and airlifted to Yellowstone, then kept in "acclimatization pens" to help them adapt to their new companions and surroundings (Figure 2.8). And as the valence of the wild has increased and its definition has become more obviously a matter of assertion rather than description, the boundaries of domestication have also blurred.

Not that they were ever especially clear. As twenty-first-century wolves belong to a long line of animals whose wildness has been compromised,

tameness has conversely also existed on a sliding scale. According to the OED, both "wild" and "tame" have persisted for a millennium, remaining constant in form as well as core meaning, while the language around them has mutated beyond easy comprehension, if not beyond recognition. But this robustness on the level of abstraction has cloaked imprecision and ambiguity on the level of application or reference. Although medieval farmers and hunters may have had no trouble distinguishing livestock animals from game or vermin, it would have been difficult to extract any general definition from their practices. The impact of domestication varied from kind to kind, as well as from creature to creature. The innate aggression of the falcons and ferrets who assisted human hunters was merely channeled, not transformed; when they were not working, they were confined like wild animals in menageries. Then, as now, people exerted much greater sway over their dogs than their cats, who were mostly allowed to follow their instincts with regard to rodents and reproduction. Medieval cattle, the providers of labor as well as meat, milk, and hides, led more constrained lives than did

FIGURE 2.9
A royal trophy.

Reprinted from John Storer,
The Wild White Cattle of Great Britain (London: Cassell, Petter, and Galpin, 1879), 169.

contemporary sheep, and pigs were often left to forage in the woods like the wild boars that they closely resembled.

With hindsight, even these relatively tame cattle could appear undomesticated, especially as wildness gained in glamour. Thus, changes in the animals' physical circumstances were complicated by changes in the way they were perceived. In the late eighteenth century, for example, a few small herds of unruly white cattle, who roamed like deer through the parks of their wealthy owners, were celebrated as aboriginal and wild. As the Earl of Tankerville, whose Chillingham herd was the most famous, put it, his "wild cattle" were "the ancient breed of the island, inclosed long since within the boundary of the park."[12] The "ancient breed" was sometimes alleged to be the mighty aurochs (the extinct wild ancestor of all domestic cattle, which had been eliminated in Britain by Bronze Age hunters; the last one died in Poland in the seventeenth century), which gave these herds an ancestry distinct from that of ordinary domestic cattle. To increase or underscore their distinctiveness, the white cattle were never milked, and if their meat was required for such ceremonial occasions as the coming-of-age of a human heir, they were hunted and shot, not ignominiously slaughtered (Figure 2.9). Through the nineteenth century, their autochthonous nobility continued to inspire the effusions of such distinguished poets and painters as Sir Walter Scott and Sir Edwin Landseer, as well as the expenditure of newly wealthy landowners eager to bask by association in the prestige of wild nobility and ancient descent.

But even at the height of their renown, it was clear that the claims of the white cattle to wildness included a large measure of wishful thinking. Skeptics persuasively wondered whether, even assuming that the nineteenth-century emparked herds lived in a state of nature, that state represented a historical constant or a relatively modern restoration.[13] Many who investigated the background of the herds concluded that they were feral at best (at

FIGURE 2.10
Still wild; a modern Chillingham bull.

Photograph courtesy of Stephen J. G. Hall.

FIGURE 2.11
Foraging for food.

National Park Service
photograph no. 11162;
photograph by
R. Robinson.

wildest, in other words)—that they were the descendants of domesticated animals, whether originally owned by Roman settlers or by later farmers. Modern anatomical and genetic research has confirmed these doubts, firmly connecting the emparked herds with the ordinary domestic cattle of the medieval period.[14] But so great is the continuing appeal of wildness, and so limited the persuasive force of scientific evidence, that a recent president of the Chillingham Wild Cattle Association has nevertheless asserted that "although there is still much that is not known about the origins of the Chillingham Wild Cattle, one fact that is certain is that they were never domesticated" (Figure 2.10).[15]

Only a few people possessed the resources necessary to express their admiration for the wild, and their somewhat paradoxical desire to encompass it within the domestic sphere, on such a grand scale. But numerous alternative options emerged for those with more restricted acres and purses. An increasing variety of exotic animals stocked private menageries. The largest of these were on a sufficiently grand scale to have also included a cattle herd, if their owners had been so inclined—for example, those of George III or the thirteenth Earl of Derby, which accommodated large animals like kangaroos, cheetahs, zebras, and antelopes. Smaller animals required more modest quarters, and parrots, monkeys, canaries, and even the celebrated but ill-fated wombats owned by the poet Dante Gabriel Rossetti could be treated as pets. Breeders attempted to enhance or invigorate their livestock with infusions of exotic blood. If they were disinclined or unable to maintain their own wild sire, they could, in the 1820s and 1830s, pay a stud fee to the newly established Zoological Society of London for the services of a zebu or zebra. In Australia, Russia, Algeria, and the United States, as well as in Britain and France, the acclimatization societies of the late nineteenth century targeted an impressive range of species for transportation and domestication, from the predictable (exotic deer and wild sheep) to the more imaginative (yaks, camels, and tapirs).[16] So difficult (or undesirable) had it become to distinguish between wild animals and tame ones that exotic breeds of domestic dogs were exhibited in Victorian zoos, and small wild felines were exhibited in some early cat shows.

The popular appeal of wild animals has continued to increase as they have become more accessible, either in the flesh or in the media. So entangled have

FIGURE 2.12
Herdwick rams
in their natural
habitat, 1900.

Reprinted from
Frank W. Garnett,
*Westmorland
Agriculture,
1800–1900* (Kendal,
UK: Titus Wilson,
1912), opp p. 156.

wildness and domesticity become that it is now necessary to warn visitors to North American parks that roadside bears may bite the hands that feed them, and it is now possible for domesticated animals to represent nature (Figure 2.11). This extended symbolic reach was demonstrated in 2001, when foot-and-mouth disease struck British livestock. Because the disease spreads rapidly and easily, the government prescribed a cull not only of all infected herds and flocks, but of all apparently healthy livestock living in their vicinity. Although outbreaks were widespread, the greatest number of cases occurred in the Lake District, the starkly dramatic landscape that had been disparaged by Daniel Defoe and praised by Thomas De Quincey; it is now the site of England's largest national park. Video and print coverage of the cull, which took the spectacular form of soldiers shooting flocks of sheep and then immolating them in enormous pyres, thus featured some of the nation's most cherished countryside as background.

The ovine victims also had iconic status. Most of them belonged to the local Herdwick breed, and at first the intensive cull seemed to threaten its very survival. What was at stake was not merely adaptation to a demanding environment, since several other British hill breeds look very like the Herdwicks and share their physical and emotional toughness. The Herdwicks' special claim to consideration was their connection to their native ground, itself a kind of national sacred space (Figure 2.12). Not only were the sheep acknowledged to possess detailed topographical information about the hills they inhabited, but their owners claimed that they transmitted it mystically down the generations, from ewe to lamb. So well recognized was their attachment to their home territories that when a farm was sold, the resident Herdwicks were conventionally included in the bargain, on the theory that if they were taken away, they would soon manage to return. And despite strong historical indications that the ancestral Herdwicks had arrived in the vicinity of the Lake District by boat, and the further fact that all British sheep descend from wild mouflons originally domesticated in the eastern Mediterranean region, they were traditionally celebrated as indigenous, "peculiar to that high, exposed, rocky, mountainous district."[17] An article in a preeminent Victorian agricultural journal asserted that the Herdwicks possessed "more of the characters of an original race than any other in the county" and that they showed "no marks of kindred with any other race."[18] Twenty-first-century journalists reporting on the threatened toll of foot-and-mouth disease adopted similar rhetoric.

As the sheep were nativized, they were also naturalized. A reporter for the *Independent* newspaper feared that if the Herdwicks disappeared, the whole ecology of the region might be changed "beyond recognition."[19] And, since the dramatic bare uplands of the Lake District have been maintained by nibbling flocks for at least a millennium, his concern was not completely unreasonable. Thus, whether technically indigenous or not, and although incontestably domesticated, the Herdwicks have become compelling symbols of the apparently untamed landscape they inhabit—more compelling than the numerous wild birds and small mammals with which they share it. Like the landscape itself, they seem wilder than they are; that is, they appear to be independent and free-ranging, but their lives (and, indeed, their very existence) are ultimately determined by human economic exigencies. They are both accessible (that is, there are a lot of them and they are everywhere, not only in the fields, but grazing and napping beside the roads and even on top of them) and also inaccessible (that is, they are skittish, and tend to

retreat when approached). The armed assault on the Herdwick sheep was, therefore, perceived as an attack on the domesticated countryside and on the unspoiled natural landscape. In both the sheep and their environment, the wild and the tame had inextricably merged.

If vernacular usage illustrates the increasing slippage between wildness and tameness in animals, scientific classification has made a similar point from the opposite direction. The species concept has a long and vexed history. The study of natural history (or botany and zoology) requires that individual kinds be labeled, but for many plants and animals (those that, unlike giraffes, for example, have very similar relatives) it has often been difficult for naturalists to tell where one kind ends and the next begins. Darwin's theory of evolution by natural selection provided a theoretical reason for this difficulty, and his shrewd observations that "it is in the best-known countries that we find the greatest number of forms of doubtful value" and "if any animal or plant . . . be highly useful to man . . . varieties of it will almost universally be found recorded" offered a more pragmatic explanation.[20] The classification

FIGURE 2.13
Lion-tiger hybrids fascinated nineteenth-century zoo-goers.

Reprinted from Richard Lydekker, *A Hand-book to the Carnivora*, pt. 1, *Cats, Civets, and Mungooses* (London: Edward Lloyd, 1896), pl. 2.

of domesticated animals has epitomized this problem—that is, none of them has become sufficiently different from its wild ancestor to preclude the production of fertile offspring (the conventional if perennially problematic definition of the line between species), and some mate happily with more distant relatives. Nineteenth-century zookeepers enjoyed experimenting along these lines, and zoogoers admired the resulting hybrids between horses and zebras, domestic cattle and bison, and dogs and wolves (Figure 2.13).[21]

Despite these persuasive demonstrations of kinship, however, from the eighteenth-century emergence of modern taxonomy, classifiers have ordinarily allotted each type of domestic animal its own species name. While recognizing the theoretical difficulties thus produced, most modern taxonomists have continued to follow conventional practice. Domestic sheep are still classified as *Ovis aries* while the mouflon is *Ovis orientalis*; dogs are *Canis familiaris* while the wolf is *Canis lupus*. The archaeozoologist Juliet Clutton-Brock explains this practice as efficient (it would be unnecessarily confusing to alter widely accepted nomenclature) as well as scientifically grounded, at least to some extent (most domestic animal populations are reproductively isolated from wild ones by human strictures, if not by biological ones).[22] But it also constitutes a simultaneous acknowledgment of the artificiality of the distinction between wild animals and domesticated ones, and of its importance and power. Vernacular understandings can trump those based on anatomy and physiology.

The implications of making or not making such distinctions extend beyond the intellectual realm. They construct the physical world at the same time that they describe it. Although the howls of the wolf may retain their primordial menace, the wolves who make them have long vanished from most of their vast original range, and they are threatened in much of their remaining territory. To persist or to return, they need human protection, not only physical but legal and taxonomic. With the advent of DNA analysis in recent decades, the taxonomic stakes have risen, so that even animals that look and act wild

may be found genetically unworthy. Thus, efforts to preserve the red wolf, which originally ranged across the southeastern United States, have been complicated by suggestions that it is not a separate species but a hybrid of the gray wolf and coyote. No such aspersions have been cast upon the pedigree of the gray wolf, but nevertheless every attempted gray wolf restoration has triggered human resistance, and local challenges to their endangered status inevitably follow even moderate success. Wildness has become a political issue as well as a zoological one—indeed, a matter of life and death. If domestic dogs were returned to their ancestral taxon, wolves would become one of the commonest animals in the lower forty-eight states, rather than one of the rarest. Their survival as wild animals depends on the dog's continuing definition as domesticated.

One of the clearest implications of Charles Darwin's theory of evolution by natural selection was that the category of species was essentially artificial. If parent species morphed gradually into their evolutionary offspring, their distinctive Latinate labels reflected the exigencies of science rather than any observable external phenomena. Although many living species were easy enough to distinguish from their closest relatives, the boundaries that separated others seemed to be the result of human assertion, which suggested that the problem of interspecific hybridization could be understood as an artifact of zoological taxonomy rather than an anomaly of nature. Even explicit acknowledgment of the constructed nature of the species category did not, however, undermine its utility, either for scholars and scientists, or for the many people who dealt with animals more pragmatically. Certainly, Darwin's theory did not end (and has not yet ended) the centuries-old debate about the definition of "species." Although the categories of "wild" and "tame" or "domesticated" are less authoritatively attested, they are equally problematic and equally powerful. Absolute wildness may be difficult to define on paper and even more difficult to identify in the world, but it nevertheless continues to determine government policies, the actions of individual humans, and the fate of many other kinds of animals.

Notes

An earlier version of this essay, "Beasts in the Jungle (or Wherever)," appeared in *Dædalus* 137, no. 2 (Spring 2008): 22–30.

1 Charles Darwin, *The Variation of Animals and Plants under Domestication* (London: John Murray, 1868). Chapters five and six are devoted to pigeons.

2 Charles Darwin, *On the Origin of Species* (1859; facsimile of the 1st ed., Cambridge, Mass.: Harvard University Press, 1964), 83.

3 "Wolf Hollow," accessed December 26, 2011, http://www.wolfhollowipswich.org.

4 Edward Lockwood, *Natural History, Sport, and Travel* (London: W. H. Allen, 1878), 237.

5 Daniel Defoe, *A Tour Through the Whole Island of Great Britain*, ed. P. N. Furband and W. R. Owens (1724–26; repr., New Haven: Yale University Press, 1991), 291.

6 Thomas De Quincey, *Literary Reminiscences: From the Autobiography of an English Opium Eater* (Boston: Ticknor, Reed, and Fields, 1851), 3:310–11.

7 Harriet Ritvo, *The Animal Estate: The English and Other Creatures in the Victorian Age* (Cambridge, Mass.: Harvard University Press, 1987), 284–89.

8 Darwin, *On the Origin of Species*, 73–74.

9 Raymond Williams, *Keywords: A Vocabulary of Culture and Society* (New York: Oxford University Press, 1976), 184.

10 William Cronon, "The Trouble with Wilderness; or, Getting Back to the Wrong Nature," in *Uncommon Ground: Rethinking the Human Place in Nature*, ed. William Cronon (New York: W. W. Norton, 1996), 69.

11 *Oxford English Dictionary*, s.v. "wild," accessed March 8, 2012, http://www.oed.com.ezp-prod1.hul.harvard.edu/view/Entry/228988?rskey=dBvZx1&result=1&isAdvanced=false#eid; and *Oxford English Dictionary*, s.v. "tame," accessed March 8, 2012, http://www.oed.com.ezp-prod1.hul.harvard.edu/view/Entry/197387?rskey=Ffdqud&result=1&isAdvanced=false#eid.

12 C. A. B. Tankerville and L. Hindmarsh, "On the Wild Cattle of Chillingham Park," *Athenaeum* 565 (August 25, 1838): 611.

13 For an extended discussion of the history of this debate, see Harriet Ritvo, "Race, Breed, and Myths of Origin: Chillingham Cattle as Ancient Britons," *Representations* 39 (Summer 1992): 1–22.

14 For summaries of modern research, see Stephen J. G. Hall and Juliet Clutton-Brock, *Two Hundred Years of British Farm Livestock* (London: British Museum, 1989); Stephen J. G. Hall, "The White Herd of Chillingham," *Journal of the Royal Agricultural Society of England* 150 (1989): 112–19; and Stephen J. G. Hall, "Running Wild," *Ark* 16 (1989): 12–15, 46–49.

15 Ian Bennet, "Chillingham Cattle," *Ark* 18 (1991): 22.

16 Ritvo, *Animal Estate*, 232–42.

17 John Bailey and George Culley, *General View of the Agriculture of Northumberland, Cumberland, and Westmorland* (1805; repr., Newcastle, UK: Graham, 1972), 245.

18 William Dickinson, "On the Farming of Cumberland," *Journal of the Royal Agricultural Society of England* 13 (1852): 264.

19 Ian Herbert, "Foot and Mouth Crisis: Cumbria," *Independent*, March 27, 2001.

20 Darwin, *On the Origin of Species*, 50.

21 Harriet Ritvo, *The Platypus and the Mermaid, and Other Figments of the Classifying Imagination* (Cambridge, Mass.: Harvard University Press, 1997), 92–95.

22 Juliet Clutton-Brock, *A Natural History of Domesticated Mammals* (Cambridge: Cambridge University Press; London: British Museum, 1987), 194–97.

CHAPTER 3

Wildness and Wilderness in Ottoman Gardens and Landscape

Manifestations of Nature through Body, Architecture, and City

B. Deniz Çalış

OTTOMAN GARDENS AND LANDSCAPES MAKE UP a newly flourishing domain of study. However, no substantial research has been conducted on Ottoman wildlife, except for concise surveys on menageries. Animals are only an occasional subtopic in studies of hunting, along with the wildlife habitats that set the scene for the endeavor. Although we are not equipped with the scientific data to assess wildlife habitats in Ottoman times, ignorance of natural elements as fundamental as animals and their habitats leaves a massive gap in our understanding of the premodern Ottoman world, including our ability to appreciate Ottoman garden and landscape traditions.

This research aspires to reconstruct historical perceptions, with the hope of inspiring contemporary studies on wildlife in the geographical area covered in the analysis.[1] It intends to shed light on the cultural meaning of the wild, and aims to examine wilderness as it was experienced in terms of space and metaphor—either as designed, inhabited, pursued, embodied, or, at times, imagined. Toward this end, the research was initially focused on hunting preserves and imperial gardens as two different domains for gaining knowledge on wildlife

habitats. Yet the study has progressed so that it now suggests an interconnected relevance between the seemingly fragmented spaces of uncultivated hunting preserves outside the city and cultivated gardens of imperial palaces within the city.

This study intends to reconstruct two different perspectives. The first is the cultural idea of "wilderness" experienced by the Ottoman sultan. We learn of this perspective by examining documents on Ottoman imperial practices associated with hunting preserves and menageries. The second involves documentation of "wild" based on accounts from foreign visitors to Ottoman lands. Thus, the study offers two layers of disparate visions: the culturally constructed idea of wilderness, and the physical reality documented mostly by foreigners from the sixteenth to the nineteenth century. Territorially, the study focuses on two cities of the Ottoman world from the sixteenth to late seventeenth centuries: Istanbul, the capital of centralized Ottoman power, and Edirne, a principal site of Ottoman frontier culture opening to the west, the Balkans.

Wilderness was a quality bestowed, granted, and inherited in the persona of the Ottoman sultan, and the research suggests that through the

FIGURE 3.1
*"My breast is a
garden for me."*
Nigari, portrait of
Sultan Selim II.

Topkapı Sarayı
Müzesi TSM H2134, 3b.

body of the sultan a connection was made between the seemingly fragmented pieces of wilderness, whether amid nature outside the city or within the city (Figure 3.1). The chest of the sultan was metaphorically the center of not only the Ottoman world, but also the House of Islam, and it was conceived as a Paradise Garden. Ottoman space was constructed, perceived, and represented in metaphorical and poetical ways; the notion of ideal space as a garden is best represented in poetry by the sixteenth-century Ottoman poet Rahmî: "Why should I contemplate the garden? My breast is a garden for me."[2]

Thus, the idea of wilderness that emerges is united, embodied, experienced, and alive in the physical and mental construction of the Ottoman sultan, his imperial persona. In different scales—as extensions of his body—his palace and his capital city, as the centers of the empire and the House of Islam, were also conceived as gardens and bestowed with paradisiacal qualities. At the same time, they were spaces displaying the magnitude of imperial power. Thus, wild animals were members of the Paradise Garden(s) accompanying the sultan, in addition to illustrating the multitude of species in his possession (Figure 3.2).

B. DENIZ ÇALIŞ

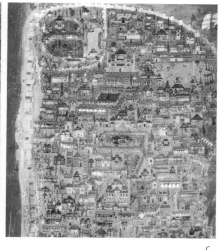

a   b   c

FIGURE 3.2

The Paradise Garden perceived, represented, and experienced in different scales, as the sultan's body, his palace, and his capital city: a) Nigari, portrait of Sultan Selim II (detail) (Topkapı Sarayı Müzesi TSM H2134, 3b); b) Topkapı Palace, from Lokman's *Hünername*, ca. 1584–85 (Topkapı Sarayı Müzesi TSM 1523, 231b); and c) Matrakçı Nasuh, sixteenth-century map of Istanbul (İstanbul Üniversitesi Kütüphanesi T5964, 8b).

Wilderness within the City

Menageries and Wild Animal Collections in Sixteenth-Century Istanbul

In sixteenth-century Istanbul, there were four imperial menageries. Two were located in the ruins of Byzantine monuments—one in a Byzantine chapel in the city center close to Hagia Sophia, and the other near the city walls within the Tekfur Palace. The second pair of menageries was located in the Old Palace, which was completed in 1458 (three years after the conquest of the city), and in the New Palace, also called the Topkapı Palace, founded in 1458–59 and used as the main imperial residence.[3] Strangely enough, at the former two locations, no habitat was created for the wild animals. These vacant Byzantine monuments were probably selected because of their vast scale and the lofty heights of their elevated domes. Special attendants looked after the wild animals. From time to time, the animals were displayed in public spaces, on the street, and as part of imperial processions and festivals.

FIGURE 3.3

A rhinoceros, a gift from Habeş, is shown to the public at Üsküdar shore before being transported by boat to the sultan's palace, from *Şehname-i Selim Han*.

Topkapı Sarayı Müzesi TSM H3595, 152a.

FIGURE 3.4
A rhinoceros,
elephants, and a lion
to be presented to the
sultan by the Persian
ambassador, from
Şehname-i Nadiri.

Topkapı Sarayı Müzesi
TSM H1124, 24b–25a.

Menageries of the Ottoman Court in the City

The first menagerie in the city—the Tekfur Palace, located near the Byzantine city walls—housed two elephants and a giraffe. In circa 1549–50, one of the elephants was about thirty to thirty-five years old, and the other was apparently over one hundred. The French naturalist Pierre Belon (who accompanied the French legation from 1546 to 1549) observed the attentiveness with which the sultan's wild animal collection—housed in these former Byzantine sites—was cared for. The animals themselves had been gathered from provinces around the empire and sent to Istanbul to display the magnitude of Ottoman rule, or they were presented as gifts from Ottoman dignitaries or other rulers of the Near East (Figures 3.3 and 3.4).[4] For example, a lion was sent to Istanbul from Tunisia, a rhinoceros from Habesh—a province bordering the Red Sea—and an elephant, lions, and a rhinoceros from Persia. Jean Chesneau (ca. 1549–50), secretary to the French ambassador

Gabriel d'Aramon, recorded that the elephants were looked after by North Africans. The German traveler Hans Dernschwam (1553–55) described the giraffe as a very strange animal that lived within a high-domed Byzantine palace, appropriate and necessary given the reach of the creature's neck.[5]

The second menagerie in the city was located rather centrally near the Hippodrome and Hagia Sophia, and was called the House of Lions—Arslanhane. It housed various wild animals, which Philip du Fresne-Canaye (1573), accompanying the French ambassador to the Levant, identified as "wild beasts."[6]

According to foreign visitors to the menagerie, this collection included lions, wolves, wild asses, hedgehogs, porcupines, bears, ermines and civets, lynx, wildcats, leopards, Siberian panthers, ostriches, and others. In another case, the pharmacist Reinhold Lubenau (1587–98) recorded that the ancient church near Hagia Sophia housed eight large lions in separate cages, in addition to two small lions, two large tigers, two panthers (one young, one old), six wild-cats, two "restless" wild asses, two dogs, several monkeys, and many leopards—which the sultan took along on hunting expeditions—as well as a cat-like beast (a hyena) believed to understand human language.[7] On the upper floors of this menagerie, the House of Lions, there was the famous workshop of the Ottoman court painters, the Nakkaşhane. This menagerie was kept intact until the early nineteenth century. But when it was severely damaged in the 1802 fire, after a devastating earthquake in 1766, the animals were taken to the Ibrahim Pasha Palace at the Hippodrome, also in the city center. Finally, in 1831, the animals were transferred to the Yedikule Dungeons, on the outskirts of the city.[8]

Menageries of the Ottoman Court in the Palaces

In addition to the menageries located within the city, wild animals were kept in the palace gardens.

In the sixteenth century, the gardens of the Topkapı Palace were built to represent a vision of the Earthly Paradise shared by Near Eastern cultures, including the plant, animal, and mineral worlds, also known as the three kingdoms of nature (Figure 3.5).[9] The Ottoman court came to be seen as a re-creation of the ancient court of Solomon, enriched by animals both real and represented. Solomon's throne was protected by lions, dragons, roosters, vultures, peacocks, and pigeons among olive, citrus, and date trees, all made out of precious materials including rubies, topaz, and gold. As an Ottoman poet noted, the ensemble "represented the seven layered heavens and the earth with its seven climes" (Figure 3.6):

They placed on four sides of the throne date, olive and citrus trees made of red gold, with leaves and fruits of turquoise, coral, beryl (chrysolite), green and red ruby (corundum), garnet and topaz. They attached on the dates

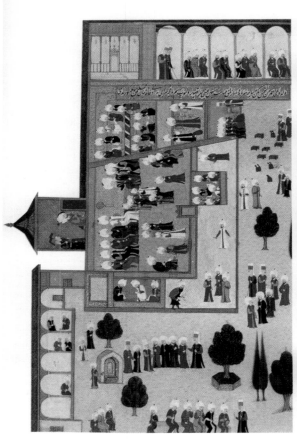

FIGURE 3.5
The second courtyard of the Topkapı Palace with gazelles wandering around freely, from Lokman's *Hünername*, ca. 1584–85.

Topkapı Sarayı Müzesi TSM 1523, 18b–19a.

two peacocks with ruby crowns, diamond necks, red ruby wings, pearl and rock crystal feet, green ruby wings, and green-ruby and topaz heads. In addition they fashioned two Egyptian vultures of red gold, studded with various jewels. The throne had seven steps; the first one of silver, the second one of red gold, the third of lapis lazuli, the fourth of green jade, the fifth of red coral, the sixth of yellow stone, and the last inlaid with seven different types of precious stones. On both sides of the throne's steps, they placed two lions of red gold that moved their tails and opened their mouths ferociously, as well as two silver dragons with seven heads and two feet. Because of the talismans the jinns and peris put into them, these animals guarded the throne by attacking those who wanted to sit on it, howling loudly, moving their wings and tails, and spouting fire. On the right and left side of the throne's center, they placed two pigeons, once again studded with various jewels, which sang every hour. A rooster perched on top of the throne's dome, which flapped its wings and croaked once every hour, was made of a solitary pearl, inlaid with precious gems. At the four sides of the throne, four mirrors were attached, on each of which talismans had been engraved with a diamond blade. One of these indicated

B. DENIZ ÇALIŞ

whether sick persons would recover or not, the other one the true face of spouses whose loyalty was suspect. On the other two sides were represented the seven layered heavens and the earth with its seven climes.[10]

Like Solomon's court, the Topkapı Palace gardens housed both cultivated and wild flora together with tamed and wild animals.[11] Animals wandered in different parts of the gardens, which were adorned with pools, fountains, and pavilions and made colorful and fragrant by tulips, narcissi, jasmines, grapevines, roses, lilacs, saffron, and herbs. As the garden came to encompass a large collection of treasures from the plant, animal, and mineral kingdoms, more such specimens were transported to it from other parts of the empire. One of the many expense reports from the sixteenth century documents the import of three hundred thousand tulip bulbs, eighty-four thousand pounds of rosebushes, and one hundred thousand hyacinth bulbs from provinces including Tripoli, Crimea, Aleppo, Diyarbakır, Edirne, and Maraş.[12]

According to historical accounts, three locations were designated for animals at Topkapı Palace: a menagerie called "tokat havlısı"; a marshy lake populated with reeds for wild geese and ducks; and an aviary.[13] Animals were let out for walks in the outer gardens surrounding the palace complex, or within the courtyards. They either wandered freely or were confined to enclosures within the garden, set off by red wooden fences. "Ostriches, peacocks, songbirds, deer, and gazelles" as well as foxes, hares, sheep, goats, and Indian cows dwelled on the grass or within the red wooden railings.[14]

In 1529, Johann Hoberdanacz recorded the presence of two elephants in the palace gardens. The animals were robed in expensive textiles. In the next year, ambassadors of the Spanish monarch Ferdinand I observed ten lions and two tigers. In 1544, a Frenchman Jérôme Maurand observed deer, roe deer, and ostriches in the gardens of the palace. And, early in the next century, Venetian representative Ottaviano Bon (1604–7) saw gazelles in the second courtyard (1603–17).[15] From the late fifteenth to the early seventeenth century, an aviary was situated in the third court of the Topkapı Palace.[16] In the

FIGURE 3.7
Sultan Süleyman the Magnificent hunting in the game preserves of the Old Palace, from Lokman's *Hünername*, ca. 1587–88.

Topkapı Sarayı Müzesi TSM H1524, 87b–88a.

seventeenth century, a new square-shaped aviary for falcons, hawks, and owls was built, centered within the courtyard with no windows, but with a fountain in the middle.

Although the sultans went on hunting expeditions outside the city, they sometimes enjoyed the same pursuits within the palace itself (Figure 3.7). In the second half of the sixteenth century, Murad III (1574–95) favored hunting in the gardens and watching his novices hunt deer, goat, wild boar, bears, and lions.[17] In 1621, during the reign of Osman II (1618–22), Louis Deshayes de Cormenin, French representative to the court of Louis XIII, describes how the act of hunting functioned as an allegory for war, with prey standing in for the enemies of the Ottoman Empire: "He (the Sultan) sometimes holds small hunts in his palace that are quite pleasant. He has many live wild boars caught, which they bring there into a place that is enclosed by canvas screens. When he wants to give them the pleasure, he has the Sultanas, eunuchs, and others whom he likes the most come there. He gives to each wild boar the name of one of his enemies, such as the King of Spain, whom he calls the Signor of Spain, the Duke of Florence, the Grand Master of Malta, and others in this manner."[18]

Wildlife and Daily Life in Sixteenth-Century Istanbul

Over the course of the sixteenth century, as Istanbul emerged as the center of the Ottoman Empire and the focus and dominion of imperial power, fragments of wildlife became part of urban culture, whether kept in royal menageries, gardens, or ruins. Foreign travel accounts show that visitors were able to observe wild animals in menageries by paying bribes, or else they simply would encounter wild animals when taken by their attendants on city streets or in public squares. In the sixteenth century, Baron Wratislaw, ambassador of Emperor Rudolf II, saw lions, lynx (vaşak), wildcats, leopards, and bears being led on chains around the city. Elephants, which were trained to perform, and lions walking in the streets were welcomed by city residents.[19]

The Private Animal Collection of Busbecq in Istanbul

The courtyard house of Ogier Ghislain de Busbecq presents an extraordinary example of locating animals within the city in a setting that was not a royal menagerie. The renowned sixteenth-century Hapsburg ambassador to the Ottoman court, Busbecq formed a private collection of animals at his residence in a "densely populated" district in the city center. Indeed, the main door of his house opened to the imperial ceremonial route. His home consisted of two stories and a large courtyard with a well at the center, but no greenery. The residence had small rooms on the second floor, which functioned as living spaces, surrounding and opening to this courtyard through a veranda. Out of personal interest, Busbecq acquired various wild animals and birds from the city of Istanbul, Anatolia, and the Aegean Islands, and kept them in his courtyard. His ironical narration of the house gives an insightful view of his private collection:

> It has no garden, in which one can take exercise, no tree or shrub, no greensward to rest the eye; on the other hand, it is infested by various animals. There are swarms of weasels, numerous snakes, lizards, and scorpions. . . .
>
> Not content with the creatures which are bred on the premises, I have filled the place with animals obtained elsewhere, the tending of which gives my household occupation and amusement, to my great satisfaction, and helps them to support with greater equanimity their longing to be back at home. For what better source is there, when we are deprived of human intercourse, than to seek oblivion of our misfortunes in the society of animals?[20]

In his courtyard, Busbecq had several horses and six camels, along with monkeys, wolves, bears, flat-horned stags, common deer, young mules, lynx, "weasels of the kinds called martens and sables," and pigs.[21] His vast bird collection included eagles, crows, jackdaws, "strange" ducks, Balearic cranes, and partridges with red beaks and red legs from the isle of Chios. Given the extent of this collection, one of Busbecq's friends compared the ambassador's house to Noah's ark.[22] Such a collection in the city center is the only one known to us from sixteenth-century Istanbul until the present day. As such, it suggests an extraordinary instance of containing wildlife in urban courtyards.

As members of urban society, so to speak, wild animals lived side by side with urban dwellers, and were allowed to be brought into public spaces as long as they were held by a chain. The cultivated and the wild were not separated from one another as we conceive today. Both existed side by side, and represented the diversity and extent of imperial power and wealth, both possessions of the sultan.

In 1582, festivities hosted by Murad III at the Hippodrome in Istanbul to mark the celebration of his sons' circumcision offer valuable illustrations of the range of wild animals in the sixteenth-century city (Figure 3.8). The procession of guilds, which lasted for fifty-two days, occasionally illustrates wild animals marching in the city center, together with the subjects of the sultan. The procession of lion trainers included a lion that confronted a wild boar at the Hippodrome, where the lion symbolized the Muslim world and the boar stood for the Christian world.[23] There were two bears marching with the bear trainers, displaying various skills and dancing to the rhythm of a drum; at one point, the bears escaped and attacked the audience.[24] There were also two elephants marching in the parade, one of them younger than the other, recalling the foreign travelers' accounts of two elephants of different ages in the sixteenth-century menageries of Istanbul.[25] Apart from the wild animals themselves, figures made from sugar were also carried and displayed during the parade. There were nine elephants, seventeen lions, nineteen leopards and tigers, one giraffe, twenty-two horses, twenty-one camels,

FIGURE 3.8
Wild animals from the procession of guilds at the Hippodrome, from Seyyid Lokman's *Şehinşahname*, 1597–98.

Topkapı Sarayı Müzesi TSM B200, 67b–68a.

twenty-five hawks and falcons, thirty-five monkeys together with 877 flowers, in addition to 308 narcissi and 281 roses identified specifically, all made out of sugar.[26] Each of the animal figures was carried by four men.[27] A gigantic model of a mountain was also exhibited, illustrating a hunting scene and adorned with caves, trees, and wild animals.

Nearly two centuries later, the Hippodrome, as one of the most important public spaces of Ottoman Istanbul, still welcomed wild animals. In October 1733, during their stroll in the city, Mr. Samuel Medley, butler to Lord Kinnoull, the British ambassador to Istanbul, recorded seeing lions among other "wild beasts" at the Hippodrome amid Byzantine and Ottoman monuments:

His Ex[cellenc]y M[ada]m Mrs Sandys and Mrs Cl[ar]k—y 2 Swedish Gent Mr Monere and Mr Lyle Jnr—& Most of us of the Retinue of my Ld past over to Constantinople Erly in the morning—to Se the famous Moskee Calld St Sophia & a very surprising building It is—we allso went to y Moskee Calld Sulltan accmet—the Lyons tigers and other wilde beasts allso was the attmedon—a very large place wher they ride and Sell Horses—all win y Citty—where is the Surprizing obelisk—the Serpentine Brass Pillar—& y old High Pillar (13 April 1734).[28]

In Ottoman cities beside Istanbul, wildlife was considered to be a natural constituent of urban life as well. For example, in Chios—as observed by Busbecq—villagers kept partridges in their households. The birds from different households would "congregate in the street, then they follow[ed] the herdsman as sheep do" and returned of their own volition, back to their homes for the night.[29] In the city of İznik, people considered nighttime visits by wild jackals to their homes to be an ordinary experience: "Hearing in the distance a loud noise as of men laughing and jeering, I asked what it was, thinking that perhaps some sailors . . . were jeering at us. . . . I was told that the noise was the howling of animals which the Turks call jackals. They are a small species of wolf, larger than foxes. . . . They go about in packs and are harmless to human beings and flocks, obtaining their food rather by theft and cunning than by violent methods."[30]

Wilderness outside the City

Consistent with Thomas Veltre's argument that "a menagerie, whatever its physical form, is primarily concerned with the symbolic role of animals within a culture,"[31] various other forms of interaction with animals, as in hunting preserves, parades, or imperial processions, also embody symbolic and metaphorical associations and represent the cultural appropriation of wilderness in diverse, yet interconnected ways.

Apart from the menageries within the city, the Ottoman court experienced wilderness during hunting expeditions, both around Istanbul and near Edirne. The tradition of hunting was a very important part of the royal Ottoman court, with its study offering scholars distinct perspectives from those provided by the menageries. Court members engaged in hunting with vigor, and the sultan was positioned both to dominate and to participate in the world of animals, both in physical and metaphysical terms (Figure 3.9).

During the classical period, hunting was part of the royal tradition. As Tülay Artan argues in her seminal work on Ottoman hunting, "God provides the hunting reserves and facilitates the hunt."[32] Hunting was not performed for sustenance but rather to conquer the world of animals and, by contrast, to also be one with the animals. Hunting established the sultan's royal existence both as part of the wilderness and as master of the animal kingdom. As Artan discusses, there were many instances when hunting was banned to commoners. Thus, as a privilege of the sultan, hunting prevented him from being a commoner—from the danger of adopting "habits and morals" of the masses.[33]

Ottoman chronicles of the lives and achievements of the sultans occasionally illustrate their hunting expeditions between military campaigns and victorious battles. In many instances, sultans are portrayed on hunting trips before, after, or during major life events, such as the birth or death of a son (Figure 3.10). They might even engage in diplomacy—for example, by accepting ambassadors—on hunting trips.[34]

Hunting also allowed the sultan to observe and to interact with a range of his subjects in many locations away from the capital. In addition, the act of chasing after prey had mystical symbolism,

standing for the search for Absolute Truth. Sultans could grow more powerful both physically and mentally by acquiring the traits of the wild animals they chased and ultimately dominated.[35]

Aside from meanings associated with power and truth, hunting allowed the sultan to escape from his comparatively static life in the capital. Artan explicitly explains and animates the circumstances and the emotional states of the Ottoman sultan during the hunting expeditions. Thus, the sultan could move about, practice, live, breathe, and make contact with the natural world. The wilderness, therefore, became an agency for personal freedom as well as a means of interacting more elementally with the natural world. Further, the sultan could achieve physical fitness and bolster his bodily and psychological strength through both observation and pursuit of his prey. Otherwise

engaged in a world of immobility, he became an actor by pursuing nature. Unlike in the capital, "he was able to push his horse to jump and to play."[36] Such movements in the city would put his dignity in peril. In the wild, however, "there were no observers and no rivals," and keepers of the hound were considered to be the closest confidants and subjects of the sultan. And the hunt constituted a safe space in other respects, as opposed to the real risks connected with leadership and war. Unlike in a war, the sultan could chase his prey and move forward without fear of injury or death causing loss in a battle.[37]

The Sultan's Body in Harmony with and against the Wild and Wilderness

In Ottoman culture, discourses pertaining to space, urban, and/or landscape cultures developed by

FIGURE 3.9
Sultan Süleyman the Magnificent hunting, from *Hünername* I.

Topkapı Sarayı Müzesi
TSM H1524, 52b–53a.

all the different features of nature. Gardens of all kinds were central in ontological, hermeneutical, and artistic traditions, enabling poetic, metaphoric, and even intertextual associations and creating layered and complex forms of cultural practices.

The philosophy that considers the body as a medium for the attainment of eternal knowledge is best explained in the teachings of the Islamic philosopher Ibn ʿArabî. ʿArabî discussed human bodies as intermediary spaces, as spaces of encounter, where physical and metaphysical worlds meet for reconciliation, for a better understanding of cosmology and eternal knowledge: knowledge of God and knowledge of all things created. Like the human body, gardens of all kinds were intermediary spaces of encounter, spaces for the attainment of knowledge.[38] Such intermediary spaces were experienced and appropriated through the act of imagination, metaphorically and poetically. One might argue that the limits and qualities of such spaces—the sultan's body, his palace, his capital city, or the range of landscape(s) he ruled—were not merely recognized by and appreciated for their physical qualities: Ottoman culture embraced and appropriated each one of these spaces to the limits of the Ottoman imagination.

The sultan's body became a space of encounter, where forces of wild nature coexisted with the harmonic beauties of tamed gardens. Thus, the relationship with nature took two disparate forms. At one extreme, the sultan posed himself in harmony with nature, as unified and one. The body of the sultan was a space where nature manifested its qualities; his body was the medium through which the sultan proudly presented the qualities of nature, whether wild or tamed. Such unification, resemblance, or representation placed the body of the sultan in the center of Ottoman cosmogony. At the other extreme, he was the master of nature, as in the act of hunting, holding supreme powers as the invincible. Such tension between harmony and mastery, comparison and contrast, formed the basis of Ottoman culture—not only limited to its vision and appropriation of nature, but also involving ontology, hermeneutics, and the arts.

Comparison and contrast were agencies to acquire eternal knowledge by means of similarities and disparities, known as *tashbîh* and *tanzîh*. Ibn ʿArabî

FIGURE 3.10
Sultan Süleyman the Magnificent hunting outside Filibe in September 1521, on the way back from Belgrade to Istanbul (a journey that would end on October 19, 1521), when he heard the news of his sons' deaths, from Arifi's *Süleymanname*, 1520–1555, 1558.

Topkapı Sarayı Müzesi TSM H1517, 115a.

poetic, metaphoric, and intertextual means. Spaces of the sultan—his body, his palace(s), his capital city as the center of his dominion, and further, the entire landscape, embracing his whole imperial terrain—were conceived and represented as gardens in different scales. These spaces unfolded into one another, sometimes physically and other times poetically and metaphorically. Adorned with gardens of diverse qualities in different scales, the territory of the Ottoman house was to be compared to the Paradise of Heavens, composed of variegated delights and eternal wisdom. Thus, whether tamed or wild, the all-embracing capacity and competence of the Ottoman house aimed to hold and possess explains tashbîh as a means to draw similarities between the unity of true knowledge and its reflections in the multiplicity of things created; it stands for the act of attaining divine knowledge through studying the similarities of all creation. However, the arts of tanzîh practice differences, asserting dissimilarity and incomparability. 'Arabî explains tanzîh as a means to attain knowledge of something by studying its opposites.[39] In this case, the mastery of wilderness and wild animals through the art of hunting can be understood as a form of contrast wherein the sultan engages in mastering nature, but desires to be as wild as wilderness can be understood, as a form of associating his body and self as one with nature. These different states—both with and against nature—did not negate one another: in totality, they introduced diverse ways of acquiring eternal knowledge through the possession of the multiplicity of all things created. Thus, the sultan's body, his palace(s), his capital city as the center of his dominion, and, further, the entire landscape embracing his imperial terrain became spaces for practicing, possessing, and experiencing the disparities and/or multiplicities of nature—in this case, the variegated qualities of the wild and wilderness—to attain the knowledge of God.

Hunting Preserves and Wildlife in the Vicinity of Istanbul

Whereas several hunting preserves were located in the vicinity of Istanbul, the most favored sites were near Edirne, the former Ottoman capital. Edirne's comparatively western location, toward the Balkans, made it an important military station. As for its wildlife, the variety was richer than in the preserves near Istanbul. Chronicles from the sixteenth century and early seventeenth century document Ottoman sultans hunting at Edirne and narrate hunting trips between Edirne and Istanbul as part of court life.

In sixteenth-century Istanbul, hunting preserves included Sarıyer, Feridun, Ayazağa, Haramidere, Hasköy, Kağıthane, Karaağaç, Halkalı, and Topkapı on the European side; with Üsküdar, Göksu, Kandilli, Tokat, and Beykoz on the Anatolian side by the Bosporus.[40] The geologist Pierre de Tchihatcheff (1847–58), who traveled to Istanbul in the mid-nineteenth century, recorded his observations on the natural environment and wildlife of the peninsula. As compared with the abundance of wild animals

in Macedonia—and against older chronicles citing hunting lions around Istanbul—Tchihatcheff noted relatively little wildlife in the vicinity of the capital. Within Istanbul, he found that the Asian side contained more animals than the European, owing to its variegated habitats with high and low altitudes.

On the European side, Tchihatcheff recorded nightingales (*Luscinia major, Luscinia philomela*) and pigeons (*Columba turtur, Columba livia, Columba oenas, Columba palumbus*) as the most common birds. He noted with disappointment, however, the absence of birdsong in the area. On the Asian side, he identified the most common birds as partridges of different varieties.[41] Among the migratory birds, quails were the most frequently spotted.[42] Two centuries before Tchihatcheff made his list, the Ottoman traveler Evliya Çelebi recorded the following as the most common birds around Istanbul: wild geese (*yabankazı*), wild ducks (*yabanördeği*), cranes (*turna*), *Otis tarda* (*toy*), heron (*balıkçıl*), and Black Francolin (*turaç*).

In the Black Sea itself, Tchihatcheff observed sixty-one species of fish. Two centuries prior, the German theologian Stephan Gerlach noted schools of two to three hundred dolphins on the Bosporus; similarly, Busbecq observed dolphins at a small seaside town en route from Edirne to Constantinople.[43]

Hunting Preserves and Wildlife in the Vicinity of Edirne

Leaving Istanbul toward Edirne, which was located about 130 miles (210 kilometers) northwest of Istanbul, the geography presented a flourishing landscape. This favorable hunting itinerary was very pleasant for the visitors, even in midwinter, as described by Busbecq: "[E]verywhere came across quantities of flowers—narcissi, hyacinths, and tulipans, as the Turks call them."[44] Wildlife proliferated around Edirne, making the area central to the Ottoman sultan's hunting endeavors: "A large area of flooded country is formed where the rivers converge, abounding in wild ducks, geese, herons, sea eagles, cranes, hawks and other birds . . ."[45] Ottoman sultans from the sixteenth to early eighteenth century favored hunting at the Edirne Palace and environs. Occasionally, they left Istanbul and went on hunting expeditions from Istanbul to Edirne, staying at Edirne for long periods and hunting in the environs of the Edirne Palace. Both in the gardens of the Edirne Palace and the imperial estates onto which the gardens opened—located up to four hours away from the royal garden—one would find twenty-one lodges, most probably all designated as stations to be used during hunting.[46] These lodges map the itinerary of the royal expeditions to areas rich in wildlife around Edirne, areas that are still protected as hunting preserves today (Figure 3.11).

From the fourteenth to the late sixteenth century, sultans were hunters. Süleyman the Magnificent was considered a "hunter-Sultan." But after Süleyman (during the reigns of Selim III, Murad III, and Mehmed III in 1566–1603), a decline in the practice occurred and sultans performed hunting only as part of a royal obligation—until Ahmed I, who was distinguished as a famous hunter, in the early seventeenth century. Following him, in the second half of the seventeenth century, sultans spent most of their time in Edirne hunting.[47]

On May 14, 1613, Sultan Ahmed I returned to Istanbul from Edirne after a five-month hunting campaign that began in December 1612. Halting for a short period in the capital city, he hunted in the environs of Istanbul for the rest of the summer. This was followed by the trend of sultans traveling back to Edirne for hunting.[48] Before Ahmed I, Süleyman the Magnificent also spent winters hunting in Edirne. It was a common royal tradition that the "Sultan would travel to Edirne, hawking and enjoying a more bracing climate," in the words of Busbecq. Such expeditions were taken in the form of royal processions where the sultan and his court would leave the city in a ceremonial way, accompanied by his courtiers and keepers of the hunt.[49] One century after Süleyman, in 1657, the Swedish ambassador Claes Rålamb witnessed and documented Mehmed IV's procession to Edirne from the Topkapı Palace. Such hunting campaigns were elaborate affairs.[50] As many as one hundred to five thousand attendants would accompany the sultan. The prospect of such a massive entourage is perhaps difficult to imagine given that wild animals roamed the streets of Istanbul. Until the early eighteenth century, these customary processions from Istanbul to Edirne and vice versa allowed for the concept of wilderness to be carried into and out of Istanbul, as well as connecting the two centers of the Ottoman court. Such mapping of the two important centers of the Ottoman domain with such massive entourages, territorializing and deterritorializing[51] the multiplicity of landscapes over and between these two centers—between the two palaces in Edirne and Istanbul—extended the bodily space of the Ottoman sultan by metaphorical, poetic, and political means. Thus, he came to embody the ever-changing seasons and landscapes of his reign, at times in harmony with and at times mastering wildness.

Like the Ottomans who had favored and visited the same hunting preserves in Istanbul and Edirne over the course of two centuries, other Near Eastern rulers, Mongolian qaghans, and Mughal emperors also had favorable hunting preserves.[52] The hunting preserves in the vicinity of Istanbul and Edirne were marked by numerous hunting lodges and/or plantings of trees imported from distant territories. They were important privileged "outposts," whether favored for military purposes or for their attractive

scenery, climate, or prey. By visiting their numerous hunting preserves, the Ottoman sultans institutionalized and embodied the city of Edirne as part of the central court outside the capital. The court's travel between several centers was a Near Eastern tradition. For example, the Seljuqs of Anatolia had several royal residences, which they visited throughout the year or favored for different purposes. Among many other palaces, they favored Alanya in winters "with view of the mountain and water," stayed in the picturesque Kubadabad during summers, used Kubadiye as a camping site for spring, but had their central palace in the official capital of Konya.[53]

Though traveling to Edirne for hunting expeditions was considered a part of court tradition in the sixteenth century, in the seventeenth century it came to denote the neglect of the capital city of Istanbul and of the royal duties of the sultan. By the end of seventeenth century, sultans hunting in Edirne were viewed as abandoning their responsibilities in Istanbul. Thus, hunting came to be perceived less as a royal duty and more as an act of irresponsibility and an unremarkable pastime.[54] The premodern cultural construction of "wilderness" embraced in the Ottoman sultan's imperial persona eroded with the changing poetic, philosophical, and political traditions that characterized the advent of early modernity in the late seventeenth and early eighteenth centuries.[55]

Conclusion

In the premodern Ottoman world, the cultural idea of wilderness constituted part of the Ottoman sultan's imperial persona. City and wilderness, nature and culture were reconciled in his body, which extended beyond its mere physical boundaries and housed fragments of the Paradise Garden bestowed on earth. In poetic terms, the sultan's body, his palace, and his capital city all contained one another and represented the Paradise Garden in different scales and mediums. Wild animals had always been part of these fragments of metaphorical paradise(s), whether kept in menageries or chased in hunting preserves. The sultan was seen to enliven, flourish from, and inhabit a paradise with wild animals, which represented the wealth and territorial expansion of his domain, his intimacy with the World of Eternity, and his understanding of eternal knowledge. In turn, animals nourished the sultan's physical and mental capacity in diverse ways. He acquired and practiced qualities of the wild as he performed with, dominated, embodied, and chased after them. In order to unite urban imperial menageries with the wildness of the open landscape, sultans undertook remarkable processions. In such spectacles, the sultan and his convoy would parade from gardens within the city to hunting preserves beyond. Multiplicity of wildness was practiced, experienced, and embodied within the culturally constructed imperial persona of the sultan, where his body extended to contain and be contained within his palaces, his imperial city, and the landscape(s) covering the vast territory of his power.

There are many questions left unanswered for further research about wildness and wilderness in the premodern Ottoman period. One such question is about the vision of wilderness practiced and appropriated by the common urban dweller. Although living in the heart of Istanbul, the Ottoman capital, a foreign visitor like Busbecq had a totally different vision of wilderness from that of the Ottoman court. Like other foreign witnesses who traveled to Istanbul, Busbecq recorded various instances of the common urban dwellers' amazement with the wild animals in the city. The question which demands an answer is about the vision of the common urban dwellers strolling in the streets of Istanbul, and dwellers of other provinces in the periphery, regarding their role in and awareness of this imperial cultural construction: how the commoners' views of wild animals and wilderness were different from the idealizations of the Ottoman sultan and his court, and how they were different from Busbecq's perspective.

Notes

1 I would like to thank Professor Nurhan Atasoy, who has encouraged and supported my studies on Ottoman gardens and wildlife, and John Beardsley, who has welcomed a historical perspective among contemporary discussions of wildlife habitats. I am indebted to Nurhan Atasoy for sharing her visual archive with me, and as well to Zeynep Çelik of Topkapı Museum Library for her sincere support and assistance in the selection of images for the publication. I would also like to thank Professor Mark Laird for his kind encouragement of the discussions covered in this paper.

2 The complete couplet as translated by Walter Andrews is:

The round burns are roses, the *elif*-like scratches are cypresses here and there

Why should I contemplate the garden? My breast is a garden for me

In his analysis of Ottoman court literature—of the *gazel* poetry—Walter Andrews proposes that gardens were essential and central to Ottoman cosmology. Each of the various levels of Ottoman cosmology was made out of interior and exterior spaces, and the Ottoman poetic tradition linked these spaces to one another: "Beginning from the private interior of the human mind a chain of interior spaces is created, a chain of gardens proceeding through the private garden to the garden of the worldly authority, to the garden of Islam, to the gardens of Paradise and the ultimate reality." Walter G. Andrews, *Poetry's Voice, Society's Song* (Seattle: University of Washington Press, 1985), 154. The interior spaces housed the superior qualities in contrast to the exterior spaces of the cosmology: "The breast, as location of the emotional faculties, is seen as equivalent to the garden, linking emotional perception to perception of the truth inherent in all the interior spaces." For a complete discussion of the "ecology" of the Ottoman gazel tradition, see Andrews, *Poetry's Voice, Society's Song*, 143–74. Similar to the examples in Ottoman poetry, Julie Scott Meisami argues that in Persian poetic tradition the imagery of the human body—of the Beloved—and gardens, also "act upon each other," and were used to acknowledge qualities of one another. See Julie Scott Meisami, "The Body as Garden: Nature and Sexuality in Persian Poetry," *Edebiyât*, n.s., 6.2 (1995): 247.

3 For a comprehensive account of the history of menageries, and, later zoos, in the Ottoman Empire from the sixteenth to the early twentieth centuries, see Feza Günergun, "Türkiye'de Hayvanat Bahçeleri Tarihine Giriş," in *I. Ulusal Veteriner Hekimliği Tarihi ve Mesleki Etik Sempozyumu Bildirileri Prof. Dr. Ferruh Dinçer'in 70. Yaşı Anısına*, ed. Abdullah Özen (Elazığ, 2006), 185–218. For a detailed study of the imperial menageries in the classical period, see Gülru Necipoğlu, *Architecture, Ceremonial, and Power: The Topkapı Palace in the Fifteenth and Sixteenth Centuries* (Cambridge, Mass.: MIT Press, 1991), 3–13; and Metin And, "The Sultan's Menageries," in *Istanbul in the Sixteenth Century: The City, The Palace, Daily Life* (Istanbul: Akbank, 1994), 148–53.

4 And refers to the sixteenth-century traveler Pierre Belon, a naturalist and a botanist, in regard to his observations about the sultan's menageries. And, *Istanbul in the Sixteenth Century*, 149.

5 Günergun, "Türkiye'de Hayvanat Bahçeleri Tarihine Giriş," 4; and And, *Istanbul in the Sixteenth Century*, 53.

6 And quotes the sixteenth-century Huguenot traveler Philippe du Fresne-Canaye in *Istanbul in the Sixteenth Century*, 152–53, 319.

7 Ibid., 152, 321.

8 Günergun, "Türkiye'de Hayvanat Bahçeleri Tarihine Giriş," 8.

9 Necipoğlu, *Architecture, Ceremonial, and Power*, 201.

10 For the description of Solomon's *divan* by the Ottoman poet Uzun Firdevsi (b. 1453) in *Süleymanname*, written for Sultan Beyazıd (1481–1512), see Serpil Bağcı, "A New Theme of the Shirazi Frontpiece Miniatures: The Divan of Solomon," *Muqarnas* 12 (1995): 102–4. In her influential article, Bağcı brings to light different versions of the court of Solomon surrounded by wild animals and beasts, from the late fifteenth to the late sixteenth century. She compares miniatures dated 1485 (from *Nizami's Khamsa*, Topkapı Sarayı Kütüphanesi H768, folios 1b–2a), where Solomon's court is depicted in open landscape, to paintings dated 1496 (from *Firdawsi's Shahnama*, Topkapı Sarayı Kütüphanesi H1508, folios 14b–15a) and 1574 (from *Firdawsi's Shahnama*, Topkapı Sarayı Kütüphanesi H1497, folios 1b–2a), where Solomon and his wife Bilqis are seated in separate kiosks within a more structured landscape, similar to the later depictions, dated 1569–70 (from *Nizami's Khamsa*, Topkapı Sarayı Kütüphanesi H750, folios 1b–2a) and 1580 (from *Nizami's Khamsa*, Topkapı Sarayı Kütüphanesi A3559, folios 1b–2a).

11 Necipoğlu, *Architecture, Ceremonial, and Power*, 202.

12 Ibid., 203.

13 Ibid., 79, 203.

14 Ibid., 53, 202n62.

15 The early seventeenth-century accounts of the Venetian Ottaviano Bon are described in Günergun, "Türkiye'de Hayvanat Bahçeleri Tarihine Giriş," 10.

16 Necipoğlu, *Architecture, Ceremonial, and Power*, 123.

17 Lorenzo Bernardo as referred in Necipoğlu, *Architecture, Ceremonial, and Power*, 83, 204.

18 Necipoğlu, *Architecture, Ceremonial, and Power*, 84, 204.

19 And, *Istanbul in the Sixteenth Century*, 148–53.

20 *The third letter* by Ogier Ghislain de Busbecq, June 1, 1560, Constantinople, in Ogier Ghislain de Busbecq, *Turkish*

Letters (1588; repr., trans. E. S. Forster, London: Eland, 2005), 65–66. Busbecq, who was an Hapsburg diplomat in Istanbul, had written four letters in Latin known to be "Turkish Letters." These letters, supposedly private correspondences addressing the diplomat Nicholas Michault, were actually revised after his return to Vienna; they documented his ambassadorial accounts and observations of the Ottoman Empire (Busbecq, *Turkish Letters*, x).

21 Ibid., 66.

22 Ibid., 67–71.

23 Nurhan Atasoy, *1582 Surname-i hümayun: An Imperial Celebration* (Istanbul: Koçbank, 1997), 107.

24 Ibid., 108.

25 Mehmet Arslan, *Türk Edebiyatında Manzum Surnâmeler Osmanlı Saray Düğünleri ve Şenlikleri* (Ankara: Atatürk Kültür Merkezi Başkanlığı, 1999), 286.

26 Atasoy, *1582 Surname-i hümayun*, 33–34; and Arslan, *Türk Edebiyatında Manzum Surnâmeler Osmanlı Saray Düğünleri ve Şenlikleri*, 184–87.

27 Arslan, *Türk Edebiyatında Manzum Surnâmeler Osmanlı Saray Düğünleri ve Şenlikleri*, 184–86.

28 Nigel Webb and Carole Webb, eds., *The Earl and His Butler in Constantinople: The Secret Diary of an English Servant among the Ottomans* (London: Tauris, 2009), 27.

29 *The third letter* by Busbecq, June 1, 1560, Constantinople, in Busbecq, *Turkish Letters*, 71–72.

30 *The first letter* by Busbecq, September 1, 1555, Vienna, in ibid., 29.

31 Thomas Veltre, "Menageries, Metaphors, and Meanings," in *New Worlds, New Animals: From Menagerie to Zoological Park in the Nineteenth Century*, ed. R. J. Hoage and William A. Deiss (Baltimore: John Hopkins University Press, 1996), 20.

32 In her work on the early seventeenth-century treatise *Tuhfetü'l-mülūkve's-selātīnı*, the Ottoman version and "translation" of the medieval Arabic *'Umdat al-mulūk*, on "Hippiatry and hippology," "Horsemanship," and "Hunting of wild beast and bird," Tülay Artan discusses the characteristics of the Ottoman tradition of hunting in many respects. Artan points out two types of hunting grounds: man-made grounds, such as a royal garden, and natural grounds, such as a forest, oak grove, or desert converted into a hunting area. Both types required maintenance. Hunting preserves called *şikârgâh-ı selâtîn* or *saydgâh-ı hâssa* were only open to the sultan's use for hunting. Tülay Artan, "A Book of Kings Produced and Represented as a Treatise on Hunting," *Muqarnas* 25 (2008): 299–330, esp. 305. For further details and accounts of hunting in the seventeenth century, see also Ibrahim Hakkı Çuhadar, ed., *Mustafa Safi'nin Zübdetü't-Tevârîh'i*, 2 vols. (Ankara: Türk Tarih Kurumu, 2003). For a diverse collection of essays on hunting in Turkish, see

Emine Gürsoy Naskali and Hilal Oytun Altun, eds., *Av ve Avcılık Kitabı* (Istanbul: Kitabevi, 2008).

33 Artan, "Book of Kings," 305–8.

34 Necdet Öztürk, "Osmanlı Kroniklerinde Av Kayıtları (1299–1500)," in Naskali and Altun, *Av ve Avcılık Kitabı*, 65–71.

35 Artan, "Book of Kings," 299–330.

36 Ibid., 308.

37 Ibid., 306–7.

38 According to Ibn 'Arabî, attainment of eternal knowledge was exercised to take place in such intermediary spaces called *barzakh*. 'Arabî reintroduced the concept of barzakh—which he borrowed from Sufi terminology and totally restructured into a new philosophy. The concept of barzakh embodies an understanding of "both/and" instead of "either/or." The presence of a barzakh enables the coexistence of ontology and epistemology; so far it enables metaphysical and physical worlds as equally important. Through the concept and practice of barzakh, 'Arabî also discussed the significance of the individual self as equal to God. Barzakh was portrayed as a space of encounter, as a third space in which the other two domains meet. Human bodies, gardens, and landscapes of all kinds were portrayed as barzakh—intermediary spaces to the extent that they allow such encounters of the opposites for a better understanding of eternal knowledge and worldly wisdom. This study proposes and questions reconsideration of the sultan's body—its reception and perception as an intermediary space—as barzakh, where all the forces of nature, wild or tamed, act upon each other. For a detailed discussion on the philosophy of Ibn 'Arabî regarding intermediary spaces in relation to body and the attainment of knowledge, see, B. Deniz Çalış, "Ideal and Real Spaces of Ottoman Imagination: Continuity and Change in Ottoman Rituals of Poetry (Istanbul, 1453–1730)" (PhD diss., Middle East Technical University, 2004), 58–82; William Chittick, *The Sufi Path of Knowledge: Ibn al-Arabi's Metaphysics of Imagination* (Albany: State University of New York Press, 1989), 117–18; Henry Corbin, *Creative Imagination in the Sufism of Ibn 'Arabi*, trans. Ralph Manheim (Princeton: Princeton University Press, 1969), 151; Ibn-i Arabi, *İlahi Aşk*, trans. Mahmut Kanık (Istanbul: Insan Yayınları, 2002), 64; and Annemarie Schimmel, *Mystical Dimensions of Islam* (Chapel Hill: University of North Carolina Press, 1975), 290–93.

39 William Chittick, *The Self-Disclosure of God: Principles of Ibn al-Arabi's Cosmology* (Albany: State University of New York Press, 1998), 8, 13, 16, 53, 106–7, 149, 169; and Chittick, *Sufi Path of Knowledge*, 68–76.

40 And, *Istanbul in the Sixteenth Century*, 154–56.

41 Among these wild animals were pheasants, eagles, starlings, finches, rabbits, roe deer, and wild boar. See

P. A. Chikhachev, *İstanbul ve Boğaziçi*, trans. Ali Berktay (Istanbul: Tarih Vakfı Yurt Yayınları, 2000), 93–100.

42 Ibid., 95–96.

43 *The first letter* by Busbecq, September 1, 1555, Vienna, in Busbecq, *Turkish Letters*, 29.

44 Ibid., 16.

45 *The third letter* by Busbecq, June 1, 1560, Constantinople, in Busbecq, *Turkish Letters*, 61.

46 These lodges were Şikar Kasrı, Aynalı Köşk, Bostancıbaşı Kasrı/Sepetçiler Kasrı, Terazu Kasrı, Adalet Kasrı, İftar Kasrı, Bülbül Kasrı, Değirmen Kasrı, Bayırbahçe Kasrı, Mumuk Sarayı, Köşkkapı Kasrı, İydiye Kasrı, Çadır Köşk, Hıdırlık Kasrı, Buçuk Tepe Kasrı, Yıldız Kasrı, Demirtaş Kasrı, Saray-ı Akpınar Kasrı, Üsküdar'da Kasır: Çömlek Akpınar'da Kasır, and Karıştıran'da Kasır. See the study of the Edirne Palace and environs in Rifat Osman, *Edirne Sarayı* (Ankara: Türk Tarih Kurumu Basimevi, 1989), 97–109.

47 Artan, "Book of Kings," 301–2.

48 Ibid., 302nn42–44.

49 *The third letter* by Busbecq, June 1, 1560, Constantinople, in Busbecq, *Turkish Letters*, 61.

50 The seventeenth-century Swedish ambassador to the Ottoman court, Claes Brorson Rålamb, narrated in his diaries the procession of Sultan Mehmed IV that took place in September 1657, in which the sultan was going on a hunting expedition from Istanbul to Edirne. There are also twenty oil paintings surviving from the Embassy of Rålamb, illustrating the procession. The compositions of these paintings are continuous almost in a cinematic fashion and are known as the Rålamb Paintings. They depict 170 men accompanying the sultan during his hunting trip. See Karin Adahl, "The Twenty Paintings Depicting the Sultan's Procession," in *The Sultan's Procession: The Swedish Embassy to Sultan Mehmed IV in 1657–1658 and the Rålamb Paintings* (Istanbul: Swedish Research Institute, 2007), 74–113.

51 Borrowing the terms from Gilles Deleuze and Félix Guattari, *A Thousand Plateaus: Capitalism and Schizophrenia*, trans. Brian Massumi (London and New York: Continuum, 2004).

52 Thomas T. Allsen, *The Royal Hunt in Eurasian History* (Philadelphia: University of Pennsylvania Press, 2006), 17.

53 Scott Redford, "Thirteenth-Century Rum Seljuq and Palace Imagery," *Ars Orientalis* 23 (1993): 220. Also see Scott Redford, *Anadolu Selçuklu Bahçeleri: Alaiyye, Alanya*, trans. Serdar Alper (Istanbul: Eren, 2008), for the study of the Seljuq palatial tradition in relation to landscape.

54 Artan, "Book of Kings," 301–2.

55 After the premodern period, menageries were placed in the newly constructed Ottoman palaces in Istanbul, and several attempts were made to open zoos in nineteenth-century Istanbul, though none of them were successful. See Günergun, "Türkiye'de Hayvanat Bahçeleri Tarihine Giriş," 185–218. For an account of the more recent history regarding a short-lived zoological station in Istanbul, see Sevtap Kadıoğlu, "Raymond Hovasse's Scientific Activities in Turkey (1926–1931) and the Foundation of the Baltalimanı Zoological Station," *Studies in Ottoman Science* 4, no. 2 (2003): 61–82.

CHAPTER 4

Spatial Scale and the
Design of Conservation Interventions

Joshua R. Ginsberg

SPATIAL AND TEMPORAL SCALE IS CRITICAL TO almost any discussion of ecology and design and is the central focus of landscape ecology, the field that bridges these two disciplines.[1] Temporal scale is linear (at least in classical physics) and predictable. Spatial scale can be real, based on quantifiable metrics, or apparent, structured by our perception of an image that lacks a spatial reference, and hence allows multiple interpretations—what T. F. H. Allen and Thomas B. Starr refer to as "observer intrusion" (Figure 4.1).[2] In his influential examination of the issues of pattern and scale in ecology, Simon A. Levin noted that even basic understanding of patterns in ecology is problematic, as patterns are often generated at scales different than those at which they are observed.[3] A specific example that complicates many spatial analyses of diversity is Carsten Rahbek's observation[4] that the scale of analysis will influence even our basic comprehension of the spatial distribution of diversity or species richness, measures often used to establish spatial priorities for conservation.[5]

A consideration of spatial scale, and how it interacts with ecological processes and human alteration of the landscape, is critical to the understanding and implementation of biological conservation interventions.[6] Spatial scale can influence how we view conservation threats, including such issues as landscape fragmentation and animal dispersal,[7] connectivity across landscapes,[8] climate change,[9] or disturbance in ecological systems.[10] In conservation, and in the design of conservation initiatives, disturbance is most problematic when the extent of the area being considered is significantly smaller than the extent at which a disturbance or threat operates.

Spatial scale can also be critical to the way in which conservation planning and priority setting are developed and implemented. Of particular importance are the grain and extent of the analysis. Grain is often determined by data resolution, while extent is often a question of the spatial scale of interest. Again, aligning these can be critical. The analysis of Eric W. Sanderson et al. of the cumulative impact of human activities produces a visual human footprint of the relative intensity of human influence at a global scale.[11] This analysis, which identifies "the last of the wild," sets clear global priorities for each biome. Because of the grain of the analysis and the need to use uniform (if deficient) data sets at a global scale, local and ecoregional planning (the scale at which

conservation is implemented) is often better served by a much finer-grained analysis of the human footprint using regional data sets with far greater accuracy and covering a much smaller extent.[12] Downscaling may not always produce more robust results. The International Union for Conservation of Nature (IUCN) Red List[13] is the arbiter of the global conservation status for the world's fauna and flora, yet national and regional analyses using the same criteria can produce significantly different assessments of threat because of the interaction of species distribution, national boundaries, and the desire of national governments to focus on something that may be locally rare but globally numerous.[14]

The diversity of the essays in this volume shows that we manage wildlife at a wide diversity of scales, and that the way in which people construct a view of nature can change with scale. Despite the complexities of scale, and of defining how scale and pattern in ecology interact, in this essay I will examine a simpler aspect of scale: How does change in scale affect the kinds of strategies and approaches we take in developing and implementing conservation activities?

Spatial scale is, of course, a continuous variable. A recent examination of conservation success at different scales avoided an explicit definition of spatial extent, but instead used three fuzzy categories (micro, meso, and macro) to define the scale of conservation action.[15] This analysis provides a useful, but relatively simplistic, analysis of scale and conservation implementation. In this essay I have made quantitative, if somewhat arbitrary, categorical definitions of different spatial extent, from tens of meters to global (Figure 4.2). For the most part I will ignore issues related to global-scale threats because their resolution at this scale is managed as a policy problem, not one of site or spatially focused conservation. Further, my focus is not on the management of diversity per se, but on the issues and management approaches that are required to manage individuals, species, and/or the communities in which they live. I will look at the impact of scale on management in four ways: the way in which different threats work across different scales; how conservation targets and actions change with scale; the way in which the behavior and ecology (and particularly how spatial requirements) of individual

JOSHUA R. GINSBERG

Scales at Which We Manage Wildlife

Scale	Example
• 10–50,000 m²	Captivity
• 1 hectare–10 km²	Natural fragments
• 10–500 km²	Isolated reserves
• 500–5,000 km²	Large reserves
• 1,000–10,000 km²	Landscapes
• >10,000 km²	Regional planning
• >1,000,000 km²	Global phenomenon

FIGURE 4.2
Spatial scale is a continuous variable, but seven categories of spatial scale can be used as a way to focus discussion.
© Joshua Ginsberg.

species interact to influence the way in which other species view these scaling issues; and finally, how management strategies are affected by scale as I have defined it. My essay is not limited to terrestrial vertebrates, but much of my discussion will focus on, and is informed by, the way in which terrestrial vertebrates, and in particular the larger mammals, both view their environment and are viewed by humans.

Threats

The classification of conservation threats has focused on establishing a framework that defines threats and establishes a standard lexicon for classifying threats.[16] These efforts are critical to developing a common language for conservationists and can allow cross-project learning and discussion. Nick Salafsky et al. harmonize previous efforts to classify direct threats and elegantly divide a complex list of direct threats into eleven categories, with a set of nested, finer classifications.[17] This approach to threat classification groups together similar kinds of threats (e.g., pollution), but each of these threats works across a diversity of scales.

Any consideration of scale and threat is vexing because of the complexities of interactions between the two. Each of the eleven categories of direct threats can operate across many scales, and can do so in several ways. For instance, pollution is so broadly defined that it can be used to refer to the extremely local impact of effluent outlets, the release of highly radioactive materials from a damaged power plant, or to the global processes of the cumulative impact of the release of persistent organic pollutants, or greenhouse gases. In the tropics, "agriculture" scales from the clearing and burning of a few hectares for swidden to the national- and regional-level impacts of the conversion of thousands of square kilometers of tropical forests to plantation agriculture of crops like palm oil, rubber, and cassava.

Many threats are also effectively fractal in their nature, with impacts being cumulative, and in some cases geometric with shifts in scale. To examine this more fully, I would argue that one has to acknowledge that the proximate impact of an individual threat may be small, but the cumulative impact of repeated instances of such a threat, the ultimate impact of that threat, may be very large indeed. For instance, one can examine the impact of a specific exurban development on local wildlife and establish the immediate and local impacts on wildlife populations.[18] The proximate impact of each development may be small, particularly at the early stages of exurban development when the majority of the landscape remains intact.[19] Yet, these developments,

Threats

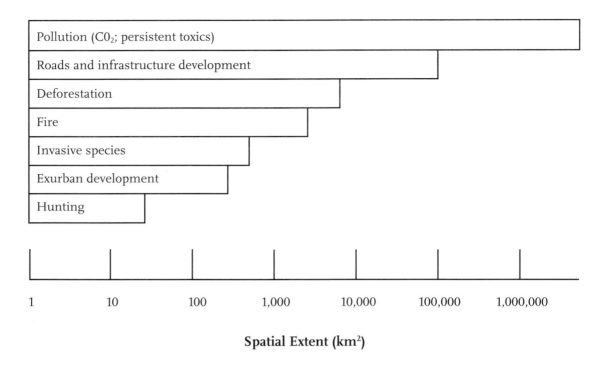

FIGURE 4.3
Human disturbance regimes, from natural to seminatural to artificial, with impacts across a range of scales.
© Joshua Ginsberg.

if poorly managed, can produce larger and more significant cumulative impacts at a local or regional scale.[20] Other factors—connectivity, the quality and type of land use (the matrix)—that surround patches of natural habitat and a species's ability to move between and among patches will, of course, also interact with threats at different scales.[21]

Similarly, hunting can be seen as a global or local problem. Kent H. Redford elegantly discussed the indirect, direct, local, and commercial aspects of hunting in the Amazon and how these actions can lead to defaunation and "empty forests," locally and regionally.[22] Poaching of elephants for ivory, or tigers for their bones, is driven by a narrow but global demand. Less than 7 percent of the original populations of tigers remains and demand for tiger bones has led to poaching and national-level extinction.[23] Such illegal trade is ultimately a global or regional threat, but is driven proximately

by local enforcement action (or inaction), as evidenced by the local nature of successful management solutions, whether for tigers[24] or elephants.[25] Interventions need to be developed in what is effectively a pincer movement, with policy initiatives aimed at banning trade and local or national institutions providing appropriate management of individual populations.[26]

Yet despite all these drivers of variation, different threats clearly act at different scales. A comprehensive consideration of how threats differ in their scaling is beyond the scope of this essay, but Figure 4.3 shows the proximate (if not the ultimate) scale at which some threats act. The examples presented are perhaps less important than the recognition that in designing for wildlife, the proximate scale at which threats act must be incorporated into the design of wildlife areas and related to both the conservation targets and the scale of conservation action.

JOSHUA R. GINSBERG

Conservation Targets and Scales of Conservation Action

Salafsky et al. define biodiversity targets as "(t)he biological entities (species, communities, or ecosystems) that a project is trying to conserve."[27] Conservationists use such focal targets in conservation planning efforts as surrogates for conserving biodiversity broadly, as a way to sharpen conservation interventions and as a means to assess and measure the impact of these interventions.[28] Salafsky et al. also develop a clear taxonomy of actions, defined as the "(i)nterventions undertaken . . . designed to reach the project's objectives and ultimate conservation goals."[29]

At its core, conservation implementation requires that actions are linked to targets at an appropriate scale. The Nature Conservancy has developed a conservation planning tool, the Conservation Action Planning process, which puts focal targets at its core and defines targets as "a limited suite of species, communities, and ecological systems that are chosen to represent and encompass the biodiversity found in your project area."[30] Implicit to any discussion of focal targets is that these targets map onto a spatial scale that is consistent with the proposed scale of conservation implementation or action.[31]

Karen A. Poiani et al. define four scales for addressing management issues for both ecosystems and species: local (meters to thousands of hectares); intermediate (one to hundreds of square kilometers); coarse (hundreds to tens of thousands of square kilometers); and larger areas defined as regional.[32] They further elaborate three types of areas: sites, landscapes, and networks. Such a system is useful for understanding that different species and ecosystems function at different scales. It also helps us see that while a target (a particular species) may remain constant, we may have to address the conservation of that target at a set of nested scales. But the system does not address the misalignment of threats and targets and how these change with scales.

The misalignment of targets and the scale at which targets are addressed can undermine the potential for conservation interventions to succeed, particularly when targets operate at an extent that is significantly smaller than that of the threats that influence them.[33] This is true in terrestrial environments, and may be particularly true in marine environments. As Tundi Agardy summarized: "in the conservation of the marine environment, where open marine ecosystems and the international nature of pollution, overexploitation, and of other threats dictate a large-scale multilateral response. The mismatch between large-scale thinking (embodied in marine policy) and small-scale conservation action has serious implications for our ability to reverse the tide of environmental degradation occurring in the world's oceans."[34] Implicit to Agardy's argument is the sometimes fundamental mismatch between conservation targets and conservation action. This mismatch is a critical issue in conservation that must be addressed.

Increasingly, we need to differentiate between the target of our conservation actions and the scale at which we take those actions. Take, for example, the management of wildebeest migration in the Serengeti-Mara ecosystem, as discussed by Johan T. du Toit.[35] The target, wildebeest, migrate over a vast area of twenty-five thousand square kilometers, and to date conservation efforts have worked at this scale to ensure connectivity and protection of the key migratory pathways. But because an even larger threat to the migration is driven by changes in the flow regime of the Mara River, the scale of action, he argues, needs to include all of the Mara River basin drainage, a further fifteen thousand square kilometers, much of which lies outside the migratory route of the wildebeest.

Issues of mismatch of scale in planning, design, and implementation of conservation efforts clearly extend well past issues of biodiversity alone. While the vast majority of forests are government-owned, increasingly decentralization and concession leasing have moved management from central to local actors.[36] Concurrently, global discussions concerning climate change mitigation, and the role of Reduced Emissions from Deforestation and Forest Degradation (REDD), create a growing quandary: negotiations on emissions are global, targets will most likely be developed and implemented at the national level, but inevitably management, implementation, and the actual conservation of forests will happen at a local or provincial level and will require a level of "nestedness" to be successful.[37]

The idea of nestedness may well be useful when planning and designing conservation interventions

Focus of Conservation Action

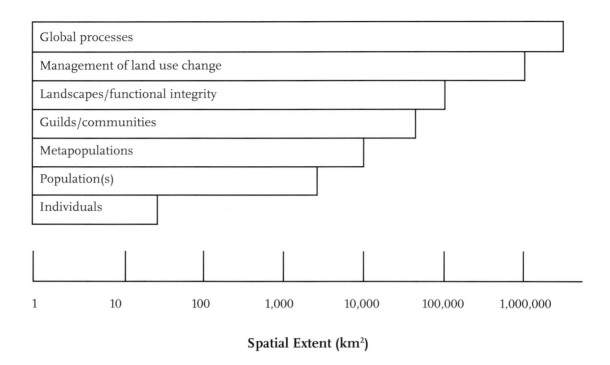

FIGURE 4.4
A model of scale relative to the various foci of conservation actions.

© Joshua Ginsberg.

for wildlife. Figure 4.4 attempts to resolve the issue of targets and scale of intervention by identifying the focus of conservation actions at different scales. Like Figure 4.3, which it parallels, the diagram is more of a heuristic tool than a quantitative analysis and does not reconcile the divergence between targets and the scale at which their threats occur. Reconciling this mismatch requires an understanding of both the proximate and ultimate scales at which threats occur, but also one needs a clear understanding of the scale at which individuals, social groups, and populations live.

Scale and Population Persistence

That individual species function at different spatial scales has long been recognized. The general relationships between size and home range have been well defined for decades, and were quantitatively defined for mammals by Brian K. McNab[38] and for birds by Thomas W. Schoener.[39] More recently, Rosie Woodroffe and I[40] showed that the persistence of large carnivores in protected areas was best predicted by the home-range size of an individual species: predators with small home ranges are able to persist in smaller reserves. Similar results have been observed for primates and ungulates,[41] birds,[42] butterflies,[43] and perhaps fishes.[44] Hence, "critical reserve size," the size of a reserve at which one expects a 50 percent chance of species persistence, can vary across two orders of magnitude, even among closely related species in the same functional guild.

More generally, Woodroffe found that carnivore persistence was negatively correlated with human-population density, although such patterns may be mediated by both cultural and management regimes.[45] Andrea S. Laliberte and William J. Ripple

JOSHUA R. GINSBERG

also showed that human influence, as measured by Sanderson's human footprint analysis, was a strong predictor of range collapse in many, but not all, large mammals of North America.[46] Again, these analyses also confirmed that there is significant interspecific variation in these effects, and that much of the variation can be driven by how wildlife adapts to human-dominated landscapes and uses the matrix surrounding protected areas: the wide distribution of leopards in human-dominated landscapes in India[47] and Africa,[48] or the prevalence of black bears who are heavily supplemented by garbage in many parts of the United States[49] are but two examples of how even large carnivores can coexist with people. Not surprisingly, what this shows is that there are few simple rules when it comes to predicting how any carnivore, or wildlife species, will adapt to human-influenced landscapes.

In the next sections, I want to examine the relationship between the scale at which we conduct conservation activities (from the intensive management of captive collections to global processes) and align these scales of management with a discussion of how threats change and are nested at proximate and ultimate levels.

The Captive World
(0.1–10 Acres)

The largest extent (smallest scale) at which we manage wildlife is the zoological collection. There is an extensive literature on the importance and value of zoos to conservation and the challenges zoos face in meeting this potential.[50] The early development of the field of conservation biology was driven, in some large measure, by a consideration of issues that were focused on the demographic and genetic ramifications of the small and fragmented populations that are commonly found in zoos.[51] Notwithstanding the potential significant conservation values of zoos, and their contributions to the development of conservation science, because of the scale at which they operate, zoos are at best an abstraction of nature.

Zoos have evolved from royal collections and nineteenth-century menageries to institutions that are on the cutting edge of management technologies and architectural and environmental design. The Bronx Zoo has two Leadership in Energy and Environmental Design (LEED) Gold buildings, one of which, the beaux-arts Lion House, is the first LEED Gold renovation of a historical landmark in New York City. Zoos balance many different requirements, but at their core is the welfare of their animals,[52] and the education and inspiration of their visitors.[53]

The Bronx Zoo (where I have my office and which is the home of the Wildlife Conservation Society) is an extensive urban park just over one square kilometer in size (125 hectares). Exhibits and built infrastructure within the Bronx Zoo, however, are a fraction of this area, comprising less than 25 percent of the footprint of the zoo (Figure 4.5). The structure of collections is one that has a strong parallel to a theater, with an "onstage" area that includes both the animal exhibit areas and those devoted to visitors, and an extensive "backstage" area that includes holding and quarantine facilities, commissaries, hospital and medical care facilities, receiving and storage areas, and shops and garages.

Threats that must be managed are focused in three areas: the prevention and mitigation of disease; the management of reproduction to avoid inbreeding; and a focus on population-level management of captive species to ensure that zoos are net producers, rather than net consumers of wildlife. Zoos are not just designed environments, but designed environments that allow for fine-scale management of all aspects of an animal's life. Predation is eliminated. Social groups are carefully managed to reduce conflict, control breeding, and mimic natural conditions as much as possible.[54]

In recent decades, the science of captive management and of animal welfare of captive animals has taken a more integrated approach and has expanded to include everything from the behavioral enrichment of zoo exhibits and facilities to engage wildlife in more naturalistic patterns of behavior, to the careful management of diet and nutrition to ensure both physical and, often, reproductive health.[55] For many species of endangered wildlife held in captivity, the threat of inbreeding is addressed through Species Survival Plan® programs, cooperative breeding programs that manage the reproduction of captive animals across multiple member institutions of the Association of Zoos and Aquariums.[56] Such measures are also critical to the management of captive

populations if they are to serve as potential assurance colonies for eventual reintroduction, although the potential to meet such objectives is uncertain.[57]

For endangered species managed in a metapopulation with captive and wild animals, the relationship between the proximate and ultimate threats is governed, to a large extent, by the differences between the ultimate threats, those factors that drive animals to extinction in the wild (habitat loss and fragmentation, direct persecution, invasive species, climate change, etc.), and the proximate threats, more closely focused challenges of maintaining a set of healthy, breeding individuals in captivity (inbreeding, selection for captivity, disease, etc.). Ultimate threats may determine which species are chosen as candidates for safe harbor or assurance colonies,[58] but the day-to-day management of these animals is governed almost entirely by proximate threats and the needs to meet welfare and exhibit goals.

Extensive Breeding Facilities (1–100 Acres)

In most captive facilities, individual exhibits cover at most several acres. But zoological collections are, at times, managed in larger areas. In the United States, there are a number of extensive captive facilities (San Diego Zoo Safari Park, The Wilds, Fossil Rim Wildlife Center, White Oak Plantation) where animals are often kept at lower densities, in larger enclosures. These facilities have the ability to provide much larger enclosures, facilitating the development of natural social groupings and a range of natural behaviors. Extensive holding areas allow for more naturalistic conditions, some grazing and browsing of naturally occurring vegetation by herbivores, and the potential for larger social groups similar to those found in the wild. Nonetheless, when it comes to disease, breeding, and diet (for most species), these collections are managed in much the same way as traditional zoos.

Fragments of Nature in Human-Dominated Landscapes (1–100 Acres)

Fragments of nature occur in all kinds of human-dominated landscapes, from urban parks to forest patches in large expanses of crop monocultures. While these fragments are of a scale similar to that of extensive breeding facilities, the way in which they and their wildlife are managed, and how threats affect them, ends at the similarity of scale. At this scale, fragments of nature are increasingly being managed to amplify their biological diversity and to provide other critical ecological functions, such as resting and feeding areas for migratory birds. For instance, while an emblem of captive collections, the vast majority of the Bronx Zoo's 125 hectares (Figure 4.5) is an urban park, with its forests increasingly being managed more carefully for their value for native biodiversity.

As a specific example, one can focus a lens on the Bronx Zoo as a fragment of nature in a sea of urban development. Migratory pathways are challenged by a number of factors, one of which is the loss of migratory stopovers as development leads to loss of forests, fields, and marshes.[59] The Bronx Park (the zoo and the adjacent New York Botanical Garden) serves as an important stopover for migratory birds and has done so for over a century.[60] The species composition through time has changed significantly, as the park shifted from relatively open farmlands to closed northeastern forests (a pattern more broadly observed across New England).[61] The species composition of the migratory species using the zoo reflects this change, and the radical change in the matrix in which the zoo is set has shifted from farmland to one of the densest human urban environments in the United States.[62] As such, while the ultimate threats to migratory species are diverse and well studied, the proximate impact of changes in the habitat, structure, and management of remaining urban fragments—and the shift in the matrix in which they are found—is far less understood.

In "Ecological Restoration Foundations to Designing Habitats in Urban Areas" (this volume), Steven N. Handel gives a wonderful summary of the values and challenges of managing small fragments of nature, using the restoration of a landfill site for his discussion. Such sites, and their larger exurban and rural cousins, face a series of similar challenges: disturbance has to be managed, invasives controlled, and restoration becomes an iterative process of active management "for" certain taxa. Management is, in many ways, a process of iterative restoration and amplification of natural features,

such as hydrology and topography. By their very nature, such fragments tend to be easily and highly disturbed and unstable, with a suite of such fragments providing a mosaic of rapidly shifting habitat patches. Yet, particularly in urban areas, conservationists are increasingly looking to these fragments of nature, and the networks of habitat they provide, as part of a network of green space where careful design and management can mitigate proximate threats and lead to a recovery of indigenous flora and fauna.[63]

From Isolated Reserves to Landscapes

As we move from fragments of nature to more contiguous landscapes, the interaction between the target of our conservation efforts and the extent and structure of the landscape becomes increasingly important. In the next sections, I want to focus on two iconic carnivores—the African wild dog, *Lycaon pictus*, and the tiger, *Panthera tigris*. In these discussions, I will look at how both scale and social ecology interact to change the way in which wildlife persists across a landscape, and how that affects the focus and scale of conservation interventions.

Wild Dogs in Managed Reserves (100–1,000 km²)

African wild dogs, like wolves, live in large packs of closely related males and closely related females. They breed and hunt communally, with reproduction being limited to a dominant pair, and with each pack having exceptionally large home-range areas (400–1,550 square kilometers, mean approximate 800 square kilometers).[64] Wild dogs exist at persistently low densities because they are subdominant predators and less directly affected by the density of prey than by the density of competing carnivore species.[65] As a result, wild dogs only persist in relatively large protected areas (50 percent probability of persistence in reserves greater than 3,500 square kilometers)[66] or in landscapes with very low human-population densities.

The ultimate threat to wild dogs is both the loss of habitat and the barriers that intensive development poses to the dispersal and the recovery of extirpated populations. The proximate threats to

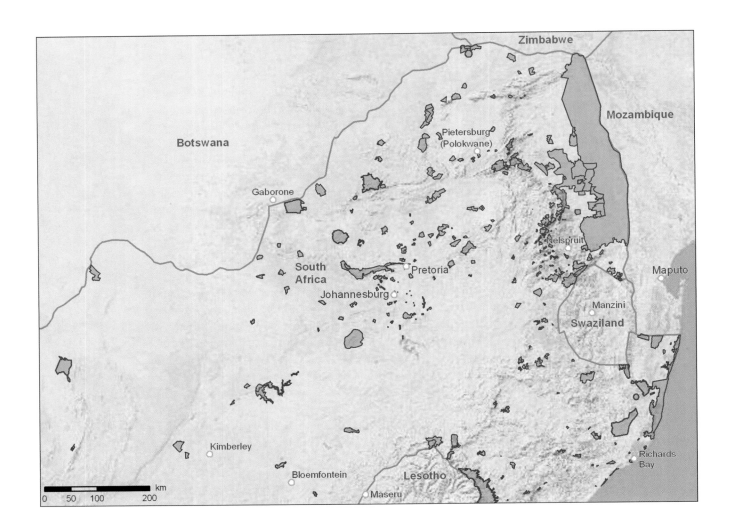

free-ranging wild dogs include direct persecution (snaring, shooting, spearing), disease, being run over by automobiles, competition with and direct mortality from other predators, and being killed by other wild dogs.[67] Direct persecution led to the extirpation of wild dogs across much of their range.[68] Wild dogs were extirpated across much of South Africa in the early twentieth century, persisting only in Kruger National Park and in parts of the Kalahari in the north of the country.[69]

I chose the wild dog to illustrate how the scale at which humans design and manage small reserves and the ecology of a wide-ranging species can collide when such a wide-ranging species is intensively managed in relatively small reserves (less than one thousand square kilometers). Such management amplifies and expands the number

of proximate threats while, at best, keeping ultimate threats at bay.

Beginning in 1980, wild dogs were reintroduced to the nine hundred–square kilometer Hluhluwe-Umfolozi Park, KwaZulu Natal, South Africa.[70] This introduction formed the first step in a much broader experiment in intensive metapopulation management, first proposed by Mills et al., that seeks to manage a metapopulation of a dozen or more packs of wild dogs spread across at least a dozen of relatively small, but not impressively small, private and public reserves (eighty to one thousand square kilometers) across South Africa (Figure 4.6).[71] Some argue that such metapopulation management is inevitable, and that in the end we will need to manage many populations of larger wildlife with this intensity. The option of such management

JOSHUA R. GINSBERG

strategies has been vetted for other large carnivores (e.g., wolves).[72]

Many of the reserves in the South African wild dog metapopulation program can support self-sustaining populations of many species of herbivores, and even relatively large populations of some of the smaller carnivores. Because of their large home-range requirements, only one or two packs of wild dogs can be established in each reserve.[73] Introduced packs have a high probability of establishing themselves once introduced,[74] but individual pack persistence is low over the medium term, and the small populations are only viable with relatively frequent additions of new social groups.[75]

Metapopulation management, while less intensive than management in captive collections, nonetheless requires much more intervention than that required to manage free-ranging populations. Hence, the financial costs of such endeavors is an order of magnitude higher than the management costs associated with free-ranging populations. P. Lindsey et al. found that the costs associated with managing the South African wild dog metapopulation were twenty times that of managing wild populations in parks like Kruger National Park.[76] Hence, in the long term, design of such small reserves will require either significantly greater financial investment to maintain wildlife populations, or require increasing connectivity and contiguousness between and among small reserves.

While data on mortality of reintroduced animals are few, Markus Gussett et al. show that one of the most important predictors of pack persistence in the small metapopulations is the integrity (length) of the fence: small, fenced reserves appear to eliminate many of the human-mediated proximate threats to wild dogs.[77] Clearly, if we pursue such a strategy, the knowledge and experience gained in captive collections to address threats such as inbreeding and disease will be critical to success.

Tigers Persisting across Scales

Tigers live across a great diversity of biomes, from tropical wet forest to the taiga of the Russian Far East. The productivity of these sytems varies widely. Because tigers are top predators,[78] their home-range size is linearly related to the density of their prey.[79]

In contrast to wild dogs, because tigers may occur at relatively high densities, they have the ability to persist in relatively small reserves when prey densities are sufficiently high (50 percent probability of persistence in reserves greater than 135 square kilometers),[80] but may require vast landscapes when densities are low.[81] In looking at tigers, this natural variation in tiger density leads us to manage this species across a diversity of scales. As such, the management of tigers allows us to look at how threats operate across scales, and how this affects conservation action.

Proximate threats to tigers fall into two broad categories: reduction in food supply[82] and the direct killing of tigers, whether because of conflict with people or for use in traditional medicine.[83] Perhaps because they are solitary and have relatively low rates of intraspecific contact, disease, while observed, is not considered a persistent or widespread population-level threat.[84] Genetic diversity, while a concern,[85] is not yet a serious proximate threat and inbreeding depression has not been observed in wild populations, only appearing to be an issue in rare circumstances in captive collection.[86] Habitat loss does not appear to be the driving force in range loss and population decline for the species as a whole as much of the current range of tigers represents good, but unoccupied, habitat, but may be important in some areas.[87]

Tigers in the Western Ghats (1,000–10,000 km²): Landscape-Level Planning

The Western Ghats of India are a critical landscape for tiger conservation.[88] The Malenad-Mysore Tiger Landscape in Karnataka is at the center of the Ghats, and covers almost forty thousand square kilometers. Of this, approximately five thousand square kilometers are under some form of protection, and the rest is a complex matrix of forest, agriculture, and human settlement with approximately ten million people living in the region (Figure 4.7).[89] The landscape encompassed has some of the most effectively managed tiger reserves in the country, ranging in size from five hundred to fifteen hundred square kilometers. The densest populations of tigers are found in areas like the contiguous Nagarahole-Bandipur National Parks (approximately fifteen

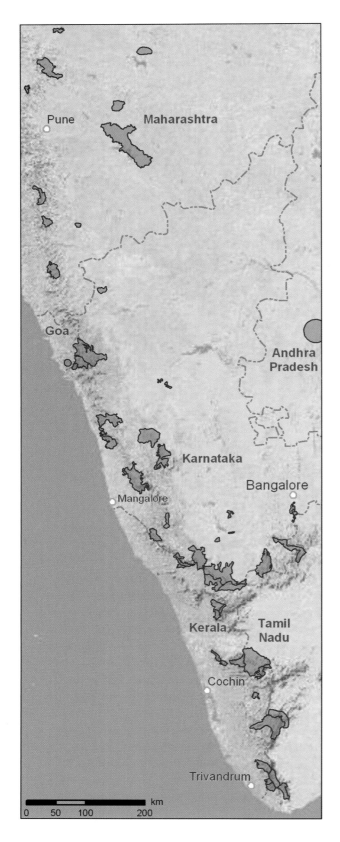

FIGURE 4.7
A mosaic of protected tiger habitat in a larger matrix of multiple use areas in the Western Ghats of India. Drawn to the same scale as Figure 4.6, the patterns of fragmentation and scale of protected areas are similar to one another.

© Wildlife Conservation Society / Kim Fisher.

hundred square kilometers). Tiger populations in this landscape are self-sustaining, and there is no evidence of genetic, behavioral, or demographic challenges to persistence. The species itself is not intensively managed; rather, the focus is on reducing direct threats to the population. When the major threats—the loss of prey and the direct poaching of tigers—are controlled, tiger populations show a direct response and predictably increase in size.[90]

Interestingly, the overall scale of the landscape, the size of the protected areas within the landscape, and the level of fragmentation of the landscape are all broadly similar to those seen in the previous example of wild dogs in South Africa, where intensive metapopulation management is being pursued. Despite similarity of scale, and a similar pattern of small reserves nested in a much larger matrix of human-dominated land use, the approach to management in the Malenad-Mysore Tiger Landscape differs in almost every way from that of South African wild dogs. The reasons are driven by the ecological and social differences discussed above, and the way in which these differences interact with the proximate and ultimate threats that are being addressed: ecologically and socially, tigers can occur at relatively high densities, and so protected areas that are of a size inadequate for wild dog persistence can harbor larger, self-sustaining population of tigers. Subpopulations are neither intensively managed nor supplemented, and natural dispersal, while uncommon, is the norm.

Instead of focusing on proximate threats that affect individuals (disease, genetics), management focuses on threats that address population-level persistence issues (e.g., prey depletion, direct hunting of tigers). By addressing these threats effectively in many of the reserves in the Western Ghats, both individual subpopulations and the overall population have expanded in numbers over the last two decades. As prey populations are restored and tiger populations approach carrying capacity, the need to further address the ultimate threat—such as habitat loss and competition for space with a growing human population—will become increasingly important.

Tigers in the Russian Far East (250,000 km²): From Landscape- to Regional-Level Planning

If small, dense populations of tigers characterize the Western Ghats (densities of one tiger per twenty square kilometers), tigers in the Russian Far East, at the other edge of the species's distribution, occur at very low densities but are spread out thinly across a vast landscape of more than 260,000 square kilometers encompassing all of Primorski Krai and the southern districts of Khaborovsk Krai. The vast majority of this landscape is potential tiger habitat, with very low human populations and relatively low human impact. Genetically not dissimilar, the ecology and demographics of this population of tigers differs significantly from those in India.[91] In this area, the density of tiger prey is extremely low and tiger densities reflect this, reaching a maximum of one tiger per one hundred square kilometers.[92] The low prey density, and overall low productivity of the taiga habitat, is also reflected in the slow potential rates of maximum growth in tiger populations when compared to tigers in more productive habitat.[93]

Mitigating the direct impact of people on tigers, whether through reduced tiger-human conflict[94] or antipoaching,[95] is critical to the persistence of tigers in this region, but because of their low densities and wide distribution, factors that may be viewed as ultimate threats elsewhere become proximate threats to tigers in the Russian Far East and northeast China.

Tigers may occupy areas in the Russian Far East that are an order of magnitude or two greater than those occupied in the Western Ghats; tens of thousands of square kilometers of habitat exist in northeast China (Heilongjiang and Jilin provinces), where tigers could potentially be restored.[96] Yet despite this vast area of relative wilderness, because tigers are found at such low densities, the persistence of tigers in the region will rely on addressing regional-scale land-use planning issues. Dale G. Miquelle et al. elaborate the details of what such planning entails, but if tigers are to persist fully, 30 percent of the land area (seventy thousand square kilometers) in the region will need to be managed for tigers.[97] Efforts to implement these conservation strategies have in some measure been successful; but as Miquelle et al. discuss, success in implementation at this scale, while informed by ecological data, is inherently a political and social process.

Conclusion: Managing across Scales

The spatial distribution of threats, both natural and man-made, is at the core of the application of landscape ecology to conservation management.[98] My discussion of wild dogs and tigers shows how the social ecology of a species and the spatial distribution and abundance of resources can interact to change the way in which we plan and execute conservation interventions. While I have focused on carnivores, this interaction between scale and social ecology (in particular, factors that influence home range) has been observed in a variety of species and biomes as diverse as flocking birds in the Amazon,[99] tropical butterflies,[100] and possibly marine fishes.[101]

Recently, David Lindenmayer et al. reviewed the key elements needed in developing landscape-level approaches to conservation.[102] They note that successful landscape-level conservation efforts work across scales and targets, focusing on individual species, suites of species of functional guilds, or larger scales of ecosystems and landscapes themselves, identifying the way in which these approaches are complementary across space and time. Further, they suggest that management should focus on "disproportionately important species and ecological processes" and that successful landscape-level management requires two key elements: "(i) a clearly articulated vision for landscape conservation and (ii) quantifiable objectives that offer unambiguous signposts for measuring progress." The Landscape Species Approach as outlined by Sanderson et al., refined by Peter B. Coppolillo et al., and applied by Karl A. Didier et al. follows these principles and allows managers to design, monitor, and evaluate the effectiveness of landscape-level conservation with interventions at different scales.[103]

As I hope my discussion and the examples I have chosen have shown, the challenge is in understanding how scale influences the decisions one makes in implementing conservation programs. At smaller scales, conservationists are forced to manage intensively, focusing not on the population persistence of individual species, but on the persistence of individuals themselves. As we increase the scale at which we effect conservation, our focus shifts first to those factors that influence the persistence of a population of individuals to factors that more broadly influence the persistence of wildlife populations. At still larger scales, we set our objectives on the management of threats that are more general in nature and use the response of individual species to threat reduction as a measure of the success of our conservation interventions. Finally, at the largest scales, the management of the landscape itself is required—through regional planning, enhancement of connectivity, and other larger-scale interventions. While scale may have absolute (if arbitrary) definitions, the ecology and behavior of a species will strongly influence how it perceives its environment, and in the context of conservation, the scale at which conservationists address those factors that threaten a species's persistence.

Notes

1 Monica Goigel Turner, "Landscape Ecology: The Effect of Pattern on Process," *Annual Review of Ecology and Systematics* 20 (1989): 171–97; and Jianguo Wu and Richard Hobbs, eds., *Key Topics in Landscape Ecology* (Cambridge: Cambridge University Press, 2007).

2 T. F. H. Allen and Thomas B. Starr, *Hierarchy: Perspectives for Ecological Complexity* (Chicago: University of Chicago Press, 1982), 29–30.

3 Simon A. Levin, "The Problem of Pattern and Scale in Ecology," *Ecology* 73, no. 6 (1992): 1943–67.

4 Carsten Rahbek, "The Role of Spatial Scale and the Perception of Large-Scale Species-Richness Patterns," *Ecology Letters* 8, no. 2 (2005): 224–39.

5 Norman Myers, Russell A. Mittermeier, Cristina G. Mittermeier, Gustavo A. B. da Fonseca, and Jennifer Kent, "Biodiversity Hotspots for Conservation Priorities," *Nature* 403 (2000): 853–58.

6 Johan T. du Toit, "Considerations of Scale in Biodiversity Conservation," *Animal Conservation* 13, no. 3 (June 2010): 229–36.

7 D. Doak, P. Marino, and P. Kareiva, "Spatial Scale Mediates the Influence of Habitat Fragmentation on Dispersal Success: Implications for Conservation," *Theoretical Population Biology* 41, no. 3 (1992): 315–36.

8 C. P. Brooks, "A Scalar Analysis of Landscape Connectivity," *Oikos* 102, no. 2 (August 2003): 433–39.

9 Mandar R. Trivedi, Pamela M. Berry, Michael D. Morecroft, and Terence P. Dawson, "Spatial Scale Affects Bioclimate Model Projections of Climate Change Impacts on Mountain Plants," *Global Change Biology* 14 (2008): 1089–103.

10 Jeffrey D. Brawn, Scott K. Robinson, and Frank R. Thompson III, "The Role of Disturbance in the Ecology and Conservation of Birds," *Annual Review of Ecology and Systematics* 32 (2001): 251–76.

11 Eric W. Sanderson, Malanding Jaiteh, Marc A. Levy, Kent H. Redford, Antoinette V. Wannebo, and Gillian Woolmer, "The Human Footprint and the Last of the Wild," *BioScience* 52, no. 10 (October 2002): 891–904.

12 Gillian Woolmer, Stephen C. Trombulak, Justina C. Ray, Patrick J. Doran, Mark G. Anderson, Robert F. Baldwin, Alexis Morgan, and Eric W. Sanderson, "Rescaling the Human Footprint: A Tool for Conservation Planning at an Ecoregional Scale," *Landscape and Urban Planning* 87, no. 1 (2008): 42–53.

13 "The IUCN Red List of Threatened Species," International Union for Conservation of Nature, accessed May 23, 2011, http://www.iucnredlist.org.

14 Ulf Gärdenfors, "Classifying Threatened Species at National versus Global Levels," *Trends in Ecology and Evolution* 16, no. 9 (September 2001): 511–16.

15 Navjot S. Sodhi, Rhett Butler, William F. Laurance, and Luke Gibson, "Conservation Successes at the Micro-,

Meso- and Macroscales," *Trends in Ecology and Evolution*, forthcoming.

16 Nick Salafsky, Daniel Salzer, Alison J. Stattersfield, Craig Hilton-Taylor, Rachel Neugarten, Stuart H. M. Butchart, Ben Collen, Neil Cox, Lawrence L. Master, Sheila O'Connor, and David Wilkie, "A Standard Lexicon for Biodiversity Conservation: Unified Classifications of Threats and Actions," *Conservation Biology* 22, no. 4 (August 2008): 897–911; Conservation Measures Partnership, *Taxonomies of Direct Threats and Conservation Actions* (Washington, D.C.: Conservation Measures Partnership, 2005); and "Authority Files for Habitats, Threats, Conservation Actions and Utilization of Species," International Union for Conservation of Nature, accessed July 28, 2011, http://www.iucn.org/about/work/programmes/species/red_list/resources/technical_documents/authority_files/.

17 Salafsky et al., "Standard Lexicon for Biodiversity Conservation," 900–901.

18 Elizabeth A. Johnson and Michael W. Klemens, "The Impacts of Sprawl on Biodiversity," in *Nature in Fragments: The Legacy of Sprawl*, ed. Elizabeth A. Johnson and Michael W. Klemens (New York: Columbia University Press, 2005), 18–53.

19 Eric A. Odell and Richard L. Knight, "Songbird and Medium-Sized Mammal Communities Associated with Exurban Development in Pitkin County, Colorado," *Conservation Biology* 15, no. 4 (August 2001): 1143–50.

20 Douglas T. Bolger, Thomas A. Scott, and John T. Rotenberry, "Breeding Bird Abundance in an Urbanizing Landscape in Coastal Southern California," *Conservation Biology* 11, no. 2 (April 1997): 406–21; Andrew J. Hansen, Richard L. Knight, John M. Marzluff, Scott Powell, Kathryn Brown, Patricia H. Gude, and Kingsford Jones, "Effects of Exurban Development on Biodiversity: Patterns, Mechanisms, and Research Needs," *Ecological Applications* 15, no. 6 (2005): 1893–905; and Heidi E. Kretser, Patrick J. Sullivan, and Barbara A. Knuth, "Housing Density as an Indicator of Spatial Patterns of Reported Human-Wildlife Interactions in Northern New York," *Landscape and Urban Planning* 84, nos. 3–4 (March 2008): 282–92.

21 Lenore Fahrig and Gray Merriam, "Conservation of Fragmented Populations," *Conservation Biology* 8, no. 1 (March 1994): 50–59; and Joern Fischer and David B. Lindenmayer, "Landscape Modification and Habitat Fragmentation: A Synthesis," *Global Ecology and Biogeography* 16 (2007): 265–80.

22 Kent H. Redford, "The Empty Forest," *BioScience* 42, no. 6 (June 1992): 412–22.

23 *Setting Priorities for the Conservation and Recovery of Wild Tigers: 2005–2015* (Washington, D.C., and New York: WWF, WCS, Smithsonian, and NFWF-STF, 2006).

24 Joe Walston, John G. Robinson, Elizabeth L. Bennett, Urs Breitenmoser, Gustavo A. B. da Fonseca, John Goodrich, Melvin Gumal, Luke Hunter, Arlyne Johnson, K. Ullas Karanth, Nigel Leader-Williams, Kathy MacKinnon, Dale Miquelle, Anak Pattanavibool, Colin Poole, Alan Rabinowitz, James L. D. Smith, Emma J. Stokes, Simon N. Stuart, Chanthavy Vongkhamheng, and Hariyo Wibisono, "Bringing the Tiger Back from the Brink—The Six Percent Solution," *PLoS Biology* 8, no. 9 (September 2010): 1–4.

25 Stephen Blake and Simon Hedges, "Sinking the Flagship: The Case of Forest Elephants in Asia and Africa," *Conservation Biology* 18, no. 5 (October 2004): 1191–202.

26 Joshua R. Ginsberg, "CITES at 30, or 40," *Conservation Biology* 16, no. 5 (October 2002): 1184–91.

27 Salafsky et al., "Standard Lexicon for Biodiversity Conservation," 898.

28 Craig Groves, *Drafting a Conservation Blueprint: A Practitioner's Guide to Planning for Biodiversity* (Washington, D.C.: Island Press, 2003); and Kent H. Redford, Peter Coppolillo, Eric W. Sanderson, Gustavo A. B. da Fonseca, Eric Dinerstein, Craig Groves, Georgina Mace, Stewart Maginnis, Russel A. Mittermeier, Reed Noss, David Olson, John G. Robinson, Amy Vedder, and Michael Wright, "Mapping the Conservation Landscape," *Conservation Biology* 17, no. 1 (February 2003): 116–31.

29 Salafsky et al., "Standard Lexicon for Biodiversity Conservation," 899.

30 The Nature Conservancy, *Conservation Action Planning: Developing Strategies, Taking Action, and Measuring Success at Any Scale*, accessed May 23, 2011, http://conserveonline.org/workspaces/cbdgateway/cap/resources/1/TNC_CAP_Basic_Practices.pdf/download.

31 Groves, *Drafting a Conservation Blueprint*, 75.

32 Karen A. Poiani, Brian D. Richter, Mark G. Anderson, and Holly E. Richter, "Biodiversity Conservation at Multiple Scales: Functional Sites, Landscapes, and Networks," *BioScience* 50, no. 2 (February 2000): 133–34.

33 Du Toit, "Considerations of Scale in Biodiversity Conservation," 231; and Akiko Satake, Thomas K. Rudel, and Ayumi Onuma, "Scale Mismatches and Their Ecological and Economic Effects on Landscapes: A Spatially Explicit Model," *Global Environmental Change* 18, no. 4 (October 2008): 768–75.

34 Tundi Agardy, "Global Marine Conservation Policy versus Site-Level Implementation: The Mismatch of Scale and Its Implications," *Marine Ecology-Progress Series* 300 (2005): 242–48.

35 Du Toit, "Considerations of Scale in Biodiversity Conservation," 230–31.

36 Arun Agrawal, Ashwini Chhatre, and Rebecca Hardin, "Changing Governance of the World's Forests," *Science* 320 (2008): 1460–62.

37 Chris Sandbrook, Fred Nelson, William A. Adams, and Arun Agrawal, "Carbon, Forests and the REDD Paradox," *Oryx* 44, no. 3 (2010): 330–34; and Mark Poffenberger, "Cambodia's Forests and Climate Change: Mitigating

Drivers of Deforestation," *Natural Resources Forum* 33, no. 4 (November 2009): 285–96.

38   Brian K. McNab, "Bioenergetics and the Determination of Home Range Size," *American Naturalist* 97 (1963): 133–40.

39   Thomas W. Schoener, "Sizes of Feeding Territories among Birds," *Ecology* 49 (1968): 123–41.

40   Rosie Woodroffe and Joshua R. Ginsberg, "Edge Effects and the Extinction of Populations inside Protected Areas," *Science* 280 (1998): 2126–28.

41   Justin S. Brashares, Peter Arcese, and Moses K. Sam, "Human Demography and Reserve Size Predict Wildlife Extinction in West Africa," *Proceedings of the Royal Society of London* 268 (2001): 2473–78.

42   Kyle S. Van Houtan, Stuart L. Pimm, Richard O. Bierregaard Jr., Thomas E. Lovejoy, and Philip C. Stouffer, "Local Extinctions in Flocking Birds in Amazonian Forest Fragments," *Evolutionary Ecology Research* 8 (2006): 129–48.

43   Ghazala Shahabuddin and Cesar A. Ponte, "Frugivorous Butterfly Species in Tropical Forest Fragments: Correlates of Vulnerability to Extinction," *Biodiversity and Conservation* 14, no. 5 (2005): 1137–52.

44   Daniel P. Egli and R. C. Babcock, "Ultrasonic Tracking Reveals Multiple Behavioural Modes of Snapper (*Pagrus auratus*) in a Temperate No-Take Marine Reserve," *ICES Journal of Marine Science* 61, no. 7 (2004): 1137–43.

45   Rosie Woodroffe, "Predators and People: Using Human Densities to Interpret Declines of Large Carnivores," *Animal Conservation* 3 (2000): 165–73; and John D. C. Linnell, Jon E. Swenson, and Reidar Andersen, "Predators and People: Conservation of Large Carnivores Is Possible at High Human Densities if Management Policy Is Favourable," *Animal Conservation* 4 (2001): 345–49.

46   Andrea S. Laliberte and William J. Ripple, "Range Contractions of North American Carnivores and Ungulates," *BioScience* 54, no. 2 (February 2004): 123–38.

47   Vidya Athreya, Morten Odden, John D. C. Linnell, and K. Ullas Karanth, "Translocation as a Tool for Mitigating Conflict with Leopards in Human-Dominated Landscapes of India," *Conservation Biology* 25, no. 1 (February 2011): 133–41.

48   R. B. Martin and T. de Meulenaer, *Survey of the Status of the Leopard (*Panthera pardus*) in Sub-Saharan Africa* (Lausanne, Switz.: CITES Secretariat, 1988), 106.

49   Jon P. Beckmann and Joel Berger, "Rapid Ecological and Behavioural Changes in Carnivores: The Responses of Black Bears (*Ursus americanus*) to Altered Food," *Journal of Zoology* 261, no. 2 (October 2003): 207–12.

50   William G. Conway, "Buying Time for Wild Animals with Zoos," *Zoo Biology* 30 (2011): 1–8; William G. Conway, "The Practical Difficulties and Financial Implications of Endangered Species Breeding Programs," *International Zoo Yearbook* 24, no. 1 (January 1986): 210–19; Alexandra Zimmermann et al., *Zoos in the Twenty-First Century: Catalysts for Conservation?* (Cambridge: Cambridge University Press, 2007); and Peter J. S. Olney, Georgina M. Mace, and Anna Feistner, *Creative Conservation: Interactive Management of Wild and Captive Animals* (London: Chapman and Hall, 1994).

51   Michael E. Soulé and Bruce A. Wilcox, eds., *Conservation Biology: An Ecological-Evolutionary Perspective* (Sunderland, Mass.: Simauer Associates, 1980); and O. H. Frankel and Michael E. Soulé, *Conservation and Evolution* (Cambridge: Cambridge University Press, 1981).

52   Joseph C. E. Barber, "Programmatic Approaches to Assessing and Improving Animal Welfare in Zoos and Aquariums," *Zoo Biology* 28 (2009): 519–30.

53   Andrew Moss and Maggie Esson, "Visitor Interest in Zoo Animals and the Implications for Collection Planning and Zoo Education Programmes," *Zoo Biology* 29 (2010): 715–31.

54   Conway, "Buying Time for Wild Animals with Zoos," 1–8.

55   Barber, "Programmatic Approaches to Assessing and Improving Animal Welfare," 528.

56   T. Foose, "Species Survival Plans: The Role of Captive Propagation in Conservation Strategies," in *Conservation Biology and the Black-Footed Ferret*, ed. Ulysses S. Seal et al. (New Haven: Yale University Press, 1989), 210–22; and Association of Zoos and Aquariums, "Species Survival Plan® Program," accessed May 23, 2011, http://www.aza.org/species-survival-plan-program/.

57   Conway, "The Practical Difficulties and Financial Implications of Endangered Species Breeding Programs," 213–15; Andrew Balmford, Georgina M. Mace, and N. Leader-Williams, "Designing the Ark: Setting Priorities for Captive Breeding," *Conservation Biology* 10, no. 3 (June 1996): 719–27; and Anne Baker, "Animal Ambassadors: An Analysis of the Effectiveness and Conservation Impact of *ex situ* Breeding Efforts," in Zimmermann et al., *Zoos in the Twenty-First Century*, 139–54.

58   Cf. Balmford et al., "Designing the Ark."

59   David Samuel Wilcove, *No Way Home: The Decline of the World's Great Animal Migrations* (Washington, D.C.: Island Press / Shearwater Books, 2008), 256.

60   C. Seewagen and E. Slayton, "Mass Changes of Migratory Landbirds during Stopovers in a New York City Park," *The Wilson Journal of Ornithology* 120 (2008): 296–303.

61   William Cronon, *Changes in the Land: Indians, Colonists, and the Ecology of New England* (New York: Hill and Wang, 1983), 235.

62   N. J. Clum and H. Brown, "Avian Species Diversity in Bronx Park: A Century of Change," forthcoming.

63   James R. Miller and Richard J. Hobb, "Conservation Where People Live and Work," *Conservation Biology* 16, no. 2 (April 2002): 330–37; Hillary Rudd, Jamie Vala, and Valentin Schaefer, "Importance of Backyard Habitat in

a Comprehensive Biodiversity Conservation Strategy: A Connectivity Analysis of Urban Green Spaces," *Restoration Ecology* 10, no. 2 (June 2002): 368–75; and Michael L. McKinney, "Urbanization, Biodiversity, and Conservation," *BioScience* 52, no. 10 (October 2002): 883–90.

64 Rosie Woodroffe, Joshua R. Ginsberg, and David W. Macdonald, eds., *The African Wild Dog: Status Survey and Conservation Action Plan* (Gland, Switz.: IUCN, 1997), 167.

65 Scott Creel and Nancy Marusha Creel, "Limitation of African Wild Dogs by Competition with Larger Carnivores," *Conservation Biology* 10, no. 2 (April 1996): 526–38; and Rosie Woodroffe and Joshua R. Ginsberg, "King of the Beasts? Evidence for Guild Redundancy among Large Mammalian Carnivores," in *Large Carnivores and the Conservation of Biodiversity*, ed. Justina C. Ray et al. (Washington, D.C.: Island Press, 2005), 154–58.

66 Woodroffe and Ginsberg, "Edge Effects and the Extinction of Populations," 2127.

67 Rosie Woodroffe, Harriet Davies-Mostert, Joshua R. Ginsberg, Jan Graf, Kellie Leigh, Kim McCreery, Gus Mills, Alistair Poles, Gregory Rasmussen, Robert Robbins, Michael Somers, and Micaela Szykman, "Rates and Causes of Mortality in Endangered African Wild Dogs (*Lycaon pictus*): Lessons for Management and Monitoring," *Oryx* 41, no. 2 (April 2007): 215–23.

68 John H. Fanshawe, Lory H. Frame, and Joshua R. Ginsberg, "The Wild Dog—Africa's Vanishing Carnivore," *Oryx* 25, no. 3 (July 1991): 137–46; and Woodroffe et al., "Rates and Causes of Mortality in Endangered African Wild Dogs," 137–47.

69 Joshua R. Ginsberg and David W. Macdonald, *Foxes, Wolves, Jackals, and Dogs: An Action Plan for the Conservation of Canids* (Gland, Switz.: IUCN, 1990), 116.

70 Ant Maddock, "Wild Dog Demography in Hluhluwe-Umfolozi Park, South Africa," *Conservation Biology* 13, no. 2 (April 1999): 412–17.

71 *African Wild Dog (Lycaon pictus) Population and Habitat Viability Assessment, 13–17 October 1997, Pretoria, South Africa* (Apple Valley, Minn.: IUCN/SSC Conservation Breeding Specialist Group, 1997); see also Harriet Davies-Mostert, Gus Mills, and David W. Macdonald, "A Critical Assessment of South Africa's Managed Metapopulation Recovery Strategy for African Wild Dogs," in *Reintroduction of Top-Order Predators*, ed. Matt W. Hayward and Michael J. Somers (Hoboken, N.J.: Wiley-Blackwell, 2009), 10–42.

72 Daniel S. Licht, Joshua J. Millspaugh, Kyran E. Kunkel, Christopher O. Kochanny, and Rolf O. Peterson, "Using Small Populations of Wolves for Ecosystem Restoration and Stewardship," *Bioscience* 60, no. 2 (February 2010): 486–87.

73 Markus Gusset, Sadie J. Ryan, Markus Hofmeyr, Gus van Dyk, Harriet Davies-Mostert, Jan A. Graf, Cailey Owen, Micaela Szykman, David W. Macdonald, Steven L. Monfort, David E. Wildt, Anthony H. Maddock, M. Gus L.

Mills, Rob Slotow, and Michael J. Somers, "Efforts Going to the Dogs? Evaluating Attempts to Re-introduce Endangered Wild Dogs in South Africa," *Journal of Applied Ecology* 45, no. 1 (February 2008): 100–8.

74 Markus Gusset, Gavin B. Stewart, Diana E. Bowler, and Andrew S. Pullin, "Wild Dog Reintroductions in South Africa: A Systematic Review and Cross-Validation of an Endangered Species Recovery Programme," *Journal of Nature Conservation* 18, no. 3 (August 2010): 230–34.

75 Markus Gusset, Oliver Jakoby, Michael S. Müller, Michael J. Somers, Rob Slotow, and Volker Grimm, "Dogs on the Catwalk: Modelling Re-introduction and Translocation of Endangered Wild Dogs in South Africa," *Biological Conservation* 142, no. 11 (November 2009): 2774–81.

76 P. Lindsey, R. Alexander, J. du Toit, and M. Mills, "The Cost Efficiency of Wild Dog Conservation in South Africa," *Conservation Biology* 19, no. 4 (August 2005): 1205–14.

77 Gusset et al., "Efforts Going to the Dogs?," 104.

78 Woodroffe and Ginsberg, "King of the Beasts?," 156.

79 K. Ullas Karanth, James D. Nichols, N. Samba Kumar, William A. Link, and James E. Hines, "Tigers and Their Prey: Predicting Carnivore Densities from Prey Abundance," *Proceedings of the National Academy of Sciences* 101, no. 14 (2004): 4854–58.

80 Woodroffe and Ginsberg, "Edge Effects and the Extinction of Populations," 2127.

81 Dale G. Miquelle, Evgeniy N. Smirnov, Troy W. Merrill, Alexander E. Myslenkov, Howard B. Quigley, Maurice G. Hornocker, and Bart Schleyer, "Hierarchical Spatial Analysis of Amur Tiger Relationships to Habitat and Prey," in *Riding the Tiger: Tiger Conservation in Human Dominated Landscapes*, ed. John Seidensticker, Sarah Christie, and Peter Jackson (Cambridge: Cambridge University Press, 1999), 71–99.

82 K. Ullas Karanth and Bradley M. Stith, "Prey Depletion as a Critical Determinant of Tiger Population Viability," in Seidensticker, Christie, and Jackson, *Riding the Tiger*, 100–13.

83 Judy A. Mills and Peter Jackson, *Killed for a Cure: A Review of the Worldwide Trade in Tiger Bone* (Cambridge: Traffic International, 1994), 52; and Kristin Nowell, *Far From a Cure: The Tiger Trade Revisited* (Cambridge: Traffic International, 2000), 110.

84 K. Quigley, J. Evermann, C. Leathers, D. Armstrong, J. Goodrich, N. Duncan, and D. Miquelle, "Morbillivirus Infection Confirmed in a Wild Siberian Tiger in the Russian Far East," *Journal of Wildlife Diseases* 46, no. 4 (2010): 1252–56.

85 P. Henry, D. Miquelle, T. Sugimoto, D. McCullough, A. Caccone, and M. Russello, "*In Situ* Population Structure and *Ex Situ* Representation of the Endangered Amur Tiger," *Molecular Ecology* 18, no. 15 (August 2009): 3173–84.

86 Y. Xu, S. Fang, and Z. Li, "Sustainability of the South China Tiger: Implications of Inbreeding Depression and Introgression," *Conservation Genetics* 8 (2007): 1199–207.

87 Walston et al., "Bringing the Tiger Back from the Brink," 1; and *Setting Priorities for the Conservation and Recovery of Wild Tigers*, 91–92.

88 Eric Dinerstein, Colby Loucks, Eric Wikramanayake, Joshua R. Ginsberg, Eric Sanderson, John Seidensticker, Jessica Forrest, Gosia Bryja, Andrea Heydlauff, Sybille Klenzendorf, Peter Leimgruber, Judy Mills, Timothy G. O'Brien, Mahendra Shrestha, Ross Simons, and Melissa Songer, "The Fate of Wild Tigers," *BioScience* 57, no. 6 (2006): 508–14; and Walston et al., "Bringing the Tiger Back from the Brink," 2, fig. 1.

89 K. Ullas Karanth, Arjun M. Gopalaswamy, N. Samba Kumar, Srinivas Vaidyanathan, James D. Nichols, and Darryl I. MacKenzie, "Monitoring Carnivore Populations at the Landscape Scale: Occupancy Modelling of Tigers from Sign Surveys," *Journal of Applied Ecology* 48, no. 4 (August 2011): 1048–56.

90 Karanth et al., "Tigers and Their Prey," 4857; and Karanth et al., "Monitoring Carnivore Populations at the Landscape Scale," 6.

91 Joel Cracraft, Julie Feinstein, Jeffrey Vaughn, and Kathleen Helm-Bychowski, "Sorting Out Tigers (*Panthera tigris*): Mitochondrial Sequences, Nuclear Inserts, Systematics, and Conservation Genetics," *Animal Conservation* 1, no. 2 (May 1998): 139–50.

92 Dale G. Miquelle et al., "Science-Based Conservation of Amur Tigers in the Russian Far East and Northeast China," in *Tigers of the World: The Science, Politics, and Conservation of Panthera tigris*, 2nd ed., ed. Ronald Tilson and Philip J. Nyhus (London: Academic Press, 2010), 403–23.

93 Miquelle et al., "Hierarchical Spatial Analysis of Amur Tiger Relationships," 80–81; cf. Guillaume Chapron, Dale G. Miquelle, Amaury Lambert, John M. Goodrich, Stéphane Legendre, and Jean Clobert, "The Impact on Tigers of Poaching versus Prey Depletion," *Journal of Applied Ecology* 45, no. 6 (December 2008): 1667–74.

94 John M. Goodrich, "Human-Tiger Conflict: A Review and Call for Comprehensive Plans," *Integrative Zoology* 5, no. 4 (December 2010): 297–308; and John M. Goodrich and Dale G. Miquelle, "Translocation of Problem Amur Tigers *Panthera tigris altaica* to Alleviate Human–Tiger Conflicts," *Oryx* 39, no. 4 (October 2005): 1–4.

95 Chapron et al., "Impact on Tigers of Poaching versus Prey Depletion," 4–5; and Steven Russell Galster and Karin Vaud Eliot, "Roaring Back: Anti-Poaching Strategies for the Russian Far East and the Comeback of the Amur Tiger," in Seidensticker, Christie, and Jackson, *Riding the Tiger*, 230–42.

96 Miquelle et al., "Science-Based Conservation of Amur Tigers," 418–20.

97 Ibid.; and Miquelle et al., "Hierarchical Spatial Analysis of Amur Tiger Relationships," 88–90.

98 See G. Arnold, "Incorporating Landscape Pattern into Conservation Programs," in *Mosaic Landscapes and Ecological Processes*, ed. Lennart Hansson, Lenore Fahrig, and Gray Merriam (New York: Chapman and Hall, 1995), 309–37; and H. Ronald Pulliam, John B. Dunning, and Jianguo Liu, "Population Dynamics in Complex Landscapes: A Case Study," *Ecological Applications* 2, no. 2 (1992): 165–77.

99 Van Houtan et al., "Local Extinctions in Flocking Birds," 223, fig. 1.

100 Shahabuddin and Ponte, "Frugivorous Butterfly Species in Tropical Forest Fragments," 1147.

101 Egli and Babcock, "Ultrasonic Tracking Reveals Multiple Behavioural Modes of Snapper," 1140–41.

102 David Lindenmayer et al., "A Checklist for Ecological Management of Landscapes for Conservation," *Ecology Letters* 11 (2008): 78–91.

103 Eric W. Sanderson, Kent H. Redford, Amy Vedder, Peter B. Coppolillo, and Sarah E. Ward, "A Conceptual Model for Conservation Planning Based on Landscape Species Requirements," *Landscape and Urban Planning* 58 (2002): 41–56; Peter B. Coppolillo, Humberto Gomez, Fiona Maisels, and Robert Wallace, "Selection Criteria for Suites of Landscape Species as a Basis for Site-Based Conservation," *Biological Conservation* 115, no. 3 (February 2004): 419–30; and Karl A. Didier, Michale J. Glennon, Andrés Novaro, Eric W. Sanderson, Samantha Strindberg, Susan Walker, and Sebástian di Martino, "The Landscape Species Approach: Spatially-Explicit Conservation Planning Applied in the Adirondacks, USA, and San Guillermo-Laguna Brava, Argentina, Landscapes," *Oryx* 43, no. 4 (2009): 476–87.

CHAPTER 5

Biodiversity, Ecosystem Functioning, and the Design of Landscapes

Shahid Naeem

Introduction: Biodiversity and Ecosystem Functioning

AS A NATURAL SCIENTIST, I WORK WITH SOCIAL scientists and those in the humanities to better understand the world we live in and share our findings with practitioners such as foresters, agriculturalists, conservation biologists, and landscape designers. We rarely, however, actually ever get together. John Beardsley, director of Garden and Landscape Studies at Dumbarton Oaks, in his prospectus for the symposium that stimulated this essay, indicated that the goal of the meeting was "to explore how designers, historians, and scientists might better collaborate to promote zoological biodiversity and how scientific ambitions might be expressed in culturally significant and historically informed design." Thus, for a few days amid the beautiful gardens of Dumbarton Oaks, the all too rare event occurred of natural and social scientists and those in the humanities coming together. In this spirit, I consider here how the abstract topic in ecological science that concerns the relationship between biodiversity and ecosystem functioning might inform landscape design. To do so requires that I consider three topics: (1) clarifying what biodiversity is from

a natural science perspective, (2) pointing to the significance of biodiversity in landscape design, and (3) considering the social implications of landscape designs that are rich or poor in biodiversity. Each topic would require its own essay, so I will focus on issues I have personally found to be important. Furthermore, as a natural scientist with little training in social science, I am rather at a disadvantage in covering social values, but I believe it is useful to see how natural scientists perceive social values as a means for contributing to a dialogue between natural and social scientists.

What Is Biodiversity?

Biodiversity is a familiar term, but scientifically its meaning sometimes surprises people. Biodiversity refers to all dimensions of the diversity of life on earth, including genetic, ecological, taxonomic, spatial, and temporal variation.[1] Biodiversity is not, as it is sometimes misconstrued, simply the number of species found in a landscape.

The number of species, or species richness, is only a measure of taxonomic diversity and does not reflect the true extent of biodiversity in an area. For example, a landscape made up of many ecosystems (e.g., wetlands, grasslands, farms, and ponds) can be more diverse than a landscape that consists solely of woodlands, even if the landscape made up of many habitats has fewer species than the landscape containing only woodlands. Similarly, if two landscapes have exactly the same number of species, but one has species that are genetically diverse (e.g., many races and subspecies) while the other does not, then the former landscape has more biodiversity than the latter. Another example concerning ecological diversity is if two landscapes have the same number of species, but one consists of species interacting with one another (i.e., competing with one another, preying upon one another, or facilitating one another) and another consists of independent species, then the former is more diverse. Species richness is, thus, important, but by itself it is insufficient for judging how diverse a habitat, ecosystem, or landscape is.

Biodiversity is also inseparable from ecosystem functioning, which concerns how ecosystems influence biogeochemical processes. In the presence of inorganic material such as nitrogen gas, water, oxygen, carbon dioxide, silicates, sulfates, phosphates, and other inorganic chemicals, when the conditions are right (temperature, humidity, substrate pH, and so forth) and there is some source of energy, usually sunlight, life will convert this inorganic material into organic material like proteins, carbohydrates, lipids (i.e., the constituents of fats and oils), and nucleic acids (i.e., DNA and RNA). Life also converts organic material back into its inorganic constituents. Ecosystem functioning concerns this dynamic: how a mass of living organisms influences the magnitudes and rates of elements cycling between organic and inorganic forms. The discipline of biogeochemistry focuses on this synthetic concept.[2]

The term biosphere reflects our understanding that life on earth is a complex web of interacting species that form a mass that covers the earth and governs the chemical and physical conditions of our atmosphere, hydrosphere, and the surface of our lithosphere.[3]

My specialty, how biodiversity influences ecosystem functioning, is a relatively new field which began only in the early 1990s.[4] More technically, I study how genetic, ecological, taxonomic, spatial, and temporal variation in the organisms that occupy ecosystems (i.e., biodiversity) influence the cycling of matter back and forth between organic and inorganic forms, or biogeochemistry (i.e., ecosystem functioning). Although we seldom think about living things as participants in biogeochemical processes, in part because life's influence over ecosystem functioning is largely invisible, most of us do know that landscapes contain plants that take in carbon dioxide, water, and mineral nutrients and produce organic masses such as wood, hay, fruits, or flowers, and we know animals do the converse by consuming organic matter (food, or vegetation for an herbivore, animals for a carnivore, or both for an omnivore) and converting it into ammonia in waste material and carbon dioxide during respiration. Although probably less well appreciated, a fair number of us also know the importance of microbial communities in decomposition, which recycles organic matter trapped in dead vegetation and animals.

The mass of life in a landscape is important, but so is its biodiversity. Few would be surprised that changes in the mass of life found in a landscape will change its ecosystem functioning. Clear-cut a woodland, for example, and its biogeochemistry is radically altered—its rate of production, or the buildup of organic material, collapses, carbon dioxide is released into the atmosphere, and nutrients in the soil dissolve in the rain and wash away. Many might be surprised, however, that changing the diversity of life, not just the mass of living things, also matters—that is, change the biodiversity of a forest and even if its mass remains constant, its production and stability will change. When it comes to understanding the biogeochemistry of landscapes, both the mass and diversity of life matter.

Measuring and managing biodiversity in the context of ecosystem functioning is challenging, but it can be done if scientists and landscape designers work together. I return to this issue later.

The Science versus Value of Biodiversity
The study of the influence of biodiversity on ecosystem functioning seems a rather dispassionate view of life, one devoid of the human values of biodiversity. When one thinks of biodiversity, one usually conjures up images of plants and animals—not matter cycling between organic and inorganic

forms. Biodiversity concerns things like penguins, wombats, blue whales, deep-sea crabs, humongous mats of fungus, rattlesnakes, hummingbirds, creosote bushes, stoats, Siberian tigers, ginkgo trees, staghorn coral, earthworms, many species of microscopic phytoplankton and zooplankton, wolves, . . . (insert several million more species here, and don't forget the bacteria, archaea, and possibly viruses), and more. To reduce life's fantastic diversity of forms, from drab to brilliant to iridescent, from dark to bioluminescent, from cryptic to flamboyant, from microscopic to gigantic, from slow to speedy, from secretive to aggressive, from timid to bold, from solitary to social, from matriarchal to patriarchal, from short-lived to long-lived, and all other aspects of variation among living forms— to reduce all this to chemical processes seems to entirely miss what we value most about biodiversity. Gardens, zoos, aviaries, and art that extols the diversity of life in paintings, tapestries, and murals, are not about chemistry, but about the amazing diversity of life's forms. Designing landscapes that maximize the diversity of life-forms one finds in a landscape seems remote from designing landscapes that maximize biogeochemical functions.

In truth, however, biodiversity and ecosystem functioning are inextricably linked, and one cannot consider one without the other. Both biodiversity and ecosystems are human constructs. Neither biodiversity nor ecosystem functioning make sense outside the light of the other. In nature, there is, in fact, no such thing as an ecosystem without biodiversity and there is no such thing as biodiversity outside of an ecosystem.

Thus, while we may value biodiversity for its inspiring range of colors, forms, and behaviors, we should also appreciate its value for governing the magnitude and stability of biogeochemical processes. This means focusing on the necessary diversity for an ecosystem to provide long-term, reliable ecosystem functions. In this context, it is the role of species, rather than their Latin binomials or their taxonomic relationships, that matter. Ecologists call this functional diversity. It is not easy to measure, but it can be done. For example, we might wish to know how fast a plant species grows, how deep are its roots, how much does a typical plant weigh, how much carbon does it sequester, how much

nitrogen does it use, how much water it needs, how much water evaporates from the plant, and so forth. These are not taxonomic traits but what ecologists call functional traits. Functional diversity is based on functional traits, not on taxonomy. By this approach, it does not matter that one site has more species than another, such as a Brazilian rainforest versus an Alaskan tundra, but what roles species play in making a rainforest or tundra a stable, functional, biogeochemical system. Although functional diversity and its measurement is a relatively new field, it has been progressing such that scientists can provide answers to questions landscape designers might have about diversity in their systems, beyond counting species.

Note that how species interact with one another is important for modeling how biodiversity dynamically influences ecosystem function and is not part of what constitutes functional diversity. Interactions are very important, but they come into play once species and their roles in ecosystem functioning are determined.

Biodiversity, Ecosystem Functioning, and Landscapes: Four Thoughts

Having considered, rather briefly, what biodiversity is, what it means in terms of habitat, ecosystem, or landscape design and function, and a little on its social values, I will now consider four ideas concerning landscape design that come to mind after these deliberations. These four are (1) the idea of the Edenic landscape, (2) the significance of biodiversity in a functioning landscape, (3) landscape typology, and (4) ecological poverty.

The Facade of the Edenic Landscape

At the outset of this symposium, Beardsley noted that "the vision of a garden shared peacefully by humans and animals is one of the most familiar landscape tropes—and one of the most elusive." It is worth considering what sort of landscape Eden might have been from an ecological perspective to understand how biodiversity fits into the picture.

While classical accounts clearly described Eden as a habitat where species coexisted in peace, there is little idea of what the habitat looked like. Paintings by Jacopo Bassano (1510–92), Jacob de Backer (1555–85),

or Jan Brueghel the Elder (1568–1625) show Adam and Eve amid landscapes lush in vegetation and populated by many species. Adam and Eve are naked, suggesting an equitable climate. Oddly, from a modern perspective, there are a number of domestic species such as chickens, sheep, goats, horses, and cows in these paintings. The domestication of plants and animals began about ten thousand years ago to provide a reliable supply of food in the form of grains, animal products like milk and meat, and work in the case of draft animals. Such animals were bred to meet human needs, yet in Eden, there were no human needs. Why would there be chickens, sheep, goats, horses, and cows—let alone wheat, maize, and rice? This theme of domesticated animals being part of Eden is seen centuries later as well, in paintings by Erastus Salisbury Field (1805–1900) (Figure 5.1). Only in Hieronymus Bosch's (1450–1516) triptych known as the *Garden of Earthly Delights* are creatures a bit less familiar, more angular, and subtly menacing in Eden; the triptych depicts a cat carrying a mouse in its mouth, a lion with its antelope kill,

and some birds attacking frog-like creatures—all of which suggests some degree of predation in Eden. But even here nature and humans are in harmony.

A world in which humanity and wildlife cohabit landscapes in peace and tranquility, however, is a world in which ecological and evolutionary processes are suppressed. Natural systems would exhibit the following properties when allowed to run their course. First, new species would be constantly emerging and extant species would be constantly going extinct. Until recently, origination generally outpaced extinction, sometimes in bursts (such as the Cambrian explosion where most modern lifeforms appeared about seventy-five million years ago), sometimes more steadily (as it has ever since the end of the Permian about 250 million years ago), in spite of some mass and minor extinctions.[5] Second, only a few species in any ecosystem come to dominate while most others are rare, a point detailed in the section below, which discusses what I refer to as "ecological poverty." Third, the natural tendency of every species is to increase its density until it exhausts its

SHAHID NAEEM

single most limiting resource, at which point its density remains stable or fluctuates around its carrying capacity. Fourth, interactions with other species that link species in a complex web involve unpleasant processes such as predation, disease, parasitism, and competition for limiting resources that generally prevent unbounded growth by any species.

The end results of ecological and evolutionary processes are the ecosystems we see around us and cherish—the woodlands, grasslands, kelp beds, rainforests, deserts, ponds, lakes, streams, swamps, alpine meadows, tundras, taigas, and so forth. These systems give rise to new species, are dominated by a few life-forms, and consist of highly dynamic populations whose potential for wild fluctuations in density are mostly kept in check by competition for limiting resources, predation, and parasitism. To those who see such natural (i.e., unmanaged) ecosystems as Edenic, the principles

of ecology and evolution are critical in understanding how to ensure that such landscapes can function even though they played no role in Eden.

I am fond of pointing out that ecology and evolution originated with original sin.

If the Eden portrayed in ancient paintings is what informs a landscape's design, then one has to counteract all ecological and evolutionary principles, much as the Creator had to have done. In Eden, there is no origination or extinction, most species are equally abundant, growth is not limited (though it must be bounded unless Eden is infinite in its extent or there are no births or deaths), and densities are low. Such a landscape would be only a facade, one held up by a structure that is highly unstable and would require enormous investments of time and energy to keep it standing.

As Carolyn Merchant suggests, the fate of nature may rest in what it is we perceive of as an Edenic

FIGURE 5.2
Edward Hicks, *Peaceable Kingdom*, ca. 1834, oil on canvas, National Gallery of Art, Washington, D.C.

Gift of Edgar William and Bernice Chrysler Garbisch, 1980.62.15.

landscape.[6] Should modern landscapes be facades? When we gaze upon the landscape we see what humans imagine Eden to be, but behind the facade is a highly unstable structure that allows no new species to emerge or enter, no species to die off or leave, and the population of every species is managed to keep them all equally abundant while suppressing the interactions among them that would favor some over others.

THE ANTHROPOCENE AND THE PEACEABLE KINGDOM

The modern world is dominated by landscapes that reflect humanity striving to achieve something akin to the Peaceable Kingdom—in the sense of having plenty of food, long lives, shelter from adverse environmental conditions, freedom from illnesses caused by disease or other factors, and improved well-being (Figure 5.2). Many would argue that we have changed things so much that we are no longer living in a world predominantly shaped by natural processes. The Peaceable Kingdom is an idea captured in the Bible by passages such as Isaiah 11:6, "The wolf also shall dwell with the lamb, and the leopard shall lie down with the kid; and the calf and the young lion and the fatling together; and a little child shall lead them," and Isaiah 65:25, "The wolf and the lamb shall feed together, and the lion shall eat straw like the bullock: and dust shall be the serpent's meat" (Authorized [King James] Version). Personally I like comedian Woody Allen's paraphrasing, "The lion and the calf shall lie down together but the calf won't get much sleep," which more accurately describes what we are likely to achieve on our own.

The result of humanity's striving to achieve the Peaceable Kingdom, in the sense that every human population seeks to improve its well-being and free itself of the vagaries of nature (which, ironically, has not been a peaceful process by any means), has created a modern world unlike any earth has ever experienced. This new world has been dubbed the Anthropocene,[7] a post-Holocene (twelve thousand years before present) world characterized almost entirely by anthropogenic processes such as biodiversity loss,[8] land-use and land-cover change,[9] elevated carbon dioxide and its attendant alterations of climate (e.g., increasing global temperatures,

sea-level rise, increasing variation in local climatic conditions),[10] biotic homogenization (e.g., extensive invasion or biotic exchange),[11] emerging diseases,[12] global N enrichment,[13] global P enrichment and source depletion,[14] hydrologic impoundment,[15] human population growth, urban growth, sub- and peri-urban expansion, widespread poverty, and food, water, and energy insecurity.[16]

Figure 5.3 illustrates the contrast between the Holocene and the Anthropocene, listing the dominant processes that shape each world. The inset box on the left of the figure indicates natural processes that predominantly shaped the world prior to the Anthropocene (demarcated by the vertical dashed line on the right). Biotic exchange (the movement of species among habitats), community dynamics (the influences of facilitation, predation, competition, parasitism, and other interactions among species on their population dynamics), succession (the natural progression of ecosystems to steady states after a perturbation), long temporal scales of ecological processes, and virtually no human "management" typify the pre-Anthropocene world. The inset box on the right summarizes the dominant processes shaping the modern world, all of which are anthropogenic. Denudation refers to the clearing of land of natural vegetation. Each graph provides predictions for future conditions up to 2050. I have adapted this figure from one provided by Jan Zalasiewcz and colleagues.[17]

Is the modern design of landscapes then to be informed by Eden, which was not shaped by ecological or evolutionary principles, or is it to further human desires to achieve something akin to the Peaceable Kingdom, in which we suppress or eliminate ecology and evolution to create a world of domestic security? An Edenic landscape is one that would allow us to experience what Eden might have been like—a diversity of life without threats of predation, disease, or competition that drive ecological and evolutionary processes. A Peaceable Kingdom landscape would differ by focusing on a sense of tranquility and security by having gardens filled with an abundance of edible fruits, vegetables, domestic flowers, and domestic animals rather than wildlife. The two landscapes are similar in that threatening species, like venomous snakes, vampire bats, stinging predatory

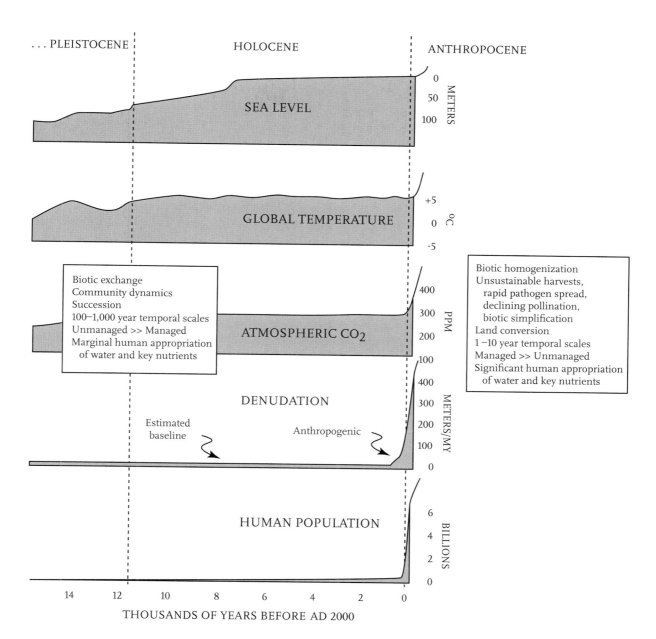

FIGURE 5.3

The Anthropocene. The modern world is no longer shaped by natural processes, but by anthropogenic processes that reflect human economic development.

© Shahid Naeem.

wasps, large cats, or bears would be present only if they could be tamed animals and fed vegetable diets (an absurd goal). Perhaps the design of modern landscapes seeking to include wildlife and animals is informed by both: the Edenic aesthetics of a world filled with a rich diversity of life-forms and the Peaceable Kingdom aesthetics of bounty, tranquility, and security, like the beautiful, rolling hills of farmland in Wisconsin where 99 percent of its prairies are gone. (Prairies are beautiful too, but from a different aesthetic.) Either way, it is unfortunate because such landscapes are not sustainable if we must forever fight off the countervailing influences of ecology and evolution.

Biodiversity and the Functioning of Landscapes

One of the most influential sets of experiments done in the 1700s was by Joseph Priestley (1733–1804), in which he placed a mouse inside an inverted jar and watched it die, placed a candle inside a jar and watched it expire, and then discovered that if one put a plant inside the jar for a time, the candle could be reignited and a new mouse could be put into the jar in which the previous mouse had died, yet it would live. His insight, long before anything was understood about oxygen, carbon dioxide, photosynthesis, or ecosystem functioning, was that plants undid what animals and candles did to the atmosphere. In his words, it is: "highly probable, that the injury which is continually done to the atmosphere by the respiration of such a number of animals, and the putrefaction of such masses of both vegetable and animal matter, is, in part at least, repaired by the vegetable creation. . . . it seems to be extremely probable that the putrid effluvium [i.e., whatever it is that extinguished candles and caused the death of mice in closed bottles] is in some measure extracted from the air, by means of the leaves of plants, and therefore that they render the remainder more fit for respiration."[18]

We know today that the term "putrid effluvium" refers to carbon dioxide and—were it still in use today—might give us a different perspective on this greenhouse gas. Priestley's simple set of experiments that anyone can do (barring the cruelty it imposes on mice) readily demonstrates the invisible cycling of material from the atmosphere to the biosphere (the air in the jar and the plants and animals in the jar) and back again. We seldom realize we live in a closed system like a jar because *our* jar is very, very big. But snowcapped mountains tell us where our habitable atmosphere begins to end, and outside the thin atmosphere within which we live lies a horrific vacuum of unimaginable cold, bathed in radiation and continuously struck by a rain of meteorites that would come down like bullets were they not burned up by friction in our atmosphere. Our jar is the atmosphere we live in filled with gases like oxygen, nitrogen, and water vapor, and greenhouse gases like carbon dioxide and methane, that are strongly influenced by life on earth.

Scaling up, if we were to put a chamber on top of a patch of land and measure the buildup of the putrid effluvium (carbon dioxide), inside that chamber we would note that by day, if there is vegetation in the chamber, the carbon dioxide could be drawn down to extremely low levels, while by night the carbon dioxide could build up to lethal levels in the chamber. Figure 5.4 provides an illustration of such an experiment done by students at the University of Minnesota when I was faculty there in 1994. The photograph in the figure shows two students, one managing an infrared gas analyzer to measure carbon dioxide in the box and the other recording the date, time, and other information about the plot. The clear plastic box is outfitted with circulating fans and a sealed portal through which the infrared gas analyzer samples the air. They put the box on the plot and immediately started measuring the amount of carbon dioxide continuously for sixty seconds. As one can see in the graph of Figure 5.4, the carbon dioxide concentration decreases dramatically from about 330 parts per million to about 300 parts per million—from current levels to preindustrial levels, all in sixty seconds! Anyone with this equipment can perform this experiment (though it is rather expensive compared to Priestley's experiment) and observe for himself that life transforms our atmosphere, a fact rarely observed in any concrete way because it happens invisibly. If one put the box out at night, of course, in the absence of photosynthesis, one would see the converse.

One could build a very large box, such as Biosphere 2—a giant, closed greenhouse costing nearly two hundred million dollars to build—with sufficient infrastructure and enough biomass to sustain twelve people for two years, though it failed miserably to do so.[19] The rich organic soil and concrete in Biosphere 2 released vastly more carbon dioxide than the vegetation could sequester, leading to nearly a tenfold increase in atmospheric carbon dioxide which forced the Biospherians (as they called themselves) to open the system slightly to vent off the excess putrid effluvium.

In the early 1990s, ecologists began to ask the question that neither Priestley nor the Biospherians asked: What is the importance of biodiversity in the mass of life that is responsible for biogeochemical processes? Returning to Figure 5.4, you will note

FIGURE 5.4
Scaling up from Priestley's jar experiments: a) students at University of Minnesota measuring carbon dioxide in a box placed on top of prairie vegetation; and b) carbon dioxide in the box, shown above, for a period of one minute.

© Shahid Naeem.

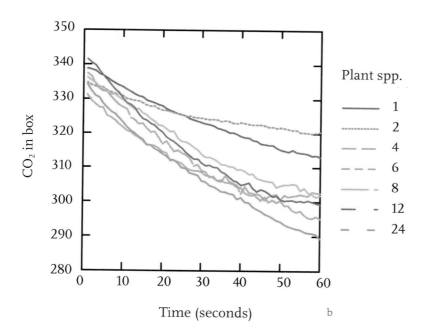

that the many trajectories represent how many plant species were in the plots where the chamber was resting. Some plots had one species, some had two, and so forth, all the way to some plots having twenty-four plant species. It is quite apparent that how fast the concentration of carbon dioxide in the chamber declined was strongly affected by how many species of plants were in the box.

Over the last fifteen years, more than nine hundred ecological studies have examined how biodiversity influences ecosystem functioning, much as the simple experiment outlined in Figure 5.4 did. The first experiment in 1994 consisted of establishing fourteen replicate communities, each in identical growth chambers with the same light, temperature, volume of soil, water, and atmospheric conditions, but varied number of plant and invertebrate species (e.g., snails, earthworms, insects, and other small organisms) among the chambers. Chambers varied in the number of species they had, but all started with equal numbers of individuals.[20] Many subsequent studies took this approach of manipulating biodiversity among replicate systems while controlling other factors. Experiments were conducted in the laboratory using bottles, test tubes, or petri dishes, in growth chambers of different sizes, in greenhouses, in field experiments, and eventually using computer models to explore how changes in biodiversity influences ecosystem functioning.[21]

These experiments were very controversial for a variety of reasons, the most prominent arguments among scientists concerning why biodiversity had the effect it did.[22] But as experiments multiplied, the debates settled, and researchers focused on more detailed, exacting experiments whose results were less subject to debate.

The field of biodiversity and ecosystem functioning is too large to cover in this short space, but several volumes, sometimes rather technical, provide summaries of the work done in the early 1990s[23] and more recently.[24] There is only one accessible account[25] and a reasonably accessible synthesis report prepared for the United Nations that came out of its Millennium Ecosystem Assessment that I discuss below.[26] There are also meta-analyses, or statistical analyses of trends across multiple studies in terrestrial and freshwater ecosystems[27] and marine ecosystems.[28]

While controversy continues to surround some of the issues in biodiversity and ecosystem functioning research, the general consensus is that biodiversity has the capacity to do two things to ecosystems. First, increasing biodiversity can increase the level of biogeochemical activity if species are complementary to one another. Second, ecosystems with greater diversity will exhibit greater stability in long-term performance if species are independent of one another. These biodiversity effects tend to diminish, however, as one adds more and more diversity in part because there is a certain amount of redundancy among species. A particular ecosystem function will not show much change if the addition of a new species brings no new functionality to the system, as the added species is redundant with those already present. For example, if most plant species in an ecosystem are shallow-rooted, the addition of another shallow-rooted species may not significantly affect the amount of water and nutrients extracted from the system's soil, but if the added species is a deep-rooted species (i.e., complementary to the shallow-rooted species), the previously inaccessible water and nutrients will now come into circulation, improving the functioning of an ecosystem. If one looks at the long-term productivity of the same system, we may also note that the addition of the deep-rooted species means that in times of drought there is less of a decline in aboveground plant production because the deep-rooted species may tap into groundwater not available to the shallow-rooted species.

In essence, the greater the diversity of life-forms in an ecosystem, the greater its efficiency in making use of all the available resources in the system and the less vulnerable it is to environmental variation.

When designing landscapes with biodiversity in mind, it is valuable to consider the key messages derived from the study of biodiversity and ecosystem functioning over the last fifteen years. The decisions one makes concerning what species will be included or excluded, what their abundances will be, and whether they are complementary to one another will affect the magnitude and stability of how such ecosystems function. It is not easy to estimate what the consequences of one's changes in biodiversity will be with respect to ecosystem functioning because the necessary experiments are too big, too costly, and take too long to conduct. Modeling approaches, in which one uses the known individual influences of species on ecosystems to predict how changes in biodiversity affect ecosystem functioning, offer much promise.[29] These methods, however, minimally require information about the biology of the majority of the dominant species in an ecosystem whose functioning one wants to predict. Such information is generally lacking even for well-studied ecosystems. But even in the absence of any ability to directly use the ecological principles uncovered by biodiversity and ecosystem functioning research, it is useful to consider at a basic level how our decisions about what to do with biodiversity will influence the way landscapes function as biogeochemical systems. Of course, that is if the client who commissions the landscape modification wants it to perform such invisible, yet invaluable, functions.

The likelihood that a client would seek such landscapes depends on how well environmental economists can value the services ecosystems provide and communicate their findings in clear and meaningful ways. The one ecosystem function that has gained considerable attention is sequestering and storing carbon. But this well-developed case for the value of ecosystems for carbon has been driven by the high-profile environmental concern over climate change. Can we achieve similar success for nitrogen cycling, oxygen production, disease regulation, pollination, and biocontrol in the absence of major environmental calamities? There is much activity in this field, and I am optimistic that environmental economists will succeed in valuing a broad array of ecosystem functions. If the economists can communicate their findings in clear and compelling ways, the number of clients who will seek ecosystem functions as part of the landscapes they wish to have designed is likely to increase.

A Typology of Landscapes from the Perspective of Biodiversity and Ecosystem Functioning

The field of biodiversity and ecosystem functioning is complex, but its central finding is relatively straightforward. If an ecosystem is at its natural level of biodiversity and experiencing conditions within the norms of recent history, it will exhibit a degree of ecosystem functioning that will decline slowly if some biodiversity is lost, but precipitously once critically low values are reached (Figure 5.5). This fundamental relationship between biodiversity and ecosystem functioning describes a saturating curve, shown in the top portion of Figure 5.5. Seven curves are plotted in Figure 5.5, the central one (curve *d*) describes the general relationship for a natural system while the other curves above and below describe how the curve would change if the ecosystem experienced either management to increase ecosystem functioning at the expense of reducing biodiversity (*a–c*) or if the ecosystem was subjected to forces that led to both a loss of diversity and ecosystem functioning at the same time (*e–g*). Thus, the basic relationship between biodiversity and ecosystem functioning is a saturating relationship, but the relationship varies (curves labeled from *a* to *g*) depending on the degree of management or degradation. For example, when exposed to different levels of stress, or a stress gradient such as pollution, increasing temperature attributable to climate change, or unsustainable extraction of natural

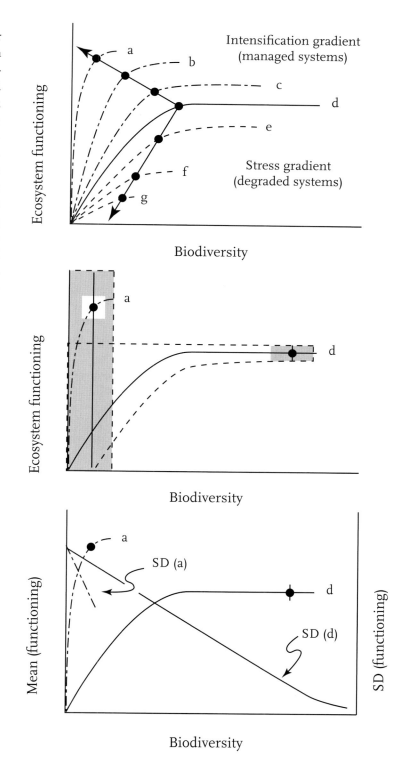

FIGURE 5.5

A graphically defined typology of landscapes based on the fundamental relationship between biodiversity and ecosystem functioning.

© Shahid Naeem.

resources, the saturation level, maximum diversity, and the "elbow" of the curve declines toward lower values of biodiversity and ecosystem functioning (curves *e–g*). By contrast, managed ecosystems may have increased levels of ecosystem function when compared to their unmanaged counterparts, such as increases in primary production when a prairie grassland is converted to a monoculture of maize or wheat. In these systems, biodiversity declines, but ecosystem functioning increases (curves *a–c*).

This simple framework presented in the top of Figure 5.5 provides a four-part typology of ecosystems or landscapes: (1) those that are managed, (2) those that are unmanaged (commonly thought of as natural), (3) those that are degraded, and (4) those that are restored from either managed or degraded states to an unmanaged system. Such a typology provides a simple way of relating the diversity of ecosystems and landscapes that make up our modern world.

Focusing on managed and unmanaged systems (curves *a* and *d*, in the middle plot of Figure 5.5), the expected boundaries of biodiversity and ecosystem functioning are shown as dashed lines that describe the set of points that an ecosystem can occupy near those curves if biodiversity is altered. The shaded area represents natural variation in biodiversity and ecosystem functioning. In this figure, monoculture crops are illustrated as highly productive (*a*), but their functioning may range from highly productive to zero (i.e., crop failure). An unmanaged system varies substantially less (smaller gray area).

The relationship between natural variation in biodiversity and both the mean and standard deviation (SD) of ecosystem functioning for curves *a* and *d*, illustrated in the bottom plot in Figure 5.5, shows how variation in system function, an inverse measure of system stability, declines with increasing biodiversity, but more sharply in managed systems. Thus, small increases in the diversity of low-diversity managed systems can improve stability much faster than in unmanaged systems, though the latter have higher stability in general. In managed systems, however, variance in function is limited (illustrated as the white square surrounding the point on curve *a* in the middle graph) by the use of subsidizations such as the addition of fertilizers if nutrients are low, irrigation if water is low, and

biocides if competition with other species or attacks by herbivorous insects occur. Managers try to keep the point in the white square, but to do so has its costs. This plot in Figure 5.5 argues that one of the costs of reducing biodiversity is contending with lower stability, often by using subsidies which are not needed in highly diverse systems, to maintain ecosystem functioning in the face of natural environmental variability.

Managed landscapes are usually managed for either biodiversity or ecosystem function, but seldom for both, even though they are intimately related.[30] Here, I use the term "managed landscape" to describe any landscape that involves significant human intervention, whether it is a farm (that is weeded, planted, irrigated, fertilized, and treated with biocides), a prairie restoration site that is burned regularly, a plantation, or even a national park or wildlife reserve where there is significant management such as burning, weed control, or culling of herds. Such sites are usually managed to increase some particular set of ecosystem functions above that which would occur without management. For example, a prairie grassland of two hundred species per hectare is converted to a cropland of one grass species (e.g., maize) in which the addition of water, fertilizer, and biocides increases production beyond anything the original prairie was likely to achieve.

In contrast, a degraded landscape is one in which both biodiversity and ecosystem functioning have declined, usually because of poor management practice (e.g., clear-cutting or poor tillage leading to erosion, overgrazing leading to desertification) or because of harmful exploitation (e.g., mountaintop removal, strip-mining, pollution).

A restored landscape, on the other hand, is one that was previously degraded, but has been successfully modified to achieve some biodiversity or ecosystem targets. Biodiversity and ecosystem functioning in a restored habitat may be both above or below the levels of the landscape prior to its degradation or abandonment if targets are not based on the original habitat. For example, restored prairies may have targets for much more plant diversity per hectare than the original prairie had, and a restored wetland may have targets for the degradation of organic pollutants much lower than what the original wetland had. If a restored landscape had exactly the same biodiversity and ecosystem functioning as the original, unmanaged landscape, then there would be no reason to call it restored, except as a matter of historical reference. For this reason there is no particular point in Figure 5.5 that is labeled as "restored," as a restored landscape is either one that is arbitrarily designated as such (so can appear in most regions of the bivariate space) or is the same as the end point of curve d.

Finally, unmanaged landscapes are those that receive no recent or current interventions from humans and have levels of biodiversity and ecosystem functioning similar to pre-Anthropocene levels.

An important point that emerges from the biodiversity and ecosystem functioning perspective is that landscapes are represented by curves, not by single points. Landscapes are dynamic and fluctuate over space and time, though over the long term they exhibit something akin to a steady or predictable state. In Figure 5.5, each curve (a–g) in the top graph represents a set of values of biodiversity and ecosystem functioning that can be expressed by a single species under natural levels of variation.

Because landscapes are dynamic, one should think of their biodiversity and ecosystem functioning as means and standard variations rather than fixed points. If we assume that it is rare that an unmanaged landscape takes on extreme values of low biodiversity and low ecosystem functioning in the absence of extreme environmental events (e.g., an unprecedented flood, fire, or drought), there is a small range, or area in the bivariate space (shown in the middle graph of Figure 5.5 as a gray area), of values an ecosystem typically exhibits. For a highly managed landscape, such as a monoculture farm of genetically engineered hybrid maize, the standard deviation is very large (shown as a large, gray area surrounding curve a in the middle graph of Figure 5.5). If you have maize or no maize, you have a lot of ecosystem functioning or none, hence the large variation compared to a prairie grassland which does not change much in ecosystem functioning when losing one or a few species (shown as a small gray area surrounding curve d in the middle graph of Figure 5.5).

The standard deviation or possible variation surrounding biodiversity and ecosystem functioning of different landscapes reflects one aspect of the system's stability. This is illustrated in the bottom graph of Figure 5.5 that shows how the standard deviation of a system's biodiversity and ecosystem functioning declines (becomes more stable) as biodiversity increases. These lines tracing the relationship between the standard deviation of ecosystem functioning and biodiversity as the latter declines are hypothetical, but coherent with current thinking in biodiversity and ecosystem functioning research that suggests that small gains in biodiversity can dramatically improve functioning and stability of a low-diversity ecosystem while small gains in biodiversity have less of an influence on the stability of unmanaged, highly diverse systems.

It is important to note that the typology does not rest on the "pristine" or "wild," which are not readily defined and probably myths. An unmanaged site is simply one that is not being cultivated, mined, burned, irrigated, or experiencing significant human interventions. All that one needs in such places is an estimate of its diversity and an estimate of where it is likely to collapse if too much biodiversity is lost. It's not easy to do such work, but again, collaborations between natural scientists and landscape designers could find ways to provide these estimates.

No More Good, Bad, or Ugly Landscapes?

What happened to the "pristine," "natural," or "wild" landscapes in this classification scheme? They do not exist in the Anthropocene in the sense that there is no place on earth that is free of influences from the activities of humans. Even if one were to find a remote area that has never been visited by a human being, it is undergoing a doubling of carbon dioxide and climate change. Some anchor the start of the Anthropocene to the rise of agriculture ten thousand years ago, while others anchor it to the more recent Industrial Revolution beginning in the eighteenth century; either way, there is too little information about most landscapes—their distribution and abundance of species and the magnitude and stability properties of their biogeochemistry—even just a couple of centuries ago, let alone thousands of years ago, to objectively determine a start date. Even today, in spite of advanced satellite imagery and detailed maps, taxonomies, and molecular tools for species identification, even with roads and modes of transportation that the early naturalist explorers like Alfred Wallace (1823–1913), Charles Darwin (1809–82), and

Alexander von Humboldt (1769–1859) could only dream about, the biodiversity of landscapes and their ecosystem functioning remain known only in the coarsest way—such as how many species of plants and vertebrates they contain and what their annual primary productivity might be. To be sure, some landscapes, especially in developed countries, are well characterized today, but we generally know very little about the biodiversity and ecosystem functioning of most landscapes around the world.

Without a clear sense of what is pristine, which would require pre-Anthropocene knowledge of landscapes as a reference point, or places long free of human influences to serve as models (and such places simply do not exist), the idea of the pristine, natural, or wild place is inoperable. Furthermore, with the current idea that a well-managed, sustainable landscape may be more desired in today's world in which one billion people remain hungry, two billion are poor, and three billion live in water-scarce habitats, unmanaged landscapes that provide no services for humans are seen as wasted or idle landscapes. The idea that some landscapes are good (pristine), bad (degraded), or ugly (managed) is difficult to apply. By the biodiversity and ecosystem functioning perspective, all landscapes can be understood from the basic scheme presented in Figure 5.5 in which all landscapes are simply near or far from the fundamental relationship between biodiversity and ecosystem functioning.

Unmanaged landscapes are what one encounters when there is no human intervention and is the place with the highest native diversity and the most stable or robust ecosystem functioning, but it may be a place with little edible food, a reservoir for human disease, or a home for dangerous animals.

For many, however, myself included, these places free of management are the Edenic places on earth, even though they pose some risk to the unwary traveler who visits them.

As biodiversity declines in any landscape, whether to shift ecosystem functioning or because of degradation in the face of unsustainable resource extraction, eventually one crosses the "elbow" in the curve where the rate of change in ecosystem functioning with respect to the rate of change in biodiversity increases rapidly. Where this elbow occurs depends on the ecosystem, but it has significant implications for the stability of ecosystems, such that a managed ecosystem with high levels of ecosystem functioning but low levels of biodiversity may have very low stability.[31]

For any ecosystem, one needs to know where the saturation point is and where the elbow is, but the actual shape of the curve is almost impossible to derive without years of extensive surveys, experiments, and modeling exercises. The generic curve, however, provides a useful heuristic for understanding how biodiversity and ecosystem functioning can help organize our thoughts about landscapes that are managed, unmanaged, degraded, or restored. This obviates the inclination to view ecosystems as good, bad, or ugly.

A MURKY BUSINESS

A shortcoming of basing typologies on a theoretical framework is that it makes the business of precisely classifying real landscapes to each type a rather murky enterprise. For example, for a landscape designer developing a plan for management, there is no easy way to determine what the biodiversity-functioning curve is, let alone the variance surrounding the curve. Given that we've already dismissed species richness as an invalid measure of biodiversity, what does the designer measure in its stead? How does one measure ecosystem function? Scientists can do such work through theoretical, experimental, and observational methods involving considerable funding and years of work, but such approaches are not practical for landscape design.

The problem of reducing the murkiness of guidelines for management based on theoretical constructs is an active area of research, but it will take some time before clear, practical, quantitative methods are developed. Quantifying biodiversity in the context of ecosystem functioning, for example, is now a well-developed field basing measurements more on what species do (how fast they grow, how much mass they contain, what their metabolic rates are) than on who they are related to (taxonomy). Quantifying ecosystem functioning can now be based on what kinds of species exist and how abundant they are in an ecosystem. But there is a long way to go, probably another five to ten years, before management plans can be quantitatively based on biodiversity and ecosystem functioning.

Ecological Poverty

If one goes for a long walk in a landscape, one encounters a certain number of species. If the next time one goes for a longer walk, say for twice as long or covering twice as much area, one encounters more species than one did in the first walk, but not as many as one would expect if species were uniformly and equally distributed across the landscape. If species were uniformly distributed, meaning they were equally abundant, one would quickly discover all the diversity in the landscape in short order. When one has to increasingly search harder to find species, then most likely only a few are abundant and the rest are rare. The relationship between the species encountered and the area one covers in looking for them is known as the species-area relationship. In nature, it is well known that one has to look harder to find more species, and some species are so rare that you may have to cover the entire landscape to find them.

The species-area relationship is one of the most well-known and well-studied relationships in ecology, dating back to the 1920s with Olof Arrhenius,[32] and invariably it tells us that in all landscapes, most species are rare while only a few are common. There is no a priori reason for species to be distributed this way, and most people tend to think that most species are distributed according to the normal distribution—that is, most people feel that most species have what one would consider an average abundance, and there are just a few that are super abundant and a few that are super rare. Such a distribution would make for a bell-shaped, normal, or Gaussian distribution. If species were distributed according to a normal distribution, rare species are anomalies, those odd creatures that avid collectors, birders, or obsessed naturalists seek out—the rare butterfly, the rare orchid, the bird so rare that it is thought to be extinct, like the Ivory-billed Woodpecker. The normal distribution works well for many familiar phenomena. For example, most people are average in height, with a few very short people and a few very tall people. The normal distribution, however, does not apply to species distributions, nor to many natural phenomena.

In nature the lognormal distribution, not the normal distribution, is more prevalent. Unlike the normal distribution, which is symmetrical, the lognormal distribution is skewed, with some values being far more likely to occur than any other. There are many distribution functions that can serve to describe such asymmetrical or skewed distributions, but the lognormal is arguably the most well known. The prevalence of the lognormal distribution in nature is astonishing,[33] describing everything from the distribution of latency periods of infectious diseases, the abundance of mineral resources, the length of words in the English language, the distribution of elements in the universe, the age of marriage in Danish women, the age of onset of Alzheimer's disease, and the income of Swiss households, along with many other phenomena. Not surprisingly, the distribution of species abundances is lognormal, though one should say lognormal-like to be more accurate. Thus, though there are many distributions that are skewed, we will focus on the lognormal distribution because of its prevalence in the literature. There are, however, sometimes better distributions for describing patterns in the distribution and abundance of species.[34]

Why most species are rare is well-studied, though what causes this pattern remains under investigation.[35] In the 1960s, Robert H. MacArthur[36] suggested that the distribution had to do with the way species divided resources among themselves.[37] Some suggest that the pattern is due to energy availability in the environment,[38] differences in geographic range among species,[39] endemism,[40] and a combination of speciation, emigration, and other processes.[41] We need not concern ourselves with speculations on the reason why the lognormal distribution describes abundances as well as it does, though it is embarrassing that ecology still struggles to understand one of the most fundamental properties of nature.

Whatever the cause for most species being rare, the implication is clear—most species command few of nature's assets while a smaller number command the rest; that is, when it comes to space, water, nutrients, and other resources that each species controls, a few species are the dominant consumers while the majority of others control little. Prairie grasslands, for example, are wonderfully diverse, but in truth what one sees if you are visiting an unmanaged prairie is, not surprisingly, mostly grass made up of a few common species. You have to look very hard to find the two

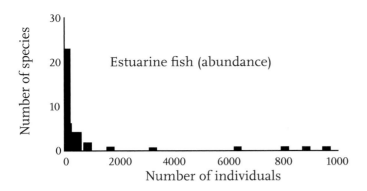

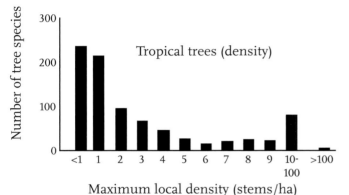

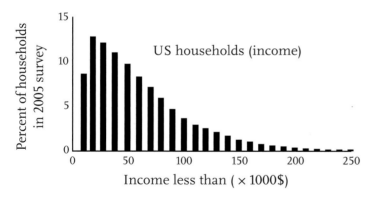

FIGURE 5.6
Ecological poverty. In nature, only a few species are common and command most of the resources in the landscape ("wealthy" species) and the vast majority of other species are rare ("poor" species).

© Shahid Naeem.

hundred species that might be there amid all that grass. Restored prairies, in my experience, actually have much more diversity than would be typical of an unmanaged prairie because prairie restorationists often seek to have as many species present in their reserve as possible, rather than worry about what the natural distribution of species should be. Another way to describe this is that most species are ecologically poor, having control over few of nature's resources while a very few are rich and control vast quantities of space, light, water, nutrients, and other natural resources.

Frank W. Preston, who noted that species abundances fit the lognormal distribution, also noticed that human income distribution, as described by Vilfredo Pareto (1848–1923), was similar to the commonness and rarity of species.[42] Preston also observed that the distribution of energy states among molecules in an ideal gas described by the Maxwell and Boltzmann laws was also similar to the Pareto law which predicted the distribution of wealth among households, and recently Jeffrey C. Nekola and James H. Brown extended Preston's observation to other properties of species distributions.[43] These distributions, although technically different, resemble lognormal distributions that describe many natural phenomena.[44] Preston suggested that perhaps human wealth (and poverty) is the outcome of the same kinds of processes that govern other patterns in nature, such as the lognormal distribution of species. The top portion of Figure 5.6 illustrates the similarities by showing the frequency of species found at particular abundances for estuarine fish (eighty species of fish collected in an estuary totaling ninety-six thousand individuals)[45] and tropical trees (density of tropical tree species in a Peruvian rainforest),[46] but I could have just as well chosen butterflies, birds, and almost any other taxa and the pattern would look similar—most species are rare while few are common. Figure 5.6 also shows the prevalence (percent) of households with particular annual incomes in the year 2005 for the United States (the distribution of wealth per US household surveyed jointly by the US Bureau of Labor Statistics and the Census Bureau). All three plots show that a few species (or households) command most of the available resources, while the majority of others do not.

The biosphere is an impoverished world in which the vast majority of species are ecologically poor (i.e., commanding few resources), much as the anthrosphere, or the global human population, is impoverished, with nearly one-third of its people in poverty (making less than US$2 a day). Landscape design, even when focusing on wildlife conservation or sustaining biological diversity, seldom concerns the ecologically poor. Even if they could, ecologists seldom know enough about rare species to help with designing a landscape that could sustain the poor.

Do the ecologically poor serve any purpose? This question, which many would find offensive and morally reprehensible to ask about poor people, is also a tough one when it comes to nonhuman species. Not only are the majority of species undescribed, perhaps 80–90 percent of them, but we also know next to nothing about their distribution, abundance, habitat preference, growth rates, diet (if animals or nonphotosynthetic microorganisms), or influence on ecosystem functioning. Without such knowledge we cannot estimate or predict what their significance is for an ecosystem, let alone what the consequences of their loss might be. In most cases, one can invoke the precautionary principle as a rationale for saving the ecological poor—just because you don't know the function of a thing does not mean it has no function. If one reaches into a complex system and randomly yanks a piece out, there is an immediate perception that the reliability of the system has declined, even if there is no visible change in the system's function. It is easier to figure out what function a part serves if the design is known or if the system were designed by a sentient being. But even in the absence of such information, if a species disappears from an ecosystem, there is a nagging concern that it might have had an important function. For example, drought-tolerant plants—uncommon in a grassland that receives a good amount of rain per year—may one day prove to be valuable to sustaining primary production when a rare drought occurs, as David Tilman and John A. Downing observed in their study of a midwestern grassland that experienced a drought.[47] Likewise, Yongfei Bai et al. showed that Inner Mongolian grassland production is more stable when there are plants that can replace one another during dry periods.[48]

The question of the significance of the ecological poor can also be illuminated by looking at book sales in the United States at Amazon.com. Although neither its sales figures nor its ranking methodology are divulged, they have been estimated indirectly.[49] Some estimates claim that a top-ranked book at Amazon.com may sell five thousand copies a day and speculators have generated formulas for converting rankings to sales figures. The distribution of sales per book, not surprisingly, is highly skewed, where a few books of high rank account for the majority of sales while the majority have comparatively few sales— just like species distributions and the distribution of wealth. In August 2008, four books by Stephenie Meyer known as the *Twilight* series were all ranked in the top ten (i.e., ranked fifth, sixth, seventh, and eighth) of Amazon.com's books, meaning that Meyer was probably collectively selling over seven thousand copies of her books per day. To describe these books, let me quote Amazon.com's own review (note that there were only three volumes in the series when the review was written): "Throughout *The Twilight Saga* (*Twilight*, *New Moon*, and *Eclipse*), Stephenie Meyer has emulated great love stories—*Romeo and Juliet*, *Wuthering Heights*—with the fated, yet perpetually doomed love of Bella (the human girl) and Edward (the vampire who feeds on animals instead of humans)." During the same period, the best-selling edition of *Romeo and Juliet*, ranked at 6,700 (more than thirty copies a day) and *Wuthering Heights* at 15,286 (about twenty copies a day), were clearly in the long, long tail of the books with impoverished sales. Mind you, these are still handsome sales figures since book rankings go as low as eight million. While Meyer's contributions to our modern culture should not be dismissed or underestimated (Charles Dickens was a best-selling, popular author in his heyday), surely it would be a mistake to assume that *Romeo and Juliet* and *Wuthering Heights* are of no significance based on their extremely small hold over the book market (as reflected by Amazon.com).

The great wealth of biodiversity is stored in its many uncommon and rare species, much the way the great wealth of our knowledge and culture consists of many, many works that are seldom seen or appreciated by the majority. It would be a mistake for a library to throw out all books that have a small readership. So too is it a mistake to dismiss all species that have small populations in our ecosystems.

Discussion and Conclusion
The Ecology of Landscapes

Landscape designers have to make a decision—pattern the biodiversity the landscape will contain after Eden or the Peaceable Kingdom, or pattern it after what is observed in unmanaged landscapes. It is interesting to speculate what species' distribution describes Eden. I suggested that the distribution may have been uniform (all species equally abundant), as most paintings of Eden or the Peaceable Kingdom show many species consisting of just one or a few individuals. If one believes in the biblical flood, then the world was started over again with just two of each species. And most botanical and zoological gardens attempt to have just a few representatives of each species, their actual numbers only occasionally adjusted when necessary to reflect natural distributions (e.g., penguin displays often have several penguins as do displays of social monkeys) or practical issues, such as costs or the solitary nature of some animals (e.g., large predatory cats). After the expulsion from Eden or after the flood, one might imagine some species reproduced quickly and reached great numbers, while others reproduced more slowly and became uncommon and remain rare today. Although ecologists argue as to why species distributions are so skewed, the fact remains that neither Eden, nor Noah's ark, nor present-day gardens and zoos reflect the realities of the world.

Can a designed landscape capture the essence of an unmanaged landscape, yet provide the aesthetic its clients desire? As I have grown older and have traveled more, I have found unmanaged landscapes to have an element of magic to them that is entirely missing from managed landscapes. I find gardens and zoos disturbing in their attempts to display as many species as they can to their visitors. I find restored habitats too manicured and eager to display what species they harbor. Perhaps that is what the landscape was designed to do in these situations—display their diversity to even the casual visitor. But when one drives across the savanna and catches a glimpse of giraffes in the distance, hikes

a woodland trail and takes in the vista of a prairie grassland with bison, cruises the Arctic ice floes and comes suddenly comes across a polar bear and her two cubs, walks quietly amid the ringing heat of the Namibian sands encountering the rare stone plants and sees a single, small, sidewinder snake hiding in the shade of a rock, or sees a tiny steenbok look back at you just before it dashes out of sight, or after many years of visiting a familiar habitat one comes across a rare flowering plant, there is a magnificence and grandeur to nature that is utterly lacking in the landscapes of our gardens, restored habitats, and highly managed national parks. It is the rarity of species that makes them special. It is the rarity of species that makes repeated visits rewarding and invites one to return. It is not surprising that titles like *Bargaining for Eden: The Fight for the Last Open Spaces in America* by Stephen Trimble, *Taking Back Eden: Eight Environmental Cases that Changed the World* by Oliver A. Houck, or *Reflections of Eden: My Years with the Orangutans of Borneo* by Birute M. F. Galdikas use Eden to describe wild spaces of incalculable value, not the managed landscapes many others feel more closely reflect Eden.

Nature's landscapes are rugged and robust, dominated by a community of species best adapted to the surrounding conditions and an enormous number of species that survive in the margins, where conditions are a little wetter or a little drier or a little colder or a little more scarce in food and nutrients than the dominant species like. When conditions vary, such as the different microclimate conditions one experiences on the north and south slopes of a hill, or the heterogeneity created by ancient, random events in geology such as glaciers dropping boulders in the middle of fields or ancient volcanic flows creating mosaics of habitat, or long-term variability in climate such as those caused by El Niño, species under one set of conditions may change from being rare to being common.

More important, what biodiversity and ecosystem functioning research highlights is that complementarity among species in the way they survive and make their living in nature leads to a much more efficient use of natural resources by the community of species that lives there. Because no organism can be a master of all trades (e.g., cacti make lousy wetland plants and parrots cannot survive the

Arctic), having millions of species that can thrive in just about every condition on earth, from hot springs to oceanic abysses, from mountaintops to underground caves, from deserts to floodplains, there is no place some species does not call home. It takes just a few species to provide most of the basic functioning of an ecosystem, but over space and time, over the incredible variation one encounters in the environment, it takes many more species to make ecosystems efficient and robust.

We return now to the ecological poor who, as it turns out, are more than likely more specialized and thrive in sets of conditions that the common species cannot. In the same way that we would never think of eliminating the elements of our culture that have smaller followings than what is popular for the moment (such as the best-sellers and the blockbusters), we would never assume that an individual who is poor has no value or serves no purpose, and we should never see species, no matter how rare, as having no significance to the functioning of their ecosystem. For a nation like the United States that believes that its proud heritage was one of gathering the world's impoverished or rejected to build a strong and robust country, one would think that we should have the same attitude about the design of our landscapes as homes for the world's ecological poor.

How does one capture the aesthetic of nature in managed or designed landscapes that are often too small to accommodate the vast diversity of an ecosystem? This is a challenge to the designer, because if a landscape truly captures the magnificence of nature in a small space, rare creatures will be even rarer than they are in nature and at horrible risk of becoming locally extinct. Local extinction is a fact of life and an essential part of nature's design, but local extinction was never a phenomenon when landscapes were vast. The great tragedy of the modern world is that local extinction for many species is now the equivalent of global extinction. Increasingly, designed or restored landscapes that focus on nature rather than on natural resource production may be the last refuge for many species.

The Relay Race that Never Was

At the beginning of this millennium, some 1,300 natural and social scientists would work together for more than five years to provide a multisectorial assessment of earth, an endeavor that was known as the Millennium Ecosystem Assessment.[50] Through a coordinated, massive effort involving many people from many countries, and with all reports subjected to a rigorous international review process, the consensus that emerged was rather remarkable. Its framework described how biodiversity influences ecosystem functioning, which in turn influences ecosystem services, or the benefits ecosystems provide for people, and how these in turn are the foundation for human well-being. Figure 5.7 provides a diagram of this framework. Biodiversity was distinctly recognized as a multidimensional factor, ecosystem functioning was recognized as the biogeochemical basis for sustaining life on earth as well as specifically benefiting humans either directly or indirectly. Ecosystem services were classified as those ecosystem functions that support life on earth (supporting services), those that provide cultural benefits (cultural services), those that provide food, fuel, fiber, timber, and other biotic resources (provisioning services), and those that provide regulatory or stabilizing benefits (regulating services, e.g., regulating climate or stabilizing soils to resist erosion). It is these ecosystem services that determine whether a nation will be able to secure or improve human well-being. Where a nation's ecosystem services cannot meet the needs of its people, then trade becomes essential.

Figure 5.7 also illustrates the linear approach social and natural scientists take in linking biodiversity to human well-being. Adapted from the Millennium Ecosystem Assessment,[51] this framework represents a considerable advance in environmental thinking because it acknowledges that the social sciences are key to a better understanding of how the diversity of life on earth is ultimately related to all the constituents of human well-being. The linear nature of the framework, however, also shows why progress is slow in incorporating this framework into the real world—natural scientists expect that social scientists will pick up where they left off, and vice versa.

The fact that the preservation of biodiversity enhances and stabilizes ecosystem functions and services and improves human well-being should resonate with people. Unfortunately, the science has had little penetrance. Martin Solan et al. found that

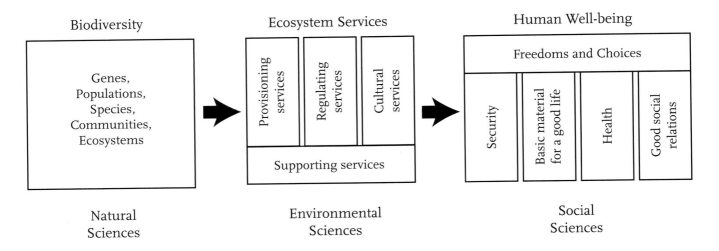

Biodiversity
Ecosystem Services
Human Well-being

Genes,
Populations,
Species,
Communities,
Ecosystems

Provisioning services

Regulating services

Cultural services

Supporting services

Freedoms and Choices

Security

Basic material for a good life

Health

Good social relations

Natural
Sciences

Environmental
Sciences

Social
Sciences

FIGURE 5.7

The biodiversity-ecosystem functioning–ecosystem service–human well-being relay race.

© Shahid Naeem.

biodiversity and ecosystem functioning research appeared rarely in nonscientific literature, management documentation, or environmental policy or legislation, in spite of some nine hundred papers published on the topic, many of which appeared in the top scientific journals.[52] Our guess as to why we failed at bringing this science to the real world may be described as a dysfunctional relay race. In a relay race, once a runner receives a baton from his or her teammate, it is their responsibility to put their best effort in taking the baton to the next runner who awaits them further down the track and will take the baton and continue the race. In the case of the failure of the natural sciences to reach the social sciences, it is as if natural and social scientists are in a relay race, only neither is passing the baton to one another.

Landscape Design with Eyes on the Invisible

The design of landscapes to serve whoever owns or wishes to derive benefits from that landscape is not so much a relay race where natural scientists pass on their findings to social scientists who pass on their baton to practitioners. Rather, it is more like a team sport in which members each have different responsibilities depending on where they are in the court or field, and all members work as a coordinated unit. The challenges, however, are more than just better integration between social and natural scientists and the humanities. Most ecosystem functions are invisible, carried out in large part by invisible species, such as microorganisms or the many small creatures that dominate earth's biota (the ecological poor) and that remain largely unknown and unseen. Can one design a landscape to capture what makes an unmanaged system both aesthetically appealing yet functionally efficient and stable if it involves diversity that one cannot see and ecosystem functions that are invisible? Can clients be convinced that it is worth incorporating biodiversity and ecosystem functioning into landscape design? As we continue into the Anthropocene with less and less land left, landscape design will play an increasingly fundamental role in ensuring that our ecosystems have the biodiversity they need to provide the ecosystem functioning and services that we need. Their charge, of course, rests with how people value nature and its services—which is complex and something, as a natural scientist, I am not prepared to adequately treat (though I made some stabs at it). Can people value an ecosystem for what it does more than what it looks like? Can people value what is invisible (small or rare species, gas fluxes, pollination)? Values do evolve, and we can all work together to help shape the environmental discourse that contributes to our understanding of nature and how we value it. I only hope there is a growth in the value people place on biodiversity and how it serves humanity before it is mostly gone.

Notes

1 Anantha K. Duraiappah and Shahid Naeem, *Synthesis Report on Biodiversity*, Millennium Ecosystem Assessment (Washington, D.C.: Island Press, 2005); and James Maclaurin and Kim Sterelny, *What is Biodiversity?* (Chicago: Chicago University Press, 2008).

2 Vladimir N. Bashkin and Robert W. Howarth, *Modern Biogeochemistry* (Dordrecht and Boston: Kluwer Academic Publishers, 2002), 561; Samuel S. Butcher, ed., *Global Biogeochemical Cycles* (London: Academic Press, 1992), 379; and William H. Schlesinger, *Biogeochemistry*, 2nd ed. (San Diego: Academic Press, 1997).

3 Vaclav Smil, *The Earth's Biosphere: Evolution, Dynamics, and Change* (Cambridge, Mass.: MIT Press, 2002), 1–26.

4 Ernst-Detlef Schulze and Harold A. Mooney, eds., *Biodiversity and Ecosystem Function* (Berlin and New York: Springer Verlag, 1993); and Shahid Naeem et al., "Introduction: The Ecological and Social Implications of Changing Biodiversity; An Overview of a Decade of Biodiversity and Ecosystem Functioning Research," in *Biodiversity, Ecosystem Functioning, and Human Wellbeing: An Ecological and Economic Perspective*, ed. Shahid Naeem et al. (Oxford and New York: Oxford University Press, 2009), 1–13.

5 James W. Kirchner, "Evolutionary Speed Limits Inferred from the Fossil Record," *Nature* 415, no. 6867 (2002): 65–68; James W. Kirchner and Anne Weil, "Delayed Biological Recovery from Extinctions throughout the Fossil Record," *Nature* 404, no. 6774 (2000): 177–80; Norman L. Gilinsky, "Evolutionary Turnover and Volatility," in *Biodiversity Dynamics: Turnover of Populations, Taxa, and Communities*, ed. Michael L. McKinney and James A. Drake (New York: Columbia University Press, 1998), 162–84; and Michael L. McKinney and James A. Drake, eds., *Biodiversity Dynamics*.

6 Carolyn Merchant, *Reinventing Eden: The Fate of Nature in Western Culture* (New York: Routledge, 2003), 320.

7 Jan Zalasiewcz et al., "Are We Now Living in the Anthropocene?," *GSA Today* 18, no. 2 (February 2008): 4–8; Will Steffen, Paul J. Crutzen, and John R. McNeill, "The Anthropocene: Are Humans Now Overwhelming the Great Forces of Nature?," *AMBIO: A Journal of the Human Environment* 36, no. 8 (December 2007): 614–21; and Paul J. Crutzen, "Geology of Mankind," *Nature* 415, no. 6867 (2002): 23.

8 *Living Planet Report 2008* (Gland, Switz.: World Wildlife Fund, 2008), 44.

9 Simon J. Butler, Juliet A. Vickery, and Ken Norris, "Farmland Biodiversity and the Footprint of Agriculture," *Science* 315, no. 5810 (2007): 381–84; and Jonathan A. Foley et al., "Global Consequences of Land Use," *Science* 309, no. 5734 (2005): 570–74.

10 Intergovernmental Panel on Climate Change, *Climate Change 2007: Synthesis Report; Summary for Policymakers* (Geneva: Intergovernmental Panel on Climate Change, 2007).

11 Julian D. Olden et al., "Intergovernmental Panel on Climate Change Fourth Assessment Report," *Trends in Ecology and Evolution* 19, no. 1 (2004): 18–24.

12 David M. Morens, Gregory K. Folkers, and Anthony S. Fauci, "The Challenge of Emerging and Re-emerging Infectious Diseases," *Nature* 430, no. 6996 (2004): 242–49.

13 Nicholas Gruber and James N. Galloway, "An Earth-System Perspective of the Global Nitrogen Cycle," *Nature* 451, no. 7176 (2008): 293–96.

14 Vaclav Smil, "Phosphorus in the Environment," *Annual Review of Energy and the Environment* 25 (2000): 53–88.

15 Taikan Oki and Shinjiro Kanae, "Global Hydrological Cycles and World Water Resources," *Science* 313, no. 5790 (2006): 1068–72.

16 Peter M. Vitousek et al., "Human Domination of Earth's Ecosystems," *Science* 277, no. 5325 (1997): 494–99; Peter Kareiva et al., "Domesticated Nature: Shaping Landscapes and Ecosystems for Human Welfare," *Science* 316, no. 5833 (2007): 1866–69; United Nations Environment Programme, *Global Environment Outlook 4* (New York: United Nations Environment Programme, 2007); and Millennium Ecosystem Assessment, *Living Beyond Our Means: Natural Assets and Human Well-Being: Statement from the Board* (Washington, D.C.: United Nations Environment Programme, 2005), 24.

17 Zalasiewcz et al., "Are We Now Living in the Anthropocene?," 4–8.

18 Eville Gorham, "Biogeochemistry: Its Origins and Development," *Biogeochemistry* 13, no. 3 (1991): 199–239.

19 Mark Nelson and Tony L. Burgess, "Using a Closed Ecological System to Study Earth's Biosphere," *BioScience* 43, no. 4 (April 1993): 225–36; and Joel E. Cohen and David Tilman, "Biosphere 2 and Biodiversity: The Lessons So Far," *Science* 274, no. 5290 (1996): 1150–51.

20 Shahid Naeem and Lindsey J. Thompson, "Declining Biodiversity Can Alter the Performance of Ecosystems," *Nature* 368, no. 6473 (1994): 734–37.

21 Michel Loreau et al., "Biodiversity and Ecosystem Functioning: Current Knowledge and Future Challenges," *Science* 294, no. 5543 (2001): 804–8; David Hooper et al., "Effects of Biodiversity on Ecosystem Functioning: A Consensus of Current Knowledge and Needs for Future Research," *Ecological Monographs* 75 (2005): 3–35; and Shahid Naeem, "Advancing Realism in Biodiversity Research," *Trends in Ecology and Evolution* 23, no. 8 (2008): 414–16.

22 Loreau et al., "Biodiversity and Ecosystem Functioning"; and Hooper et al., "Effects of Biodiversity on Ecosystem Functioning."

23 Schulze and Mooney, *Biodiversity and Ecosystem Function*; and Michel Loreau, Shahid Naeem, and Pablo Inchausti, eds., *Biodiversity and Ecosystem Functioning: Synthesis and Perspectives* (Oxford: Oxford University Press, 2002).

24 Shahid Naeem et al., *Biodiversity, Ecosystem Functioning, and Human Wellbeing.*

25 Yvonne Baskin, *The Work of Nature: How the Diversity of Life Sustains Us* (Washington, D.C.: Island Press, 1997).

26 Duraiappah and Naeem, *Synthesis Report on Biodiversity.*

27 Bradley J. Cardinale et al., "Effects of Biodiversity on the Functioning of Trophic Groups and Ecosystems," *Nature* 443, no. 7114 (2006): 989–92.

28 Boris Worm et al., "Impacts of Biodiversity Loss on Ocean Ecosystem Services," *Science* 314, no. 5800 (2006): 787–90.

29 Daniel E. Bunker et al., "Species Loss and Aboveground Carbon Storage in a Tropical Forest," *Science* 310, no. 5750 (2005): 1029–31; Martin Solan et al., "Extinction and Ecosystem Function in the Marine Benthos," *Science* 306, no. 5699 (2004): 1177–80; Peter B. McIntyre et al., "Fish Extinctions Alter Nutrient Recycling in Tropical Freshwaters," *Proceedings of the National Academy of Sciences of the United States of America* 104, no. 11 (2007): 4461–66; and Mathew E. S. Bracken et al., "Functional Consequences of Realistic Biodiversity Changes in a Marine Ecosystem," *Proceedings of the National Academy of Sciences of the United States of America* 105, no. 3 (2008): 924–28.

30 Shahid Naeem, "Biodiversity and Ecosystem Functioning in Restored Ecosystems: Extracting Principles from a Synthetic Perspective," in *Foundations of Restoration Ecology,* ed. Donald A. Falk, Margaret A. Palmer, and Joy B. Zedler (Washington, D.C.: Island Press, 2006), 210–38; and Justin P. Wright et al., "Restoring Biodiversity and Ecosystem Function: Will an Integrated Approach Improve Results?," in Naeem et al., *Biodiversity, Ecosystem Functioning, and Human Wellbeing,* 384.

31 Naeem, "Biodiversity and Ecosystem Functioning in Restored Ecosystems," 210–38; and Wright et al., "Restoring Biodiversity and Ecosystem Function," 384.

32 Olof Arrhenius, "Species and Area," *Journal of Ecology* 9, no. 1 (1921): 95–99.

33 Eckhard Limpert, Werner A. Stahel, and Markus Abbt, "Log-normal Distributions across the Sciences: Keys and Clues," *BioScience* 51, no. 5 (2001): 341–52.

34 Mark Williamson and Kevin J. Gaston, "The Lognormal Distribution Is Not an Appropriate Null Hypothesis for the Species-Abundance Distribution," *Journal of Animal Ecology* 74, no. 3 (2005): 409–22; Stephen P. Hubbell, *The Unified Neutral Theory of Biodiversity and Biogeography* (Princeton: Princeton University Press, 2001); and R. G. Hughes, "Theories and Models of Species Abundance," *The American Naturalist* 128, no. 6 (December 1986): 879–99.

35 Robert M. May, "Patterns of Species Abundance and Diversity," in *Ecology and Evolution of Communities,* ed. Martin L. Cody and Jared M. Diamond (Cambridge,

Mass.: Belknap Press of Harvard University Press, 1975), 81–120; George Sugihara, "Minimal Community Structure: An Explanation of Species Abundance Patterns," *The American Naturalist* 116, no. 6 (December 1980): 770–87; John Harte, Adam B. Smith, and David Storch, "Biodiversity Scales from Plots to Biomes with a Universal Species Area Curve," *Ecology Letters* 12, no. 8 (2009): 789–97; Stephen P. Hubbell, "Neutral Theory in Community Ecology and the Hypothesis of Functional Equivalence," *Functional Ecology* 19, no. 1 (2005): 166–72; Fangliang He and Pierre Legendre, "Species Diversity Patterns Derived from Species-Area Models," *Ecology* 83 (2002): 1185–98; and Joshua B. Plotkin et al., "Predicting Species Diversity in Tropical Forests," *Proceedings of the National Academy of Sciences of the United States of America* 97, no. 20 (2000): 10850–54.

36 Robert H. MacArthur, "On the Relative Abundance of Species," *The American Naturalist* 94, no. 874 (January–February 1960): 25–36.

37 Sugihara, "Minimal Community Structure."

38 David H. Wright, "Species-Energy Theory: An Extension of Species-Area Theory," *Oikos* 41, no. 3 (December 1983): 496–506; John L. Wylie and David J. Currie, "Species-Energy Theory and Patterns of Species Richness: I. Patterns of Bird, Angiosperm, and Mammal Species Richness on Islands," *Biological Conservation* 63, no. 2 (1993): 137–44; John L. Wylie and David J. Currie, "Species-Energy Theory and Patterns of Species Richness: II. Predicting Mammal Species Richness on Isolated Nature Reserves," *Biological Conservation* 63, no. 2 (1993): 145–48; and David Storch, Karl L. Evans, and Kevin J. Gaston, "The Species-Area-Energy Relationship," *Ecology Letters* 8, no. 5 (2005): 487–92.

39 Ilkka Hanski and Mats Gyllenberg, "Uniting Two General Patterns in the Distribution of Species," *Science* 275, no. 5298 (1997): 397–400.

40 John Harte and Anne P. Kinzig, "On the Implications of Species-Area Relationships for Endemism, Spatial Turnover, and Food Web Patterns," *Oikos* 80, no. 3 (December 1997): 417–27.

41 Hubbell, *The Unified Neutral Theory of Biodiversity and Biogeography*; and David Alonso, Rampal S. Etienne, and Alan J. McKane, "The Merits of Neutral Theory," *Trends in Ecology and Evolution* 21, no. 8 (2006): 451–57.

42 Frank W. Preston, "Gas Laws and Wealth Laws," *The Scientific Monthly* 71, no. 5 (1950): 309–11.

43 Jeffrey C. Nekola and James H. Brown, "The Wealth of Species: Ecological Communities, Complex Systems, and the Legacy of Frank Preston," *Ecology Letters* 10, no. 3 (2007): 188–96.

44 Limpert, Stahel, and Abbt, "Log-normal Distributions across the Sciences."

45 Anne E. Magurran and Peter A. Henderson, "Explaining the Excess of Rare Species in Natural Species Abundance Distributions," *Nature* 422, no. 6933 (2003): 714–16.

46   Nigel N. C. A. Pitman et al., "Tree Species Distributions in an Upper Amazonian Forest," *Ecology* 80, no. 8 (1999): 2651–61.

47   David Tilman and John A. Downing, "Biodiversity and Stability in Grasslands," *Nature* 367, no. 6461 (1994): 363–65.

48   Yongfei Bai et al., "Ecosystem Stability and Compensatory Effects in the Inner Mongolia Grassland," *Nature* 431, no. 7005 (2004): 181–84.

49   Judith Chevalier and Austan Goolsbee, "Measuring Prices and Price Competition Online: Amazon.com and BarnesandNoble.com," *Quantitative Marketing and Economics* 1, no. 2 (2003): 203–22.

50   *Ecosystems and Human Well-Being: A Framework for Assessment*, Millennium Ecosystem Assessment (Washington, D.C.: Island Press, 2003), 245; and *Ecosystems and Human Well-Being: General Synthesis* (Washington, D.C.: Island Press, 2005).

51   Anantha K. Duraiappah and Shahid Naeem, *Ecosystems and Human Well-Being: Biodiversity Synthesis*, Milllennium Ecosystem Assessment (Washington, D.C.: Island Press, 2005).

52   Martin Solan et al., "Biodiversity-Ecosystem Function Research and Biodiversity Futures: Early Bird Catches the Worm or a Day Late and a Dollar Short?," in Naeem et al., *Biodiversity, Ecosystem Functioning, and Human Well-being*, 30–46.

CHAPTER 6

"That's Real Meat"

Birds, Native People, and Conservation in the Neotropics

SHEPARD KRECH III

CHAN CHICH, NORTHWESTERN BELIZE. MARCH 16, 2002. Less than an hour before sundown. I lay quietly on the side of a narrow old limestone road bordered closely by forest. My guide, Gilberto Vasquez, a man of Maya descent born just over the border in Mexico, was nearby (Figure 6.1). We spoke softly. Birds, mostly quiet, were winding down with the day, but with a sudden "whoosh!" a Pale-billed Woodpecker swooped low overhead to the trunk of a tree nearby, where it announced itself with a powerful double rap signaling kinship with (and the same genus as) the Ivory-billed Woodpecker (Figure 6.2). The distraction was momentary. We were after more elusive quarry: a large, shy, ground-dwelling bird known as the Great Tinamou, which had just started calling (Figure 6.3). Frequently heard, especially at dusk, but far less often seen, its haunting call evokes the forest itself. Gilberto imitated it perfectly and the tinamou responded. Gilberto whistled again, and the tinamou again, either closer or throwing its voice. But these birds are wary and this one broke off the duet. Seventeen degrees north of the equator, night comes fairly quickly, so when the tinamou went silent we picked ourselves up and headed back to the lodge while we could still see the

road. Gilberto—salivating, I thought—remarked, "That's real meat." He recalled that in his natal village he learned to make wooden traps for tinamous and set them in the forest, and he clearly relished the memory of eating his catch fried in a pan with tomatoes and cilantro.

I had come to Chan Chich for the birds, and it is natural to wonder if there was any tension between a birder—many of whom would be horrified at the thought of killing and consuming that which they wished to see—and the native guide, for whom a bird like the Great Tinamou, which weighs slightly over one kilogram, represents meat. Actually, there was none. Not only had I grown up thinking it normal to shoot and eat game birds, but I am trained as an anthropologist.

I had met Gilberto at the lodge known as Chan Chich—from the ancient Maya site on which it is located. Chan Chich is at the heart of a 130,000-acre estate named Gallon Jug, which in essence is a private nature reserve consisting of 127,000 forested acres protected ever since sixty years of selective logging came to a close decades ago, as well as a three-thousand-acre working farm devoted to coffee and cacao production and pasture for cattle.

FIGURE 6.1
Gilberto Vasquez with the author, Chan Chich, Belize.

Photograph by Sheila ffolliott.

FIGURE 6.2
Pale-billed Woodpecker (*Campephilus guatemalensis*), Costa Rica.

Photograph by Dr. Hays Cummins, Miami University.

FIGURE 6.3
Great Tinamou (*Tinamus major*), Gamboa, Panama.

Photograph by Kevin J. Zimmer.

A larger, forested state conservation area known as Rio Bravo is just to the north. It and Gallon Jug together represent a major part of the effort in Belize to join Guatemala and Mexico in preserving "La Selva Maya," the Maya Forest.[1] In theory, Gallon Jug's faunal assets are safe from hunters, even if it took persuasion to bring all on board. Some assets are undeniably more precious than others. Among birds, they include the Great Tinamou, which since 1988 has been on the International Union for Conservation of Nature (IUCN) Red List as "threatened," albeit of less concern than more endangered birds racing toward extinction.[2]

Gilberto's remarks were not surprising then and they would not be now. Four years earlier, I had come across the remains of Ocellated Turkeys and Great Curassows on a dirt road in the Sian Ka'an Biosphere Reserve near the town of Felipe Carillo Puerto in the southern Yucatan. They had been shot. And in Panama in 2009, I asked an Embera man if he considered tinamous good tasting. Without missing a beat, he replied with a smile, "¡Oh, sí!"

These incidents raise several questions: Do they indicate a wider desire on the part of local indigenous or nonnative people for these particular birds or for other ones? If so, is the harvest of birds by local people, especially local indigenous hunters, sustainable, or is it of conservation concern? And if it is of concern, then what role might or should these people play in the management of lands, or the re-imagination of landscapes, set aside for purposes of conservation and biodiversity? These questions are of global importance, but I address them here for neotropical forests.

Landscape and Birds

I focus on neotropical forests because they represent the most endangered ecosystems and their birds the most threatened in the Western Hemisphere—and among the most endangered worldwide (Figure 6.4). Nearly everywhere, both ecosystems and birds are under assault. They represent the biodiversity hotspots: the most biologically valuable ecoregions in which there is a high degree of endemic species of rarity and restricted range, most of which are under threat today.[3] The long-term prospects of tropical forest birds of a certain type—relatively large, of low fecundity or mobility, or in need of restricted habitat or resources—are not bright. Nearly everywhere,

FIGURE 6.4
Forest at San Isidro, Ecuador, with Steve N. G. Howell.

Photograph by Sheila ffolliott.

habitat loss and transformation loom. Just to take one example, over the last forty years, the forest surrounding the fifth- to eighth-century Maya city-state of Palenque in present-day Mexico has been subject to such severe pressure from human population growth, road construction, timber extraction, and the conversion of land into cattle ranches and agricultural farms that it has been deforested and fragmented, and nearly 20 percent of all bird species have either been extirpated or have suffered significant declines. Particularly hard hit have been large-bodied birds and canopy-dwelling birds that eat fruit or insects—the frugivores and insectivores. Among the extirpated birds are the Great Curassow—the same species whose remains I had seen in Sian Ka'an Biosphere Reserve—and the Crested Guan, which together with other big, fruit-eating gallinaceous birds are known as cracids from their avian family, Cracidae (Figure 6.5). At the same time that these birds and certain small forest specialists have disappeared, more than one dozen species of open-habitat birds have colonized Palenque. If studies of fragmentation elsewhere can be extended to the environs of Palenque, it will take these forest remnants a long time to recover, if they ever do.[4]

If forest fragmentation and deforestation were not bad enough for forest viability, the loss of the large fruit-eaters or frugivores such as cracids, toucans, and various parrots and macaws (known from their family as psittacines) means the disappearance of the very birds that provide ecosystem services. It is these birds that disperse seeds from the fruit they eat, thus ensuring not simply the propagation of trees on which they and other animals depend, but the complexity of the forest itself.[5]

The alarm on forests and their birds has sounded loudly for decades. This is an important and much-discussed topic. The processes that plague Palenque bedevil nearly all neotropical forests. Here I'll explore briefly two other examples—in Costa Rica and along coastal Brazil, Paraguay, and Argentina—and then turn to the people living in neotropical forests.

In Costa Rica, deforestation has been extreme. What was formerly forest now consists of agroecological systems—coffee plantations, for example, with plants beneath shade or canopy trees, or "technified" plantations with only short trees or no trees at all; or cacao trees; or pasture for domesticated stock. Compared to forest, these systems are structurally simple—pasture in particular. The impact of this conversion process can be seen even in a place like the Amistad Biosphere Reserve montane forest—one of World Wildlife Fund's "Global 200" valuable ecoregions—which is deeply threatened by conversion to agricultural land branded "inhospitable" to one-third of the forest birds.[6] Deep-forest species (for example, antbirds) are especially vulnerable, but other categories of birds like flycatchers, tanagers, thrushes, and saltators fare better in some replacement agroecological systems.[7] Yet no matter the degree of attraction, agricultural landscapes are "depauperate" in birds. The exception is agroforestry that retains floristic diversity and structural complexity brought by canopy trees, for example shade-grown coffee, cacao, and rubber plantations (though less so in banana agroforestry) (Figure 6.6). Far better than the alternatives of pasture or plantain monoculture—both essentially worthless as avian habitat—these agroforestry systems nevertheless remain unattractive to specialized forest species from the forests they replaced.[8]

The Atlantic Forest of Brazil, Paraguay, and Argentina, a global biodiversity hotspot, is also gravely threatened. Globally, it might be the most devastated ecosystem in existence. Only 7 percent remains and it is fragmented, under pressure from selective logging, surrounding farms and ranches, roads, and other factors (including hunting). Despite interest in conservation and corridors linking disparate pieces, the trajectory is downward, especially in

FIGURE 6.5
Crested Guan
(*Penelope purpurascens*),
Costa Rica.

Photograph by Dr. Hays Cummins, Miami University.

fragments representing less than one-third of their former size. Large frugivores such as the cracids and the toucans suffer here as elsewhere (Figure 6.7).[9]

Here, the fate of forest birds is linked to the fate of remnants invariably compromised by the mono-cultural or otherwise anthropogenically disturbed landscapes surrounding them; by agroforestry inside them; and by lack of official protection to enforce laws against encroachment, illegal cutting, and wildlife poaching. While they provide an important source of cash, eucalyptus plantations (an exotic) bordering forests do not help the survival of forest species unless they contain a mixed understory. As in other fragmented forests, the fruit-eaters (cracids again) fare poorly, but ground-seed-eaters like doves and pigeons do comparatively well. The Atlantic Forest in northeastern Brazil has lost one curassow (the Alagoas); it is extinct. Other endemics hang on by a thread.[10]

Given fragmentation and loss, questions have been raised about the efficacy of landscape designed to link forest remnants. These days, fragmented landscape consists variably of native forest patches, a matrix of income-producing lands farmed or ranched (e.g., pasture, sugar cane, plantains, soya, eucalyptus, or another monocultural crop), and agroforest woodlots (often within forest remnants). Some efforts have been undertaken to link patches by riparian gallery forests and other corridors, by what are known as stepping stones (small natural areas), and by living fences (whose "posts" are living trees)—and to make agroforestry woodlots more friendly (Figure 6.8). The aim is to preserve biodiversity by helping animals, including birds, move safely between optimal patches of forest. Of these, corridors and agroforest woodlots are most comparable to forest patches in diversity. No matter where they might be, connected forests are more optimal for birds than isolated forests.[11] Remnant forest strips also retain sometimes surprising avian diversity, as do shade cacao plantations and a complex mix of habitat types. Habitat heterogeneity greatly increases biodiversity over homogeneity; and canopy trees are often—for certain species, always—important.[12] Yet even oil palm plantations—a major source of income and a major cause of deforestation—can contain a rich assemblage of birds if the landscape makes room for tall grasses and an understory of shrubs.[13]

FIGURE 6.6
Shade-grown coffee, Olancho, Honduras.

Photograph by Guillermo Velasquez, Velasquez Family Coffee.

FIGURE 6.7
Keel-billed Toucan (*Ramphastos sulfuratus*), Mexico.

Photograph by Jason Dirks.

FIGURE 6.8
Living fence,
Costa Rica.

Photograph by
Walter Kuentzel.

The environmental history of landscapes in Costa Rica and the Atlantic Forest, as well as others in the neotropics, nearly always boils down to long-term anthropogenic disturbance, whose most recent iteration has seen a massive deforestation and conversion of forest to agricultural lands for pasture and industrial monoculture. Today, anthropogenic disturbance is due not only to large-scale farming and livestock ranching, and consequent soil degradation, but to selective logging and collecting trees and wood for fuel and other purposes, fires set deliberately (e.g., for slash-and-burn) as well as carelessly, and the harvest of forest biota, including birds. In many places the conversion of forest to agrobusiness has been rapid.[14] Savanna landscapes disturbed by human activity also invite new predators and garbage, as well as parasitic birds, adversely affecting the nesting success and survival of finches, tanagers, and other birds.[15] In many cases the impact on birds is predictable: clear-cut forests lose specialist forest bird species and gain generalist or nonspecialist species. Selectively logged forests have variable short-term consequences, depending on time since logging, burning, and other factors, but the long term ends uniformly in reduced avian diversity.[16] A narrow, specialized, or structurally complex niche stands against the long-term viability of certain bird species.[17]

For forest birds, then, health is correlated with forest size and complexity. Optimal complexity includes canopy, understory, and ground cover as well as trees growing and dying, bearing fruit and flowers, and attracting insects. Remove these and you remove the birds. Needless to say the conversion of forest into monoculture is bad for biodiversity, including birds. But stepping stones, riparian gallery forest strips, living fences, and complex agroforest woodlots can mitigate some of the worst consequences of forest loss and fragmentation for some forest species. Forests connected are better for birds than isolated forest islands. The implications for landscape design in which one goal is to restore or optimize habitat for birds, among other fauna, are clear.

SHEPARD KRECH III

Birds and People: Impacts

Before returning to the gustatory interests of Gilberto and others in the Great Tinamou, Great Curassow, Crested Guan, and other birds, we should keep in mind that as long as their lives have intersected, people and birds have had an impact on each other. The impact has varied greatly across space and through time. Today it can be seen where people, indigenous or immigrant, regard birds as meeting subsistence, economic, and other cultural ends. It is also apparent when birds are unintentionally caught up in human design ranging from loss of habitat to suburbs, golf courses, roads in previously roadless areas, oil and gas wells, and the like. Or when resources crucial for birds are commodified for other ends; for example, horseshoe crab eggs, which could not be of greater importance to Red Knots stopping at Delaware Bay en route from South America to the Arctic, went into free fall (as did the birds) with the intensive and unsustainable harvest of crabs commodified in fishing and other industries. Or when communication towers and brightly lit, tall buildings together kill millions of migrating birds annually; or climate change adversely affects avian habitats, breeding success, and migration patterns.[18]

Furthermore, *Avatar*—that 3-D paean to noble indigenousness whose predecessors are as varied as *Pocahontas* (the animated film), *Dances with Wolves*, and Jean-Jacques Rousseau[19]—notwithstanding, indigenous people did not all walk lightly in their moccasins when it came to having an impact on fauna. While there were surely numerous occasions when they had virtually no lasting effect on birds, there were without doubt many times when their footprint was heavy. For example, from 3,500 years BP on (and prior to the arrival of Europeans), Pacific Islanders extinguished thousands of species of birds. In New Zealand the birds included approximately one dozen species of large, flightless ostrich-like birds known as moas, which Maoris sent to their doom from the thirteenth to fifteenth centuries, with ample evidence of conscious selection of certain parts but not others for consumption.[20]

In the continental Western Hemisphere, native people living on the shores of San Francisco Bay from ca. 1600 BC to AD 1300 systematically extirpated geese, ducks, shorebirds, and cormorants.

Drawing attention is not just the inventory but the scenario: American Indians first killed off large geese, then small geese; then large ducks and after them small ducks; then cormorants; then finally large shorebirds and, last of all, small shorebirds. First they killed the large birds and then the small birds, first in the families of largest size and weight and then in the families of smaller size. First they killed birds that were nearby and then they turned on birds at a distance. They killed and extirpated colonial nesters. All this makes sense if the goal is energy efficiency. That is, it makes energetic sense to focus on the largest and closest prey first and the smallest and most distant last. This is far from the imagined prudent predation of the noble *indigène* setting aside prey out of concern for future generations. Rather, it is the all too common opposite: opportunistic predation.[21]

But what about prohibitions or taboos against waste, extirpation, or extinction, which conventional wisdom—*Avatar* again as the most recent iteration—conditions us to assume were strongest in societies closest to nature? If they existed in the cases noted above, they were not in evidence. The moa hunters wasted meat—the necks of their large prey, discarded barely touched or untouched—conspicuously. There is no evidence for restraint on San Francisco Bay, only opportunistic predation. Closer in time to today, the seventeenth-century explorer and colonist John Smith said that Virginia Indians killed birds regardless of sex or season: "at all times of the yeare they never spare Male nor Female, old nor young, egges nor birds, fat nor leane, in season or out of season with them, all is one." There is no evidence among native people here or elsewhere in the American South for what we would consider today to be the conservation of birds.[22]

If restraint lacked in these North American Indian examples—and there is good evidence that it did when it came to hunting not just birds but animals like buffalo, deer, beaver, and various sea mammals—it can be seen in part as a result of the widespread belief in reincarnation. If one believed, as was common in native North America, that prey, properly (culturally) respected in thought and action, would reanimate, then conservation as it developed and is understood today in the West is antithetical. Respect seemed to have had little or nothing to do, at least at first, with conservation, but rather everything to do with culturally variable practices like thanking an animal for giving itself up that you might live, refraining from thinking or speaking ill of an animal, returning an aquatic animal's bones to the water whence they came so that flesh might reclothe them, keeping bones away from dogs that might desecrate them, or keeping weapons away from menstruating women. Far more rarely (and more recently) it pertained to what Western-trained scientists consider the conservation of animal populations. Indeed, as long as respect is a constant, its content is open to additions and change. Conservation as understood today can become part of its inventory. Given the vagaries of historical memory, the precise origins of different forms of respect can easily be forgotten. Given the universality of the process by which cultural invention becomes traditional, the content of respect is not just perceived as timeless but authoritative.[23]

Neotropical Cracids and Tinamous

With these reflections on the romanticized image of indigenous man and the comparative data on avian-human relationships as a frame, let's return to the neotropics—where, indeed, Gilberto's story of "real meat" suggests their utility. First we take up several examples of indigenous and other local people hunting cracids and other big forest birds; then we consider their role in conservation management.

Tinamous, the Ocellated Turkey, and cracids—approximately fifty species of chachalacas, guans, and curassows—can be found in neotropical forests from Mexico to Argentina. Like Gilberto, native people throughout the neotropics love to eat these forest birds. This should not be surprising: as birds, they are big, weighing from roughly three hundred grams to three and one-half kilograms, and it makes sense from an energetic standpoint to focus on what brings most meat to the hunter. For both native people and campesinos or colonists, they constitute an oft-important source of protein—of "bushmeat," as it is known. Birds are never in first rank, which (again for energetic reasons) is reserved for the larger mammals, but often of secondary importance. Formerly, birds were used extensively not just for subsistence but as raw material for products

ranging from fletching for arrows to bones for tools or ornaments. Nearly everywhere these other uses have been in sharp decline or have disappeared. The exception is the continuing use of feathers, especially as a marker of indigenousness, but the feathers employed tend to be from birds other than the cracids and others considered here.[24]

In 1990, half of all neotropical guans and curassows were listed as endangered, threatened, or vulnerable because of habitat loss or hunting.[25] Then and now, people hunt them widely without consistent (or any) regard to laws, which go largely unenforced, or boundaries of places set aside as reserves or for protection. (Globally, the hunt for animals for subsistence is of such magnitude that there is talk of a "bushmeat crisis" that seems resistant to the alleviation of poverty.)[26] Yet, and perhaps not surprisingly, over the last thirty years the impact of hunting on birds has varied from one locale to the next, as can be seen in the following examples from Venezuela, Ecuador, Panama, Paraguay, and Brazil.

In Venezuela, both indigenous people (Ye'kwana, Sanema, Pemon, and Hoti) and campesinos have a taste for and hunt cracids. Yet despite pressure and mortality, cracid populations have not been extirpated or hunted to extinction—probably because people prefer bushmeat from primates and other mammals over birds. Moreover, campesinos and indigenous people seem to hunt differently: armed with guns, campesinos hunt more efficiently and at times for sport, not consuming all that they kill; indigenous people are as likely to hunt with bows and blowguns as with guns, eat what they kill and rotate hunting areas, thus allowing cracid populations to rest and recover—critical for birds whose populations grow and recover slowly. Ominously (for cracid populations), indigenous people have been arming themselves more with guns and converting to Seventh-Day Adventism, which allows the consumption of birds and deer but forbids piglike mammals typical of South American fauna. One cracid, the Northern Helmeted Curassow, is endangered (see IUCN) in Venezuela (Figure 6.9). Some argue that because it is endemic, taxonomically unique, and considered charismatic and therefore of high public appeal, it deserves to be the highest-priority bird in Venezuela for conservation attention. The equally endangered Tawny-breasted Tinamou

FIGURE 6.9
Northern Helmeted
Curassow (*Pauxi
pauxi*).

Photograph by
José Maria Mateos.

and the less-threatened, vulnerable Wattled Guan rank much lower for purposes of attention.[27]

In Ecuador's Napo province, the Huaorani, who live in the Huaorani Ethnic Territory Reserve, the eastern part of which is surrounded by Yasuni National Forest, kill more than one hundred species of birds but focus on the usual big-bodied cracids and the Great Tinamou (as well as toucans, parrots, and the trumpeter). In the 1990s, Huaorani hunters increasingly used shotguns, which increased kill rates by 15 percent over an earlier era when they were armed with bows and blowguns. Hemmed in by other native people and colonists—Shuar, Quichua, and mestizos—they intensified the pressure on large birds, which seemed to remain (the analysis was admittedly impressionistic) essentially unchanged in number. Yet the forecast was that they would not change their hunting patterns—even to the end point of the extirpation of species—until they possessed alternative sources of protein. Moreover, they lacked an ideology that might promote conservation—to them nothing was or could

be scarce—as well as social mechanisms to establish or enforce rules even if they existed.[28]

In western Panama, where two separate indigenous people (Buglé and Ngöbe) and mestizos live, the indigenous Buglé attract many species of birds to a mosaic of gardens, orchards, and fallows, interspersed with fragments of undisturbed forest, reflecting their form of shifting cultivation. Hunters (including boys armed with slingshots) easily kill more than one hundred species of birds. They eat them all, including hummingbirds. Adult hunters set snares in openings of vegetation fences in order to catch Great Tinamous (also trapped) and Great Curassows. Armed with guns, they undertake trips to kill Crested Guans and various mammals. What is of interest is that despite desire and hunting pressure (and unlike many other neotropical cases), the big forest birds—Great Curassows and Great Tinamous especially, Crested Guans somewhat less so—remain available quite near settlements. In fact, 90 percent of the bird kills take place within two kilometers of hunters' homes. What appears to be

FIGURE 6.10
Scarlet Macaw (*Ara macao*) feeding on almond fruit, Costa Rica.

Photograph by Dr. Hays Cummins, Miami University.

critical to this nearby success is a large, surrounding, unspoiled forest area that serves as a source for birds to repopulate the sink, or habitat of lower quality, that nearly always develops near the villages where hunters dwell.[29]

The importance of a source to the sink can also be seen in the Mbaracayú Reserve in Paraguay. Here, at first glance, the indigenous Ache hunt unsustainably in the reserve within a six-kilometer radius of their village—a fifty-six-square-kilometer zone—which tends to be depleted of game. But if the five-hundred-plus-square-kilometer reserve is considered as the source, they hunt sustainably. They need the help of guards at the entrances to the reserve, for also hunting there (illegally) are Paraguayan and Brazilian frontiersmen and indigenous Guarani Indians, all of whom target three cracid species.[30]

From the hunting patterns of the Ache, Bolivian Siriono, and other native people, it is possible to calculate that sustainable hunting in the neotropics often requires three to five square kilometers per person. Thus a village of five hundred people would require from 1,500 to 2,500 square kilometers for sustainability. This does not change the fact that lands near villages—the sinks—are largely depleted of game; the same is true of most hunters who depart from a central place: concentric rings define their impact, with the innermost depleted of game and the outermost richest in game. Once more, this is a sign of opportunistic, not prudent, predation—unless the hunters can ensure that the source beyond the perimeter of their hunting will replenish the sink their hunting has produced.[31]

Despite variability, no one doubts that in nearly all cases, hunting pressure adversely affects cracid populations. At nearly two dozen Amazonian sites, the density of curassows, large tinamous, and

FIGURE 6.11
Hyacinth Macaw (*Anodorhynchus hyacinthinus*).

Photograph by Kevin J. Zimmer.

trumpeters was far less at heavily or moderately hunted sites than at lightly hunted or unhunted ones; all three categories of birds are labeled sensitive to pressure, which need not be great to precipitate decline.[32] The pressure can be devastating, as with the Black-fronted Piping Guan or Jacutinga, an endangered species of forest remnants of the deforested Atlantic Forest of Brazil. Easily shot, it has always been a favorite with indigenous people, killed by the thousands from the 1940s on, and is still hunted today in unpatrolled and understaffed reserves. Not coincidentally, it is present in greatest number where poachers, thieves (of palm hearts), and native and other local people are least in evidence.[33] While undeniably lethal, hunting in some instances tips birds over edges reached because of habitat loss and forest fragmentation, the absence of an adequate source from which to replenish depleted sinks, and other systemic factors.[34]

Before turning to conservation management, it should be mentioned that while the focus here is on the relationship between people and cracids and tinamous, the lives of tropical forest people have intersected with many other birds, notably parrots, macaws, and parakeets (collectively psittacines) harvested widely by native people for food, pets, domestic and international commercial cage trades, and feathers employed to different ends—from aesthetics (beauty) pleasing to the spirits to indigenousness in today's world. Like the cracids, the populations of the larger psittacines are not helped by slow reproductive rates. In the 1980s and 1990s, the international parrot and macaw trade was huge—in the 1980s, more than seven hundred thousand neotropical parrots and macaws of nearly one hundred species came into the United States in a five-year period alone. Argentina was the largest exporter, America the largest importer. The multibillion-dollar trade, which not surprisingly saw most profits flow into the hands of dealers, not suppliers, continued despite illegalities at every turn, from removing chicks from nests to trade by those who endorsed the Convention on International Trade in Endangered Species of Wild Fauna and Flora (CITES). Some species plunged in numbers, famously the Hyacinth Macaw, which was extirpated in northeastern Brazil where it had once been numerous (Figures 6.10–6.11).[35]

Conservation and Management

It has rightly been claimed that many indigenous people, in particular those who grew up and continue to live on ancestral lands, possess formidable knowledge about the biota and systems that comprise their environments—granting these people a depth of ethnoecological and ethnoethological understanding that one might, indeed should, expect to be specific to culture and therefore distinct from the knowledge or understanding possessed by a Western-trained conservation scientist. But environmental knowledge does not necessarily translate into conservationist action—not in neotropical forests, not globally—and it is of course folly to assume that people from radically different cultural backgrounds possessing different knowledge systems will share identical conservation goals. Conservation, in the widely accepted sense used here, is about intentionality: a conservationist intends to and does conserve. Actions might have sustainable consequences but this does not make them conservationist unless intended as such.[36]

If there is no necessary link between, on the one hand, knowledge (of the ecosystem and its parts) and belief (the cultural meanings of the cosmos, earth, spirits, persons, kin, the animate, and so on) and, on the other, behavior (conservationist or not), then should native (or other local) people be given a role in design and management for biodiversity or in the development of systems of sustainable extraction of resources?

Since the late 1980s, the answer has often been no. Scholars have pointed out or argued that indigenous people have often failed to privilege biodiversity per se or to conserve, and they have attributed this failure variously to the lack of a conservation ethic and/or to ever more influential links to external markets and cultural worlds—some with global reach. Not only did some native people hunt primates and other mammals and birds unsustainably, "no one, most of all native people themselves," one scholar remarked, "can agree" on what "saving the rainforest" means or how it should be done.[37] Some scholars called for an end to the romantic received wisdom that neotropical indigenous people always were and always would be conservationists, and argued that local native communities "cannot be trusted with conserving nature."[38]

Given their role in ecosystem functioning, one might think that a case to conserve large birds like cracids could be made more easily than when it comes to other birds or mammals. As remarked before, cracids eat seeds, leaves, and fruit, and eject feces full of intact seeds. Because of the size and strength of their bills, they eat and disperse what other birds cannot, thus ensuring not simply propagation of trees on which they and other animals depend but the health and complexity of the forest itself.

But the weight of this role is clearly not sufficient to override gustatory interest in these and other large birds, actual or perceived subsistence needs, or the importance of hunting to social status and ethnic identity. For example, in 1990 Maya hunters in Quintana Roo in Mexico were reported to be "at a loss" on how to make their hunting patterns sustainable; two of their favored birds, the Ocellated Turkey and Great Curassow, were said to be in danger of extirpation (Figures 6.12–6.13). Hunters themselves attributed the declines to their own overhunting, but other factors might have contributed to the ebbing numbers of game birds. The Mexican government has instituted hunting seasons, bag limits, and other regulations, but there is little if any enforcement of these rules. For hunters to develop a conservation ethic, they had to agree that it was desired and they needed to develop comanagement relations with the government—in part community-based, modeled perhaps on those percolating elsewhere in Mexico—or something like systems of rotation (as in Venezuela).[39] But at the time nothing was a sure thing.

Complicating the options or actions of indigenous people even further are nonnative people: today, native people are increasingly less isolated in hunting or residences from people who do not have status as indigenous people (even though they might possess native ancestry) variously labeled campesinos, colonists, mestizos, ribereños, and others. Indeed, one conclusion for the neotropics is that "incursion and/or circumscription" is one of the most significant challenges to sustainable hunting; the others are "sedentarism, population growth, market involvement, [and] technological enhancements."[40] To be effective, any strategy promoting conservation developed by the state or a nongovernmental organization

(NGO) either alone or in conjunction with indigenous people would also often need the cooperation of nonnative, local people.[41]

That people of mixed descent are as interested as indigenous people in cracids can be seen not only in cases alluded to earlier in this essay but in northeastern (Amazonian) Peru, where in the 1990s ribereños were engaged in an unsustainable (and illegal) harvest of Common Piping Guans and Razor-billed Curassows in the Pacaya-Samiria National Reserve,[42] and in Bolivia, where the Siriono, who were always keen hunters (including of cracids, tiger herons, and other birds), might now live in their own lands (the Siriono Territory) consisting largely of forest and savanna, but find themselves increasingly pressed on the periphery by colonists. Their lands are penetrated by a road bringing in commercial and sport hunters and others who, despite laws prohibiting them, are unfettered in harvesting birds and mammals. Given the Siriono need for protein from mammals, birds, and fish, as well as (from the hunter's perspective) for the status that accrues to the successful and generous hunter, and given the encroachment by outsiders on Siriono territory, it was clear that the hunt for certain animals—peccaries, tapirs, marsh deer—was not sustainable. Could the harvest of these animals, which (with others, including birds) the Siriono do not consider to be owned until dead, be halted? As yet, this question has no answer. Whether it will could depend on the Siriono themselves—but ominously, history might repeat itself: by the 1990s, primates common in Siriono forests forty years before had been extirpated.[43]

These cases and others—like that of the Panamanian Kuna, who in the context of population growth, external markets, and the increasing influence of the outside world and its people, and despite massive NGO support for conservation and their own (Kuna) respect for nature, overexploited turtles and lobsters—suggest that even with control of their lands (which they want above all), indigenous people, left to themselves, would be ineffective managers of increasingly scarce yet still desired resources.[44]

Some would argue that with exposure to the outside world of traders and missionaries, the traditional moral order of many native societies has eroded severely and that the market in bushmeat,

FIGURE 6.12
Ocellated Turkey (*Meleagris ocellata*), Mexico.

Photograph by George Harrison, United States Fish and Wildlife Service.

FIGURE 6.13
Great Curassow (*Crax rubra*), Costa Rica.

Photograph by Dr. Hays Cummins, Miami University.

satisfied in mammals or birds, beckons irresistibly to cash-hungry hunters. One survey of fourteen indigenous communities in Peru along a tributary of the Amazon concluded that hunters admitted to ignoring the traditional custom of ceasing to hunt when they had met subsistence needs and instead continued to kill in order to satisfy far greater commercial desires; that guns heightened the carnage; and that "fully aware of the consequences of their own actions, they continued to both lament the disappearance of wildlife species and hunt them to extinction." There seems to be no easy solution. Paramount in the minds of many, as mentioned, is title to land, toward which significant strides have been taken. Yet wherever the mercantile, religious, and governmental agents of colonists and the greater world presses on them—and where does it not?—the temptation to satisfy one's own or the market's needs through bushmeat is too strong to resist. "Biodiversity," as the author of this analysis titles his piece—and switching to the voice of the native—"won't feed our children."[45]

In some instances, there is reason to soften this gloomy outlook.[46] Some cases are admittedly driven by hope rather than by hard evidence. For example, in Ecuador the Siona-Secoya, who once hunted Salvin's Curassow and the Grey-winged Trumpeter unsustainably, have secured land, organized against outsiders, and might just turn to conservation as a new economic strategy. Also in Ecuador, one Huaorani acknowledges that oil company exploration, loggers, road builders, and population growth will adversely affect the numbers of guans and trumpeters (other large forest ground birds), which, added to Huaorani pressure on game, will ultimately surely undermine the traditional belief in "natural plenty."[47]

Raising the prospect more convincingly that native people, alone or in conjunction with other local people, might be better managers than outsiders, or at least comanagers with outside organizations and institutions, are cases like the Reserva Comunal Tamshiyacu-Tahuayo in northeastern Peru, where, since establishment, the larger community (greatly varied in origin) together with government agencies, NGO extension workers, and wildlife researchers directed a program of biodiversity and conservation management. They instituted rules restricting hunting access, installed a quota system, and actually halted the unsustainable harvest of primates (but not other animals).[48] In the Bolivian Gran Chaco, Izoceño-Guaraní hunters have changed their habits in response to declining numbers of game and increasing pressure from outsiders, now leaving one chick in each parrot nest harvested for the trade, ceasing the hunt for tapir, and instituting rotation of hunting areas.[49] In Brazil, the Kaxinawá gained legal title to more than one thousand square kilometers of land, trained with an NGO in natural resource management, collected data on wildlife harvests, banned nonindigenous people from their lands, ceased hunting with dogs in the forest, forbid killing newborns or pregnant females—and discovered that several animals extirpated in 1993 (including several cracids and tinamous) were again available, repopulating the sink from a much-larger and better-managed source.[50]

Despite the need for realism in predicting the course of any single people or in any single indigenous land, cases like these should give pause to the naysayers. Where title over land or rights over use of land has passed to native people, nearly anything becomes possible, including a variety of conservation alliances such as those that have emerged in the Brazilian Amazon.[51] Indeed, we end with the indigenous Xavante of Brazil—one of approximately a dozen indigenous groups indicating declining wildlife harvests—who asked the World Wildlife Fund and another NGO to evaluate harvest rates of game and the sustainability of their hunting, and who changed their ways when it became clear that their course was destructive. Like other people, Xavante hunters killed what was nearest to their villages and what was largest, regardless of sex and age. Following recommendations, they rested areas depleted of game, and gave time and space to the animals most affected so that their populations might recover. In addition to rotation, they started again to use traditional weapons instead of guns and to instruct youth in traditional ways, emphasizing community responsibility rather than the individual right of hunting.[52] Here, then, developed an exchange between Western and indigenous science—with regard to each other, the two are far from hermetically sealed[53]—in a scheme developed for comanagement at the start and indigenous management at the end.

Coda

These stories do not yet possess endings. Nevertheless, they begin to provide answers to questions posed at the outset regarding the desire of local indigenous or nonnative people in neotropical forests for particular birds, the harvest of birds as sustainable or not, and the role that local people might or should play in the re-imagination of landscapes or management of lands set aside for purposes of conservation and biodiversity. In a nutshell, while nothing is guaranteed (because indigenous and other local people possess gustatory interests that adversely affect populations of cracids, tinamous, and other large forest birds), with control over land comes the possibility of control over resources, which, enhanced by regimes of comanagement, raises the possibility of sustainability.

Needless to say, for those fortunate enough to have a hand in the design of reconstituted or revitalized neotropical habitats intended to emulate an earlier time when the demands of human inhabitants weighed less heavily on them, the clarion call (insofar as the conservation of birds is concerned) should be not merely to work from start to finish hand in hand with local people, indigenous and other, but to develop canopy trees and understory—vertically layered habitats—in stepping stones, corridors, islands, riparian gallery forests, agroforestry plots, and the like, and to promote structural complexity and floristic diversity. Privilege mess over neatness, asymmetry over symmetry, cover over cleared sight lines, and complex agroforestry enterprise over monoculture. The cleaner and more sculpted the habitat, the less useful it proves to be for many birds, in particular ones that have become severely stressed in the world's threatened and endangered neotropical forests.

Notes

1 *Chan Chich Lodge*, accessed April 19, 2010, http://www.chanchich.com. The Rio Bravo area is more than twice as large as Gallon Jug.

2 *Tinamus major*. "The IUCN Red List of Threatened Species," International Union for Conservation of Nature, accessed March 1, 2010, http://www.iucnredlist.org. The Great Tinamou is of "low risk."

3 Norman Myers, Russell A. Mittermeier, Cristina G. Mittermeier, Gustavo A. B. da Fonseca, and Jennifer Kent, "Biodiversity Hotspots for Conservation Priorities," *Nature* 403, no. 6772 (2000): 853–58; Russell A. Mittermeier et al., "Biodiversity Hotspots and Major Tropical Wilderness Areas: Approaches to Setting Conservation Priorities," *Conservation Biology* 12, no. 3 (1998): 516–20; David M. Olson and Eric Dinerstein, "The Global 200: A Representation Approach to Conserving the Earth's Most Biologically Valuable Ecoregions," *Conservation Biology* 12, no. 3 (1998): 502–15; Stuart L. Pimm and Peter Raven, "Biodiversity: Extinction by Numbers," *Nature* 403, no. 6772 (2000): 843–45; and Osvaldo E. Sala et al., "Global Biodiversity Scenarios for the Year 2100," *Science* 287, no. 5459 (2000): 1770–74.

4 Michael A. Patten, Héctor Gómez de Silva, and Brenda D. Smith-Patten, "Long-Term Changes in the Bird Community of Palenque, Chiapas, in Response to Rain Forest Loss," *Biodiversity and Conservation* 19, no. 1 (2010): 21–36; and Bryan J. Sigel, W. Douglas Robinson, and Thomas W. Sherry, "Comparing Bird Community Responses to Forest Fragmentation in Two Lowland Central American Reserves," *Biological Conservation* 143, no. 2 (2010): 340–50.

5 Alejandro R. Giraudo, Silvia D. Matteucci, Julián Alonso, Justo Herrera, and Raúl R. Abramson, "Comparing Bird Assemblages in Large and Small Fragments of the Atlantic Forest Hotspots," *Biodiversity and Conservation* 17, no. 5 (2008): 1251–56.

6 Catherine A. Lindell, Walter H. Chomentowski, and Jim R. Zook, "Characteristics of Bird Species Using Forest and Agricultural Land Covers in Southern Costa Rica," *Biodiversity and Conservation* 13, no. 13 (2004): 2419–41; and David M. Olson and Eric Dinerstein, "The Global 200: A Representation Approach to Conserving the Earth's Most Biologically Valuable Ecoregions," *Conservation Biology* 12 (1998): 502–15.

7 Catherine A. Lindell and Michelle Smith, "Nesting Bird Species in Sun Coffee, Pasture, and Understory in Southern Costa Rica," *Biodiversity and Conservation* 12 (2003): 423–40.

8 Celia A. Harvey and Jorge A. González Villalobos, "Agroforestry Systems Conserve Species-Rich but Modified Assemblages of Tropical Birds and Bats," *Biodiversity and Conservation* 16, no. 8 (2007): 2257–92; and Robert B. Matlock and Peter J. Edwards, "The Influence of Habitat Variables on Bird Communities in Forest Remnants in Costa Rica," *Biodiversity and Conservation* 15, no. 9 (2006): 2987–3016.

9 Giraudo et al., "Comparing Bird Assemblages"; Susan G. W. Laurance, "Rainforest Roads and the Future of Forest-Dependent Wildlife: A Case Study of Understory Birds," in *Emerging Threats to Tropical Forests*, ed. William F. Laurance and Carlos A. Peres (Chicago: University of Chicago Press, 2006), 253–67; and Pedro Ferreira Develey and Jean Paul Metzger, "Emerging Threats to Birds in Brazilian Forests: The Role of Forest Loss and Configuration in a Severely Fragmented Ecosystem," in *Emerging Threats to Tropical Forests*, 269–90.

10   Stuart J. Marsden, Mark Whiffin, and Mauro Galetti, "Bird Diversity and Abundance in Forest Fragments and Eucalyptus Plantations around an Atlantic Forest Reserve, Brazil," *Biodiversity and Conservation* 10, no. 5 (2001): 737–51; Juan Mazar Barnett, Caio J. Carlos, and Sonia A. Roda, "Renewed Hope for the Threatened Avian Endemics of Northeastern Brazil," *Biodiversity and Conservation* 14, no. 9 (2005): 2265–74; and Giraudo et al., "Comparing Bird Assemblages."

11   Alexandre Uezu, Dennis Driesmans Beyer, and Jean Paul Metzger, "Can Agroforest Woodlots Work as Stepping Stones for Birds in the Atlantic Forest Region?," *Biodiversity and Conservation* 17, no. 8 (2008): 1907–22; Benjamin S. Seaman and Christian H. Schulze, "The Importance of Gallery Forests in the Tropical Lowlands of Costa Rica for Understorey Forest Birds," *Biological Conservation* 143, no. 2 (2010): 391–98; and Alejandro Estrada, Pierluigi Cammarano, and Rosamond Coates-Estrada, "Bird Species Richness in Vegetation Fences and in Strips of Residual Rain Forest Vegetation at Los Tuxtlas, Mexico," *Biodiversity and Conservation* 9, no. 10 (2000): 1399–416.

12   Joseph Hawes et al., "The Value of Forest Strips for Understorey Birds in an Amazonian Plantation Landscape," *Biological Conservation* 141, no. 9 (2008): 2262–78; Renata Pardini et al., "The Challenge of Maintaining Atlantic Forest Biodiversity: A Multi-Taxa Conservation Assessment of Specialist and Generalist Species in an Agro-Forestry Mosaic in Southern Bahia," *Biological Conservation* 142, no. 6 (2009): 1178–90; and Rua S. Mordecai, Robert J. Cooper, and Rebecca Justicia, "A Threshold Response to Habitat Disturbance by Forest Birds in the Choco Andean Corridor, Northwest Ecuador," *Biodiversity and Conservation* 18, no. 9 (2009): 2421–31.

13   Andrea Najera and Javier Simonetti, "Can Oil Palm Plantations Become Bird Friendly?," *Agroforestry Systems* 80 (2010): 203–9.

14   Huw Lloyd and Stuart J. Marsden, "Bird Community Variation across Polylepis Woodland Fragments and Matrix Habitats: Implications for Biodiversity Conservation within a High Andean Landscape," *Biodiversity and Conservation* 17, no. 11 (2008): 2645–60; and J. Barlow et al., "The Responses of Understorey Birds to Forest Fragmentation, Logging, and Wildfires: An Amazonian Synthesis," *Biological Conservation* 128, no. 2 (2006): 182–92.

15   Fábio Júlio Alves Borges and Miguel Ángelo Marini, "Birds Nesting Survival in Disturbed and Protected Neotropical Savannas," *Biodiversity and Conservation* 19, no. 1 (2010): 223–36.

16   Stefan Woltmann, "Bird Community Responses to Disturbance in a Forestry Concession in Lowland Bolivia," *Biodiversity and Conservation* 12, no. 1 (2003): 1921–36.

17   Lloyd and Marsden, "Bird Community Variation."

18   Shepard Krech III, "Birds," in *Encyclopedia of American Environmental History*, ed. Kathleen A. Brosnan (New York: Facts on File, 2011), 1:176–80.

19   Daniel Mendelsohn, "The Wizard," *The New York Review of Books*, March 25, 2010.

20   R. N. Holdaway and C. Jacomb, "Rapid Extinction of the Moas (Aves: Dinornithiformes): Model, Test, and Implications," *Science* 287, no. 5461 (2000): 2250–54; Jared Diamond, "Blitzkrieg Against the Moas," *Science* 287, no. 5461 (2000): 2170–71; and David Steadman, "Prehistoric Extinctions of Pacific Island Birds: Biodiversity Meets Zooarchaeology," *Science* 267, no. 5201 (1995): 1123–31.

21   Jack M. Broughton, *Prehistoric Human Impacts on California Birds: Evidence from the Emeryville Shellmound Avifauna*, Ornithological Monographs 56 (Washington D.C.: American Ornithologists' Union, 2004).

22   Holdaway and Jacomb, "Rapid Extinction"; Shepard Krech III, *Spirits of the Air: Birds and American Indians in the South* (Athens: University of Georgia Press, 2009), 178.

23   Shepard Krech III, *The Ecological Indian: Myth and History* (New York: W. W. Norton, 1999); and Shepard Krech III, "Beyond *The Ecological Indian*," in *Native Americans and the Environment: Perspectives on the Ecological Indian*, ed. Michael E. Harkin and David Rich Lewis (Lincoln: University of Nebraska Press, 2007), 3–31.

24   Stuart D. Strahl and Alejandro Grajal, "Conservation of Large Avian Frugivores and the Management of Neotropical Protected Areas," *Oryx* 25, no. 1 (January 1991): 50–55; Alfredo J. Begazo and Richard E. Bodmer, "Use and Conservation of Cracidae (Aves: Galliformes) in the Peruvian Amazon," *Oryx* 32, no. 4 (October 1998): 301–9; and José L. Silva and Stuart D. Strahl, "Human Impact on Populations of Chachalacas, Guans, and Curassows in Venezuela," in *Neotropical Wildlife Use and Conservation*, ed. John G. Robinson and Kent H. Redford (Chicago: Chicago University Press, 1991), 37–52.

25   Strahl and Grajal, "Conservation of Large Avian Frugivores."

26   Elizabeth L. Bennett et al., "Hunting the World's Wildlife to Extinction," *Oryx* 36, no. 4 (2002): 328–29; and John G. Robinson and Elizabeth L. Bennett, "Will Alleviating Poverty Solve the Bushmeat Crisis?" *Oryx* 36, no. 4 (2002): 332.

27   Silva and Strahl, "Human Impact on Populations"; and Jon Paul Rodríguez, Franklin Rojas-Suárez, and Christopher J. Sharpe, "Setting Priorities for the Conservation of Venezuela's Threatened Birds," *Oryx* 38, no. 4 (2004): 373–82.

28   Patricio Mena V. et al., "The Sustainability of Current Hunting Practices by the Huaorani," in *Hunting for Sustainability in Tropical Forests*, ed. John G. Robinson and Elizabeth L. Bennett (New York: Columbia University Press, 2000), 57–78, 77. See also Jorge Trujillo León, "The Quichua and Huaorani Peoples and Yasuní National Park, Ecuador,"

in *Traditional Peoples and Biodiversity Conservation in Large Tropical Landscapes*, ed. Kent H. Redford and Jane A. Mansour (Arlington, Va.: The Nature Conservancy, 1996), 75–92; and Flora E. Lu, "The Common Property Regime of the Huaorani Indians of Ecuador: Implications and Challenges to Conservation," *Human Ecology* 29, no. 4 (December 2001): 425–47.

29 Derek A. Smith, "The Harvest of Rain-Forest Birds by Indigenous Communities in Panama," *The Geographical Review* 100, no. 2 (2010): 187–203; Derek A. Smith, "Garden Game: Shifting Cultivation, Indigenous Hunting, and Wildlife Ecology in Western Panama," *Human Ecology* 33, no. 4 (2005): 505–37; and Derek A. Smith, "The Spatial Patterns of Indigenous Wildlife Use in Western Panama: Implications for Conservation Management," *Biological Conservation* 141, no. 4 (2008): 925–37.

30 Kim Hill and Jonathan Padwe, "Sustainability of Ache Hunting in the Mbaracayu Reserve, Paraguay," in Robinson and Bennett, *Hunting for Sustainability in Tropical Forests*, 79–105.

31 Hill and Padwe, "Sustainability of Ache Hunting."

32 Carlos A. Peres, "Evaluating the Impact and Sustainability of Subsistence Hunting at Multiple Amazonian Forest Sites," in Robinson and Bennett, *Hunting for Sustainability in Tropical Forests*, 31–56.

33 Mauro Galetti et al., "Ecology and Conservation of the Jacutinga *Pipile jacutinga* in the Atlantic Forest of Brazil," *Biological Conservation* 82, no. 1 (October 1997): 31–39.

34 Aidan Keane, M. de L. Brooke, and P. J. K. Mcgowan, "Correlates of Extinction Risk and Hunting Pressure in Gamebirds (Galliformes)," *Biological Conservation* 126, no. 2 (2005): 216–33.

35 Jorgen Bent Thomsen and Amie Brautigam, "Sustainable Use of Neotropical Parrots," in Robinson and Redford, *Neotropical Wildlife Use and Conservation*, 359–79; and E. E. Inigo-Elias and M. A. Ramos, "The Psittacine Trade in Mexico," in Robinson and Redford, *Neotropical Wildlife Use and Conservation*, 380–92.

36 Kim Hill, in consultation with Tito Tikuarangi, "The Mbaracayú Reserve and the Aché of Paraguay," in Redford and Mansour, *Traditional Peoples and Biodiversity Conservation*, 159–96. On conservation and intentionality, see Krech, *The Ecological Indian*; and Krech, "Beyond *The Ecological Indian*."

37 Allyn Stearman, "A Pound of Flesh: Social Change and Modernization as Factors in Hunting Sustainability Among Neotropical Societies," in Robinson and Bennett, *Hunting for Sustainability in Tropical Forests*, 249; Kent H. Redford and Allyn Maclean Stearman, "Forest-Dwelling Native Amazonians and the Conservation of Biodiversity: Interests in Common or in Collision?," *Conservation Biology* 7, no. 2 (June 1993): 248–55; Janis B. Alcorn, "Indigenous People and Conservation," *Conservation Biology* 7, no. 2 (1993): 424–26; and Kent H. Redford and Allyn Maclean

Stearman, "On Common Ground? Response to Alcorn," *Conservation Biology* 7, no. 2 (1993): 427–28.

38 Flora Lu Holt, "The Catch-22 of Conservation: Indigenous Peoples, Biologists, and Cultural Change," *Human Ecology* 33, no. 2 (April 2005): 199–215.

39 Jeffrey P. Jorgenson, "Wildlife Conservation and Game Harvest by Maya Hunters in Quintana Roo, Mexico," in Robinson and Bennett, *Hunting for Sustainability in Tropical Forests*, 251–66.

40 Allyn Stearman, "A Pound of Flesh," in Robinson and Bennett, 234.

41 See Richard E. Bodmer, "Managing Wildlife with Local Communities in the Peruvian Amazon: The Case of the Reserva Comunal Tamshiyacu-Tahuayo," in *Natural Connections: Perspectives in Community-Based Conservation*, ed. David Western and R. Michael Wright (Washington, D.C.: Island Press, 1994), 113–34.

42 Begazo and Bodmer, "Use and Conservation of Cracidae."

43 Wendy R. Townsend, "The Sustainability of Subsistence Hunting by the Siriono Indians of Bolivia," in Robinson and Bennett, *Hunting for Sustainability in Tropical Forests*, 267–81.

44 Jorge Ventocilla et al., "The Kuna Indians and Conservation," in Redford and Mansour, *Traditional Peoples and Biodiversity Conservation*, 33–56.

45 Richard Chase Smith, "Biodiversity Won't Feed Our Children: Biodiversity Conservation and Economic Development in Indigenous Amazonia," in Redford and Mansour, *Traditional Peoples and Biodiversity Conservation*, 198.

46 John G. Robinson and Kent H. Redford, "Community-Based Approaches to Wildlife Conservation in Neotropical Forests," in Western and Wright, *Natural Connections*, 300–19.

47 Holt, "The Catch-22 of Conservation," 208 and passim; and William T. Vickers, "Hunting Yields and Game Composition Over Ten Years in an Amazon Indian Territory," in Robinson and Redford, *Neotropical Wildlife Use and Conservation*, 53–81.

48 Richard Bodmer and Pablo E. Puertas, "Community-Based Comanagement of Wildlife in the Peruvian Amazon," in Robinson and Bennett, *Hunting for Sustainability in Tropical Forests*, 395–409.

49 Andrew J. Noss, Erika Cuéllar, and Rosa Leny Cuéllar, "An Evaluation of Hunter Self-Monitoring in the Bolivian Chaco," *Human Ecology* 32, no. 6 (December 2004): 685–702.

50 Pedro de Araujo Lima Constantino et al., "Indigenous Collaborative Research for Wildlife Management in Amazonia: The Case of the Kaxinawá, Acre, Brazil," *Biological Conservation* 141 (2008): 2718–29.

51   Stephan Schwartzman and Barbara Zimmerman, "Conservation Alliances with Indigenous People of the Amazon," *Conservation Biology* 19, no. 3 (2005): 721–27.

52   Frans J. Leeuwenberg and John G. Robinson, "Traditional Management of Hunting in a Xavante Community in Central Brazil: The Search for Sustainability," in Robinson and Bennett, *Hunting for Sustainability in Tropical Forests*, 375–94.

53   David Gordon and Shepard Krech III, eds., *Indigenous Knowledge and the Environment in Africa and North America* (Athens: Ohio University Press, 2012).

CHAPTER 7

Designing a Wilderness for Wildlife

The Case of the Pilanesberg National Park, South Africa

JANE CARRUTHERS

AFRICA'S NATIONAL PARKS AND GAME RESERVES are world-renowned. Famed for the wilderness landscapes they conserve and for the herds of charismatic large mammals they succor, these protected areas attract many thousands of international tourists every year and contribute substantially to the economies of a number of African countries. In one important respect these reserves are all alike: they appear "natural," are inhabited by creatures that evolved there, and are free from the intrusion of cityscapes, ploughed lands, or other evidence of modernizing transformations. As even a casual Internet search will reveal, this Edenic perspective is how many parts of Africa choose to market themselves internationally. It is not often appreciated that these protected areas all have different historical origins and are professionally managed in ways that have changed over time in order to become successful hubs of economic and animal production. Many are also the consequence of social engineering, with local people removed in the interests of what is referred to as "fortress conservation"[1] (a fenced, protected area devoid of humans), or more latterly engaged in various forms of "community conservation" and thus becoming part of rural development

schemes that have a protected area as its core economic driver. Whatever their size or locality, Africa's protected areas are not neutral spaces but active in the resource utilization and developmental strategies of the national states concerned, with participation by politicians, scientists, community developers, tour operators, resource economists, and local people.

Although there has been active management intervention in African nature conservation over many decades, the first national park to have been conceived on the designer's drawing board and created specifically for tourist entertainment and local economic improvement (rather than wildlife and/or biodiversity protection) was the Pilanesberg National Park.[2] Its conception and inception therefore marks an important milestone. The Pilanesberg was established in 1977 in what was then the western part of the Transvaal province of South Africa in an African reserve that was about to transform from an apartheid Bantustan, or "homeland," into an "independent state" named Bophuthatswana. Despite the inauspicious political start and the initial unease in many quarters as local people and their livestock were removed, evidence

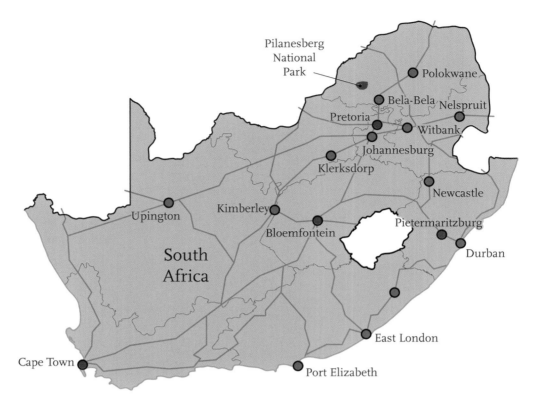

FIGURE 7.1

The general location of the Pilanesberg National Park, North West Province, Republic of South Africa.

Map by Tim Sheasby.

of croplands was erased, wildlife translocated into the area, and rest camps were established, over the past thirty years (and despite its small size) the Pilanesberg has established itself as a leading example of the current protected area estate in southern Africa. Because of its proximity to the large cities of Gauteng (Johannesburg in particular), its beautiful landscape, its competent wildlife management, and the absence of malaria, the pioneering project of "playing God" that was the Pilanesberg has been extremely successful in meeting most of its objectives. This essay will explain how and why this specifically designed national park came about, situating its beginnings in the political context of the time and charting the first decade of its existence. In doing so, I am building on the literature that critiques African nature conservation, eschewing Western paternalism and values that Europeans place on nature, while avoiding paying homage to an idealized precolonial harmonious "state of

nature." I also question the foundations of biodiversity conservation and present the argument that ecological restoration may be possible. The need to use wildlife sustainably and consumptively to facilitate economic development and meet the needs of modern African people is emphasized here as it eclipses the need for any ersatz, middle-class "wilderness experience."[3] As is argued at length in the book *The Myth of Wild Africa* by Jonathan Adams, a conservationist and writer, and Thomas McShane, Africa program officer for the World Wide Fund for Nature in Switzerland, the way in which ecological systems are managed has less to do with science than it does with ideology, competing developmental models, and even global politics.[4] This essay illuminates many of these issues through the prism of the creation of the Pilanesberg National Park, the history of which resonates strongly with the title of ecologist Alistair Graham's now classic, iconoclastic book *The Gardeners of Eden* (1973) (Figure 7.1).

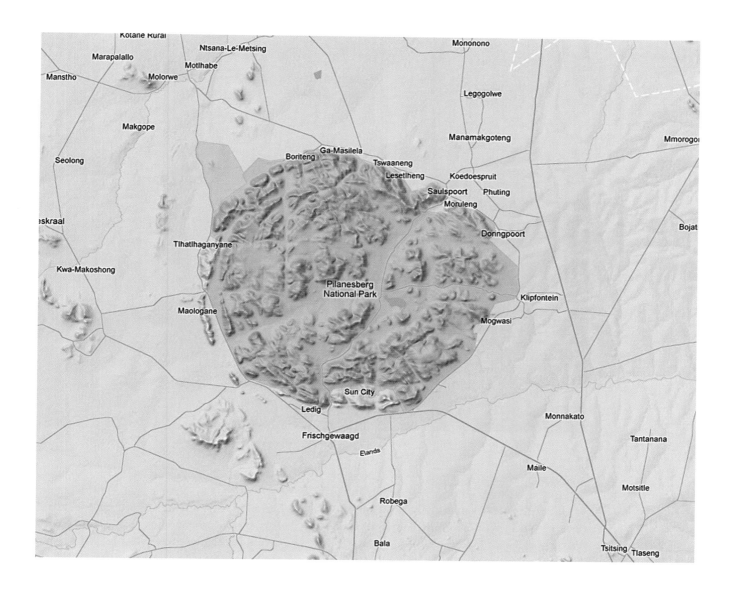

Location, Geology, and Natural History

The Pilanesberg National Park, a roughly circular area some 572 square kilometers (about fifty thousand hectares) in extent and between twenty-three to twenty-eight kilometers in diameter, is situated about fifty kilometers north of Rustenburg in the North West Province, one of South Africa's nine provinces. The Pilanesberg is a unique geological feature in South Africa, the root zone of a volcanic crater that erupted about 1,200 to 1,300 million years ago, containing a number of rare rocks and elements. After being covered beneath the Karoo sediments, it now presents as a complex series of eroded rings of low mountains and hills that rise

about three hundred to six hundred meters above the surrounding land. There is only one perennial river, but there are a number of freshwater and saline springs at upland and lower levels. The largest permanent body of water is Mankwe Dam (approximately two kilometers by one kilometer), which was constructed by white farmers in the late 1950s. The climate is benign; the average rainfall is six hundred to seven hundred millimeters per year, although droughts are a regular occurrence (Figure 7.2).[5]

While—as discussed in detail below—sociopolitical and economic factors played the major role in the design and creation of the Pilanesberg National Park, the interesting crater formation had

FIGURE 7.2
Geological landform of the Pilanesberg. The national park is situated in the crater of an extinct volcano that presents as a series of eroded concentric rings of hills rising about three hundred to six hundred meters above the surrounding land.

Map by Tim Sheasby.

FIGURE 7.3
The scenery of
the Pilanesberg
National Park
provides evidence
of the volcanic
origin of the
landscape.

Photograph by
Bruce Brockett.

been remarked upon by a number of nineteenth-century hunters and explorers. For example, the artist-explorer Thomas Baines was captivated by the views he obtained of the Pilanesberg in 1869 and painted watercolors of the scenery.[6]

In terms of vegetation, the Pilanesberg is currently classed as "SVcb5 Pilanesberg mountain bushveld."[7] This veld type is botanically significant because it is a transition zone between the Arid Savanna and the Moist Savanna Biome.[8] Because of the complex substrate, there is a wide variety of landscapes and habitats for both plants and animals. As the game reserve's designers explained in the initial planning and management proposals, the crater lent itself to biodiversity restoration and conservation because "due to the ring within ring sequence of hill ranges and valleys, a striking catena sequence of geomorphic surfaces and habitats is found . . . [and] . . . a rich biogeographic system has evolved where forest, thicket, moist savanna and arid savanna components meet and overlap" (Figure 7.3).[9]

Although specific records for the Pilanesberg do not exist prior to 1980, the whole region was once rich in wildlife, and the names of the majority of the settler farms of the nineteenth century—Rhenosterkraal (Rhinoceros corral), Vogelstruisfontein (Ostrich spring), Elandsfontein (Eland spring), Kameelkuil (Giraffe pit), Wildebeestkuil (Wildebeest pit), Buffelskloof (Buffalo ravine), Leeuwfontein (Lion spring), etc.—bear witness to precolonial abundance. Indeed, once trade and settlement began to move northward from the Cape Colony, the northwestern region of southern Africa became renowned for its big game. Given the hunting pressure after the introduction of firearms and the development of an export market, however, it did not take long for the large herds of game to be decimated.

Pilanesberg Politics circa 1840 to the Mid-1970s

In the nineteenth century, the northwestern region of southern Africa was inhabited by clans of people with a common Tswana cultural and linguistic base. There was some cultivation of crops, such as sorghum and maize, but the economies of these communities were based principally on pastoralism and some internal trade, while wildlife hunting, which was sometimes ritualistic, provided an additional source of fresh meat (Figure 7.4).

One of the major clans that lived in the region of the Pilanesberg in the nineteenth century was the Bakgatla baKgafela.[10] When Boers arrived in the district from the Cape Colony during the mid- and late 1830s, the *kgosi* [chief] of the Bakgatla was Pilane (died 1850) and the settlers named the mountains after him. The Boer conquest met little resistance from the Bakgatla, who had been weakened by Mzilikazi's intrusions from the Zululand area and the general instability of the 1820s and 1830s. Indeed, the Bakgatla even became allies of the Boers, assisting them in exploits of war and further conquest, human trafficking for indentured labor (*inboekeling*), and ivory hunting. But once Boer hegemony had been secured, the communal lands of the Bakgatla—including the Pilanesberg

crater—were commandeered by the white settlers and carved up into private farms. The Bakgatla then living on these properties became labor tenants of their new landlords.[11] In 1913, after the four colonies in South Africa had been united (1910), the Natives Land Act confined black South Africans to clearly demarcated and spatially limited areas of South Africa. The Native Trust and Land Act (1936) was an attempt to provide more land for Africans by designating what were called "released areas." These took the form of about sixty-two thousand square kilometers (seven million hectares) of what was then white-owned land that, once "released," was to be purchased by the South African Native Trust and added to African areas. The Pilanesberg was one of the "released areas" and white-occupied farms were gradually expropriated. So slow was the process that it was only in the early 1960s that farming by whites in the Pilanesberg eventually came to an end. The area reverted to the Bakgatla (as state land owned by the South African Native Trust), and they were once again able to use the crater to graze their livestock as they had done in the nineteenth century.

FIGURE 7.4
The Tswana settlement at Dithakong, as painted by Samuel Daniell in 1801.

Photograph courtesy of the Museum Africa, Johannesburg.

Designing a Wilderness for Wildlife 111

FIGURE 7.5
The "Tswana
islands" within
"white" South
Africa that
comprised the
"independent" state
of Bophuthatswana
from 1977 to 1994.

Map by Tim Sheasby.

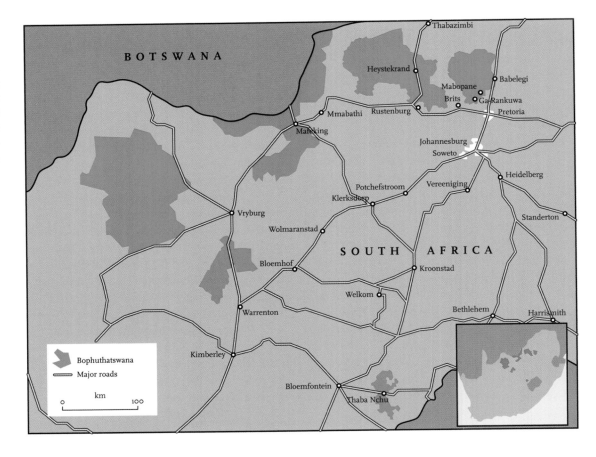

After 1948, when the National Party came to power in South Africa, the more stringent policies of apartheid were introduced. In 1961, a so-called Tswana homeland was established in the northwestern part of South Africa, and this meant that Tswana speakers in South Africa were physically grouped into a single political entity. For some years during the mid-1960s, Tidimane Pilane, kgosi of the Bakgatla, was chairman of this body, but he was ousted in 1972 by Lucas Mangope, head of the Bahurutshe clan and leader of the Bahurutshe Tribal Authority.[12] During the 1970s, the apartheid plan was to convert these "tribal homelands" first into "self-governing states" and then into "independent" nations.[13] The Pilanesberg area became part of Bophuthatswana, a polity about forty thousand square kilometers in extent which, in its final form, consisted of islands surrounded by white South Africa. Rivalry between Mangope, who supported apartheid, and Pilane, a disciple of the African National Congress (ANC), and their followers was intense and sometimes violent. Nonetheless, until a final coup in March 1994, on the very eve of democracy in South Africa and the coming to power of the ANC, Mangope ruled Bophuthatswana as a virtual dictator, sustained by the South African government (Figure 7.5).[14]

Although real political independence was a chimera, the aim of regional economic development held promise. The area of Bophuthatswana included rich mineral resources, and there were also generous tax breaks and other benefits to "border industries" that could be established adjacent to the homelands and to white South Africa and that employed "homeland" labor and generated gross domestic product. Agricultural improvement was another element in Bophuthatswana's economic progress, and this was the responsibility of the Department of Agriculture, which had been set up in 1972. After "full independence" had been granted to Bophuthatswana in 1977, this department was tasked with promoting national self-sufficiency and a parastatal body, and the Agricultural Development Corporation of Bophuthatswana (Agricor) was established in 1978 to execute this mission.[15] As will be explained below, Agricor played a decisive role in setting up the Pilanesberg National Park.

Landscape Architecture and Wildlife Conservation in Bophuthatswana in the 1970s

Before about 1960, wildlife was routinely eradicated in Africa so that land might be used more "productively" for domestic livestock or cultivation.[16] But greater ecological understanding, together with ideas around sustainability, thereafter gained ground.[17] In southern Africa, the new thinking was given substance by rangeland scientists Raymond Frederic Dasmann, Archie S. Mossman, and Thane Riney, who worked as Fulbright scholars in Southern Rhodesia in the mid-1960s and who were advocates of the "Aldo Leopold school of thought."[18] Their scheme was to make use of the total productivity of an ecological system, not only to crop its wildlife, although the latter was the most important immediate outcome.[19] At the same time, veterinarians were developing and refining darts, drugs, and capture and translocation equipment that enabled live wildlife to be transported safely en masse from one area to another. South Africa is unusual in that it is one of few countries in the world where indigenous wildlife can be traded, resulting in game sales (usually auctions) becoming increasingly frequent and lucrative. In the 1960s, the environmental movement was growing in South Africa, and there was considerable excitement and speculation as to its implications for the region.[20] These ideas were to come together in the formation of the Pilanesberg National Park.

Even as the independent Tswana homeland took political shape, there were suggestions that the Pilanesberg should become a game reserve. In South Africa at that time, the provinces were responsible for game reserves that were formalized through provincial ordinances (even though some, particularly in the province of Natal, were referred to as "national parks"), while there was a national body, the National Parks Board of Trustees, that had oversight of protected areas that had been declared by acts of parliament.[21] In 1969, a recommendation was made that the Pilanesberg crater become a recreation resort and nature reserve, but the implications in evicting and resettling the Bakgatla scotched the plan. But the idea was raised again in 1973, and the following year Mangope established a committee to investigate the feasibility of such a project.[22]

Part of the rationale of the "independent" homelands was to encourage a varied economy, and in this regard tourism was important, as it was also for showcasing these "nations" to the international community. Specifically, the Southern Sun hotel group, under the dynamic leadership of business entrepreneur Sol Kerzner, planned to extend its operations in Bophuthatswana, taking advantage of the Pilanesberg's proximity to Johannesburg, particularly in the light of the fuel restrictions of the time, which had curtailed traveling long distances. In 1976, the location of a new hotel was under discussion and, having at first considered Mankwe Dam in the crater's center as ideal, the present site of Sun City on the southern boundary was chosen.[23] Construction of the multimillion rand project began in 1978.[24] At this time, the hotel developers joined the call for a game reserve that would form an additional attraction for its visitors in that they could foray out a short distance and observe wild animals—this being a change from gambling, sitting around the swimming pool, or playing golf (Figure 7.6).

Initial funding for a game reserve of some four hundred square kilometers was raised by David Beuster, the managing director of Agricor, and so it was that in 1977, the same year that Bophuthatswana gained its independence, the Pilanesberg was formally proclaimed a nature reserve. At the time the area was home to many cattle-owning Bakgatla and other people, and was crisscrossed with fences and farm roads. It contained derelict, abandoned farmhouses that had once belonged to whites, invasive alien vegetation, and abandoned cultivated farmlands. Because of its potential as a rural development project and not a nature conservation project, administration was given to Agricor rather than to the Department of Nature Conservation, as would more usually have been the case. This bureaucratic move was significant because Agricor was a parastatal organization, tasked with economic and

FIGURE 7.6
Sun City Hotel,
a recreation and
golfing complex
located on the
southern boundary
of the Pilanesberg
National Park.
© Sun International.

community development in the rural sector, not with conserving nature, or what today would be referred to as biodiversity conservation.

Even more significant—and far more adventurous—was the fact that landscape architects were employed by the South African Department of Bantu Affairs, a move instigated by Beuster and Mangope. The firm involved was Farrell & Van Riet, Landscape Architects and Ecological Planners, then a recently established, Pretoria-based company, and it was instructed to act as consultants and to draw up a management plan. At the time, landscape architecture was a new discipline in South Africa. A four-year degree program at the University of Pretoria was first offered in 1971 through the initiative of the innovative Joane Pim, whose book *Beauty Is Necessary: Preservation or Creation of the Landscape* was to become a classic of South African landscape and horticultural literature. As the founder, in 1962, of the South African Institute of Landscape Architects, Pim's work in South Africa was extremely significant. She was a talented landscape planner and horticulturist who engaged in creative

town planning (particularly for mines and mining towns), promoted the use of indigenous plantings, and believed that people's lives were improved—and their spirits uplifted and refreshed—by attractive surroundings, whether urban or rural.[25]

While not an environmentalist in the modern sense of the term, Pim paid tribute to Ian L. McHarg, the renowned US landscape architect, commending him for "fighting a tremendous contemporary battle against all environmental abuses" and for recognizing how humans "consistently refuse to realize how efficient nature really is, if allowed to play her part."[26] Leading progressive thinking in the field of landscape architecture in South Africa in the mid-1970s, and cementing its disciplinary association with ecological planning, was Willem van Riet. Van Riet had qualified as an architect at the University of Cape Town and thereafter, from 1972 to 1975, studied under McHarg at the University of Pennsylvania.[27] McHarg had started the interdisciplinary Department of Landscape Architecture and Regional Planning on the basis of "human ecological planning" or "human ecology."[28] On his return to South Africa in 1975, Van Riet enthusiastically adopted McHarg's philosophy to "design with nature," seeing in it many ideas that could profitably be transferred to South Africa.[29] Today, Van Riet is a renowned and leading conservationist, involved in South African National Parks,[30] the World Wide Fund for Nature, and the Peace Parks Foundation. His career has been somewhat similar to that of Frederick Law Olmsted, the first formally named landscape architect and designer of New York's Central Park, who was also a conservationist actively engaged with many aspects of the formation of the United States' national parks.

Ecological efficiency, design, veld restoration, and productivity became melded in the creation of the Pilanesberg through the collaboration between two men who were inspired by McHarg: Ken Tinley, an ecologist, and Willem van Riet, a landscape architect. While still at university, Tinley advocated McHarg's *Design with Nature* (the writing of which was apparently suggested to McHarg by Raymond Dasmann and Russell Train, both then in the Conservation Foundation) to his fellow students and acquaintances.[31] Tinley was one of an emerging new generation of wildlife ecologists in South Africa whose contribution has been lasting in terms of integrating social as well as biological ecology into conservation and management. He and his colleagues, many of whom graduated from the University of Natal, were English-speaking ecologists, some with a Southern Rhodesian background and training.[32]

Botanist Eugene Moll attributes the University of Natal's preeminence in ecology to its long history of ecological studies, including pioneers of the early 1900s John Bews and John Phillips, both of whom had worked closely with Arthur Tansley in Britain.[33] Among other university contemporaries of Moll and Tinley was Brian Huntley, a zoologist by training and former head of the South African National Botanical Institute, and Jeremy Anderson, an ecologist and wildlife management specialist. They recall the synergy of their student group, but also the disciplined and almost Victorian grounding in zoology they received from their sympathetic and supportive professors, as well as their teachers' insistence on fieldwork and field knowledge, not only laboratory expertise.[34]

By the early 1970s, early in his career as an ecologist, Tinley had gained a deserved reputation for his innovative ideas about protected area management. Like other English speakers, he was not welcomed within the Afrikaner-dominated fold of the National Parks Board or provincial wildlife authorities, and he thus worked in the South African black "homelands" of Pondoland and Maputaland (with Van Riet) and in the Gorongosa National Park in Mozambique.[35] What the Pilanesberg report by Tinley (as ecologist) and Van Riet (as designer) suggested was revolutionary in terms of how it contrasted with existing wildlife management in South Africa. Elsewhere in the country, fortress conservation was firmly in place in national and provincial parks and game reserves, which were administered in paramilitary style, local people and neighbors were ignored in terms of their interests as regional stakeholders, and national parks and provincial game reserves were managed as islands. In large wilderness areas, for example in the United States, people were allowed to enjoy the outdoors and to hike and appreciate the grandeur of the scenery. In Africa, owing to the prevalence of dangerous wildlife even in small national parks and game reserves, visitors were obliged either to remain in their motor vehicles or, if on foot (as was far more unusual), to be accompanied by a qualified, armed game ranger. But in the United Kingdom the link between national parks and landscape management was being recognized in a manner similar to McHarg's holistic, ecological design ideas, and this kind of thinking was taken up in South Africa for the first time in the Pilanesberg.[36] As a template or design for biodiversity restoration, the Farrell & Van Riet and Tinley report, which was entitled "Pilanesberg National Park, Bophuthatswana: Planning and Management Proposals for Department of Agriculture, Republic of Bophuthatswana, August 1978" is worth summarizing in some detail. (It is also worth noting that the Pilanesberg was to be called a "national park"— as befitting the new nation of Bophuthatswana— rather than a "game reserve.")

The report began with what was then a provocative statement, namely, that the survival of wildlife in Africa was dependent on the attitudes of rural African people and that any conservation measure would ultimately be futile unless wildlife and nature could deliver tangible, visible benefits to humans. The main argument was that protected areas should not be conceptualized as atolls in seas of antagonistic humanity, but viewed in their regional, ecological, and economic contexts as productive primary (ecological services) and secondary (tourism, education, and wealth-creation) landscapes. The report warned against urban-based, romantic, middle-class attitudes toward "nature," "wilderness," and recreation, and the authors insisted that protected areas had to be considered in their socioeconomic and geographic milieu. In other words, a national park is a site-specific economic resource of "inestimable cultural and education value." The report paid particular attention to wildlife as a source of protein as well as of traditional medicine and other natural products that might be sustainably harvested by local people, together with wildlife tourism as a benefit to local employment and income. What is currently referred to as "community conservation" in a formally named national park got its first official airing in South Africa with this report.

Together with the radical idea of using national parks sustainably as engines of economic and social development, Van Riet and Tinley introduced a novel concept of planning and design that impacted on the ecological restoration that they envisaged. What was important about the Pilanesberg project was that they had a free hand and a flexible institutional, bureaucratic, and policy environment. They were not burdened with an entrenched public service, decades-old conservation ideas of "preservation," or outmoded tourist facilities by way of accommodation, ill-sited roads, or other amenities, as was the case in parks administered by the National Parks Board or the provincial authorities.[37] Nature had provided the ideal design: from within the alkaline rings of the crater one cannot see the plains beyond them; it all appears quite natural, although it is a geographically confined landscape bounded by the crater's walls. While at the start there existed cultivated lands, evidence of stock grazing and farmsteads, alien vegetation, roads, etc., once these—and the people—were removed, the crater presented an almost clean slate for design. The report noted the rich geomorphology, the variety of habitats, and the vegetative biodiversity that had survived centuries of human use, and a full ecological survey was provided. To maximize wildlife

viewing in the small area and utilize it to best advantage, the report proposed that all major tourism facilities should be on the boundaries of the park (as was the Sun City complex), thus preserving the interior of the crater from large crowds in specific places, unsightly camps, restaurants, and other amenities. This peripheral development, which was particularly appropriate to a small area such as the Pilanesberg that was too limited in scale to have allowed for large hotels or campgrounds in its interior, was contrary to the design of other larger national parks and game reserves that had sited major visitor accommodation within the protected area. Moreover, using the internal watersheds as ecological borders, the report proposed dividing the crater into distinct activity zones; this, too, was a departure from the accepted norm. There were seven zones in all (later amended and reduced to five)[38]: wilderness and special-use zones in which there would be no roads or amenities; a buffer zone around these two zones; resource utilization areas; rest camp areas; and intensive-use areas for historical, archaeological, and cultural projects. Specific recommendations for planning and use of each of these different zones were made in order that the activities would harmonize with each other. Adaptive wildlife management had not then come into its own, and although not expressly stated, the fact that carrying capacity was the benchmark for wildlife introductions and that the Phillips/McHarg model was followed indicates that the restoration and maintenance of a controlled and stable ecosystem was the aim at that time (Figure 7.7).[39]

In a recent book, *From Bauhaus to Ecohouse*, Peder Anker has argued that McHarg's vision of landscape management was based "on cabin ecological research" and a "closed" system that owed much to prevailing ideas around space exploration at the time, together with ideas of "spaceship earth" that accorded with the growing environmental movement that had begun to consider matters such as overpopulation, alternative energy sources, and ultimately "seeing local initiatives in a global context." Anker argues further that McHarg only came to apply ecology to his approach after South African ecologist John Phillips's yearlong visit to Pennsylvania in 1966.[40] An admirer of Jan Smuts, Phillips brought Smuts's philosophy of "holism" to McHarg and his colleagues who were working in the field of landscape design. Apparently

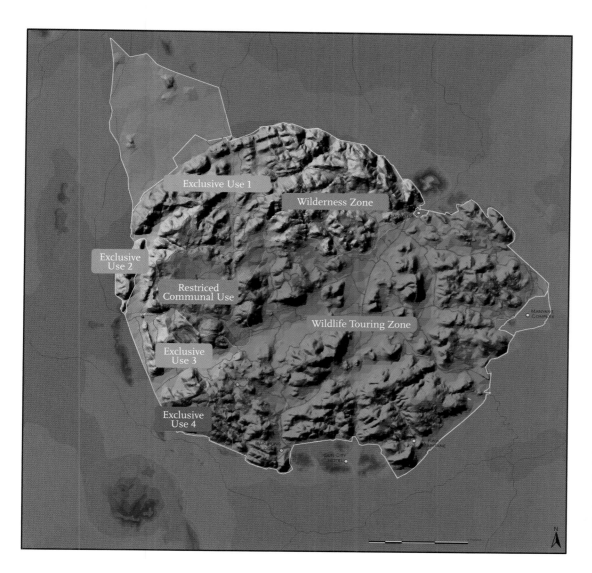

FIGURE 7.7
Pilanesberg
National Park
was innovative
because the area
was divided into
various zones for
particular uses.

Illustration by
Willem Boonzaaier.

"McHarg adopted Phillips as his chief mentor,"[41] although McHarg did not go along with Phillips's endorsement of "the South African government's design of the Bantustan landscape." Combining the intellectual elements—or as Phillips had expressed it, "I do not restrain ecology to a study of vegetation, I mean the *full* ecology . . . that of man, other animals and vegetation."[42] McHarg advocated a conceptual model for "landscape architecture on Earth." First, an ecosystem inventory should be made, its processes investigated and limiting factors identified. Thereafter, "values should be attributed to the ecological aspects of the landscape [and] permissible and prohibited changes should be determined."[43]

This template and this mode of thinking about planning methods resonate clearly in the Farrell & Van Riet and Tinley report.

In other path-breaking departures from the accepted management of national parks in which selected culling of certain species was done by wildlife managers, the report recommended that commercial (safari) trophy hunting be factored into the allowable activities in the Pilanesberg and also that environmental education be prioritized. In the section on "Management Proposals" (Chapter 5), the report lists the various species of mammals that should be introduced, and this was worked out on an agricultural model, bearing carrying capacity in mind (large bulk grazers, small bulk grazers, specialist feeders, etc.). No fewer than twenty-seven species were listed as appropriate, and optimum herd sizes were determined.

In short, the report designed a five-hundred-square-kilometer national park, literally from the bottom up. In this regard, the fact that its objectives were made so explicit at the outset had an influence on the eventual direction of protected area management in southern Africa, which now pays more attention to sustainable utilization and adaptive management within this objective than to preservation or to the conservation of biodiversity for its own sake.[44]

The First Five Years: 1978–1983

The Van Riet and Tinley master plan was compiled by scientific men—ecologists and landscape architects—not politicians and sociologists. In the opening chapter of their report, they made strong statements about the holistic philosophy of sustainable national parks and about the need to benefit local people by creating protected areas, but their primary tasks were to analyze and plan the future ecological management of the Pilanesberg. Unlike other national parks and protected areas in South Africa (which had involved forced removals), the idea on this occasion was that the Bakgatla would be willing participants in decisions about the new national park, would vacate the crater area voluntarily, and would contribute to its social and economic planning and design as well as to its management thereafter.

Early in 1979, the discussions between Van Riet and Tidimane Pilane, and in turn between Pilane and the other Bakgatla chiefs,[45] were successfully completed and the Bakgatla, through their kgosi, agreed to give up their grazing rights and rights to land in the crater.[46] They did so on the basis that they would be allocated two nearby state farms for communal grazing, and that they would be fully compensated for land and structures that were required by the national park. They would also be recompensed for the full costs of removal, and they would retain the right to enter the reserve in order to visit graves or to collect firewood, thatching material, and medicinal plants. In addition, they would

receive an (unspecified) portion of entry ticket sales and Tidimane Pilane would be a member of the national park's governing and management board of trustees, thus ensuring a Bakgatla voice in a form of joint management.[47] None of these details was secured in writing, and it subsequently emerged that Pilane, a political opponent, had been threatened by Mangope with eviction from other state land if he did not agree to the Pilanesberg National Park.[48] Moreover, in later years complaints surfaced that Pilane had not adequately consulted with the rest of the community before agreeing to these conditions.[49]

The Bakgatla were not the only people in the region, however. Inside the crater itself on the farm lived a long-standing community who owned part of the property in their own right; they too agreed to move, providing they were fully compensated, and this agreement was put into formal documentation. (On the basis of this evidence, the community has subsequently been awarded a land-restitution claim on this farm, and the land has been leased back to the Pilanesberg National Park.[50]) But it was impossible to consult every individual, and many were dissatisfied with the arrangements. To the south of the Pilanesberg, the farm Ledig was occupied by the Tswana-speaking Bakubung, part of a disunited group that had been forcibly removed from the outskirts of the small town of Boons where they formed a "black spot" within white South Africa and were therefore obliged to relocate in the late 1960s. There were also large numbers of Nguni speakers, many of whom had also been forced into this homeland from urban areas or white farms. As far as these people were concerned, "care was taken to ensure that all talk of the project was kept away from the Bakubung notables and strictly confined to official circles" and soon, without warning, there were reports of "a giant game fence snaking across the Pilanesberg" and excluding them and their livestock.[51] It seems evident from oral sources such as this (and later comments) that while negotiations and participation had occurred at top political levels, the views of ordinary people had not been solicited or taken into account, particularly those who were not part of the formal "tribal" structures of the district, and who perhaps would pay the heaviest price in terms of losing access to land.[52]

The establishment of the Pilanesberg National Park and its ambitious "Operation Genesis"—the mass reintroduction of many species of wildlife—received considerable local and international publicity, not all of it complimentary. Moreover, development did not proceed smoothly according to the grand plan. Agricor was responsible for the national park; many officials lacked experience and, for this and other reasons, they were either removed from their posts or encouraged to resign.[53] Competent personnel were sorely needed and in October 1980, Jeremy Anderson—whose doctoral research on nyala ecology in Zululand and subsequent study on lion management in the Umfolozi Game Reserve (Natal) had gained him a reputation as a competent and knowledgable wildlife manager—was recruited as director. Anderson had also studied wildlife management under Mossman in Zimbabwe and had been influenced by his innovative ideas on ecological productivity. According to his colleagues, Anderson—with his scientific expertise, energy, enthusiasm, and familiarity with Mossman's philosophy and the new scientific thinking emanating from East Africa (R. M. Laws and Hugh Lamprey)—was tailor-made for the job.[54] He was joined by Willem Boonzaaier as chief administrative officer, whose task it was to handle the financial side of the operation. They took care to appoint qualified and appropriate staff, including ecologists Roger Collinson and Peter Goodman in 1981.

Soon Sun City began to prove itself as a successful resort, to the extent that it was expanded in 1981 and again in 1984. Obviously, the Bophuthatswana elite in the Mangope government were extremely supportive of the Sun City development, as was the South African regime. But Tidimane Pilane was less enthusiastic. As a member of the opposition party espousing a different vision for Bophuthatswana, he was probably always going to disagree with government policy, but he also felt strongly that the local Bakgatla were not benefiting sufficiently from Sun City and saw employment going to those he believed to be outsiders to the district.[55] While laborers were also required by the budding national park, tourist revenue—which was to be shared with the Bakgatla—was minimal.

At the same time that local resentment began to simmer, the first introductions of wildlife into the Pilanesberg had also not been without serious hitches. Because some species were being given away freely by South African conservation bodies that had problems of overstocking, while others were very expensive to acquire, the Pilanesberg became stocked with an incorrect balance of wild animals and some habitats were overgrazed.[56] At times it was difficult to obtain the correct species because South Africa has strict controls on moving wildlife from areas in which cattle diseases (e.g., anthrax, foot-and-mouth) are endemic, so animals had to be sourced from disease-free populations a long distance away such as Namibia or the Eastern Cape (buffalo, for example, came from the Addo Elephant National Park), and transport was thus extremely costly. Because adult elephant males can be dangerous during the capture and transport process, fewer of them were translocated in comparison with females and young, and thus subsequent breeding success was low and herd sizes and composition were skewed. The mixing of gene pools was also a matter of scientific concern. Some introductions were made before the fencing was complete and animals were kept in a holding camp that was too small; once the grazing inside it was depleted, many of them died (Figure 7.8).[57]

Writer Michael Brett gives an indication of the far-flung origins of the animals that were moved into the Pilanesberg: black-and-white rhinoceroses and hippopotamuses came from Zululand; many zebras, gemsbok, hartebeest, eland, and giraffes were sourced from Namibia; sable antelope, waterbuck, wildebeest, springbok, impala, and kudu were translocated from the Transvaal and from state land in Bophuthatswana. The elephants and buffalo came from the Addo Elephant National Park and, interestingly, among them were two nineteen-year-old elephants that were repatriated Kruger National Park individuals from the United States. (They had been circus elephants there and television stars in Kenya before finally making their way back into the wild in 1982, at considerable—some said "wasted"—expense.[58])

Other translocations brought other problems. For example, cheetahs were introduced and they flourished, but later had to be removed because they were feasting on too many calves of the rarer species like waterbuck and tsessebe.[59] Moreover, only

one of the eight elephants introduced from Addo in 1979 survived; another escaped through the fence and killed a farmer in nearby Brits, which brought adverse publicity. In 1981, eighteen young elephants were translocated after a culling program from the Kruger National Park; two years later, another twenty-four youngsters arrived.[60]

The Bophuthatswana government did not have the funding to pay for these very costly introductions of large mammals. There was, however, an organization that was prepared to foot the bill: the South African Wildlife Foundation (SAWF), founded in 1968. SAWF had come into being as a branch of the World Wildlife Fund (WWF), but was distinct from WWF in restricting membership to companies and corporations, not allowing individual members. SAWF been founded by Afrikaner business magnate Anton Rupert, who was a trustee of South Africa's National Parks Board and who had close ties with the National Party. According to a sympathetic biography of Rupert, in the 1970s SAWF funded Mlilwane nature reserve near Mbabane in Swaziland, the Sehlabathebe reserve in Lesotho, and an ichthyology project in Malawi, as well as several other

projects in South Africa. Given Rupert's personal belief in cultural and linguistic ethnicity, assistance to the "nation" of Bophuthatswana through SAWF was entirely in character. Indeed, Bophuthatswana may have held special significance for the Rupert family, for his wife, Huberte (née Goote), came from the western Transvaal and spent some years at Derdepoort (presently in the Madikwe Game Reserve), near the Botswana border.[61]

Those involved in the early years of the establishment of the Pilanesberg emphasize the difficulties they had to overcome. There was no existing institutional policy framework—either scientific or bureaucratic—within which to operate. Although there was some grassland restoration (for example in places where farmhouses had been located), the general policy was to allow the veld to recover at its own pace.[62] Given the small number of rangers and laborers, the process of restoring a natural environment was extremely slow. Anderson recalled that in terms of basic infrastructure, the perimeter fence had to be constructed to keep the wildlife within the park, but that inside that fence, off-loading ramps, translocation stations, bomas, feedlots, and pens

FIGURE 7.9
Bulldozers were active in the Pilanesberg National Park for many months, as buildings, alien vegetation, and other indications of human settlement and habitation were removed.

Photograph by Willem Boonzaaier.

had to be built for the introduced animals, which then had to be monitored after they were released. More than one thousand kilometers of internal farm fencing had to be removed, as did the many solid concrete cattle dips, farm reservoirs, and windmills, about thirty large farmhouses, and more than one hundred smaller houses, outbuildings, and huts. Borrow pits, landscape scars, and old lands had to be rehabilitated and general farming detritus (e.g., old vehicles and heavy, rusted implements) cleared. Invasive alien plants were abundant, not only jointed cactus (*Opuntia* spp.), but huge old trees, especially Australian eucalypts; all of them had to go (Figure 7.9).

There was debate over the fate of the 1936 magistrate's court situated in the center of the Pilanesberg and thus contrary to the peripheral plan. First it was used as office and storage space, and in the end it was agreed that it would not be demolished but would become an information and recreational center, despite it being in a central position. At the start there was no accommodation for game guards, management staff, stores, or offices. Prefabricated buildings were erected to meet some of these needs, but for a few years all management personnel and their families lived in caravans. Workshops and vehicle maintenance points were also needed. The construction of permanent buildings, game-viewing hides, and visitor amenities such as camps and

entrance gates proceeded slowly—as did replanning of roads to make them suitable for game drives (old straight farm roads had to be obliterated). Local staff were unskilled and thus training, education, and mentorship were needed. At this time there was no regular telephone communication in the park and only radio phones could be used—a scarce and expensive resource (Figures 7.10–7.11).[63]

Veld and wildlife monitoring systems had to be established from scratch, and these had to proceed hand in hand with applied management tools such as a burning regime and game capture and release. Jules Turnbull-Kemp—a senior game ranger recruited by Agricor from Rhodesia who later became warden of the Pilanesberg—was put in charge of the southern part of the national park and was responsible for receiving the wildlife introductions. At the time there were no formal studies concerning the ability of different species to survive or thrive on old farmlands, and only by observation and experience did it emerge how animal populations coped with, and altered with, the recovery and restoration of the habitat. For example, red hartebeest did well initially on old cultivated lands, but their numbers plummeted once nutrients had been exhausted.[64]

Fire policy also had to be determined from scratch because large-scale models (such as the Kruger National Park) could not be applied to a small area like the Pilanesberg. An innovation in

FIGURE 7.10
The magistrate's court in the Pilanesberg, ca. 1936.

Photograph by Michael Brett.

FIGURE 7.11
Restoration work
around the old
magistrate's court
to be utilized as an
information center
and restaurant.

Photograph by
Willem Boonzaaier.

terms of management philosophy was that stocking was done at a high rate (i.e., many animals at
one time) so that the takeoff rate (reducing numbers through hunting) was optimized as soon as
possible.[65] Not surprisingly—given the dearth of
wildlife and the abundant, unsightly evidence of
former fields, houses, and roads in the crater—
tourism did not take off quickly. Anderson, who
doubted that gate revenues from day visitors were
likely to produce any substantial income,[66] took
the decision to introduce trophy hunting to generate some immediate revenue.

Management ideas did not emanate from park
personnel alone, and the tourist industry was able
to put pressure on Bophuthatswana's president
Mangope, sometimes to the benefit of the park. For
example, in the early 1980s Sol Kerzner complained
that Sun City's tourists were not seeing enough
game in the Pilanesberg. Mangope therefore

instructed Pilanesberg's management to increase
the stocking rates so that no tourist would be dis-
appointed. Anderson had to inform the president
that the park was already stocked to carrying capacity and that the problem would be solved if funding
to expand the network of roads was made available
so that tourists could access more of the area of the
park. Money was quickly allocated.[67]

The initial master plan had identified a critical area of concern to the Pilanesberg management: environmental education. The Gold Fields
Foundation (a South African mining house) funded
the educational center's buildings, and the program
offered by Pilanesberg under Peter Hancock eventually became renowned for its success and dynamism. Many thousands of black schoolchildren
were brought by the busload to the center named
"Goldfields" in Bosele Camp in order to benefit
from the programs that were subsidized by the government of Bophuthatswana.[68] In the first decade,
some ten thousand local schoolchildren attended
environmental education classes. Adults were also
welcomed and special projects were established for
this more advanced level of student.[69]

Because the Pilanesberg National Park was an
Agricor initiative, and was the only project of this
nature in its stable, the administrative and financial arrangements were as independent as—and
could be as experimental as—those of the wildlife
management. As administrative officer, Boonzaaier
adapted commercial systems to the national park's
requirements, and much of what he introduced still
operates satisfactorily today. There was no model to
follow: the park had to be up and running as quickly
as possible, and as profitably as possible. The first
question was: Where was an initial income to come
from? In this regard, wildlife management and
administration were able to dovetail. Anderson's
idea of revenue-producing trophy hunting could
only take place if there were surplus animals to
shoot. To determine the optimum stocking rate
that would be needed to manipulate species numbers for the best returns, Anderson, Collinson, and

Boonzaaier designed a complex model to determine how many (and which) species were required so as to profit most from game sales, hunting, meat production, or tourist viewing. Wildlife populations were therefore predicated on formulas that demonstrated the best return on investment per land unit. The Pilanesberg's management was innovative because instead of a few wild animals of various species being introduced and then allowed slowly to build up their numbers, large populations were introduced at the start and thus numbers increased very quickly, providing a surplus after only a year or two in the case of some species. Very careful records were maintained of net production versus utilization. What was novel about these calculations was that they were being done for the first time in a protected area: wildlife was being taken into account as a financial asset, not merely a "nature conservation" ethical good. Just as cattle and game farmers entered their herds into their accounting books and measured the profit from them, so too did this national park.[70]

All this, however, took time to consolidate. To compound the birth pains of the Pilanesberg National Park, the 1980s saw one of the subcontinent's worst droughts of the century. This meant that the rehabilitation and restoration of the Pilanesberg grasslands and vegetation took far longer than anticipated; it also meant that the displaced Bakgatla and others were short of grazing on the farms to which they had been relocated, and many looked longingly at the recovering (albeit slowly) veld in the Pilanesberg that had been free of grazing cattle for a few years.[71] During the drought, mobile Pilanesberg animals wrought havoc on properties outside the reserve, baboons in particular climbing over the perimeter fences and ravaging the maize fields of neighboring Africans in Ledig and elsewhere (Figure 7.12).[72]

The Plan Revised: 1983–1984

By 1983, circumstances had changed so substantially that the enterprise required revised planning on the basis of a comprehensive overview.[73]

Designing a Wilderness for Wildlife

On this occasion, Ken Tinley was not involved, and the new report, "A Five Year Development Plan for Pilanesberg National Park as Requested by the Bophuthatswana Government and the Bophuthatswana National Parks Board, September 1983," was authored by Willem Boonzaaier, Roger Collinson, and Willem van Riet. The report began with a warning. Because the construction of tourist facilities within the national park had been so slow, there was a real danger that the investment of the previous five years in management, rehabilitation, and wildlife introductions might be wasted. Clear objectives needed to be established. The report aimed to set these firmer goals and to outline them against a background of the rational attitude of the International Union for Conservation of Nature World Conservation Strategy of 1980 and in the context of a developing country in which meeting basic needs was the most difficult challenge. The primary objective was to "maintain and where necessary create an ecosystem comprising a biota of as wide a variety of indigenous plant and animal species" as possible. The secondary objective was defined as "to utilize the area and its natural resources in ways that will yield the greatest benefits to Bophuthatswana and its people, both now and in the future."[74]

The zoning of the park was also altered. It was recommended that there be two types of areas, a "managed natural area" and a "natural environment recreation area," each subdivided into zones. Within a "managed natural area" (i.e., well within the park's boundaries), accommodation would be limited in numbers and cater to very small groups (around twelve to fifteen), and the only permissible activities would be walking trails and trophy hunting. The "natural environment recreation area" would be devoted to general visitor and multiple uses, and there would be peripheral development of restaurants, shops, lodges, bungalows, campsites, swimming pools, and other amenities at Manyane, Bakubung, and Bakgatla gates. All these plans would, however, be extremely expensive and the Pilanesberg would probably run at a loss while development was done in various phases.[75]

In 1984, the year after the report was submitted, the organizational structure of the Pilanesberg changed with the creation of a National Parks and Wildlife Management Board for Bophuthatswana along the lines of a parastatal. This new structure (which was formalized in 1987 with the National Parks Act No. 24) came about as the result of a merger between the Division of Nature Conservation of the Department of Agriculture and Forestry and Agricor, thus ending their somewhat competitive and even acrimonious relationship. The change in structure may also have been related to the fact that Bophuthatswana was economically stressed and, in fact, had "an acute financial crisis"[76] around this time. Fundamental to the escalating political dissension was the growing impossibility of maneuvering between the policies of the ANC dissidents in Bophuthatswana, including Tidimane Pilane, and the ideal of an ethnic Tswana nation in an artificially segregated South Africa.[77]

The new national parks organization was to be managed overall by a board, but importantly, the new appointees to this body did not include kgosi Tidimane Pilane.[78] This marginalized the Bakgatla, although it was they who had vacated the land in order that the park might be established. Together with the fact that no monetary compensation was accumulating for the Bakgatla, which is what they had been promised (this has subsequently been addressed), and because there were few visitors and thus little by way of gate fees, relations between the national park and the neighboring communities worsened. Perhaps the promises of beneficiation had been overgenerous at the start, and certainly the administrative beginnings had not been auspicious. The Bophuthatswana government had apparently reneged on agreements about land and financial compensation. Goodwill evaporated in consequence. Magome and Collinson believe that the breakdown in communication owed much to the heavy demand for very rapid development and effective wildlife and administrative management, which meant that reserve authorities had little time to devote to community relationships.[79]

The year 1984 was significant not only for the establishment of the National Parks Board but also because a sociologist, Jeremy Keenan from the University of the Witwatersrand,[80] was appointed to report on community relations in the same way in which Boonzaaier, Collinson, and Van Riet had done with respect to ecological and tourist issues. At the request of Roger Collinson and Jeremy Anderson, for the first time in the history of wildlife management and nature conservation certainly in Africa, and possibly in the world, Keenan and his researchers conducted a detailed survey of the neighbors of the Pilanesberg.[81] They detected seriously negative perceptions of the national park. There was discontent over the initial verbal arrangements regarding the evacuation of the crater and inadequate financial and property compensation. Cattle rustling took place during the removals and there was theft of property. Many local people, it seems, took the opportunity to complain to Keenan not only about the national park but also about the many unsatisfactory aspects of their lives. The survey gave them a chance to have their voices heard. The Bakgatla resented the structures of governance, which they perceived as "dictatorial and deceitful," and they alleged that farms intended for compensation had been given away to government ministers and Mangope cronies. They had decided that they wanted to take back their land, and to this end had begun a court action (although this did not eventuate).[82] The fact that Tidimane Pilane had political aspirations of his own and was a leading figure in opposition politics exacerbated the situation further. People involved at the time were aware that the Pilanesberg was used to score political points in these oppositional politics at a time of tension in South Africa, dividing even Bophuthatswana Parks Board staff members.[83]

But despite the grievances and the misunderstandings that were reflected about the function of a national park, the Keenan Report also indicated that there was some local support for the national park and for its educational outreach program in particular.[84] Because the report was leaked to the media by Keenan himself (whose anti-Bophuthatswana views were made explicit), it attracted a great deal of attention, and the managers of the Pilanesberg were caught in the middle of the fracas between the government and the Bakgatla.[85]

Conclusion

Since 1994, there have been many alterations to the management philosophy, objectives, and style in the Pilanesberg and other game reserves in what is now North West Province. With the change in government, the priority of urban and rural development, service provision, and capacity building has dominated South Africa's economic and political thinking—with effects on biodiversity conservation. It is instructive to reflect on how the creation of the Pilanesberg National Park and its management during its early years pioneered a number of significant changes in South African natural resource management and conservation. These innovations include peripheral development, the consumptive use of wildlife in protected areas, the provision of a variety of accommodation, community engagement, reclamation of farmland, translocation of wildlife, trained African senior personnel, environmental education, and a commercialization and concession policy. South African National Parks and other provincial protected-area authorities have followed in many of its footsteps, particularly in the training and development of capable black staff, outsourcing of facilities, trophy hunting, the need to cater for the luxury market, private-public partnerships, local community participation, and professional managerial expertise. Because the Pilanesberg was so successful in many respects, other game reserves in the Bophuthatswana area followed its design, and the idea of using wildlife and ecotourism as drivers of rural development became uncontroversial.[86] In the North West Province today, tourism is a priority and wildlife is used to meet that need. Many management decisions are taken with tourism and income generation (through game sales) rather than with biodiversity conservation in mind.

This essay has argued that national park and wildlife management is not static. In this regard, what was an artificial "nation" created at the height of apartheid unexpectedly played a leading role in designing an economically viable game reserve from degraded farmland, and this has provided an example that has been widely followed in the region. Together with a changing paradigm toward adaptive ecological management that was a later introduction, the Pilanesberg has become a model that has informed—and some would argue that it has even transformed—protected-area management in southern Africa.

Acknowledgments

I am most grateful to John Beardsley for the invitation to participate in "Designing Wildlife Habitats," the symposium that was organized by Garden and Landscape Studies and held at Dumbarton Oaks in May 2010. It was a great pleasure to have been included in this stimulating meeting, and I would like to thank everyone associated both with it and with the subsequent publication of the papers that were presented there. I would also like to thank the following individuals for their generous assistance in providing inspiration, guidance, information, documentation, discussion, and for correcting factual and editorial errors: Jeremy Anderson, Willem Boonzaaier, Bruce Brockett, Vincent Carruthers, Roger Collinson, Brian Huntley, Cynthia Kemp, Hector Magome, Bernard Mbenga, Eugene Moll, Archie S. Mossman, Sue Mossman, Norman Owen-Smith, Alexis Schwarzenbach, Ken Tinley, Jules Turnbull-Kemp, Rudi van Aarde, Willem van Riet, and Brian Walker. I am indebted for photographs to Willem Boonzaaier, Michael Brett, Bruce Brockett, and Vincent Carruthers. Financial support from the University of South Africa and the National Research Foundation is gratefully acknowledged.

Notes

1 The term has been introduced into the lexicon of the social sciences through publications such as Dan Brockington, *Fortress Conservation: The Preservation of the Mkomazi Game Reserve, Tanzania* (Oxford: International African Institute; Bloomington: Indiana University Press, 2002).

2 The name means "Pilane's Mountain" [*"berg"* means "mountain" in both Afrikaans and Dutch]. This is sometimes rendered as "Pilansberg," "Pilandsberg," or "Pilands Berg."

3 John A. Livingston, *The Fallacy of Wildlife Conservation* (Toronto: McClelland and Stewart, 1981); and Alistair D. Graham, *The Gardeners of Eden* (London: Allen and Unwin, 1973).

4 Jonathan S. Adams and Thomas O. McShane, *The Myth of Wild Africa: Conservation without Illusion* (Berkeley: University of California Press, 1996), 102–5.

5 Lester Charles King, *South African Scenery*, 2nd ed. (Edinburgh: Oliver and Boyd, 1951), 275–76. Mucina and Rutherford summarize its geohistory as "subsequent fracturing, emplacement of intrusions, collapse and resurgence of magma and radial emplacement of dykes." Ladislav Mucina and Michael C. Rutherford, eds., *The Vegetation of South Africa, Lesotho and Swaziland*, Strelitzia 19 (Pretoria: South African National Biodiversity Institute, 2006), 463. See also Michael R. Brett, *The Pilanesberg: Jewel of Bophuthatswana* (Sandton, South Africa: Frandsen, 1989), 98–103; Terence McCarthy and Bruce Rubidge, *The Story of Earth and Life* (Cape Town: Struik, 2005), 144; and Farrell &

Van Riet Landscape Architects and Ecological Planners and K. L. Tinley, "Pilanesberg National Park, Bophuthatswana: Planning and Management Proposals for Department of Agriculture, Republic of Bophuthatswana, August 1978" (unpublished report, Pretoria, 1978), 16.

6 Thomas Baines, *The Northern Goldfields Diaries of Thomas Baines*, ed. J. P. R. Wallis (London: Chatto and Windus, 1946), 1:30.

7 Mucina and Rutherford, *Vegetation of South Africa, Lesotho and Swaziland*, 462–63; and Farrell & Van Riet and Tinley, "Pilanesberg National Park, Bophuthatswana," 13.

8 Farrell & Van Riet and Tinley, "Pilanesberg National Park, Bophuthatswana," 17.

9 Ibid., 47.

10 This community can also be referred to as the "Kgafela-Kgatla," "Bakgatla-baga-Kgafela," or "Bakgatla-ba-ga-Kgafela," the meaning of which is the "Kgatla people of Kafela" in various forms of the Tswana language. Kgafela was the chief who originally gave his name to the "tribe." The current head of the clan is Kgosi Kgafela II, who resides in Mochudi, Botswana, while Kgosi Nyalala Pilane leads the group at Saulspoort. The tribal totem is the monkey.

11 For Bakgatla history and details of the history of this region, see Bernard Mbenga and Andrew Manson, "The Evolution and Destruction of Oorlam Communities in the Rustenburg District of South Africa: The Cases of Welgeval and Bethlehem, 1850s–1980," *African Historical Review* 41,

no. 2 (2009): 85–115; P. L. Breutz, *The Tribes of Rustenburg and Pilansberg Districts*, Ethnological Publications 28 (Pretoria: Government Printer, 1953), 246; Bernard K. Mbenga, "The Bakgatla-baga-Kgafela in the Pilanesberg District of the Western Transvaal from 1899 to 1931" (DLitt et Phil thesis, University of South Africa, 1996); Isaac Schapera, *The Tswana* (London: International African Institute, 1953); Bernard Mbenga and Fred Morton, "The Missionary as Land Broker: Henri Gonin, Saulspoort 269 and the Bakgatla of Rustenburg District, 1862–1922," *South African Historical Journal* 36, no. 1 (May 1997): 145–67; Fred Morton, "Slave-Raiding and Slavery in the Western Transvaal after the Sand River Convention," *African Economic History* 20 (1992): 99–118; Bernard K. Mbenga, "Forced Labour in the Pilanesberg: The Flogging of Chief Kgamanyane by Commandant Paul Kruger, Saulspoort, April 1870," *Journal of Southern African Studies* 23, no. 1 (1997): 127–40; C. John Makgala, *History of the Bakgatla-baga-Kgafela in Botswana and South Africa* (Pretoria: 2009); and Fred Morton, "Land, Cattle, and Ethnicity: Creating Linchwe's BaKgatla, 1875–1920," *South African Historical Journal* 33, no. 1 (November 1995): 131–54.

12   Peris Sean Jones, "'To Come Together for Progress': Modernization and Nation-Building in South Africa's Bantustan Periphery—The Case of Bophuthatswana," *Journal of Southern African Studies* 25, no. 4 (December 1999): 586; and Jeffrey Butler, Robert I. Rotberg, and John Adams, *The Black Homelands of South Africa: The Political and Economic Development of Bophuthatswana and KwaZulu* (Berkeley: University of California Press, 1977): 33, 74–78, 88–90.

13   The apartheid grand plan was that there would be separate "nations" for the Ndebele-, Pedi-, Sotho-, Venda-, Xhosa-, and Zulu-speaking peoples. Each of these ethnic groups became self-governing, and Transkei and Bophuthatswana became "independent" in 1976, with Venda following in 1979 and the Ciskei in 1981.

14   Michael Lawrence and Andrew Manson, "The 'Dog of the Boers': The Rise and Fall of Mangope in Bophuthatswana," *Journal of Southern African Studies* 20, no. 3 (September 1994): 447–61.

15   J. H. Drummond, "Rural Land Use and Agricultural Production in Dinokana Village, Bophuthatswana," *GeoJournal* 22, no. 3 (1990): 337.

16   Jane Carruthers, "'Wilding the Farm or Farming the Wild': The Evolution of Scientific Game Ranching in South Africa from the 1960s to the Present," *Transactions of the Royal Society of South Africa* 63, no. 2 (2008): 160–81.

17   See, for example, S. K. Eltringham, *Wildlife Resources and Economic Development* (Chichester and New York: Wiley, 1984); and Aldo Leopold, *Game Management* (Madison: University of Wisconsin Press, 1986).

18   Mossman attended classes given by Aldo Leopold (personal communication, November 2009); see also

S. R. Johnson, W. Boonzaaier, R. Collinson, and R. Davies, "Changing Institutions to Respond to Challenges: North West Parks, South Africa," in *Evolution and Innovation in Wildlife Conservation: Parks and Game Ranches in Transfrontier Conservation Areas*, ed. Helen Suich, Brian Child, and Anna Spenceley (London and Sterling, Va.: Earthscan, 2009); Sue Lee Mossman and Archie S. Mossman, *Wildlife Utilization and Game Ranching: Report on a Study of Recent Progress in this Field in Southern Africa* (Morges, Switz.: National Union for Conservation of Nature and Natural Resources, 1976); Raymond Fredric Dasmann, *Environmental Conservation* (New York: Wiley, 1959); Raymond Fredric Dasmann and Archie S. Mossman, "Commercial Use of Game Animals on a Rhodesian Ranch," *Wild Life* 3, no. 3 (1961): 7–14; Raymond Fredric Dasmann and Archie S. Mossman, "The Economic Value of Rhodesian Game," *Rhodesian Farmer* 30, no. 51 (1960): 17–20; and Raymond Fredric Dasmann, *African Game Ranching* (Oxford and New York: Macmillan, 1964).

19   Archie S. Mossman, personal communication, November 2009.

20   As McHarg explains: "In 1959 the environment was not a topic, there was no lobby, there were no persons identified as environmentalists. There were conservationalists [sic], although very few, ecologists were fewer still. Those precious few who would give intellectual leadership to the environmental movement were intent on learning of the operation of natural systems. Tending to exclude man as a source of destruction and pollution. . . ." See Ian L. McHarg, *A Quest for Life: An Autobiography* (New York: Wiley, 1996): 158.

21   For example, provincial protected areas included the Royal Natal National Park and Umfolozi and Hluhluwe Game Reserves, while the National Parks Board managed Kruger National Park, Kalahari Gemsbok National Park, Mountain Zebra National Park, and a number of other small national parks.

22   Brett, *Pilanesberg*, 111–12; Johnson, Boonzaaier, Collinson, and Davies, "Changing Institutions to Respond to Challenges," 290; D. T. (Hector) Magome and Roger F. H. Collinson, "From Protest to Pride: A Case Study of Pilanesberg National Park, South Africa," The World Bank/WBI's CBNRM Initiative, accessed July 16, 2007, http://srdis.ciesin.org/cases/south_africa-0003.html.

23   According to Willem Boonzaaier (personal communication, March 2010), David Beuster and Willem van Riet persuaded Sol Kerzner to change the position of the hotel site.

24   *Bophuthatswana at Independence* (Pretoria: Bureau for Economic Research re Bantu Development [Benbo], 1978), 99.

25   Joane Pim, *Beauty Is Necessary: Creation or Preservation of the Landscape* (Cape Town: Purnell, 1971).

26   Pim, *Beauty Is Necessary*, 28. McHarg's autobiography mentions visiting South Africa, but he does not elaborate on the people or places he encountered. See McHarg, *A Quest for Life*, 299.

27 In *A Quest for Life*, McHarg describes landscape architecture as emerging quickly, almost fully formed, as a discipline thanks to the early efforts of Frederick Law Olmsted and later of Thomas Church and Roberto Burle Marx (among others). McHarg also emphasizes his initial intention to improve the quality of students in landscape architecture by recruiting trained architects (such as Van Riet) into the postgraduate program and by providing generous financial grants. See *A Quest for Life*, 123–34.

28 Ian L. McHarg, "Human Ecological Planning at Pennsylvania," *Landscape Planning* 8, no. 2 (June 1981): 109–20.

29 Ian L. McHarg, *Design with Nature* (Garden City, N.Y.: American Museum of Natural History, 1971). It may be postulated that the Pilanesberg owes something to "Pardisan" (planned between 1973 and 1979), which was a response to the vision of the Stockholm World Conference on the Human Environment. At "Pardisan," McHarg and his colleagues aimed to create a landscape that epitomized sustainable adaption and provided examples of the world's major ecosystems. When the Shah of Iran was overthrown, the project collapsed. See R. Terry Schnadelbach, "Ian McHarg," in *Fifty Key Thinkers on the Environment*, ed. Joy A. Palmer (London and New York: Routledge, 2001): 228–41. Schnadelbach describes the project as an "ecological theme park, a model not too dissimilar to Disneyworld." This description certainly resonates with the link between Sun City and the Pilanesberg. See also McHarg, *A Quest for Life*, 290–96.

30 After 1994, the name of the organization changed from the National Parks Board of Trustees to South African National Parks, or SANParks.

31 Brian Huntley, personal communication, March 22, 2010. McHarg explains that the genesis of his book lay in a meeting between McHarg, Russell Train (president of the Conservation Foundation) and the foundation's chief scientist, the noted ecologist Ray Dasmann. Apparently Train said, "Ian, Ray and I have decided that the time has come for a book on ecology and planning," and McHarg agreed to write it. See McHarg, *A Quest for Life*, 199–200. In his autobiography, McHarg mentions visiting South Africa but does not give further details.

32 For example, Brian Walker, Norman Owen-Smith, Jeremy Anderson, Brian Huntley, and Anthony Hall-Martin. At the time, the South African national park bureaucracy was dominated by Afrikaners.

33 Eugene Moll, personal communication, February 2010. See also Jane Carruthers, "Influences on Wildlife Management and Conservation Biology in South Africa c. 1900 to c. 1940," *South African Historical Journal* 58 (2007): 65–90; Jane Carruthers, "Conservation and Wildlife Management in South African National Parks 1930s–1960s," *Journal of the History of Biology* 41, no. 2 (2008): 203–36; and Peder Anker, *Imperial Ecology: Environmental Order in the British Empire, 1895–1945* (Cambridge, Mass.: Harvard University Press, 2001).

34 Huntley, personal communication, March 22, 2010.

35 Farrell & Van Riet Landscape Architects and Ecological Planners, "Planning and Management Proposals for the Dwesa Forest Reserve, Transkei; Prepared for the Department of Forestry and Nature Conservation, Umtata, South Africa, 1975" (unpublished report, 1975), 1–29; and K. L. Tinley, "Mkambati Nature Reserve: An Ecological and Planning Study" (unpublished report, 1978). Around this time Van Riet also laid out the trails at the Victoria Falls. Jules Turnbull-Kemp, personal communication, March 1, 2010. Van Riet recalls that he and Tinley did the planning for the three parks in Pondoland (for the old Transkei) as well as compiling a study for Maputaland (Willem van Riet, personal communication, March 26, 2010).

36 Ann MacEwen and Malcolm McEwen, *National Parks: Conservation or Cosmetics?* (London: Allen and Unwin, 1982), 68–69.

37 Brian Child, "Recent Innovations in Conservation," in Suich, Child, and Spenceley, *Evolution and Innovation in Wildlife Conservation*, 277–87.

38 Trails zone, hunting zone, general visitor zone, multiple use zone, and peripheral development zone.

39 For a full discussion on the evolution of wildlife and protected area management in South Africa's national parks, see Carruthers, "Influences on Wildlife Management," 65–90; and Carruthers, "Conservation and Wildlife Management," 203–36.

40 Peder Anker, *From Bauhaus to Ecohouse: A History of Ecological Design* (Baton Rouge: Louisiana State University Press, 2010), 104–6.

41 In his autobiography, McHarg referred to Phillips as "the legendary South African ecologist" who contributed "scientific insights to the enterprise." See McHarg, *A Quest for Life*, 331–32.

42 Phillips quoted in Anker, *Imperial Ecology*, 130.

43 Anker, *From Bauhaus to Ecohouse*, 101–8.

44 Child, "Recent Innovations in Conservation," 277–87.

45 J. Keenan, "Report on the Socio-Economic Effects of the Pilanesberg Game Reserve on the Surrounding Population and the Attitudes of the Surrounding Population to the Game Reserve, University of the Witwatersrand, on Behalf of the Pilanesberg Game Reserve, South Africa, 1984" (unpublished report), 14–15. The final version of this report is not available in any library, and I am grateful to Professor Bernard Mbenga for photocopying the draft version of the report in his possession.

46 This consisted of freehold land of eighty-five square kilometers, obtained directly from the Bakgatla: Schaapkraal, Welgeval, and portions of Legkraal, Koedoesfontein, Kruidfontein, Saulsport, Rooderand, and Doornpoort. Some

forty-five square kilometers came from the Bakubung, namely Wydhoek and portions of Ledig and Koedoesfontein. In addition, ten square kilometers were obtained from private owners and the remaining 460 square kilometers was state land that had been purchased from whites by the Department of Bantu Affairs as mentioned previously. See Keenan, "Report on the Socio-Economic Effects of the Pilanesberg Game Reserve," 14.

47 Makgala, *History of the Bakgatla-baga-Kgafela*, 319–22; and Magome and Collinson, "From Protest to Pride."

48 Keenan, "Report on the Socio-Economic Effects of the Pilanesberg Game Reserve," 16–17.

49 Makgala, *History of the Bakgatla-baga-Kgafela*, 330–35, states that Tidimane was an unpopular chief.

50 Mbenga and Manson, "Evolution and Destruction of Oorlam Communities," 97.

51 Charles van Onselen, *The Seed Is Mine: The Life of Kas Maine, a South African Sharecropper 1894–1985* (New York: Hill and Wang, 1996), 470–510.

52 Keenen, "Report on the Socio-Economic Effects of the Pilanesberg Game Reserve," 39–43.

53 Brett, *Pilanesberg*, 112.

54 Willem Boonzaaier, personal communication, March 1, 2010.

55 Makgala, *History of the Bakgatla-baga-Kgafela*, 322–23. See also Truth and Reconciliation Commission, Human Rights Violations, Submissions Questions and Answers, Case JB3606, May 7, 1997, which relates to the testimony of Catholic bishop Kevin Dowling.

56 Rudi Van Aarde, personal communication, March 11, 2010.

57 R. F. Collinson and J. L. Anderson, "Problems, Principles, and Policy in the Reintroduction of Large Mammals in Conservation Areas," *Acta Zoologica Fennica* 172 (1984): 169–70.

58 Brett, *Pilanesberg*, 115–16. The story goes that in 1966 elephants named Durga and Owalla had been translocated from the Kruger National Park to the United States, where they performed in a circus for five years. They were then taken to Kenya in order to star in a television film, but after five months of filming they were deported. Sun International (the hotel group) offered to pay for them to be translocated to the Pilanesberg, but after a sea voyage from Kenya they were not allowed to land in Durban because of quarantine regulations. The elephants therefore had to return to the United States, where they were kept in quarantine, after which they were finally allowed to enter South Africa.

59 Turnbull-Kemp, personal communication, March 1, 2010. See also J. L. Anderson, "Restoring a Wilderness: The Reintroduction of Wildlife to an African National Park," *International Zoological Yearbook* 24/25 (1986): 192–99.

60 Again in 1992 and 1993, a further fifty-seven young elephants were introduced from the Kruger National Park, and six large bulls in 1998. See Marion E. Garaï, Rob Slotow, Robert D. Carr, and Brian Reilly, "Elephant Reintroductions to Small Fenced Reserves in South Africa," *Pachyderm* 37 (2004): 28–36.

61 Ebbe Dommisse, *Anton Rupert: A Biography* (Cape Town: Tafelberg, 2005), 353; see E. J. Carruthers, *Game Protection in the Transvaal 1846 to 1926* (Pretoria: Government Printer, 1995), 146–54. After 1986, when WWF became the World Wide Fund for Nature, SAWF changed its name to the South African Nature Foundation. In 1979, Rupert presented the Pilanesberg as a project to WWF International and the International Union for Conservation of Nature and received approval to fund it. I am grateful to Alexis Schwarzenbach, author of a commemorative history of the World Wide Fund for Nature (as yet unpublished), for this information.

62 Turnbull-Kemp, personal communication, March 1, 2010.

63 Jeremy Anderson, personal communication, February 23, 2010. I am extremely grateful to Dr. Anderson for his detailed comments on an early draft of this paper.

64 Turnbull-Kemp, personal communication, March 1, 2010.

65 Jules Turnbull-Kemp and Willem Boonzaaier, personal communication, March 1, 2010.

66 Boonzaaier, personal communication, March 1, 2010.

67 Anderson, personal communication, February 23, 2010.

68 W. V. Boonzaaier, R. F. H. Collinson, and W. F. Van Riet, "A Five Year Development Plan for Pilanesberg National Park as Requested by the Bophuthatswana Government and the Bophuthatswana National Parks Board, September 1983" (unpublished report, 1983).

69 Magome and Collinson, "From Protest to Pride"; and Makgala, *History of the Bakgatla-baga-Kgafela*, 322.

70 I am very grateful to Willem Boonzaaier for the detailed explanation of this innovative model.

71 Mbenga and Manson, "Evolution and Destruction of Oorlam Communities," 96.

72 Van Onselen, *The Seed Is Mine*, 510.

73 R. F. H. Collinson and P. S. Goodman, "An Assessment of Range Condition and Large Herbivore Carrying Capacity of the Pilanesberg Game Reserve, with Guidelines and Recommendations for Management," *Inkwe* 1 (1982): 1–55.

74 Boonzaaier, Collinson, and Van Riet, "Five Year Development Plan for Pilanesberg National Park," 4–5.

75 Ibid., 7–11.

76   Jones, "'To Come Together for Progress,'" 603; Peris Seab Jones, in "The Etiquette of State-Building and Modernization in Dependent States: Performing Stateness and the Normalization of Separate Development in South Africa," *Geoforum* 33, no. 1 (2002): 37, states that financial problems had arisen on account of the Bophuthatswana government having to pay for all the "prestige" projects that had begun.

77   Jones, "'To Come Together for Progress,'" 604.

78   Makgala, *History of the Bakgatla-baga-Kgafela*, 321; and Magome and Collinson, "From Protest to Pride."

79   Magome and Collinson, "From Protest to Pride"; and Makgala, *History of the Bakgatla-baga-Kgafela*, 322.

80   Keenan had been involved in research concerning agribusiness in Bophuthatswana in the early 1980s: see Drummond, "Rural Land Use and Agricultural Production," 342.

81   Keenan, "Report on the Socio-Economic Effects of the Pilanesberg Game Reserve," 5.

82   Ibid., 15–17, 67–74.

83   Boonzaaier, personal communication, March 1, 2010.

84   Keenan, "Report on the Socio-Economic Effects of the Pilanesberg Game Reserve," 67–74.

85   Magome and Collinson, "From Protest to Pride"; see also Richard Summers, "Legal and Institutional Aspects of Community-Based Wildlife Conservation in South Africa, Zimbabwe, and Namibia," *Acta Juridica* (1999): 188–210; and Marc J. Stern, "The Power of Trust: Toward a Theory of Local Opposition to Neighboring Protected Areas," *Society and Natural Resources* 21, no. 10 (2008): 859–75.

86   It may well again become controversial as socialist advocates consider what they regard as the commodification of nature for tourist consumption with distaste, and see in it the rise of a neoliberal approach to nature. See for example, Bram Büscher, "Seeking 'Telos' in the 'Transfrontier'? Neoliberalism and the Transcending of Community Conservation in Southern Africa," *Environment and Planning* 42 (2010): 644–60.

CHAPTER 8

Wildlife Habitat Design for Biodiversity Conservation and Conservation Education

Two Case Studies: Alice Springs Desert Park and the Cambodia Wildlife Sanctuary

STUART GREEN

THE ALICE SPRINGS DESERT PARK (ASDP) IN Central Australia was designed to re-create natural habitats of the region, while the Cambodia Wildlife Sanctuary's Observation Zone was designed to preserve existing habitats within a large wildlife sanctuary. This essay draws on both of these projects to discuss the possibilities and challenges of designing wildlife habitats for biodiversity conservation and conservation education.

The first and second parts of the essay introduce the wildlife habitat designs in each study by discussing the background and design objectives, design challenges, and design processes, and by highlighting the way in which the conservation education experience is tendered to the visitor. The third part of the essay draws on these case studies to analyze the major factors that can influence the success (or otherwise) of design initiatives that integrate biodiversity conservation with conservation education. A basic model containing five main factors is introduced, including: the designer's ability to work with the indigenous and local communities; the role of government and financial resources; the economic and social opportunities available to local communities; conservation education as a resource pre- and

post-design; and access to scientific research. The paper concludes that open collaboration between government, indigenous groups, and the design team is critical to the success of biodiversity conservation and education projects.

Alice Springs Desert Park

Background and Design Objectives

The landscape of the arid "Red Centre" of Australia is dominated by iconic rock formations of which Uluru (Ayers Rock) is the most well known. The ocher sandy soils, mountain ranges, and vegetation of this desert region provide habitats for a diverse array of unique wildlife.

The ASDP project was initiated by the Northern Territory Government of Australia in response to the demand for enhanced facilities for visitors to Central Australia. The main aim of the park was to provide an area that would combine zoological, botanical, and natural history elements to not only become an educational resource for local, national, and international visitors, but also to re-create wildlife habitats that would assist in the conservation of the biotic diversity of the Centre. The park was also intended to establish Alice Springs as a focal point for ecotourism.

To achieve these bold aims, the park was required to provide visitors with educational opportunities that combined the indigenous community's ecological knowledge and relationship to the land with the experiences of the rich and diverse flora and fauna of this arid desert zone in one facility. The park was also required to complement the resources of other national parks in the region, such as Uluru-Kata Tjuta (Ayers Rock-Mount Olga), by stimulating visitor interest in the biodiversity of the desert zone, often seen as a dead zone, and encouraging visitors to extend their stay in the region.

A master plan for the park was developed by Land Systems EBC using the concept plan developed by the Conservation Commission Northern Territory to "establish a major wildlife park and botanical desert gardens."[1] Green & Dale Associates was appointed in 1994 to provide the detailed design and construction phases of the wildlife habitats, bringing to fruition the only site in Australia which presents the fauna of the arid zone—an area which covers 70 percent of inland Australia.

Location and General Site Description

The site of the park is located on the lower northern aspect of the West MacDonnell Ranges on the outskirts of the town of Alice Springs in Central Australia. The park covers about 1,300 hectares and includes an impressive portion of the West MacDonnell Ranges, running east–west, that rise 350 meters above the surrounding plains. Mount Gillen provides a strong landmark towering above the park. The "core area" of the park covers about forty hectares.

Today the West MacDonnell Ranges are the mere worn-down stubs of once Canadian Rocky–sized mountains.[2] The geographical features of the foothills of the ranges are low hills, rocky outcrops, and dry creek beds. These features provided a natural landscape as a basis for the design and formation of the riverine and the woodland habitats in the park. The majority of soil types are poor and infertile, with weathered quartz sands being dominant.

The dominant plant species occurring naturally on the core site include *Acacia kempeana* (witchetty bush—source of the famous witchetty grub), *Acacia*

FIGURE 8.1
Alice Springs Desert Park: existing landscape in 1994.

Photograph by Stuart Green, Green & Dale Associates.

estrophiolata (ironwood), *Atalaya hemiglauca* (white-wood), *Hakea suberea* (corkwood), *Acacia aneura* (mulga), and one of the icons of Central Australia, the ghost gum (*Eucalyptus papuana*).[3] The dominant grass of Central Australia and covering 22 percent of the continent, spinifex (*Triodia*), a hummock grass, does not occur naturally within the core site.

Design Challenges

The major design challenges for the park were: re-creating authentic wildlife habitats; communicating the design team's perspective of the requirements for biological conservation to the indigenous community; enabling the Aboriginal people to feel comfortable sharing their knowledge and culture; working within the project budget of Aus$20 million; and incorporating engineering works to prevent flash flooding of the site after heavy rains (Figure 8.1).

HABITAT RE-CREATION

The flora and fauna were to be presented through habitat-immersion exhibits. This involved in situ habitats—mulga, gorge, range, and woodland—and the creation of ex situ habitats—sand dune and sand plain, claypan, salt pan, gypsum pan, and desert rivers. In establishing the habitats only the sand country habitat required extensive remodeling of the existing landscape (Figure 8.2). In re-creating the habitat, the design team benefited greatly from visits to the existing habitats in the Centre's national parks, guided by local Aboriginal guides as well as botanical and wildlife park rangers. The botanist and author Peter K. Latz introduced the design team to the desert environment of Central Australia from a Western as well as an Aboriginal perspective. Latz was brought up in an Aboriginal community in Hermannsburg, west of Alice Springs, where he amassed an incredible knowledge of how Aboriginal people look after the land and plants, and how people use plants for food, medicine, and tools.[4] It's not often one gets the opportunity to be shown a tropical vine growing behind the Alice Springs sewerage plant! It was all the more incredible as this vine dates back to when the Centre was a tropical rainforest (twenty million years ago), with many of its plants having affinities with today's rainforest plants of New Guinea. This knowledge formed a basis for the design of the park's landscape.

FIGURE 8.2
Mulga woodland on site with Mount Gillen in background.

Photograph by Stuart Green, Green & Dale Associates.

FIGURE 8.3
Consulting with
the indigenous
community.
© Alice Springs
Desert Park.

COMMUNICATION

It was important to build trust through cross-cultural communication. The design team needed the indigenous community to share their traditional knowledge so habitats could be replicated authentically. The indigenous community needed to know that their knowledge and culture would be respected and that they would continue to be involved with the park as educators, guides, rangers, and ultimately managers and Traditional Owners (Figure 8.3).

The Aboriginal custodians of the land identified areas of landscape that could not be developed because they were sacred sites. For example, the caterpillars are the major creative ancestors of Mparntwe (Alice Springs area). In their creation stories, the caterpillars started to the east of Alice Springs and moved westward creating ranges, hillocks, and rocky outcrops.[5] The Yeperenye caterpillar is the most important of the caterpillars to the Arrernte people.[6] The activities of the wild dog (*Akngwelye*) formed most of the features of the Heavitree Range escarpment with Mount Gillen as a dominant landmark (the backdrop to the desert park).[7] The challenge here was to respect these sites,

ensuring that they were not disturbed by earthmoving equipment during construction.

BUDGET AND PROGRAM

The re-creation of the sand dunes required massive quantities of red sand to be trucked long distances. Dead trees and rocks needed to be sourced from disturbed areas such as roadworks, or removed from under bridges following flooding of the rivers, and to be moved across vast areas. These works were major costs in the construction of the park. An overall site budget of Aus$20 million was established, of which Aus$5 million was set aside for the establishment of the wildlife habitat and restoration of disturbed areas.

The design program commenced in 1994, with construction starting in 1995 and completed in late 1996 in readiness for the public opening. The design team and Parks & Wildlife Commission of the Northern Territory (PWCNT) worked together to source materials for the site, with the design team directing on-site construction, which included the formation of the riverine creek and the sand country dunes. Much of the design team's time was spent showing construction workers, who were used to building roads and railways, that we were creating natural habitats and not landscaped gardens. After six months, a construction expertise in habitat-creation started to evolve.

ENGINEERING WORKS

The site for the park, 1,300 hectares (three thousand acres), was chosen in an area that had several existing habitats (mulga, range, gorge, and woodland) at the base of the West MacDonnell Ranges to the west of Alice Springs. In this Central Australian arid zone, rainfall is unpredictable. Due to the steep slopes of the West MacDonnell Ranges, the local geology, and the sparse vegetation cover, there is the potential in the park for flash flooding along the existing dry creek beds and watercourses. Complex hydraulic engineering was therefore necessary, in the design of the sand dune system and its pans, to allow floodwater to flow through the site unobstructed and to prevent the flooding of the nearby residential development in Alice Springs. This consisted of diversionary sluice gates and pipelines, which accommodate the large water flows, and retarding basins that are part of the landscape within the exhibits, as floodplains and pans.

Design Process

While the park is seen as a botanical and zoological park, its guiding goals are the story lines that take an ecosystemic approach to display and interpretation and an educational approach to conservation—to increase appreciation and an understanding of the natural habitats of Central Australia. The design process required scientific research information for the botanical, zoological, and landform elements, as well as the traditional ecological knowledge of the indigenous community. This information influenced the design team's choice of habitats suitable for the site, and ultimately provided a strong story line for conservation messages, enabling an informative and exciting experience for the visitor.

The research for the re-creation of the habitats was coordinated with the zoological researchers at the Arid Zone Research Institute of Australia's Commonwealth Scientific and Industrial Research Organization (CSIRO), and the research of botanist Peter K. Latz.[8] The design team worked on-site in Alice Springs, with in-house earth scientists—ecologists, botanists, and native animal specialists—from the PWCNT and the park's Aboriginal custodians, the Arrernte people. The design team also researched in situ habitats in other areas of the Northern Territory as well as sourcing materials such as dead trees and rocks for use in the park. This research enabled the design team to replicate, as accurately as possible, the soils, landforms, flora, and fauna of the ecosystems of the salt pans, gypsum pans, and claypans, desert water holes, and floodouts (after heavy rainfall the water in the creek floods out into sandy areas).

Research into a desert dune system that allowed for the greatest diversity of habitat species to be displayed resulted in a choice of the linear dunes, which are the most prolific landforms of Central Australia, as seen in the Simpson Desert with its sand drifts and wind-blown dunes. The Great Sandy Desert is a system of red sand ridges (dunes), with the Tanami Desert having large areas of red sand plains. These systems also support a range of groundwater evaporation pans: salt, clay, and gypsum.[9]

Research conducted in the early 1980s in Central Australian deserts revealed that more than one-third of the desert's terrestrial mammals had vanished in the previous fifty years.[10] "The Aborigine's use of fire for hunting, regeneration of food plants and signalling . . . provided an environmental diversity that favoured the mammals."[11] The Aboriginal use of fire is based on regular "cool fires," where the patch-burning, low-intensity fires occurred in winter over a number of years to create a mosaic of habitats.[12] These fires maintained the "open" eucalypt woodland, reducing dense undergrowth, and promoted native grasses which in turn encouraged grazing animals such as kangaroos, wallabies, and Emus. Fires were lit when there was little fuel load and weather conditions were most suitable.

The study revealed that mammals disappeared after the indigenous population gave up their nomadic lifestyle on traditional lands and began to move into European settlements and missions. It was concluded that even though exotic predators and competition from nonnative herbivores may have been factors, it was the change in fire regimes that was the main cause of the decline of the mammals. Fire was an event of nature, usually started by lightning, causing infrequent, extensive, very hot summer wildfires, which destroyed the mammals' habitats, leading to their decline and extinction.[13] This information emphasized the importance of the mammals in Aboriginal culture and demonstrated the relevance of an aspect of biodiversity conservation which could be best interpreted by the indigenous peoples.

Design Influences

The design process included a review of the existing master plan and the development of a sub-master plan for the three proposed habitats with regard to their suitability for the site. This followed detailed analysis and research of these habitats in their natural setting in the region and was assisted by the government's scientific research and by the indigenous peoples' knowledge of the ecosystems of these habitats. Botanists and horticulturists determined the plant species that were appropriate for the specific habitats. Plants and seeds were collected in the wild and used for cultivation and propagation. All these elements influenced the design of the park (Figure 8.4).

Detailed assessment was made of the sites chosen for the three habitats—woodland, riverine, and sand dunes—to enable their design to integrate with the existing landscape. The natural landscape of the park, with its small rocky outcrops and dry creek beds, allowed reasonably easy adaptation of the woodland and riverine habitats. The sand country habitat required the most extensive construction.

Woodland Habitat

The woodland habitat demonstrates the greatest change in habitats throughout the desert region due to degradation caused by the introduction of grazing stock as well as feral animals, such as rabbits, cats, and foxes. The vegetation of the existing woodland habitat was restored to represent the original diversity of plant life. Ghost gums, ironwoods, mulga, and witchetty bushes are examples of the woodland flora in this habitat, and further planting of these species was undertaken to create a more dense woodland ecosystem in the park. The large

FIGURE 8.4
Alice Springs Desert Park: Stage One Habitat Plan. Stuart Green, Green & Dale Associates— Plan of ASDP.

Reproduced courtesy of Catherin Bull, *New Conversations with an Old Landscape: Landscape Architecture in Contemporary Australia* (Mulgrave, Vic.: Images, 2002), 54–55.

FIGURE 8.6
Desert river habitat.

Photograph by Stuart Green, Green & Dale Associates.

FIGURE 8.5
Woodland habitat with iconic bloodwood tree.
© Alice Springs Desert Park.

mammals in this habitat include the Red Kangaroo and the Emu. Many of the smaller endangered species, such as the Bilby and reptiles, are exhibited in the Nocturnal House. The Bilby (*Macrotis lagotis*) has also recently been displayed in the protected mulga habitat (Figure 8.5).

Riverine Habitat

A naturally occurring riverine habitat incorporates the seasonally dry, sandy, river or creek beds and its surrounding flora. The dominant tree specimens include the river red gum, coolabah, and ghost gum, which line the edges of the sandy rivers. These rivers, which are dry most of the time, are referred to as "streams of life." To re-create a riverine habitat within the park and to reduce the impact of seasonal "flash floods" on the park landscape, existing creek beds were widened (from a width of two meters and depth of one meter) to a

wider, shallow creek of ten meters in width, filling them with sand and alluvial sediment.

The ecosystems of the riverine habitat were enhanced by the construction of the clay and gypsum pans, which became a water resource during heavy rainfall. These pans were created by constructing low depressions and compacting heavy clay soils

FIGURE 8.7
A claypan.

Photograph by Melanie Couyant, Green & Dale Associates.

to form the base. The gypsum pans required clay with a high level of gypsum. The pans also serve as retarding basins, which help to reduce the hydraulic impact of fast-flowing watercourses in the wet season.

Within the riverine habitat, many species have adapted to survive the rain/drought cycles of this arid region. Typical fauna of this habitat are such mammals as the Long-haired Rat and the Nail-tail Wallaby, birds such as the White-plumed Honey-eater, fish such as the Spangled Grunter and rain-bowfish, reptiles such as the Perentie and Pygmy Goanna, and invertebrates such as the Yabby and the Desert Bulldog Ant (Figures 8.6–8.7).

Sand Country Habitat

A degraded area of the park was identified (formerly a dirt track used by locals in their hot rod cars) and a sand dune landscape was created. More

FIGURE 8.8
Newly formed sand dune.

Photograph by Stuart Green, Green & Dale Associates.

than thirty-two thousand square meters (approximate coverage of eight acres) of sand was sourced from major roadworks and landholdings from as far away as Uluru (Ayers Rock)—a distance of about five hundred kilometers (three hundred miles). The red sand, chosen for its stability due to its high clay content, was trucked to the site over the course of several months. The base of the sand dunes was formed using fill from site building and roadworks, compacted to a height of one and one-half meters. The sand was then brought in and compacted in layers to achieve the dune shape. The final layer of sand contained a high quartz content and was very mobile in the prevailing winds, creating a mini-sandstorm at times of high winds. The dunes had to be stabilized, and this was achieved by the use of ground cover planting, aided by the installation of a temporary drip line irrigation system. The park has a water tank storage system, which is partly used for the built facilities, as well as providing irrigation (which includes recycled gray water) for the establishment of the new plants. Once planting is established, the irrigation lines are closed and removed.

This habitat has been very successful, with the dunes now stabilized with planting of the dune systems, including spinifex, the dominant sand dune grass species. These dunes are sculpted daily by prevailing winds, resulting in the dune system "moving" several inches per year.

An integral feature of sand country is the salt pan, forming a strong visual feature among the dunes and the backdrop of the West MacDonnell Ranges. The construction of the salt pan involved the same process as the claypan, but included a waterproof butyl membrane lining on the pan base and edges, then overlaid with a compacted clay floor. This prevented the surrounding dune system and its planting from suffering from excessive salination seepage. Salt was sourced from existing commercial, natural salt pans found in the Eyre Peninsula of South Australia. The dry blocks of salt were dissolved into the pan water using high-pressure hoses for several days. Evaporation of the water over a three-month period completed the creation of a salt pan. It functions naturally, dehydrating in the dry season and filling slowly with groundwater runoff after summer rains. Dominant spinifex shares

FIGURE 8.9
Spiky spinifex provides a good home for many desert lizards, snakes, birds, and small mammals.

Photograph by Melanie Couyant, Green & Dale Associates.

FIGURE 8.10
An aviary in the sand country habitat.

Photograph by Stuart Green, Green & Dale Associates.

FIGURE 8.11
Red Kangaroo in open enclosure.

© Alice Springs Desert Park

the habitat with clumps of tea tree and a distinctive eucalyptus tree, marble gum (*Eucalyptus gongylocarpa*), on the fringe of the salt pan (Figure 8.8).

Many small mammals—such as the Marsupial Mole, Sandhill Dunnart, and Spinifex Hopping Mouse—as well as reptiles (arid Australia is the "land of the lizard," and the coexistence of lizards has no ecological parallel anywhere else in the world), amphibians, and invertebrates represent some of the fauna of the sand country habitat. The flora of the sand dune, sand plains, and salt lake habitat include *Spinifex* species, *Grevillea* species, and saltbushes.

The park incorporates approximately 120 species of desert animals and more than four hundred species of plants into the habitats to represent the desert ecosystems (Figure 8.9). A central feature of the park is the Nocturnal House, which provides an introduction to the animals of the sand and woodland habitats that would be otherwise impossible to see—the reptiles, lizards, and many endangered nocturnal species such as the Bilby, Dunnart, Mulgara, Mala, and Marsupial Mole. Larger animals such as the Red Kangaroo, Emu, Dingo, and birds of prey are displayed in large, open enclosures (varying from five thousand to twenty thousand square meters in area). The park attracts a wide variety of free-ranging birdlife, ranging from the Wedge-tailed Eagle, Whistling Kite, Mulga Parrot, Budgerigar, and Bronzewing Pigeon, to name a few. The desert ecosystems are also represented in large walk-in and smaller aviaries of the habitats. The aviaries have been designed to integrate with the natural vegetation and landforms of each habitat type (Figures 8.10–8.11).

Future development of Stage Two of the park will include the range, gorge, and mulga (an *Acacia* species that covers a large proportion of the Australian mainland) habitats. Research and design concepts for these habitats have been undertaken to integrate them into the existing (created) desert habitats of the site. It is intended that a number of underground or concealed observation facilities will be incorporated into the landscape to reduce the impact of built facilities. Each of these centers will be based in the proposed range, gorge, and mulga habitats, incorporating interpretation and small animal exhibits. This stage has commenced with the development, by ASDP, of the mulga habitat.

CONSERVATION STORY LINES
AND INDIGENOUS INTERPRETATION

The conservation story lines and indigenous interpretation formed the basis of the habitat designs. The traditional knowledge of indigenous Australians, handed down through millennia, of the wildlife habitats of Central Australia, and indigenous peoples' management and use of the land and the native animals, were at the heart of the biodiversity conservation message that the park wanted to impart to visitors.

VISITOR EDUCATION EXPERIENCE

The park delivers conservation education through its extensive interpretation of the habitats. "The ASDP takes a 'holistic, habitat-based, story-driven' approach to display and interpretation, which maximizes the park's environmental education potential."[14] The interpretation of Australia's desert environment in the park is of fundamental importance to the conservation of the biodiversity of Central Australia. Visitors to the park are presented with a great variety of media techniques used to convey information, such as interactive displays, audio guides, and films.

One of the most successful aspects of the park is the cultural interaction between visitors and local indigenous peoples. The indigenous people employed in the park play a key role in education through their storytelling and explanations of the use and management of the flora and fauna of the region. The Traditional Owners of the park, the Arrernte people, control which aspects of their culture they will share with the visitor, and the education programs are developed around these elements, thereby ensuring authentic cultural interpretation.

The Aboriginal people, through their storytelling, explain to visitors how they use and manage the arid-zone flora and fauna for medicine, bush tucker (food), tools, and as artifacts, giving the visitor a rich and rewarding "one-on-one" experience of the Centre. The Arrernte language is used on signage extensively throughout the park, including storyboards, plant identification signs, and animal species identification signs. The Aboriginal rangers and guides also explain the effect feral animals have had on wildlife habitat. In the park visitor center, a local artist, Kaye Kessing, displays her colorful, thought-provoking images of feral animals destroying wildlife habitat.

The visitor experience provides short-term and long-term walks. Short-term visitors may choose an overview of all habitats via the Primary Circuit to maximize their experience of the desert habitats. The Primary Circuit provides an introduction to each of the habitats and the key habitat messages, such as: "desert life is most abundant in the riverine areas"; "plants and animals have adapted to the sand dune habitat's poor soils and unpredictable rainfalls"; and "people and animals have been instruments of change in woodland areas since prehistoric times." The circuit provides orientation shelters at the beginning of each habitat, which display the interpretive information and serve as key scenic vantage points. The magnificent West

MacDonnell Ranges and Mount Gillen in the background greatly enhance the park's desert landscape. Long-term visitors may follow the Habitat Loop Circuits, which provide a more developed story line for each of the habitats and develop the key habitat messages in greater detail (Figure 8.12).

Opportunities abound for a natural animal-viewing experience of the free-ranging wildlife such as lizards, snakes, and birds. Sightings are enhanced by the provision of watering and feeding stations throughout the park, while the animals are protected from predators and from any excessive disturbance from visitors. Birds, like mammals and reptiles, need a constant supply of food and water. Therefore, bird populations shift rapidly in response to changing conditions.[15] Nomadic and migratory birds have quickly relocated to the park water holes, encouraged by feed stations and the provision of lush plant growth and insect activity. It is not uncommon to see visiting flocks of Budgerigars and Zebra Finches descending on the water holes, followed by the occasional Wedge-tailed Eagle in search of food. While constructing the park, it was not unusual to sight a "wild" Dingo family and wallabies roaming the new landscape, even with the site security fence in place.

The weather conditions in this arid region mean that animals are more active in the early mornings,

evenings, and at night. The park has developed nocturnal tours where visitors are able to spotlight rare and endangered species. The Mulga Walk—which now forms part of the nocturnal tour—has been created by revegetating the area, installing predator-proof fencing, and releasing many nocturnal mammals, including the threatened Bilby, into this habitat.

The birds of prey, such as Wedge-tailed Eagles, hawks, owls, and Whistling Kites, along with larger animals such as Red Kangaroos and Emus, are displayed in open exhibits. Hidden fencing encloses them, with all animals provided with food and water. A great number of the park's animal species are endangered and nocturnal, therefore requiring enclosed, confined facilities where visitors can view them in a suitable environment. The park's Nocturnal House also exhibits the small ground-dwelling desert mammals, such as the Bilby, Dunnart, Spinifex Hopping Mouse, and Stick-nest Rat. Many of these species range freely within the park, only being seen during the supervised nocturnal tours. Larger species such as the Dingo are introduced to visitors in the supervised setting of an outdoor amphitheater.

Conservation education continues through local school programs where the park's staff assist students with seed collection and plant propagation to establish bush gardens at their schools.[16] Bird

FIGURE 8.12
A park habitat path.

© Peter Bennetts; reprinted from Catherin Bull, *New Conversations with an Old Landscape: Landscape Architecture in Contemporary Australia* (Mulgrave, Vic.: Images, 2002), 54–55.

posters with the common names of bird species found in indigenous communities have been developed in five Aboriginal dialects to increase awareness of the species in these areas.[17]

The breeding programs for threatened species in 2008 and 2009 were 100 percent successful in the breeding of the Bilby, Mala, Red-tailed Phascogale, Western Quoll, and Central Rock Rats.[18]

ASDP is highly committed to biodiversity conservation and conservation education, and its success can be attributed to the habitat-immersion design and its interpretation. Information is presented in a way that allows the visitor to discover how all the elements of an ecosystem, including humans, are interconnected.

Visitor numbers have plateaued at approximately seventy-five thousand for the last three years, but there has been an increase in visiting schoolchildren, up a total of 30 percent since the park opened, and visitor satisfaction is steady at 95 percent.[19] The park has given economic and logistic support to the Traditional Owners of the park to develop a cross-cultural program that gives tours of the park and nearby Alice Springs.[20] The park is a major drawcard for ecotourism visitors and received two tourism awards in 2008.[21]

FIGURE 8.13
Kulen Promtep Wildlife Sanctuary.

Photograph by Stuart Green, Green & Dale Associates.

The habitat-based approach to design has placed the park firmly in the worldwide zoological and environmental discussion. While the park is largely seen as zoological and botanical, it provides an introduction to Central Australia's wildlife habitats and is an opportunity for visitors to further explore the National Parks of the Centre.

Legendary naturalist and filmmaker Sir David Attenborough, while filming a wildlife documentary for the British Broadcasting Corporation in the park, exclaimed, "There is no museum or wildlife park in the world that could match it."[22]

Cambodia Wildlife Sanctuary

Location and Geographical Features of the Site

The Cambodia Wildlife Sanctuary (CWS) is located within the much larger Kulen Promtep Wildlife Sanctuary (KPWS), a site of 440,000 hectares (approximately one million acres) that lies in the Siem Reap, Oddar Meanchey, and Preah Vihear provinces of the northern plains of Cambodia. It is one of the largest and richest surviving examples of an Indochina dry forest habitat. The defining feature of this vast, largely flat landscape is extensive lowland, savanna-like deciduous dipterocarp forests, which occur in a complex mosaic with seasonal wetlands, semi-evergreen forests, and grasslands (Figure 8.13).[23] Geographical features of the CWS are a series of flat undulations with low areas susceptible to flooding in the wet season. Dry creeks cross the landscape in a southwesterly direction. To the far south of the proposed CWS site, along the edge of the KPWS forest, dry woodland and open grassland dominate and are inundated with floodwater in the wet season. To the north, the park boundary is defined by a village, and to the west the Main National Highway. The eastern boundary is the vast expanse of the forest of the Kulen Promtep Wildlife Sanctuary.

Background and Design Objectives

Green & Dale Associates, landscape architects with expertise in wildlife habitat design,[24] were selected to design the Observation Zone of CWS, a two-thousand-hectare (five-thousand-acre) site, located within the overall KPWS and located one hundred kilometers (sixty-two miles) north of Angkor Wat (in Siem Reap).

The Cambodia Wildlife Sanctuary was founded in March 2004 as a government/private partnership initiative.[25] The objective of the sanctuary is to protect the existing wildlife habitats within the area, thereby encouraging biodiversity conservation, and to offer refuge for rescued captive wild animals. The Observation Zone, which will encompass existing habitats, is designed to allow visitors to view the wildlife in its natural habitat, although within fenced enclosures. The establishment of ecotourism in the area is also an important consideration in the design. The facility will also incorporate veterinary services to enable care of the animals and to serve as an education facility for the training of Cambodian people in veterinary and habitat conservation practices.

Design Challenges

There were many challenges for the design team in Cambodia. Degradation and destruction of the forest caused by illegal activities and land encroachment occurs in the sanctuary. There is a threat to personal safety from those who are protecting the sanctuary, either by poachers or remnants of the Khmer Rouge. Personal safety is also threatened by undetected landmines from the civil war and by free-roaming wildlife such as tigers. Identification of habitats was difficult and time-consuming without detailed surveys of the sanctuary site. Limited cross-cultural communication with local communities meant the design team was unable to incorporate local knowledge into their research. And funding and government support for the project and for the local communities was not forthcoming at the outset. The overall design intention was to retain and conserve the existing habitat of the selected area, developing built facilities in disturbed or open areas.

DEGRADATION AND DESTRUCTION OF THE FOREST

Illegal Activities

The major causes of forest degradation within the sanctuary are illegal logging and the clearing of land for subsistence farming. Every day, hectares of the forest are cleared indiscriminately by fire, tree felling, and "resin tapping."[26]

Resin tapping entails the collection of liquid resin from the *Dipterocarpus* species and the solid resin from the *Shorea* species, which is then used by local villagers for wood varnishing, caulking boats, and traditional medicine.[27] In most cases this has led to severe damage to the trees and their eventual loss as an important habitat. Tapping of resin (oleoresin) occurs within the protected area of cws. Offenders who are caught risk serious penalties such as jail and/or fines, but in practice are rarely prosecuted. Much of the design team's time on the ground was spent convincing the park rangers of the importance of protecting the large mature trees and habitat, even going to great lengths to demonstrate our reverence of the trees by "hugging" them with outstretched arms. While this had an amusing effect, the design team soon realized it was lost on the rangers when it discovered that a ranger's truck contained recently cut rosewood round tabletops destined for home use or the illegal market (Figures 8.14–8.16).

FIGURE 8.14
Land degradation: clearing for subsistence farming plots.
Photograph by Stuart Green, Green & Dale Associates.

FIGURE 8.15
Tapping of resin can lead to loss of habitat trees.

Photograph by Stuart Green, Green & Dale Associates.

Land Encroachment

The construction of new roads, in particular the north–south national highway that dissects the sanctuary site, has made this area more accessible for communities displaced by increasing urbanization in regional cities. Villages are located on the northern boundary of the forest and to south on the open woodland perimeter of the sanctuary. Communities within these settlements are dependent on subsistence farming,[28] which is now spreading into the sanctuary in the form of blocks of forest cleared using "slash-and-burn" techniques. "Illegal land grabbing" practices, by landless farmers and real estate developers within the region, are rife.

Personal Safety

Armed rangers were required to accompany the design team on the ground and in the air at all times. This was a source of anxiety for the design team, and it also created a barrier for free communication with local communities who also felt threatened by our presence.

IDENTIFICATION OF HABITATS

The survey information provided by the government was general for the overall KPWS and not detailed for the specific area of CWS. The design team was therefore required to inspect the site on foot using GPS (Global Positioning System) mapping when habitats were identified. Mapping was difficult, as all supplied paper maps were from the civil war. Recent government surveys were used to identify broad areas of habitat. For larger areas, aerial surveys were also undertaken to assess the broader nature of the study site.

COMMUNICATION

Cross-cultural interaction was limited because there were no government or NGO (nongovernmental organization) strategies in place to facilitate this—for example, workshops that included the local communities. Due to time and financial constraints, there was no opportunity to liaise with the local communities to glean their perspective on biodiversity conservation or to gauge their reaction to the development of the sanctuary.

FIGURE 8.16
Local villagers and forest products.

Photograph by Stuart Green, Green & Dale Associates.

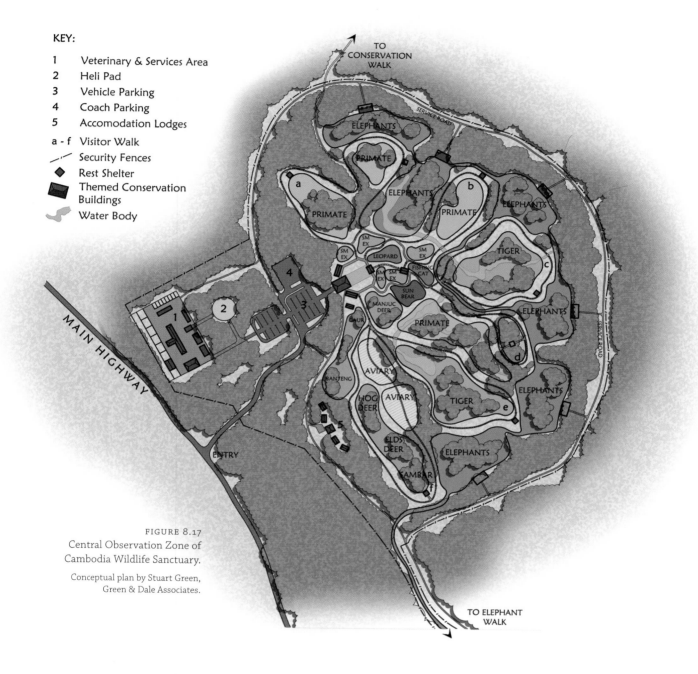

KEY:

1   Veterinary & Services Area
2   Heli Pad
3   Vehicle Parking
4   Coach Parking
5   Accomodation Lodges
a - f   Visitor Walk
—·—   Security Fences
◆   Rest Shelter
▰   Themed Conservation Buildings
〰   Water Body

FIGURE 8.17
Central Observation Zone of
Cambodia Wildlife Sanctuary.

Conceptual plan by Stuart Green,
Green & Dale Associates.

FUNDING

This project is a combined private/government-funded development. It was anticipated that private benefactors and NGOs working with the government would support this initiative. But the project requires more exposure to these organizations in an attempt to build a working relationship that will

enable the sanctuary to be established as planned. More promisingly, in August 2011, the sanctuary finally received formal recognition from the Cambodian government with an official opening, and also joined forces with the Elephant Nature Park in northern Thailand, a successful elephant rescue and rehabilitation center where volunteers are a key element in running the park. Founder and director of the Elephant Nature Park Sangduen "Lek" Chailert, well known in the international elephant conservation and animal rights world, will help in the running of the sanctuary, attracting recognition in the NGO world.

An initial budget of US$5 million has been set for construction of the Observation Core Area, with three visitor zones. The costs include a more developed site establishment and opening of the key facilities as depicted on the master plan. It will also allow for the future inclusion of other animal facilities.

Design Process

Given the many challenges outlined above, the design process was limited to the development of a preliminary conceptual master plan for the CWS. The design was influenced by the site location, research information of the existing habitats within the CWS boundary, and the animals to be included in the sanctuary. These factors, in turn, influenced the design for the enclosures and buildings as well as the visitor education experience (Figure 8.17).

Design Influences

ESTABLISHMENT OF THE SITE AND MASTER PLAN GUIDELINES

The client introduced to the design team a panel of international experts in animal management (including Ed Stewart of the Performing Animal Welfare Society [PAWS][29]), animal health care, and water treatment. A series of workshops was held with design team members in order to structure a preliminary working master plan for the site. Guidelines for the master plan included the establishment of the CWS site boundaries, the locations of water bodies, and the possibilities for water storage on site. An area which contains a range of existing habitats, and scope to develop further habitats suitable for the wildlife of the area, was chosen for the development of the central Observation Zone of the sanctuary. This area is substantial, with an area of fifteen kilometers by fifteen kilometers set aside for habitat restoration. Areas of degraded landscape were identified to site the sanctuary's buildings. Visitor entry and parking facilities, visitor accommodation, and veterinary and education facilities were also sited.

RESEARCH OF EXISTING HABITATS

The design team, working on site, identified that the diversity of the vegetation ranged from a structure of closed canopy forest of low trees five to eight meters (twenty-five feet) in height, to a typical woodland structure with 50 to 80 percent canopy cover and an open understory dominated by grasses. In undisturbed areas, emergent trees reached heights of ten to fifteen meters (forty-five feet). The dominant element of the area is the deciduous dipterocarp forest. Only six species of the approximately 550 dipterocarps in the world are deciduous, and all of these occur in this area.[30] Rosewood (*Dalbergia* sp.) is one of four deciduous dipterocarp species that form the dominant biomass and cover (Figure 8.18).[31] Climbing high among these trees are the "strangling figs"—*Ficus bengalensis* and *Ficus religiosa*—a highlight in the forest canopy with their twisting forms.

FIGURE 8.18
A towering rosewood tree.

Photograph by Stuart Green, Green & Dale Associates.

On the forest floor, bamboo and grasses dominate, with the occasional errant rattan vines that test visitors' capacity to absorb cruel lacerations.

The task of identifying the flora and fauna was aided by survey information containing sightings of key mammals, birds, and vegetation types of the region, provided by the Cambodia Ministry of Environment and Conservation Wildlife Society Cambodia. This information was complemented by fieldwork on foot with local sanctuary rangers, during which a range of habitats was identified and recorded using GPS mapping. A highlight of one of the field surveys was the discovery of an open savanna forest with groundwater surface pools, a typical habitat of elephants that would have roamed there in large numbers prior to the occupation by the Khmer Rouge during the civil war (Figure 8.19). This area is now frequented by wild deer and visited infrequently by tigers. The design team's surveys identified existing forest tracks to be used for site access as well as identified and recorded areas destroyed by illegal logging and land clearance.

FIGURE 8.19
Open forest woodland.

Photograph by Stuart Green, Green & Dale Associates.

ANIMAL SPECIES TO BE INCLUDED IN THE SANCTUARY

KPWS supports a rich mammal fauna (including elephants, two species of wild cattle, four species of deer, and the many attendant carnivores such as tigers, leopards, and wild dogs), inviting comparison with the more famous animal concentrations on the East African plains. The avifauna of the biome is also globally outstanding, especially for the abundance and diversity of large breeding waterbirds including ibis (two species), storks (four species), and the Sarus Crane. In contrast to almost all other surviving tracts of this habitat type, KPWS retains virtually a full complement of the existing native large mammal species of this biome, many in healthy populations, and a complete set of the large bird species, almost all of them nesting in the reserve.[32]

The animal species to be included in CWS comprise various elephant, tiger, leopard, Sun Bear, leaf-eating monkey, deer, banteng, gaur, and avifauna. Where possible, multiple species can be placed together, but this will largely consist of hoofed animals and birdlife. Predators will be restricted to their own enclosures.

DESIGN FOR ENCLOSURES AND BUILDINGS

Zones for planned animal enclosures were identified according to existing vegetation and specific habitat requirements. Enclosure areas were restricted to the sloped sites or well-drained topography. Sizing of enclosures will be large to accommodate the bigger animals and to protect the habitat—for elephants an enclosure size of ten to fifteen hectares is anticipated. These enclosures are fenced and hidden from the visitors' view. For groups of hoofed species, larger enclosures of twenty to thirty hectares are planned. Areas of flood inundation were retained as watercourse corridors with no development sited on them. Siting of buildings and facilities utilized existing areas of disturbed forest or habitat of poor or degraded value.

Visitor Education Experience

The key visitor area is the Observation Zone—the refuge for rescued captive wild animals and endangered species. The Observation Zone provides protection and shelter for indigenous wildlife that is either under veterinary care or not able to be released into the wild. In the planned enclosures, they will roam large areas of their natural habitat, living in natural groupings (where possible). These areas will take the form of large fenced enclosures.

It is anticipated that professionally trained local Cambodian guides and rangers will welcome visitors and interpret the flora, fauna, and local culture. The welfare and safety of the individual animals will always be a principal priority, and the needs of the animals will always take precedence over the wants of the humans. Thus, there will be no direct visitor-animal contact. Visitors will be able to view these animals in large natural settings, rather than small, contained areas. The animal enclosures will have screened safety restraint fencing. Visitors reach the key viewing areas via a circuit of well-screened paths, elevated walkways, and observation platforms that extend into the enclosed areas. These viewing areas will also allow close observation of the animals by veterinary staff and by researchers for scientific study.

Visitors will discover a wide range of Cambodia's wild animals—elephants, tigers, Fishing Cats, Clouded Leopards, various species of primates, Sun Bears, muntjacs, slow lorises, banteng, and the impressive giant gaur—in spacious enclosures of their natural habitat. A highlight for the visitors will be the Elephant Trail, consisting of a forest walk with the elephant and its keeper at the edge of the sanctuary, where the forest meets the seasonal wetlands and wooded grasslands. Here, visitors can experience the free roaming of the elephant and hoofed stock in an open-range environment. Interpretation is envisaged to convey conservation messages and cultural interaction, as has been implemented so successfully in ASDP.

Factors Affecting Successful Design Projects

Based on the author's experience of the ASDP and CWS projects, the major factors that can influence the success or otherwise of design initiatives that integrate biodiversity conservation with conservation education include: the designer's ability to work with the indigenous and local communities; the role of government; the type and amount of funding available; the economic and social opportunities available to local communities; the relative prioritization of conservation education within the project; and access to scientific research. Each of these factors is discussed below in the context of the ASDP and the CWS projects. This comparative analysis is then used to draw some final conclusions about the elements needed to successfully integrate landscape architecture design, biodiversity conservation, and conservation education.

Working with Indigenous and Local Communities

In designing ASDP, the design team collaborated with the indigenous community on all aspects of habitat design. Aboriginal culture and indigenous interpretations of biodiversity conservation were then integrated into the park's design. Differences in cultural perspectives on biodiversity conservation between indigenous and nonindigenous participants in the project were resolved openly through interactive discussion, shared learning, and openness to new perspectives, which enabled the design process to run smoothly. The willingness of local indigenous people to share their knowledge and culture, and also to learn a Western perspective of conservation that relies on scientific research and designers' skills—and vice versa—became central to the establishment and ongoing success of the park.

In the design of the Observation Zone in the CWS, the design team had limited access to local communities. The rangers of the sanctuary, while assisting and protecting the design team on field trips, had limited knowledge of the area's flora and fauna. Most people were not indigenous to the region but rather were new settlers from other parts of Cambodia. There was little in the way of cultural interaction between the Cambodian people and the design team. This impaired the design team's awareness of the local communities' feelings about the intercession of Westerners or their understanding of the reasons for conservation. It is possible that locals also felt that the project would not offer them a means of survival if their illegal subsistence activities were to be stopped.

The Role of Government and Financial Resources

ASDP was funded by the Northern Territory Government at a cost of Aus$20 million. There were no corporate sponsors or nongovernmental organizations involved. The government had sufficient resources to fund the project and continues to make sufficient resources available to ensure its viability. The government also recognizes the benefits of working with local indigenous communities and has used its institutional and organizational power to bring local groups together with government experts and consultants to collaborate in an inclusive way, thereby helping to break down cultural barriers that could have inhibited the project.

The government has also brought its policy-making capacity to bear on the project, using ASDP as a platform to develop indigenous employment, training, and cultural heritage initiatives with multiple policy, economic, and social benefits. The return of the ownership of the park to the Traditional Owners; the initiatives undertaken to educate, train, and employ indigenous peoples; and the value and respect held for Aboriginal culture all manifest the government's ongoing support for the project and demonstrate how the financial commitment and cultural sensitivity of government can affect the success of conservation projects such as this one.

In contrast, the Cambodian project is reliant on private funding. Beyond allocating the land and providing official recognition for the sanctuary, Cambodian government authorities have had limited involvement in the project. Only eight rangers have been employed as caretakers, and the designers were not able to draw on government expertise and local resources. The private funding for the project and interest from NGOs has been insufficient to proceed with the project to date. Moreover, governmental authorities lack the regulatory capacity and resources to enforce local laws (e.g., against deforestation) or to provide opportunities for sustainable development to local communities, resulting in a disjuncture between the government's aims

for the sanctuary and the incentives and realities facing local communities on the ground.

Economic and Social Opportunities

Australia is a developed economy and home to a world-class tourism industry. These fundamental economic realities have undoubtedly made ASDP easier to establish and sustain. But the Northern Territory is also home to chronically underdeveloped local economies in which many indigenous people face developing-world conditions and opportunities. In many remote and urban Aboriginal communities, there exists widespread poverty, passive welfare, unemployment, and social dysfunction. The Northern Territory Government has shown that by making a project such as ASDP inclusive of indigenous peoples, economic and social opportunities can be created in ecotourism and biodiversity conservation projects.

The government of Cambodia is still recovering economically from the many years of civil war and rule by the Khmer Rouge. Due to strong demand for wood and animal products, and an absence of superior economic opportunities, local groups living in and around the wildlife sanctuary face perverse economic incentives to *destroy* the biodiverse plants and wildlife of their region in order to subsist. Meanwhile, laws to protect Cambodian wildlife habitats from deforestation, illegal logging, resin tapping, hunting, and poaching are difficult to enforce in remote areas such as KPWS. In recent years, there have been many NGOs offering incentives to communities to use sustainable farming methods and to become involved in community-based conservation and ecotourism to improve their economic and social situations. Ultimately, such programs will need to be successfully expanded if the sanctuary is to be preserved and the CWS project is to succeed. The limited financial and government support for the project makes this an acute challenge.

Conservation Education as a Resource Pre- and Post-Design

The indigenous communities of Central Australia brought to the project an extraordinary depth of traditional knowledge of the ecosystems of this arid area. Their willingness to share this knowledge with the design team—often taking them into the desert to see the animals in their natural habitats and introducing the designers to elders in the Aboriginal communities—was invaluable to the successful recreation of the wildlife habitats.

Education is the cornerstone of understanding. ASDP provides an awareness of the need for the conservation of biodiversity and imparts the information in a variety of ways and at many different levels. The visitor is able to experience biodiversity throughout the park and question or inquire deeper into the value and meaning of conservation from both a Western and an indigenous point of view. The visitor is able to take from this experience a much greater understanding of how the indigenous peoples have managed the use of the land for millennia, seeing themselves as belonging to the ecosystems, not as separate from them.

The Australian Aborigines are hunter-gatherers, able to live off what nature provides, which therefore has given them the greatest incentive to conserve their ecosystems. This knowledge of indigenous Australians contrasts starkly with the level of knowledge conveyed to the design team by the local communities in the area of the CWS. A major reason is that there is not an indigenous population living there due to the occupation of armed forces during the civil war, when indigenous communities were removed. Now people are settling here from other areas, mostly driven out of cities by urbanization. The Cambodian people live off subsistence farming and use the timber and non-timber products of the forest to survive. At the time of designing the sanctuary, Cambodian education in biodiversity conservation was limited due to lack of government funding and the limited choices for sustainable and legal employment for local communities. Again, this is improving because of the involvement of NGOs establishing a working relationship with the government and the local communities.

It is hoped that the education experience for visitors to the Observation Zone will impart messages about the value of habitat conservation with participation from local communities. A great deal more research, cross-cultural interaction, and involvement with government and NGOs will be necessary if conservation education in the sanctuary is to be successful.

Access to Scientific Research

The availability of scientific research to the design team working on ASDP, such as soil types, sand dune formations, and the flora and fauna of the region, was crucial for the establishment of the authentic recreation of the habitats. This was provided through government agencies such as CSIRO and PWCNT. ASDP has its own herbarium, and botanical propagation and research into arid flora is ongoing.

The Cambodian government's Ministry of Environment assisted the design team with relevant surveys for KPWS. The vegetation and sightings of flora and fauna were presented as an overall representation of findings in KPWS, but there was limited specific detail of local ecosystems. This meant that the design team had to survey many areas of the sanctuary site on foot and use GPS tracking to record habitats within the sanctuary's boundaries.

Conclusion

The success of ASDP was influenced by the strong collaboration between the government, the indigenous peoples, and the design team. The government provided funding, human resources, and scientific research, and was inclusive of indigenous peoples, investing in them a sense of ownership of the project. The indigenous peoples were willing to share their extensive ecological knowledge and their culture while being open to the involvement of outsiders on their traditional lands. And the design team was able to extract from all these elements the necessary ingredients to design, and to supervise the construction of, such a successful project.

Important as ecological and conservation goals of the Alice Springs project were, arguably the greatest strength of ASDP has been its attention to cultural, socioeconomic, and educational details. The ability to work with the local communities has greatly improved the quality of cross-cultural relationships to the point where the park and its educational programs are beneficial to all parties. ASDP has been a springboard for biodiversity conservation and conservation education programs throughout Central Australia.

This contrasts to the Cambodia project, where these elements have yet to be fully realized. Cross-cultural barriers, lack of government support for the sanctuary and for the viability of local communities' livelihoods, insufficient scientific research into ecosystems, and limited traditional knowledge are all factors contributing to the stagnation of this project. It is hoped that the lessons drawn from these two case studies and the basic "success model" consisting of the five factors identified here can be applied to the design of future wildlife habitats seeking to promote biodiversity conservation and conservation education. This model should be of particular relevance to practitioners working to conserve native habitats in complex political, cultural, and economic environments, especially those involving interaction between local indigenous groups and nonlocal project proponents.

Notes

1   Land Systems EBC, *Desert Wildlife Park and Botanic Gardens—Alice Springs* (master plan, 1994), 1.

2   Penny van Oosterzee and Reg Morrison, *The Centre: The Natural History of Australia's Desert Regions* (Balgowlah, N.S.W.: Reed Books, 1991).

3   Graham Phelps and Anne Scherer, "Habit-Based and Story-Driven," *Roots* 1, no. 27 (December 2003), accessed March 10, 2010, http://www.bgci.org/resources/article /0415.

4   Peter K. Latz, *Bushfires and Bushtucker: Aboriginal Plant Use in Central Australia* (Alice Springs: IAD Press, 1995).

5   David Brooks and Shawn Dobson, *The Arrernte Landscape of Alice Springs* (Alice Springs: Institute for Aboriginal Development, 1991), 5.

6   Ibid., 6. Arrernte is the native language of the Mparntwe indigenous peoples of Alice Springs.

7   Ibid., 7.

8   Latz, *Bushfires and Bushtucker.*

9   Mary C. Bourke, "Paleoflood Geomorphology in Central Australia," Planetary Science Institute, accessed April 12, 2010, http://www.psi.edu/about/staff/mbourke/ bourkeprojects/HaleRiver.html.

10   Andrew A. Burbidge, Ken A. Johnson, Phillip J. Fuller, and R. I. Southgate, "Aboriginal Knowledge of the Mammals of the Central Deserts of Australia," *Australian Wildlife Research* 15 (1988): 9.

11   Ibid., 35.

12   Rhys Jones, "Firestick Farming," *Australian Natural History* 16, no. 7 (1969): 224–28.

13   Ibid.

14   Phelps and Scherer, "Habit-Based and Story-Driven."

15   Van Oosterzee and Morrison, *The Centre: The Natural History of Australia's Desert Regions*, 110.

16   Northern Territory Government, Department of Natural Resources, Environment, The Arts and Sport, *2008–2009 Annual Report* (Darwin: Northern Territory Government, 2009), 140.

17   Ibid.

18   Ibid., 139.

19   Ibid.

20   Ibid., 140.

21   Ibid.

22   "Desert Park Reptiles Star in Upcoming BBC Production," Northern Territory Government, Department of Natural Resources, Environment, The Arts and Sport, media release, November 15, 2006, accessed March 15, 2010, http://www.alicespringsdesertpark.com.au/about/pdf/mr/ bbc151106.pdf.

23   "Central Indochina Dry Forests (IM0202)," World Wildlife Fund, accessed March 21, 2010, http://www .worldwildlife.org/wildworld/profiles/terrestrial/im/ im0202_full.html.

24   Green & Dale Associates habitat design projects include Lowland Gorilla, Sumatran Tiger; Trail of the Elephants and Orangutan Sanctuary (Melbourne Zoo); Rainbow Valley Lorikeets and Jungle Jewels Hummingbirds (Singapore); Backyard to Bush and Wild Asia (Taronga Zoo, Sydney).

25 D. Casselman, an attorney from Los Angeles, in association with a prominent Cambodian businessman, and the Ministry of Environment, Cambodia.

26 The resin is extracted by cutting a hole into the tree trunk. When the resin is collected, any remaining resin is used as fuel to burn in the hole for a few minutes in order to stimulate the flow of resin. This practice of collection and burning may last for two weeks.

27 Hong-Truong Luu, *Dipterocarp oleoresin in Vietnam and Cambodia: Harvesting Techniques, Resource Management, and Livelihood Issues; A Report from an Exchange Visit to Cambodia*, accessed April 8, 2010, http://www.ntfp.org/ntfpadmin/publications-pdf/Resinstudy_Cambodia_May07.pdf.

28 Subsistence farming typically involves the planting of cashew nuts and fruit trees among the remains of giant dead forest trees.

29 Ed Stewart is cofounder of the Performing Animal Welfare Society (PAWS).

30 "Central Indochina Dry Forests (IM0202)," World Wildlife Fund.

31 *Shorea siamensis* (Rang), *Shorea obtusa* (Teng/Phchek), *Dipterocarpus obtusifolius* (Theng), and *Dipterocarpus tuberculatus* (Khlong) are the other three deciduous dipterocarp species.

32 "Northern Plains," Wildlife Conservation Society Cambodia, accessed April 10, 2010, http://www.wcscambodia.org/saving-wild-places/northern-plains.html.

CHAPTER 9

Orongo Station Master Plan

NELSON BYRD WOLTZ LANDSCAPE ARCHITECTS
THOMAS L. WOLTZ, PRINCIPAL AND DESIGNER

THE ORONGO STATION MASTER PLAN FOR A three-thousand-acre sheep farm in New Zealand establishes a vision for the extensive regeneration of native ecologies devastated by standard farming practices. The landscape design, developed by Nelson Byrd Woltz Landscape Architects (NBW), combines innovative restoration ecology with best practices in crop and livestock production in the context of a cultural landscape rich in history. Designed in collaboration with a team of public officials, private stakeholders, and local experts, the project serves as an important model that can expand the current definitions of sustainability and landscape architecture in the context of contemporary agricultural practices.

In 2003, when NBW began the design of the master plan, Orongo Station was a typical sheep farm on the east coast of New Zealand's North Island. Nearly all of the three thousand acres were grazed by cattle and sheep despite steep cliffs, brutal wind exposure, salt spray, and erosion on the windward slopes. The station's primary notoriety came from the prominent cliffs on its northern peninsula—Te Kuri a Paoa, also called Young Nick's Head. This promontory is important to the history of New Zealand both as the landing site of the Horouta Canoe, bringing

Maori settlers to the island, and as the first land spotted by Captain Cook's crew, the first Western explorers to visit the island in 1769.

The ecology of Orongo Station, like that of much of New Zealand, has been under assault ever since the arrival of humans in the thirteenth century. Lush, temperate rainforest covered the North Island and teemed with a rich diversity of birds, amphibians, and invertebrates. Early Maori settlers cut much of the forest for fire, shelter, and agriculture. The later arrival of English colonists brought further destruction of the forests for lumber and grazing while introducing mice, cats, weasels, rabbits, and other alien mammals that quickly decimated native bird and amphibian populations.

Assisted and inspired by a talented team of conservation biologists and ecologists, NBW developed a unique opportunity for a significant wildlife conservation area on the peninsula of Young Nick's Head. A predator-proof fence isolates the headland, which is otherwise protected by steep cliffs plunging to the Pacific Ocean on three sides, creating a sanctuary ideal for nesting migratory birds. Existing rodents and pests were eradicated and a dense planting of coastal woodland tree saplings was installed to

153

initiate the reestablishment of temperate rainforest, the primordial ecology of the site. The ultimate goal for the sanctuary is the reintroduction of the tuatara, a highly endangered prehistoric reptile that once inhabited the exposed cliffs of the North Island. The effectiveness of the restoration efforts are supported by a vigilant and aggressive pest control regime. The improved habitat and reduced predation has already attracted new arrivals of threatened nesting bird species that include blue penguins and Fluttering Shearwaters. An innovative audio system developed by the team's conservation biologist plays recorded birdcalls that have attracted the endangered Gray-faced Petrel to nest and breed, the first success of its kind in the world.

To support the efforts of the Tuatara Preserve, the landscape architect initiated an extensive plan for restoring the adjacent Orongo wetland, a once vibrant tidal wetland that was previously drained for expanded grazing paddocks. To provide a diversity of habitats, the master plan proposed the construction of a freshwater wetland in addition to the restoration of the saltwater wetland. A large sinuous earthen embankment divides the watersheds and diverts rainwater to the inland freshwater wetland. While the saltwater wetland is tidal, the freshwater wetland is designed to accommodate seasonal flooding. A winding ribbon of deep water flows year-round and the broad surrounding flatlands flood during the wet season. To create and maintain habitats throughout the year, islands were designed and shaped from fill created by excavation of the channel. The islands' slopes and sizes are carefully calibrated to provide protective habitat for specific amphibians, invertebrates, and flightless birds.

Reforestation on the uplands above the wetlands is part of a larger effort that extends southward from the Tuatara Preserve five and one-half miles along the coast. These highlands are exposed to battering winds and rain, and they are slowly eroding into the sea. Reforestation helps stabilize the vulnerable coastline while creating valuable habitat and increased connectivity through wildlife corridors. To date, five hundred thousand trees have been planted at Orongo Station, a bold step toward restoring the coastline to an imagined pre-settlement state.

The land of Orongo Station is sacred to the local Maori tribe—the Ngai Tamanuhiri. Remnants of earthen defensive structures, fishing encampments, and pits created to store the staple food crop (a sweet-potato-like tuber called kumara) are found throughout the landscape. The master plan engaged the tribe to restore a cemetery on the property that suffered from poor access and neglect. Simple design strategies raise the prominence of the cemetery in the river valley and protect adjacent historic earthen defensive structures. These efforts have fostered a positive relationship with the tribe and create a regional model for integrating agricultural practices with the restoration of Maori cultural landscapes. Moreover, the ecological restoration projects are a source of pride for the tribe. The design team worked with the Ngai Tamanuhiri to start a nursery that allows the tribe to supply some of the trees required for the reforestation effort. This provides much-needed employment and invites the community to share their wisdom of local plants and participate in the ecological regeneration.

The efforts to celebrate the Maori cultural landscape and to restore ecologies and habitats for endangered species are unique in their integration with an active, working, and profitable agricultural operation. In their search for more balanced farming practices, the designers sought methods to integrate these efforts while designing some of the primary functional pieces of the farming operation. The architecture of the farm, the shearing sheds, vehicle and equipment storage, and staff housing have been composed to create a multifunctional courtyard. A bridge and road over the Maraetaha River were designed by the landscape architect to provide improved farm connectivity and to compose the river floodplain in a way that celebrates the surrounding physical and cultural landscapes. The road and bridge strike a straight axis across the floodplain to align with the peak of the prominent hill of Taranaki beyond, a site of sacred significance to the Ngai Tamanuhiri. Also, the designers collaborated with farmers to lay out the citrus fields and inscribed a sweeping arc of shelter-belt trees to mark its outer boundary. The perimeter is reforested with native riparian trees that will filter sediment and stabilize the riverbanks. A journey across the field pierces the broad arc which parallels the natural course of the river and reveals the unfolding landscape in dramatic views to the Pacific. The bridge design keeps a low, elegant profile to respect views from adjacent properties and roads.

Finally, the efforts to knit ecology, farming, and the cultural landscape together have been distilled into a series of gardens and buildings at the owner's residence. The complex is anchored by a historic house; the gardens create formal and informal spaces for entertaining, play, and discovery. They are rich in narrative, using plants and earthworks to tell important stories about New Zealand ecology and culture. The gardens create a lens for visitors to understand the efforts of the nationally important conservation efforts on Orongo Station and the new vision that they represent.

FIGURE 9.1
The conservation master plan for Orongo Station (which includes Maraetaha and Mapere Station) encompasses three thousand acres and weaves together multiple ecological restoration strategies with a working sheep farm and a rich cultural landscape.

Image courtesy of Nelson Byrd Woltz Landscape Architects.

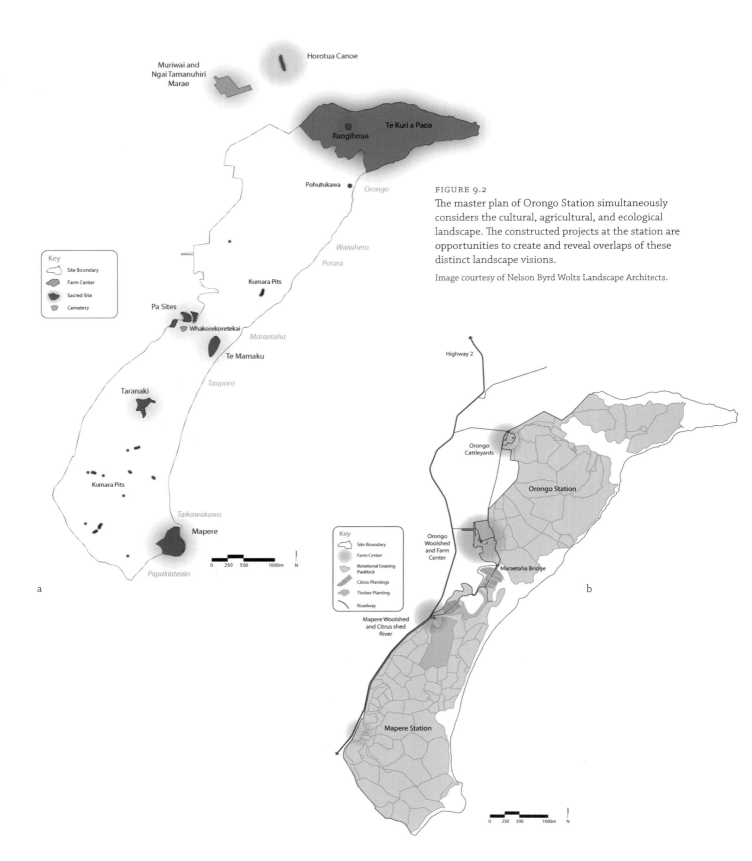

FIGURE 9.2
The master plan of Orongo Station simultaneously considers the cultural, agricultural, and ecological landscape. The constructed projects at the station are opportunities to create and reveal overlaps of these distinct landscape visions.

Image courtesy of Nelson Byrd Woltz Landscape Architects.

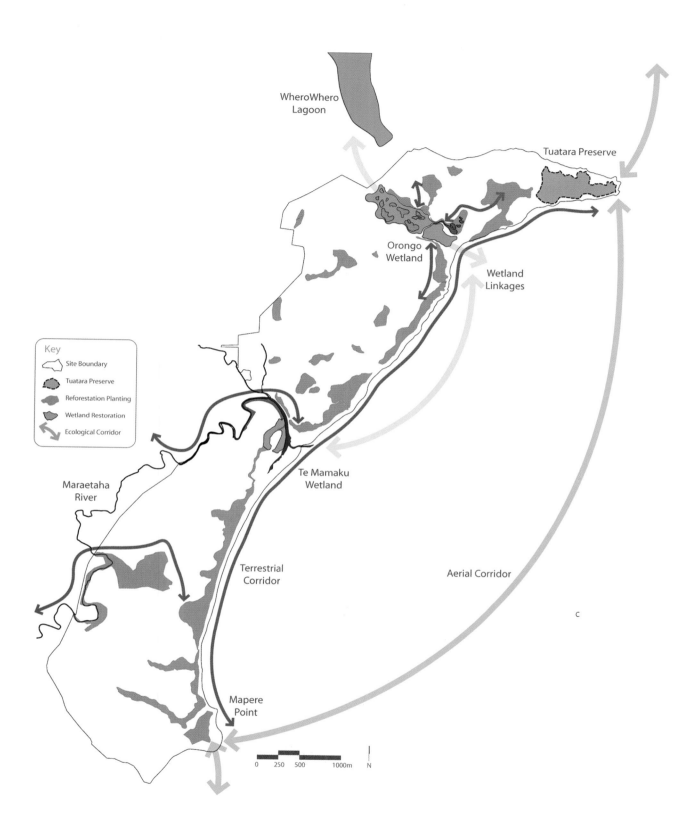

Key

- Site Boundary
- Tuatara Preserve
- Reforestation Planting
- Wetland Restoration
- Ecological Corridor

WheroWhero Lagoon

Tuatara Preserve

Orongo Wetland

Wetland Linkages

Maraetaha River

Te Mamaku Wetland

Terrestrial Corridor

Aerial Corridor

Mapere Point

0   250   500   1000m

N

c

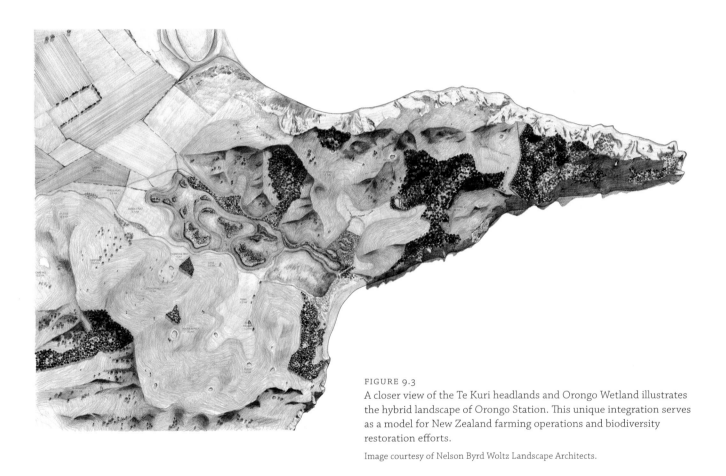

FIGURE 9.3
A closer view of the Te Kuri headlands and Orongo Wetland illustrates the hybrid landscape of Orongo Station. This unique integration serves as a model for New Zealand farming operations and biodiversity restoration efforts.

Image courtesy of Nelson Byrd Woltz Landscape Architects.

FIGURE 9.4

A closer view of the primary restoration projects at Orongo Station. The Tuatara Preserve has achieved unprecedented success in New Zealand in developing coastal scrub and grassland habitat and in attracting targeted species including Fluttering Shearwaters, Grey-faced and Sooty Petrels, and gannets. The Orongo Wetland project, still underway, is one of the most ambitious in the country.

Image courtesy of Nelson Byrd Woltz Landscape Architects.

FIGURE 9.5
The 1,640-foot-
long Excluder
Fence includes a
flange at the top to
discourage climbing
rodents. A below-
grade flange repels
any attempt to dig
under the barrier.

Image courtesy of
Nelson Byrd Woltz
Landscape Architects (a);
© Marion Brenner (b).

a

b

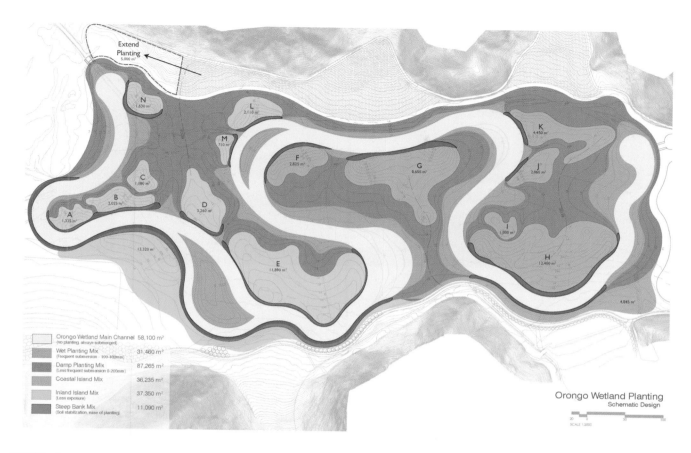

Orongo Wetland Planting
Schematic Design

Orongo Wetland Main Channel (no planting, always submerged)	58,100 m²	
Wet Planting Mix (Frequent submersion - 100-400mm)	31,460 m²	
Damp Planting Mix (Less frequent submersion 0-200mm)	87,265 m²	
Coastal Island Mix	36,235 m²	
Inland Island Mix (Less exposure)	37,350 m²	
Steep Bank Mix (Soil stabilization, ease of planting)	11,090 m²	

FIGURE 9.6

The planning of the wetland included careful arrangement and sizing of the islands to provide distinct habitat types for birds and amphibians. The steep banks help provide protection from predators during critical nesting periods.

Image courtesy of Nelson Byrd Woltz Landscape Architects.

FIGURE 9.7
Completed road networks, shoreline reforestation, beach restoration, salt and freshwater wetlands, and re-fenced grazing paddocks demonstrate the complete landscape vision for the Orongo Valley.

Image courtesy of Nelson Byrd Woltz Landscape Architects.

a

b

FIGURE 9.8
a) Wetland under construction in 2008, showing the sinuous channel that retains water throughout the year (image courtesy of Kim Dodgshun); and b) wetlands in 2012, showing the salt and freshwater wetlands that provide seventy-five acres of restored habitat for plants and wildlife (image courtesy of Nelson Byrd Woltz Landscape Architects).

FIGURE 9.9
The 1,890-foot-long earthen dam separates the freshwater (to the left) from the saltwater wetland (to the right). It also provides a mowed walking path through the wetland environment.

Image courtesy of Nelson Byrd Woltz Landscape Architects.

Orongo Station
Staff Housing & Office

Orongo Station
Work Yards & Woolshed

Maraetaha Bridge
56 meter freespan (183 feet)

Riverbank Restoration
1.9 km (1.2 mi) of riverbank
8.5 hectares

Maraetaha Citrus Blocks
9.6 hectares

Te Mamaku Wetland
5.9 hectares

Whakorekoretekai
Ngai Tamanuhiri Cemetery

Citrus Blocks
4.3 hectares

Mapere Station Woolshed

Maraetaha
River

Pa Sites

Maraetaha
(Highgate)

Te Mamaku

Orongo Station

Pacific Ocean

Maraetaha

Key

Reforestation Initiated
Planned Reforestation
Sheep Paddock
Citrus Block
Shelterbelt Row
Project Boundary

0   125   250m   N

FIGURE 9.12

Master plan of the Maraetaha River floodplain incorporating ecological restoration, the cultural landscape, and working farm components.

Image courtesy of Nelson Byrd Woltz Landscape Architects.

FIGURE 9.15
At Orongo Station's Homestead, a narrative series of seven gardens interpret the natural and cultural histories of New Zealand. The Earthworks Garden above, encircled by a collection of native hebes, honors the shaping of the land as an important legacy of the New Zealand landscape.

Image courtesy of Nelson Byrd Woltz Landscape Architects.

FIGURE 9.16
The earthworks echo the shapes of defensive structures constructed by the native Maori and later trimmed smooth by grazing sheep. This garden interprets these powerful landforms and the severe effects that grazing and deforestation have on shaping the land.

© Marrion Brenner; image courtesy of Nelson Byrd Woltz Landscape Architects.

CHAPTER 10

Ecological Restoration Foundations
to Designing Habitats in Urban Areas

Steven N. Handel

Restoration Ecology
for the Urban Theater

HOW CAN ECOLOGISTS BE INVOLVED IN THE future design of our cities? Urban life has traditionally been defined as a contrast with natural, rural settings. But the twenty-first century has brought new understanding of the value of habitats and ecological services to city dwellers. Most people throughout the world, as well as in North America, live in urban centers. Their needs for energy conservation, water supplies, and a release from the stresses of modern life have put ecological urban landscapes into a positive new focus. Academic ecologists, interested in the structure and functioning of living plant and animal communities, are being brought to the table to discuss urban planning with design professionals. The separate traditions of academic ecology and urban design must now find a common idiom toward improving urban conditions.

Restoration ecology is defined as bringing back the structure and functions of nature to areas where they have been removed by past land-use disturbances.[1] The removal is often for construction or for clearing land for agriculture or commerce. Sometimes the disturbance has a natural

origin, such as a flood or fire, which has substantially removed the previous living community. In both scenarios, the restoration process is similar in responding to physical and biological site intervention needs.

Restoration ecology contrasts with conservation biology. Conservation aims at securing and sustaining those patches of nature that still persist, often surrounded by intense human activities. Restoration aims to add back more habitat patches to the landscape mosaic, increasing our natural capital. As urban and suburban areas change with economic and demographic progressions, very often land patches become available, which could be the stage for new ecological expressions. Sometimes these patches are quite small or are of peculiar shape—such as very thin, linear transportation corridors. Each available patch has its own potential future and ecological constraints that determine its potential for restoration design.

Available urban spaces for restoration actions are often scattered, surrounded by the infrastructure of modern life: our roads, residences, and commercial districts. The available spaces are landscape islands in a sea of development. These paved and human-dominated lands around areas being considered for restoration, the matrix for our efforts, can be barriers to ecological functions.[2] For example, they challenge processes such as dispersal, colonization, community assembly, and population growth of plants and animals.[3] The matrix is an ecological design constraint that limits and molds the type of natural community that can be successfully restored. This is similar to the types of decisions landscape architects must make about transportation, infrastructure, zoning, and financial resources when designing public space. But it is the requirements of living species that define this ecological constraint—not public policy or engineering needs.

Almost all urban areas have some unused land that can be opportunities to add new habitat. Here, we define as degraded land any space with neither its historic soil horizons intact nor its historic ecological communities present due to past land-use decisions or disruptions. In many urban areas, these landscape opportunities can be sanitary landfills, abandoned industrial zones (including brownfields), and port and other commercial parcels that are neither economically viable nor serve current government agency needs. The need for economically useful and healthy environments never disappears, however, and focusing on the role of restored nature in satisfying those needs is our concern here.

Ecosystem services are recognized as having great value for public landscapes.[4] These are the processes that plant and animal communities offer human communities, usually at no cost. To replace the ecoservices with infrastructure and high-technology equipment would be very expensive. Although the value of ecosystem services has often been ignored, considered an externality to municipal budgets, this attitude is changing. Among the services restored habitats offer us are the generation and preservation of soils and the cycling of nutrients in the soil and ground water. The shade and moisture that living communities offer give us partial stabilization of local climate, as well as purification of air and groundwater. This is also understood as a public health benefit, as fewer chemicals and particulates in the air lower respiratory stresses on the human population. Living communities also help mitigate against droughts and floods by holding precipitation and floodwater, then slowly releasing it. In

these ways, restored natural communities are bioengineering features as well as cultural amenities.

Restoration Ecology and the Design Process

Landscape architecture professionals have many criteria to embrace during their design decisions that directly involve the structure of the new landscape. In contrast, restoration ecology is grounded in the functioning of the landscape, particularly the ability of the new plant community to reproduce, to modify the physical environment, and to be an acceptable habitat that satisfies the many niche requirements of animals. Also, a functioning restored habitat undergoes undirected change through the years—some species fading out of the community, others migrating in and spreading.

In contrast, many high design gardens are built to remain static over many decades, except for the inevitable growth of the initial plants installed during construction. Over time, if any of the plants die, they are usually replaced in kind. If there is an invasion of new plant species on the ground, then they will often be removed during routine maintenance. Many of the design decisions, such as ground treatment with stones or barrier fabrics, are made to keep the design true to the original vision. This maintains a purposeful design expression and a historic look rooted in the aesthetics of the time when the park was built. The human cultural goals are paramount. This approach fights ecological function (e.g., seedling recruitment, successional change, availability of microsites for animal habitats) and is never included in the criteria of success for habitat restoration.

Similarly, modern lighting design can be stylish, energy efficient, and carefully calibrated to answer a specific site's needs for high- or low-intensity illumination. But all outdoor lighting has significant effects on the organisms in the landscape.[5] Research into the impacts of lighting regimes on the area biodiversity is needed as a complement to design decisions involving human requirements for the lighting system. Design decisions for the night environment can have profound ecological impacts.

Among the critical differences between restoration ecology and landscape architecture is a concern about tempo of vegetative change. An ecological community of many species includes those with subtle but real physiological differences. Some plants tolerate and need high light intensities; others only succeed in the shade. These differences have well-understood biological bases, such as photosynthetic chemistry and water balance adaptations. For example, many beautiful woodland wildflowers, such as trilliums (*Trillium* spp.) and mayapple (*Podophyllum peltatum*), can only survive in the shade. Installing them early in the construction process leads to death. These plants can only be added years after the initial canopy is installed and the woodland surface is suffused with shade. The tempo of a successful woodland restoration is slow and can stretch to over a decade.

Similarly, the structure of a restored plant community is multilayered from ground level to shrubs, to subcanopy trees to the canopy. This vertical structure develops over time as plant reproduction and dispersal by many species progresses. Although high design gardens often do have ground treatments and canopy layers, the model is based on aesthetics, not the dynamic and multigenerational character of natural communities.

Successful plant communities always change over time. Ecological succession is seen throughout the living world, though the pace of change can be rapid or very long-term.

Species move across the regional landscape in response to disturbances, opportunities, or long-term environmental change. Over time, the successful species of an ecologically restored site may be very different from what was installed during the first stages of a construction.[6] One reasonable hypothesis might be that a successful restoration may contain completely different plant species and individuals over time than what were initially installed. This change in plant identity is rooted in demography. Changes in birth rates and death rates determine which species will persist. In a natural plant community, each species has different rates, which are integrated into changing population numbers.[7] As each species expands or contracts its population, the overall community changes, sometimes dramatically. The expectation of demographic change is one of the foundations of ecological restoration, although it is missing from the idiom of the high design garden. Those landscapers who wish to include restored natural communities also must accept the inevitability of change and recognize its role in creating sustainable habitats and their services for the public.

Defining the Target Community to Be Restored

Determining which plant species should be installed, the ecological target for the site, is usually based on some attempt to re-create the past. This can be based on historic documents, photographs, on-site evidence of remnant plants, or memories of local residents.[8] But the past is not prologue in restoration ecology because our urban sites have so dramatically changed. Even if detailed and quantitative records of past vegetation are available, the hypothesis that the former community can be reiterated on the site can be challenged on many grounds. Modern urban sites are fragmented, small, and distant from any healthy adjacent sites, which can buffer and support local populations.

The physical environment of modern cities is also quite stressful and different from the past.[9] The landscape matrix around project sites is often paved and constructed, very inhospitable to the movement and needs of living species. Air quality is polluted, soil is modified both chemically and physically, human intrusions are usually common and destructive, and the small size of urban project sites means that many plants are near the edges. Edge conditions are themselves stressful, being hot, dry, and having many shafts of light, resulting in no part of the project site being in an interior condition of high humidity and filtered light.[10] The types of plants and animals that can live in these modern, urban sites are most likely quite different from what were there in the distant, uninhabited past.

An additional concern is the quality and membership of the plant and animal communities that might remain around an urban project site today. Many of the original plants and animals are long gone because of human actions and past land uses.[11] In addition, most urban sites, on a worldwide basis, have hundreds of species that have invaded from other continents and challenge one's ability to re-create historic habitats.[12] These invaders are usually aggressive, have rapid population growth, and are damaging not only at the beginning of a project but also in maintaining the target community in the years ahead.

Any design plan that wishes to include native habitats must take a cautious view that only some of the species of the past can survive today and into the near future. Consequently, performance of the persisting native plant species in contemporary urban sites should be studied in some detail, as these are the winners of the contest of what is feasible in modern stressful cities.

Experimental Precedents on Degraded Lands

Several experimental studies of urban restoration have been completed, testing the links in nature that can be rebuilt. These studies are usually collaborations between an experimentalist, designing the tests so that results can be applied elsewhere, in collaboration with design firms that contribute the requirements of land regulations, site access, and compatibility with other project goals. These design professionals have been civil engineers, landscape architects, planners, and construction managers. Almost no urban restoration can be completed without the multiple perspectives of science and design.

Soil in the Meadowlands

In determining pragmatic protocols and targets for restoration ecology, a series of formal experiments has been conducted in the New York–New Jersey metropolitan area. These studies are putting boundaries on the ecological realities of urban habitat design. One study in the New Jersey Meadowlands, adjacent to the New Jersey Turnpike, studied the effect of soil conditions on plant invasion and growth. The original site was a sixteen-acre sanitary landfill operated by the town of Kearny. The site had been closed to additional dumping, and then left unmanaged. After twenty years, the vegetation was predominantly a dense population of nonnative mugwort (*Artemisia vulgaris*) with some scattered tree of heaven (*Ailanthus altissima*) stems. Although standard ecological theory would have predicted a significant succession of many native plant species to this site, the isolation of this urban infrastructure and the surrounding matrix

of wide highways, railroad yards, and large industrial areas made this landfill an island surrounded by an utter lack of native habitat. Very few plant species were available to migrate in and begin population growth and community development there.

The site conditions lacked any soil horizon over the decaying household debris. The surface was a clutter of old trash, twisted bicycles, discarded automobile tires, and broken glass (Figure 10.1). The sweeping stand of mugwort was not surprising, as this weedy species thrives in degraded, alkaline conditions. New soil material was located by the New Jersey Meadowlands Commission and trucked to the site. Two feet of sandy loam from Manhattan was spread across the landfill. This was clean material from a glacial riverbed that had been buried for more than ten thousand years and was free of debris and weed seeds. This was covered by approximately one foot of composted leaf litter from Teaneck, New Jersey, garden waste (Figure 10.2). The site was hydroseeded with fescues, as required by soil erosion rules for municipal landfills. Sixteen small clusters of native trees and shrubs (including *Acer rubrum, Cornus amomum, Morella pensylvanica, Prunus serotina, Robinia pseudoacacia, Sambucus canadensis,* and *Viburnum dentatum*) were scattered over the newly covered site, and then recruitment of seedlings from these clusters was recorded over the years.[13] In 2010, twenty years after the initial planting, the site was again monitored and was found to be a dense forest of American ash and some scattered mulberries. Neither of the species was planted in the initial installation. They migrated in and are thriving in the now deep and favorable soil structure. The site has gone from weed patch to woodland after soil rehabilitation. Similar studies on other degraded lands also have shown the stimulating effects of appropriate new soil horizons.[14]

Generally, urban soils are chemically and physically stressful.[15] Because of past land use, they are often compacted; contain concrete dust, construction debris, and other pollutants; and have very restricted drainage and aeration properties. Also, urban soils often lack beneficial microbes necessary for nutrient cycling and mycorrhizae to assist in plant growth.[16] Addition of new soil must always be considered in urban restorations if a high-biodiversity and low-maintenance future are to be achieved.

FIGURE 10.1
Initial conditions at the sanitary landfill in the New Jersey Meadowlands lacked soil cover over the refuse and a species-poor plant community dominated by mugwort (or common wormwood), *Artemisia vulgaris*.

Photograph by S. N. Handel.

Larger urban sites are often a mosaic of parcels with very different land-use histories. Consequently, soil conditions can vary wildly from lot to lot within the site. A detailed mapping of current conditions and necessary amendments is a requirement for future ecological success. Additions of organic matter, chemicals to modify pH toward an appropriate level (usually somewhat acidic in eastern woodlands), or depth of soil to aid in water retention must always be considered as a design requirement before the living palette is added.

Ecological restoration requires new seedlings and clonal offshoots to increase the population size by growing away from the initial planted material. The soil conditions surrounding the initial plantings cannot be inappropriate for seedling germination, emergence, and growth—the complete ecological

sequence for population increase. Without a birth rate on site, sustainable populations are impossible.

Dispersal Mutualisms at Fresh Kills

A large-scale ecological restoration program was set up at the Fresh Kills Landfill in Staten Island, New York. With approximately two thousand acres, this is the largest landfill in North America. It is becoming a new recreational park, Freshkills Park, following the master plan of James Corner Field Operations.[17] One of the high garbage mounds at Fresh Kills is 150 feet high and was closed in a regulated manner by a clay cap covered by two to three feet of clean fill, then hydroseeded with a mixture of perennial grasses and legumes. Onto this site, the research team under my direction installed twenty patches of native trees and shrubs, ranging from seven to seventy plants.[18] Many data were collected, but the focus here is on the mutualisms between plants and animals that were reestablished on these new plantings. Plant species have many interactions with surrounding animals. Those which are beneficial to both members of the interaction are termed mutualisms, and this partnership increases the population levels of both members of the interaction. Could habitat to attract and maintain animal mutualists be designed here? If so, this interaction could be a possible facilitator to advance designed, ecological landscapes.

The first mutualism investigated was seed dispersal by birds. All seven of the plant species installed at Fresh Kills have fleshy fruit (Table 10.1). Birds eat

FIGURE 10.2
Addition and grading of composed leaf mulch over clean fill from a glacial riverbed. This new substrate over refuse allowed for adequate rooting media for restoration plantings.

Photograph by G. R. Robinson.

TABLE 10.1

Native plant species installed on Fresh Kills Landfill to test the potential of reestablishing ecological mutualisms in a restored woodland. These plants were installed in patches of seven, twenty-one, forty-two, and seventy plants, representing one, three, six, and ten of each species.

Hackberry	*Celtis occidentalis*
Sumac	*Rhus copallina*
Shadblow	*Amelanchier canadensis*
Beach Plum	*Prunus maritima*
Blueberry	*Vaccinium corymbosum*
Blackberry	*Rubus allegheniensis*
Wild Rose	*Rosa nitida*

these, and when they leave the seed-producing tree, the seeds are deposited away at some distance.[19] The bird gets a nutrient advantage and the plant gets its seed dispersed at a distance from the shade and competition of the mother tree. The experimental plantings were in the middle of a large industrial zone with very little natural habitat and the Rutgers University researchers did not know whether this mutualism could be reestablished. But even in the first year after planting, we recorded the presence of thousands of seeds brought in by the bird community from surrounding areas. These were deposited in cloth traps placed under the tall hackberry trees in each patch. These seeds represented more than twenty species that we had not planted on the site (Figure 10.3). These new species included many native East Coast trees and shrubs from the region, including *Parthenocissus virginiana*, *Viburnum dentatum*, *Nyssa sylvatica*, *Rhus copallina*, *Morella pensylvanica*, and *Sassafras albidum* as the most abundant taxa. Even the smallest patches of seven plants yielded hundreds of seeds from elsewhere dropping into the seed traps.[20] This supported an initial observational finding that new seeds are quickly dispersed into this landfill site.[21]

These data are evidence that a landscape designer, even in degraded urban areas (the continent's largest landfill!), can have a project that is strongly impacted by this dispersal mutualism in the future.[22] By this mutualism bringing in seed-yielding new species that were not part of the design palette, the surrounding habitat is a source of plant material that will intrude upon and change

the original design complex. For this setting, the birds were de facto landscape architects. Given the extensive numbers of alien, aggressive plant species in our urban centers, the look and functioning of these sites may be very different in the decades ahead.[23] Dispersal mutualisms are both a source of biodiversity and a sink for the retention of the initial landscape design. This process can only be managed by an understanding of the surrounding vegetation, and then a protocol for long-term management to control the seed-dispersal dynamic as the site matures.

Although many North American woody plants have fruit dispersed by birds, other dispersal modes are common and must be considered. Wind-dispersed seeds are present in both woody and herbaceous plant species and can move broadly across the landscape.[24] The distance is determined by the physical interaction of seed shape and mass with the wind velocity and vector. In the Fresh Kills experiment, few wind-dispersed tree seeds were found, as the traps were hundreds of yards away from any source tree. But over time, the slow rain of wind-dispersed seeds can reach any site in our urban centers. Some of these will be unwanted, invasive species (e.g., *Ailanthus altissima*, *Acer platanoides*). Again, management of the site to control the changing palette is required for a designer to realize a specific habitat target.

A large number of our woodland herbs (such as *Sanguinaria canadensis*, *Trillium grandiflorum*, many *Viola* species, *Carex pedunculata*, and *Asarum canadense*) have seeds specifically dispersed by ant

a

b

FIGURE 10.3
More than just passive objects creating shade in the landscape, trees are focal points of dynamic ecological processes. a) Cloth traps placed under young trees tested how these plants attract perching birds, which can bring in seeds of other species; and b) the collection of seeds from traps shows that single trees can assist in enriching the diversity of a new natural community.

Photographs by S. N. Handel.

species.[25] These plants are important for nutrient retention as well as for landscape beauty. The seeds of these plant species have a fatty reward, the "elaiosome," surrounding the seed. The ants pick up the seed and fat unit, carry it to their nest where the fat is eaten, and the seeds, unharmed, are discarded and may grow. This interaction is important for a complete and functioning understory in restored woodland, but it is very difficult to initiate this mutualism without a proactive effort. Small plantings of these herbs must be installed by the contractor as ants will not typically carry the seeds widely, and certainly not across dangerous, urban infrastructure like roads and railways.

Similarly, woodland ant colonies invade new restoration sites slowly. Queen ants fly, but it often takes years before colonies are large enough to yield enough workers that can efficiently carry plant seeds across a woodland site.

These ant-dispersed plants and their insect partners usually live in shady environments with rich soils. It may take several or many years for a new restoration ecology site to have rich soil and a closed canopy. Consequently, adding these herbaceous plants to create a full biodiversity suite for the habitat may be a phase that must be postponed for several years. This delay requires institutional and financial resources that are kept active for years after the initial landscaping contract. This is atypical in landscape architecture and requires new administrative frameworks.

Pollination Mutualisms at Fresh Kills

The production of seed at a restoration site is a necessary process for long-term sustainability. Will pollinators visit plants installed at an urban site distant from the nesting and foraging habitats typical of these insects? If not, can these types of habitats be designed on site, and will bees colonize the new venues? These must be compatible with the other goals of the ecological and human landscape programs. At the Fresh Kills Landfill experiment, my field research team recorded the number, diversity, and distribution of insect pollinators on the installed plants.[26] The general pattern of the results was very optimistic, with more than sixty bee species found on these modest plantings.[27] This was similar to the number of bee species found at populations of same plant species in city parks where the plants had been established for many years. There, the habitats around the study plants were substantially natural, with many resources for healthy bee populations. Also, the percentage of flowers that made seed on the landfill plantings was statistically similar to the percentage of successful flowers in the native areas.

When the spatial distribution of the pollinators was recorded, many bees were found even 350 meters from the edge of the landfill, where there was a remnant native forest. In fact, the frequency of bees in the middle of this large site was higher than at test plantings near to the edge. It was discovered that the very successful central plantings were close to erosion gullies on the landfill surface, where many bees were nesting. Many native bees nest in the soil and would have difficulty digging and maintaining nests where there is a dense grass cover. But thick grass cover is the typical closure requirement on landfills. In this way, what was an engineering problem, an erosion gully, could be redefined as an ecological advantage.

Contrasts between engineering and ecological needs are common and must be overcome for the "value added" of ecological services. In this setting, the addition of piles of loose soil of various densities on the surface of the landfill would satisfy both requirements: the landfill surface is intact and there is open, loose soil in which bees can dig new nests, and then forage on and pollinate the new restoration plantings.

Urban Genotypes for Restoration Plantings

Landscape architects are trained to always use plant species appropriate for the soil type and hydrology of the project site. Sometimes water supply can be added as part of the construction mandate to expand the palette possible at a relatively dry site. For restoration ecology, with its emphasis on low maintenance and long-term sustainability, artificial watering regimes are inappropriate. In addition, the stressful nature of urban sites suggests that the variety of plants used during the construction phase must be different from the traditional, regional supplies available from the commercial nursery industry. The plant selection in commercial catalogs varies broadly in color, shape, and fruiting ability.[28] Given the atypical soil structure and the hot, dry stresses of smaller urban plots, a special suite of plant varieties may be needed for restoration. These should have physiological traits to sustain them in these unfavorable conditions.

Plant exploration is typically done in wild areas, but the source of new urban varieties might more reasonably be found in older urban areas where natural selection for persistence in degraded conditions has occurred for many years. It is known that selection for some urban genotypes can occur quite quickly.[29] For example, lead-tolerant perennial plants were found adjacent to roadways.[30] This condition falls off abruptly within a few meters of the roadside. Other weedy perennials in regularly mowed areas have evolved prostrate forms, saving leaves and stems from destruction by decapitation.[31] This information, so analogous to what has been found in natural settings, suggests there may be many opportunities to discover successful urban ecotypes in our old cities. These could yield plant populations that are most sustainable in the increasing urban stresses of the near future.

STEVEN N. HANDEL

The warning from the science of ecotype biology, the study of adaptation to local conditions, is that plant populations vary in their tolerances from place to place, even over very short gradients. Attention to plantings in stressful areas such as urban centers requires that project specifications are precise as to where the plant material is obtained. Attention to microsite needs during the design process should yield a much lower maintenance cost and a much higher success rate of installed plant material. Genotypic specificity would lead to economic sustainability.

Urban Case History: East, Wet, and Commercial into a Park

Restoration of urban habitats can yield interesting, attractive, and welcoming public spaces. Even intensely built-up spaces can be transformed into plant communities that mimic local, wild models. The master plan for the Brooklyn Bridge Park in New York City included a rich example of how an old industrial site can be transformed.[32] This site is a one-and-three-tenths-mile strip between the East River and a residential and commercial urban neighborhood. The park's eastern boundary, facing the river, includes the Brooklyn-Queens Expressway,

old hardscape, which rises above parkland to the neighboring residences in Brooklyn Heights. The master plan was developed by the Michael Van Valkenburgh Associates team and aims to bring back sustainable elements of the historic, undeveloped Brooklyn waterfront.[33] This site has been commercial since colonial days, but it has lost much of its economic potential in an age of large container ships. The original coastal vegetation was completely removed by centuries of commerce. The shoreline is concrete and riprap, and even the subtidal zone has been scraped flat to accommodate commercial shipping. The original shoreline ecological zonation and shape has been replaced by bulkheads, paved parking areas, and industrial structures. The hardscape can be removed, but what is an appropriate green solution to revive the site?

The site is narrow, with a distinct transition from tidal saltwater to dry upland. Several vegetative zones can be installed here (Figure 10.4). For this site, the master plan includes elements across the entire gradient: submarine saltwater habitat, salt marsh, halophytic shrubs, coastal meadows, freshwater wetlands and swales, and shrublands and woodlands typical of the East Coast. The inclusion of so many habitats for a coastal zone park was not an attempt to inappropriately present a "Sears Catalog" of possible solutions.

FIGURE 10.4
At Brooklyn Bridge Park, New York City, a diversity of habitats, from salt marsh grasses through coastal halophytic shrubs to early successional woodlands is being restored. The site had been a commercial shipping facility since colonial days. Above the site is a major highway and Brooklyn Heights, a dense urban community.

Photograph courtesy of Michael Van Valkenburgh Associates.

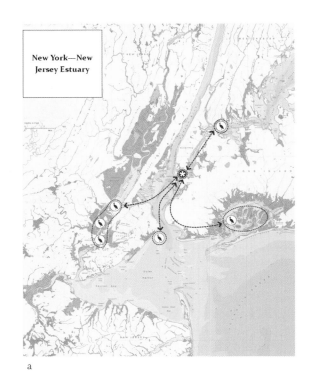

New York—New
Jersey Estuary

a

b

c

STEVEN N. HANDEL

Rather, the complexity of adjacent small habitats was meant to answer the needs of many animal species that might be attracted to the site.

Few animal species use only one habitat type throughout their life history. Different types of adjacent habitats are needed to respond to developmental and seasonal requirements. For many animals, feeding sites change through time, from cool mornings to warm afternoons, and also across the seasons. Even animals that spend much of their foraging time in open meadow habitats retreat to woodlands for protection from predators and storms. Also, climate is changing rapidly in this area and the presence of several habitat types during the construction phase allows for some to retreat and others to expand as climate conditions change over the decades. This helps ensure ecological functioning and low-maintenance habitats through the years. By increasing the number of habitat types in the mosaic, we decrease the risk of system-wide failure. Finally, the most common species in this park will be humans, and by having a variety of habitats on-site the designer presents a richer experience for human visitors. This encourages repeated visits and civic concern for the future of the new park. Without stewardship from its visitors, the park will not get the political and financial support needed in the decades ahead. In this way, the ecological advantages of a diverse habitat also support the political realities of maintaining a distinctive public park in the country's largest metropolitan area.

Another advantage of wild habitats in this small park is that there are still very few natural areas across the New York harbor region. This park by the East River can be a refuge for animal species fleeing disturbances elsewhere. For example, there are heron rookeries on small islands near the western, New Jersey border of the harbor. These are close to industrial zones, including oil refineries, and have a history of being disrupted by oil accidents.[34] Offering habitats on the Brooklyn shore gives birds fleeing such episodes a new place to rest and recover (Figure 10.5). Consequently, this park can be part of a broad landscape ecology interplay and has value far beyond the needs and values of this thin stretch of land by itself. The park acts as one patch in a metapopulation network, advancing sustainability across the metropolitan area. If one population fails, this park can be a refuge for survivors, or a source of new individuals that can become migrants to the stressed habitat as it recovers. This adds ecological functions elsewhere around the harbor.

At Brooklyn Bridge Park, some of the port infrastructure is being retained, such as the large piers reaching out into the river. These can be reprogrammed as habitat parcels as their size, strength, and location are appropriate for dense plantings, and as targets for coastal birds to use for their ecological needs. Infrastructure does not always have to be removed to advance ecological agendas. In this case, a useful and cost-effective solution is reusing existing man-made structures for valuable biological resources.

Urban Case History: West, Dry, and Military into a Park

The closure of the four-thousand-acre El Toro Marine Air Station in Irvine, Orange County, California, presented the local government with an

FIGURE 10.5

a) Few rookeries for harbor herons still exist in the New York–New Jersey Estuary. Addition of new foraging and perching habitats at the Brooklyn Bridge Park can add ecological redundancy and help secure the birds' populations across the landscape. b) Pier One salt marsh and pile field at Brooklyn Bridge Park is a constructed salt marsh planted with smooth cordgrass, framed by salvaged granite from the demolished Willis Avenue Bridge. Bird-watchers have sighted a number of migratory and resident bird species in the park, including falcons, herons, cormorants, blackbirds, warblers, and a variety of native ducks and geese. Beyond the granite blocks is a managed succession planting that includes several species of sumac along with little-leaf linden, gingko, plane tree, catalpa, and sweet gum. c) The terraced water gardens on Pier One gradually descend down the west side of the pier, forming a productive tidal ecosystem. Excess stormwater is cycled through lushly planted rain gardens and stored underground for park irrigation. Along the path is a managed succession planting, which includes hawthorn and sumac, while the water garden terraces contain numerous species of shrubs, wildflowers, wet and moist plant mixes, and several species of sedges and ferns.

Photographs courtesy of Michael Van Valkenburgh Associates.

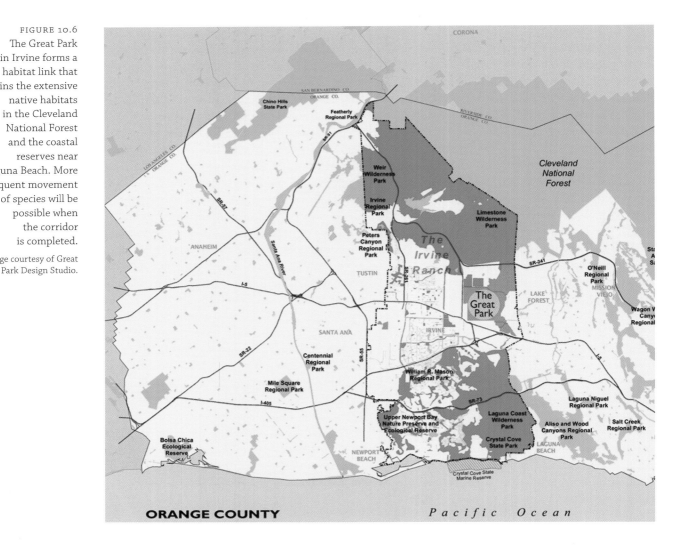

opportunity to solve a variety of social and ecological needs. Much of the land was sold for residential development to raise capital to supply new public functions. About 1,500 acres were reserved for a new public park, which was defined as having social and landscape ecology requirements.[35] A public, international competition to design the new Orange County Great Park was completed in 2007 and a multidisciplinary team design was chosen, led by New York landscape architect Ken Smith, working with collaborators Mia Lehrer + Associates, TEN Arquitectos, Green Shield Ecology, and Fusco Engineering. The project from the beginning used a core team of principals to develop the design. This group representing landscape architecture, architecture, ecology, and civil engineering created a schematic design

that embraces ecological function across many spatial scales.[36]

At the landscape scale, this park, in the middle of Orange County, includes restored Southern California habitats that physically link preserves on the north and south sides of the park (Figure 10.6). This new corridor will allow the movement of animals and seeds across the landscape and allow for more sustainable populations on the coast and in the mountains. Over time, if there is a disruption such as a fire in one area, individuals can move across the Great Park through its wildlife corridor (off-limits to people) and replenish populations on the other side.[37] Southern California has a Mediterranean-style climate of cool, moist winters and hot, dry summers and harbors many unusual species of plants and animals. Connecting currently disjunct populations is particularly useful here.

The demographic advantages are married with genetic advantages, as moving individuals bring new traits and genes from one population to another. This is an advantageous microevolutionary process and is particularly valuable in this century, as rapid climate change is projected for Southern California.

There is great public support from environmental groups in the community for this wildlife corridor. These groups were also a strong political force in the decision to use this large landscape for park facilities and not commercial development. Maintaining their interest will be critical in order to supply docents and stewards in the future to nurture the ecological restoration. Without long-standing public support, urban restorations often become degraded again. Problems include arson, invasive species, and vandalism.[38]

The restoration target for the new park included several habitat types analogous to the Brooklyn Bridge Park. Stream corridors are present on the site, and the park design also included creation of high earthen berms framing the water corridors' edges. Although most of the landscape is coastal sage scrub (the historic habitat type of this landscape, which only receives about thirteen inches of rain per year), there were opportunities for pockets of other plant communities. Along the streams are willow and cottonwood riverine habitats of great value for birdlife and freshwater aquatic species. The sides above the waterways are mostly dry shrub vegetation. Various shrub communities are included to match changes with aspect, elevation, and soil type. Scattered on the ridges are California oak and hickory woodlands and native grasslands and meadows. Higher reaches also contain native conifers for ecological and visual diversity.[39] The plant palette here was

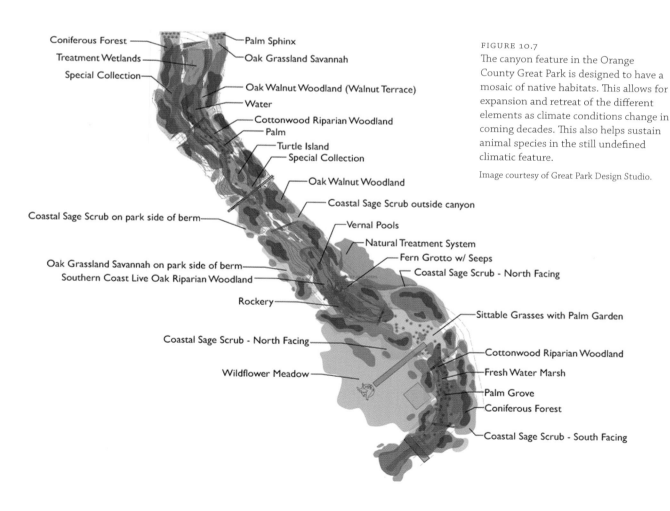

FIGURE 10.7
The canyon feature in the Orange County Great Park is designed to have a mosaic of native habitats. This allows for expansion and retreat of the different elements as climate conditions change in coming decades. This also helps sustain animal species in the still undefined climatic feature.

Image courtesy of Great Park Design Studio.

Ecological Restoration Foundations to Designing Habitats in Urban Areas

rigorously defined as "California Friendly" species. These are plants which have low water needs, can thrive with minimum maintenance in the local climate, and are not aggressive, invading species that could biologically pollute surrounding lands. These plantings are also aimed at educating visitors about the value of native species, encouraging their use in residential and commercial land. The restoration here may influence landscape design decisions outside the park borders.

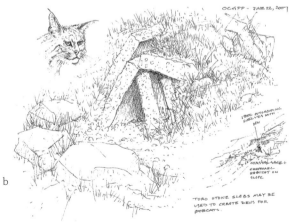

FIGURE 10.8

Microsites in the canyon, including woodland, cactus scrub, and aquatic habitats, would serve life history requirements of small animals. a) Dead wood and logs are preferred microsites for oviposition and refuge by lizards and many insects. b) Small crevasses constructed of reserved concrete runway pieces can become cryptic caves for bobcats, coyotes, and other small mammals.

Images from Handel et al., *Ecological Guidelines*, 100 and 197; drawn by D. D'Alessandro, courtesy of Great Park Design Studio.

The physical arrangement of these habitat types answers several ecological requirements. Zones varied by hydraulic condition from stream edges to dry, upland ridges. In addition, attention was paid to the expectation of changing climate and the inability to precisely measure microclimatic differences from place to place in the Great Park. Design needs required that the schematic design and plant placements be determined in advance so that cost estimates and initial construction bidding could occur. This all was done before landforming so that the variation in temperature and moisture across the projected elevations was unknown during these design phases. The approach was to scatter different vegetation formations throughout the park, knowing that some of the habitats types would expand into the most favorable microsites. This is often a prudent procedure in urban design projects for native species. The eventual microhabitat conditions are revealed only after construction is well under way, too late to redefine the habitat details that should have been installed.

For example, in the diagram of the Great Park Canyon, a two-and-one-half-mile feature stretching across the park landscape, the various habitat types form a fine-scale mosaic of vegetation (Figure 10.7). The design team concluded this was the most appropriate arrangement of parts as the vegetation grew in and spread. Embedded in the general vegetation types is a series of small ecological features to accommodate initial niche requirements of many animals. For example, there are sandy islands in the stream to allow for egg laying by reptiles, rocky outcrops to allow for thermoregulation by the many lizards of Southern California, crevices throughout the slopes for bat nesting and small mammal burrows, and open sandy patches for insect life that hunts and mates in these sunny microhabitats (Figure 10.8). The ability to have hundreds of native species on this landscape requires design specifications for surface conditions that are widely heterogeneous.

Elegance in ecological diversity needs a jumble of microsites, not cool simplicity. The neat and regular surface of many modern park designs would not permit this biodiversity to live. At this small scale, the park design offers an irregular surface, not a smooth one. The contractors will be instructed to create ridges and valleys, varying by inches, to accommodate the diverse seed germination and nesting and refuge requirements of small animals, including many insects. In addition, the surface will be left irregular before planting. It will have a wide array of pebbles and cobbles of various diameters scattered about, and many well-rotted pieces of dead wood of different dimensions.

The wooden debris will be salvaged during the demolition of the original Marine air-base structures and their foundation plantings. The wood can be stockpiled at the edge of the construction site and then moved out into the ecological zones after landforming has advanced. Saving, stockpiling, then relocating this dead wood is not a common procedure. But the ability to maintain growing populations of native biodiversity requires that these types of organic microhabitats be available. Dead wood is a habitat for many insects that are the base of terrestrial food webs. Dead wood is where some lizards bask, and others oviposit or hide from predators (Figure 10.8). Then, when dead wood rots, it creates small zones of high organic-matter soil, which is the preferred germination microsite for many plant species. Although this wood is dead by one definition, it is the source of life in many other ways. Not saving and distributing dead wood across this park would give us a relatively sterile environment inappropriate for populations of dozens of species. These microhabitat features of stone and wood can be arrayed in interesting ways that do not interfere with many human activities, such as hiking and picnicking. On balance, these small features, of little interest to those concerned with neat, simplified surfaces, offer the visiting public a chance to see, understand, and celebrate the remarkable natural heritage of Southern California.

The cultural features of the Great Park—hiking, biking, festivals, sports, and exhibit spaces—were then arrayed around the ecological backbone, satisfying the many human ecological desires that are wanted by the public corporation that determines the civic direction of this park (detailed at the Orange County Great Park website). Having the ecological plan done up front allowed a better mesh of landscape architecture and ecological design decisions.

From Nightmares to Dreams of Restoring Nature

In these several ways, the principles of ecological science can yield useful and beautiful habitats for public spaces and add new spatial processes and interpretations that add to the landscape designer's toolbox. Ecological services have great value, and the appearance and sustaining of local biodiversity support many public needs. Ecological function in public space enhances a designer's product.

But there are significant ecological constraints to a designer's ability to reiterate historic landscape biodiversity. In a world festering with human populations, fragmented, and changed in many physical and chemical ways, a realistic restoration ecology program must confront these constraints.[40] Dispersal of seeds and animals across urban areas is limited. For example, the movement of airborne milkweed seeds through a block of high-rise buildings is the botanical equivalent of ping-pong balls bouncing through a maze. Small animals moving through human population centers face physical barriers and common predators, such as feral cats and dogs. The pockets of remaining native plant and animal communities in our urban centers are usually degraded, missing many of the species that were present before wide-scale urbanization. Consequently, whatever dispersal does occur into designed spaces is from depauperate biological communities.

Physically, urban landscapes are not accommodating too many of our native species. Soil quality and biota are generally poor. Pollutants are common. Fragmentation, extensive hardscapes, and lack of water flow are formidable barriers to allowing living communities to persist. Natural disturbances, necessary for the persistence of certain early successional communities such as meadows, are often lacking in habitats that are dominated by human needs. For example, many of our meadows require occasional burning to persist. Although people often admire the colors and textures of a species-rich meadow, many municipalities do not permit disturbance by fire because of danger to property and concern for minimizing air pollution. If no disturbance regime is permitted, the design opportunities for meadows are constrained.

Biologically, the threat of invasive species is continuously growing and a few aggressive species always have the ability to overwhelm an intricate species-rich design solution. Even when a well-researched palette of species is included in the habitat design plan, genotypes appropriate for changed and stressful urban conditions may not be available. Contract growing of plant material is possible to secure species the designer wants, but often this takes a few years of preparation time, which may not be possible given tight construction schedules.

These biological constraints march next to social constraints. Not all residents using a yard or park want natural landscaping, as it is asymmetric, often dense, and can be uncomfortable within which to walk or throw a baseball. Enjoyment of natural habitat is a learning experience for urban dwellers, whose experience in and education about natural habitats is not deep. Similarly, agencies that control public lands may not want natural habitat despite its many financial advantages through ecological services. Often active recreation zones or construction of a building or restaurant is given high value. Even the most appealing sites for habitat restoration may be zoned differently. Designers interested in adding ecological services must always make the case against competing programmatic desires. Lobbying for design priorities is always part of the work of a landscape designer, but natural habitat is a new petitioner in a crowded field.

Many urban sites are small, and although habitat for certain lovely native species of birds and plants may be desired by the local public, the ecological designer cannot secure sustainable populations in all available settings. For example, beautiful woodland wildflowers often require moisture and shade, which are unavailable in narrow and small urban parcels. Certain birds have large territorial requirements, which are unavailable in many urban settings.[41] The romantic idea of bringing back diversity that was here three hundred years ago must be tempered with the ecological requirements of the species of interest. The physical pattern of urban spaces will not support species needing large, dark, or secluded habitats.

The institutional and political requirements necessary to restore native habitats to cities are enormous. Public officials have many public needs to satisfy. The advent of the interest in ecological restoration has given a complex, new possibility to urban planning and design. It is sometimes difficult for public agencies, rarely staffed at appropriate levels, to have the time to research, review, and approve completely new land-use elements. Also, the professions traditionally charged with land-use planning and reviews do not receive extensive ecological training as part of their academic preparation. Continuing education opportunities rarely include advanced ecological progress. The interest in ecological services may require modification of professional training regimes before these can be included broadly in future design solutions.

During the planning phases, design teams and municipal planning departments have always had rosters that include many technical skills such as lighting, transport, public safety, graphic arts, and cost estimation. The interest in ecological habitat structure and ecosystem services suggests that these teams must be enlarged to include professionals with biological training. Although this suggestion in itself is not radical, changing institutional processes and enlarging already financially strapped agencies is extremely difficult. But new skills are more than just new expenses. They represent new value that can, in time, make our urban life more cost-efficient, more valuable, and offer new definitions of joy to urban populations.

The opportunity to restore elements of our natural heritage to urban lands as well as ecological functions is real and expanding on an international basis. Emphasis by designers on how these interesting and complex small habitats can reduce management and financial needs as well as offer a new venue for environmental education must be stressed on many fronts. The landscape perspective may be the most useful in these dialogues. Improving biodiversity in small, urban patches gives value well beyond the borders of the project site. Native animal and plant species additions on any one site might through time improve ecological services across the whole region. In this sense, the costs of ecological restoration are investments for the wider community as well as at the project site. This ecological process of spread continues every year, and biodiverse habitats can continually yield living dividends and functions.

Notes

1 Society for Ecological Restoration International, Science and Policy Working Group, *SER International Primer on Ecological Restoration* (Tucson: Society for Ecological Restoration International, 2004), 3.

2 Richard T. T. Forman, *Urban Regions: Ecology and Planning beyond the City* (Cambridge: Cambridge University Press, 2008), ch. 9.

3 Vicky M. Temperton, *Assembly Rules and Restoration Ecology: Bridging the Gap between Theory and Practice* (Washington, D.C.: Island Press, 2004).

4 Gretchen C. Daily, ed., *Nature's Services: Societal Dependence on Natural Ecosystems* (Washington, D.C.: Island Press, 1997).

5 Catherine Rich and Travis Longcore, *Ecological Consequences of Artificial Night Lighting* (Washington, D.C.: Island Press, 2006).

6 Donald A. Falk, Margaret A. Palmer, and Joy B. Zedler, eds., *Foundations of Restoration Ecology* (Washington, D.C.: Island Press, 2006), ch. 9.

7 Michael Begon, Colin R. Townsend, and John L. Harper, *Ecology: From Individuals to Ecosystems*, 4th ed. (Malden, Mass.: Blackwell Publishing, 2006), 89–119.

8 Dave Egan and Evelyn A. Howell, eds., *The Historical Ecology Handbook: A Restorationist's Guide to Reference Ecosystems* (Washington, D.C.: Island Press, 2001).

9 Oliver L. Gilbert, *The Ecology of Urban Habitats* (New York: Chapman and Hall, 1989), 25–54.

10 Mary L. Cadenasso and Stewart T. A. Pickett, "Effect of Edge Structure on the Flux of Species into Forest Interiors," *Conservation Biology* 15, no. 1 (2001): 91–97.

11 Michael L. McKinney, "Urbanization, Biodiversity, and Conservation," *BioScience* 52, no. 10 (October 2002): 883–90; and Michael L. McKinney, "Effects of Urbanization on Species Richness: A Review of Plants and Animals," *Urban Ecosystems* 11, no. 2 (2008): 161–76.

12 Petr Pyšek, "Alien and Native Species in Central European Urban Floras: A Quantitative Comparison," *Journal of Biogeography* 25, no. 1 (1998): 155–63; and Julie L. Lockwood and Michael L. McKinney, *Biotic Homogenization* (New York: Kluwer Academic/Plenum Publishers, 2001), ch. 1.

13 George R. Robinson and Steven N. Handel, "Directing Spatial Patterns of Recruitment during an Experimental Urban Woodland Reclamation," *Ecological Applications* 10, no. 1 (February 2000): 174–88.

14 Anthony D. Bradshaw and Michael J. Chadwick, eds., *The Restoration of Land: The Ecology and Reclamation of Derelict and Degraded Land* (Berkeley: University of California Press, 1980), 73–83.

15 Peter Bullock and Peter J. Gregory, eds., *Soils in the Urban Environment* (Oxford: Blackwell Scientific Publications, 1991), chs. 4, 6, and 7.

16 Amy S. Karpati, Steven N. Handel, John Dighton, and Tim R. Horton, "Quercus Rubra-Associated Ectomycorrhizal Fungal Communities of Disturbed Urban Sites and Mature Forests," *Mycorrhizae* 21, no. 6 (2011): 537–47.

17 Peter Reed, *Groundswell: Constructing the Contemporary Landscape* (New York: Museum of Modern Art, 2005), 156–61.

18 George R. Robinson, Steven N. Handel, and Jennifer Mattei, "Experimental Techniques for Evaluating the Success of Restoration Projects," *Korean Journal of Ecology* 25, no. 1 (2002): 1–7.

19 W. G. Hoppe, "Seedfall Pattern of Several Species of Bird-Dispersed Plants in an Illinois Woodland," *Ecology* 69, no. 2 (April 1988): 320–29.

20 Steven N. Handel, "Restoring Plant Population Dynamics to New Urban Habitats," in *Proceedings of the Congress on Urban Green Spaces* (New Delhi, 2012), in press.

21 George R. Robinson and Steven N. Handel, "Forest Restoration on a Closed Landfill: Rapid Addition of New Species by Bird Dispersal," *Conservation Biology* 7, no. 2 (June 1993): 271–78.

22 Jennifer H. Mattei, Steven N. Handel, and George R. Robinson, "Lessons Learned in Restoring an Urban Forest on a Closed Landfill (New York)," *Ecological Restoration* 21, no. 1 (2003): 62–63.

23 Myla F. J. Aronson, Steven N. Handel, and Steven E. Clemants, "Fruit Type, Life Form, and Origin Determine the Success of Woody Plant Invaders in an Urban Landscape," *Biological Invasions* 9, no. 4 (2007): 465–75.

24 John L. Harper, *Population Biology of Plants* (London and New York: Academic Press, 1977), 33–54.

25 Steven N. Handel and Andrew J. Beattie, "Seed Dispersal by Ants," *Scientific American* 263 (1990): 76–83A.

26 Mary E. Yurlina, "Bee Mutualists and Plant Reproduction in Urban Woodland Restorations" (PhD diss. Rutgers, The State University of New Jersey, 1998).

27 Steven N. Handel, "The Role of Plant-Animal Mutualisms in the Design and Restoration of Natural Communities," in *Restoration Ecology and Sustainable Development*, ed. Krystyna M. Urbanska, Nigel R. Webb, and Peter J. Edwards (Cambridge: Cambridge University Press, 1997), 111–32.

28 Steven N. Handel, George R. Robinson, and Andrew J. Beattie, "Biodiversity Resources for Restoration Ecology," *Restoration Ecology* 2, no. 4 (1994): 230–41.

29 David Briggs, *Plant Microevolution and Conservation in Human-Influenced Ecosystems* (Cambridge: Cambridge University Press, 2009), ch. 10.

30   Janis Antonovics, "The Effects of a Heterogeneous Environment on the Genetics of Natural Populations," *American Scientist* 59, no. 5 (1971): 593–99.

31   Briggs, *Plant Microevolution and Conservation in Human-Influenced Ecosystems*, 151–63.

32   Anita Berrizbeitia, ed., *Michael Van Valkenburgh Associates: Reconstructing Urban Landscapes* (New Haven: Yale University Press, 2009), 222–53.

33   Ibid.

34   Joanna Burger, *Oil Spills* (New Brunswick, N.J.: Rutgers University Press, 1997).

35   Leslie McGuire, "Restoring Native Landscapes," *Landscape Architect and Specifier News* (March 2008): 128–36.

36   Steven N. Handel, Milan J. Mitrovich, Elizabeth Hook, and Rebecca Aicher, *Great Park Ecological Guidelines—Park Ecology and Natural Habitats* (Irvine: Orange County Great Park Corporation, 2009).

37   Andrew F. Bennett, *Linkages in the Landscape: The Role of Corridors and Connectivity in Wildlife Conservation* (Gland, Switz.: International Union for the Conservation of Nature, 2003), 61–62.

38   Shannon L. Galbraith-Kent and Steven N. Handel, "Lessons from an Urban Lakeshore Restoration in New York City," *Ecological Restoration* 25, no. 2 (2007): 123–28.

39   Handel, Mitrovich, Hook, and Aicher, *Ecological Guidelines—Park Ecology and Natural Habitats*, 9–53.

40   Andrew Goudie, *The Human Impact on the Natural Environment*, 5th ed. (Cambridge, Mass.: MIT Press, 2000).

41   Robert A. Askins, *Restoring North America's Birds: Lessons from Landscape Ecology* (New Haven: Yale University Press, 2000), 99–129.

CHAPTER 11

Biodiversity and Climate Change in Cities

Kristina Hill

IN THIS ESSAY, I WILL PRESENT EVIDENCE TO support three main points: First, in response to climate change trends, the focus of conservation planning needs to shift from species conservation alone to the broader goal of conserving ecosystem functions. Second, cities can play a significant role in supporting ecosystem function during times of rapid environmental change, if the links between spatial patterns and functional dynamics are understood. And third, several cities that have already taken significant steps in this direction offer the benefits of experience as planners and designers in other cities consider the opportunities and challenges they face.

Cities, Climate, and Biodiversity: Critical Linkages

In the past, changes in climate have been linked to the evolution of biodiversity and the development of human cities. This is likely to be the case in the future as well. In this section, I will first introduce the links between climate and biodiversity, then the link between climate and human settlements, and finally the link between human cities and biodiversity.

Changes in biodiversity are closely linked to climate. Throughout the geologic record, major warming periods have been noted as a factor in five or more major extinction events and the subsequent periods of increasing biodiversity that followed these mass extinctions.[1] Climate change brings not just changes in average temperatures, as the term "global warming" might imply. Climate change also brings much more rapid increases in sea level (currently forecast at a rate of four to seven and one-half times faster than in the last century),[2] changes in the timing and intensity of rain (which can lead to droughts, fire, and pest outbreaks as well as flooding), and extreme wind or storm events. Species that are unable to tolerate new temperature or moisture extremes, or whose food resources are reduced by these trends, will suffer from these changes. But how does this occur, and how is it relevant to human behavior?

Environmental processes, driven by larger phenomena like climate change, create advantages and disadvantages for individual species. Those advantages and disadvantages are created because organisms possess specific traits—that is, characteristics or behaviors that an animal or plant displays. These traits include abilities to demonstrate flexibility in

FIGURE 11.1
A coyote rests on a seat after jumping onto a MAX light-rail train on Wednesday, February 13, 2002, at Portland International Airport in Portland, Oregon.

Associated Press / Port of Portland; photograph by Dennis Maxwell.

FIGURE 11.2
Ninety-five percent home range contours for resident coyotes in downtown Schaumburg, Illinois.

Illustration courtesy of Stanley Gehrt and Cook County Coyote Project / Max McGraw Wildlife Foundation.

resource use. An insect species that can change host plants, for example, might survive a change in climate, while a species that cannot survive on new hosts might become extinct. The trait that allows the insect to use a new host plant may be passed on to future generations, which is a key component of evolution. Through this selection of characteristics, significant adaptations can evolve in the same species.[3] Adaptation can be both structural—in which heritable physiological characteristics such as color allow higher survival rates because they provide advantages under particular conditions—and behavioral, involving changes in how an animal interacts with its environment. Within the category of behavioral adaptations, biologists consider both ontogenetic factors, which accumulate during the lifetime experience of an organism (such as learned avoidance behaviors), and mechanistic factors—physiological processes such as behaviors driven by hormonal fluctuations (such as increased aggression or nurturance).[4]

Human traits are also likely to be affected by changes in the environment. For example, a theory has been advanced that a fourfold increase in human brain size resulted from repeated periods of rapid climate change during the Pleistocene via the mechanisms of physiological responses to dietary restrictions.[5] This theory is relevant to questions of how and why human settlements emerged after the last glacial period, since the enlargement of the brain occurred partly in areas that support problem-solving and creativity.[6]

When climate shifts, the context for humans, other animals, and plants changes in many ways. Geomorphological changes can also occur on a large scale as climates change, which creates different opportunities for some species to flourish and others to decline. For instance, major river deltas form during periods of relatively stable coastline positions. Where rivers meet the ocean, they deposit the sediment load they have carried from their headwaters. A stable position of the coastline allows river sediment to be deposited in the same area over hundreds and thousands of years, forming large deltas of fertile soil with shallow groundwater that supports plant growth. Rates of sea-level rise after the most recent period of glaciation have typically been much more rapid than in the last ten thousand years. As the rates of relative sea-level rise slowed significantly, approximately twelve thousand to nine thousand years ago, the world's major deltas formed. Many early human cities were in delta locations—perhaps most famously in the Mesopotamian region, but also in the Indus Valley of southern Pakistan and the Nile delta of Egypt.

In geologic and even human evolutionary timescales, cities are new. They appear only in the last nine thousand years, initially as a rare cultural phenomenon. As a common geographic occurrence or cultural experience, they are far more recent than that. In 2007, the United Nations noted that for the first time more than 50 percent of the world's population lives in cities. Of the world's poorest people, 75 percent now live in urban areas.[7] In a very short amount of time, living in cities has gone from being a truly exceptional human experience to being the most common way of life around the world. In that context, it is hardly surprising that humans struggle to manage the social and technological complexities of urban systems. Humans are still actively learning how to live in dense settlements, and inventing what cities can become.

The change in human behavior that has led a majority of us to live in large cities has had a major impact on global biodiversity, demonstrating the complexity of the linkages between climate change, species traits, and the biophysical environment. As urban areas expand, bringing paved surfaces, piped water, and large numbers of humans, they replace other ecosystems (such as forests and wetlands) that are incompatible with an urban density of human dwellings and activities. While cities can imitate some of the functions of their preexisting ecosystems, they cannot sustain the full range of functions of those ecosystems. Global losses of biodiversity have been driven over the last several hundred years by expansions in urbanization and the intensification of agricultural production that typically accompanies urbanization. Climate change is a new factor in biodiversity loss, and may alter the role of cities from replacement to refuge for some species if the strategies for conservation planning can shift to recognize this potential (Figures 11.1–11.2).

Conservation Strategies in Industrialized Regions

The basic strategies for conservation of biodiversity in both urban and agricultural regions have been changing rapidly over the last twenty-five years, even before the recognition of climate change effects. Conservation planners have come to realize that reserves cannot actually be "walled off" from the processes that surround them in the way exhibits in a zoological park can be separated from an urban neighborhood. The *matrix*, or surrounding land uses, affects the survival of species in the reserve. Connectivity among reserves also matters, arguing for corridors that follow topographic features and serve to guide animal and plant dispersal. In addition, the number and size of conserved patches that exist as "stepping stones" in a region are also a factor, supporting species that can move easily—such as birds—but need specific resources or isolation from predators to survive.[8] Given these spatial insights, the last couple of decades have been characterized by a "turn to spatial pattern" in biology.

This change of focus in ecological science has facilitated an era of more explicitly biological approaches in landscape planning and design. These applied fields have always had a spatial emphasis but have struggled in the past to incorporate ecological ideas in fundamental ways. Over the last thirty years, many designers and planners began to use the concept of optimal spatial configuration to generate ecological strategies for biological conservation reserve design on a regional and even national level. The idea of the optimization approach is to identify the best pattern of reserve location, size, and connectivity that would support characteristic regional biodiversity. Some of the unique elements of that pattern would be fixed in space, and others might shift in space over time, like lights blinking on and off, while still maintaining the same percentages of critical ecosystems in terms of acres (a concept known as the "shifting mosaic," described and advocated as a valuable component of planned landscapes by the prominent American landscape ecologist Richard T. T. Forman, among others).

This approach has been used to develop specific proposals for conservation land acquisition in cities as well as rural areas. The metropolitan planning authority that includes Portland, Oregon, used the basic principle of connecting patches along topographic features such as river valleys to identify land for an expanded regional park system in the 1990s, and again in the last five years. The concept was familiar historically, since Frederick Law Olmsted and other American landscape architects had popularized the concept of park systems as integral parts of well-designed cities in the nineteenth century. Those historic park systems were designed primarily for human use and were connected by roads for human travel. But they also protected water supply reservoirs and were linked by topographic valleys with streams. The idea of building or conserving an optimal system of connected parks is not new to American cities, but the idea of combining human recreational goals for those systems with the goal of sustaining characteristic regional biodiversity is a contemporary idea, dating back to the 1960s.[9] It would not have made sense in an urban world that existed as patches in a non-urban matrix, but it has come to seem essential in a world where urban lands have literally become the matrix. In London, as I will describe in the case study section of this chapter, the corridor park system along rivers is being planned as a buffer against the negative impacts of climate change.

Dynamic Systems in Landscape Planning and Design

One of the problems with the strategy of identifying and constructing an optimal spatial configuration for conservation is that the relationship between spatial patterns and biological processes can change. There are few, if any, necessarily one-to-one relationships between patterns and processes.

Scientists have struggled to understand this dynamic set of linkages between patterns and processes, and have developed a critical skepticism that emphasizes observation and seeks to avoid premature conclusions.[10] One preliminary conclusion is that the linkages are often scale-dependent. Processes and patterns that interact at the same spatial and temporal scales are more likely to exert strong mutual influences. Processes that occur at much-slower rates than changes in pattern may influence those patterns, but a reverse direction of influence is unlikely. Similarly, patterns that change very slowly are more likely to influence faster processes than the reverse—that is, those faster-changing processes are less likely to influence the slower-changing patterns.[11] Processes may also be highly influenced by context. For instance, when conservation planners try to provide habitat structure for rare species in an urban environment, it may turn out that predators or parasites actually limit the success of those rare species as much as habitat structure; in these cases, it is not enough to provide habitat structure alone.[12] The dynamics of relationships among species, as well as material cycling and climate fluctuations, are often not determined by pattern and may be disconnected from spatial variables at a given scale.

The tendency to emphasize the predictability of ecological relationships, rather than dynamic examples that may be stochastic (random) or chaotic (in the sense of chaos theory and complexity), or even in the sense of relationships that are expressed as gradients, has been characteristic of landscape planning and design in the past.[13] Efforts have occurred to preserve sand dunes in particular locations, or to delineate wetlands with fixed boundaries that do not include their watersheds, or to assign stable water-use allowances in regions with unstable water supplies. Even Ian L. McHarg's method, described in *Design with Nature* and on his television program in the late 1960s to early

1970s, relied on static patterns as a kind of proxy for dynamic processes.

Perhaps one of the most important areas in which planners and designers have grappled with the concept of dynamics—both cultural and ecological—is in defining and supporting so-called native species. The term "native" and the concept of conserving native plants and animals became a flash point for cultural and ethical concerns after a historical research paper was published that described the focus on nativism and plants in Germany during the National Socialism era.[14] This paper came out during a decade in which scientific knowledge was becoming more important to landscape design and planning in the United States, and was read by an audience only slightly familiar with the concepts of biological evolution and adaptation. Many readers reacted by subsequently questioning any focus on native plants in design and conservation planning. The perception of an ethical conflict persists informally among some practitioners, although professionals with more scientific training seem to apply the expectation that native plants are more likely to support native insects and birds, and are therefore of high value for functional reasons.

Species and Climate Change in Urban Conservation Planning

Policy makers, planners, and designers are beginning to recognize the dynamics of climate change in North America, as their colleagues in Europe have for more than a decade. New conceptual problems are arising for planners and designers everywhere as they try to shift from thinking about ecological communities, defined by species assemblages (using species type and dominance), to considering ecological regime shifts, which are being defined using fairly sophisticated mathematical tools to analyze change over time across multiple variables.

For example, recent studies suggest that bioclimatic plant hardiness zones, which are mapped on the basis of average temperature and are used as a guide to plant selection for different regions, have already shifted northward based on the last two decades of temperature records.[15] While planners and designers are increasingly aware of this research, misunderstandings can occur about whether this means that the plant and animal species currently associated with those zones will therefore shift northward as well, without management intervention. This northward movement is possible but not likely without active management, given (1) the number of barriers to species movement, and (2) the likelihood that invasive species might successfully fill gaps that open up due to mortality in species that cannot tolerate new climate conditions.[16] Research from the 1960s by Margaret B. Davis provided conclusive evidence that plant species responded individualistically to climate changes in the past, and supports the prediction that future plant communities under new climate regimes will not be analogous to today's communities in their composition.[17]

Meanwhile, a complex strategic, ethical, and conceptual problem has emerged from the focus on species when defining "biodiversity" rather than directly examining the diversity of traits as a basis for measuring ecosystem functions. If particular species that are already declining in population size will be disadvantaged by the climate conditions that are predicted for their region, should the conservation of those species continue to be the goal of conservation design and planning? An animal or plant may become very rare in one region, while it becomes more common in an adjacent region. Or it may become locally extinct, but its functions could be replaced by a different species. The historical focus on species has been codified into law in many countries and in international agreements; even if scientists, planners, and designers agreed to substitute traits or ecosystem functions as the targets of conservation, laws and policies would have to be significantly restructured.

Implementing Spatial Patterns in Relation to Dynamic Processes

The fundamental challenge is that it will be impossible to identify optimal spatial patterns for new regional species (or trait) assemblages until the planet reaches a new stable climate period. Even then, species will continue to adjust their roles and locations in response to other community and population variables that may be novel in new surroundings, such as competition, herbivory, parasitism, and other dynamics that influence reproductive success. It would be like measuring someone for a suit who is in constant motion; the badly dimensioned clothes wouldn't fit once the person did stand still (in relative terms). A system of stable conservation reserves can't be effectively designed until we know more about where our climate trajectory is going to put us during the next several hundred years.

So what can we do to adapt our urban and urbanizing landscapes to support ecosystem functions during an era of rapid environmental change? According to a thorough recent literature review by Nicole E. Heller and Erika S. Zavaleta in 2009, changes in regional conservation strategies have been discussed in relation to observed climate trends for at least the past twenty-two years, although very few of these ideas have been developed using region-specific research. Even fewer have been accepted or implemented broadly by managers. The discussion has included a strong focus on increased research and dialogue with stakeholders. Some authors have recommended moving away from an emphasis on spatial patterns, replacing it with a focus on processes. Others have called for adapting spatial patterns in specific ways. All of these recommendations are relevant for urban design and planning, which has important stakeholder as well as ecological processes with which to contend. But for the sake of a discussion focused on the implications for change in design and planning practice, I will limit my review of these ideas to the key recommendations regarding the relationship between ecological processes and spatial patterns.

The most common idea in the scientific literature for adapting conservation strategies is to create more of an emphasis on corridors that facilitate the geographic dispersal of animals and plants. The other most common ideas are to integrate climate change into planning scenarios, to study how species actually respond to climate trends, to physically relocate species, and to mitigate other problems that will accelerate the rate of biodiversity loss, such as fragmentation and pollution. Another group of ideas is mentioned less frequently but could still be considered common: to increase the number and size of reserves, to create and manage buffer zones around reserves, to increase the number of stepping-stone reserves around large reserves, and

to decrease the degree to which matrix land-use types around the reserves create a hostile environment for species that are in decline. Less frequently mentioned ideas include: protecting current and future areas that might function as refuges for species that are negatively impacted by climate change, expanding reserves along their northern borders, locating reserves at the northern edge of species' ranges, making greater efforts to anticipate surprising changes, making special efforts to protect high-elevation areas (mountains) as well as urban green spaces, and to use triage principles to protect as many species as possible in the short term, even if it means not protecting all species at risk.[18]

In spatial terms, these ideas might have specific meaning for conservation planning and design. One interpretation of the call to emphasize corridors is that new corridors (or enlarged versions of existing corridors) should provide easier movement to higher elevations and to higher latitudes. The best short-term corridor implementation strategy might be to emphasize corridors that link to higher elevations, since it is much more efficient for species to migrate a few hundred feet higher on steep slopes than it is to capture the same temperature benefits by moving hundreds of miles in latitude.[19] But since mountain ranges provide less area as they rise higher in elevation, migrating upward is essentially the equivalent of "walking the plank" for species in need of cooler temperatures, unless a second set of corridors is available that allows them to migrate in latitude once they run out of space by moving up in elevation. The best longer-term solution might be to provide north–south corridors within and between mountain ranges, in addition to providing corridors that allow species to climb their local mountains with minimal mortality losses.

The concept of identifying places of climate refuge for vulnerable species, known as *refugia*, dates back to Quaternary paleoecological studies that tried to pinpoint the locations in which species found refuge during the ice ages of the last two million years.[20] In cooling periods, south-facing slopes and other small pockets of warmer temperatures were valuable, but only if animal and plant movements were not blocked by east–west-trending mountain ranges. Appalachian cove forests were important refugia in North America in part because the

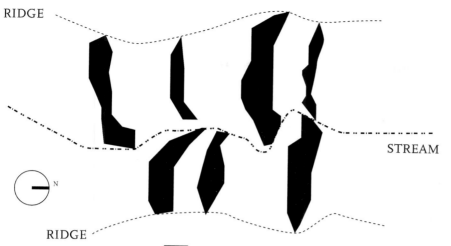

RIDGE

STREAM

RIDGE

■ north-facing slopes

N

FIGURE 11.3
Corridor and patch structures: elevational gradients, ridgelines, stream corridors, and aspect gradients. Patches with northern aspects may act as corridors and stepping stones ("ladder rungs") for species migration within regional landscapes.

Illustration by Kristina Hill.

Appalachian Mountains trend north–south. In a new era of increasingly high temperature extremes, animals and plants that are vulnerable to more extreme upper limits on local temperature ranges may benefit from access to cooler north-facing slopes and deep valleys with extended shade.

The pattern of north-facing slopes and deep valleys often generates a kind of "ladder" spatial conservation strategy at the landscape scale, in which the slopes provide the "rungs" and stream valleys provide the "legs" of the ladder. Reserve networks could incorporate this spatial pattern as additions to existing reserves, as a strategy for extending them into higher latitudes and higher elevations. Reserve managers could also use them as a spatial framework for monitoring strategies in order to track the response of vegetation to climate change, and also to determine whether parts of the landscape are actually functioning as refugia (Figures 11.3–11.4).

Refugia are only effective for the species that must migrate into the refuge patches when these patches are accessible via animal and plant dispersal mechanisms. The ability of migrating species to reach these refugia is critical to their function. The current fragmentation of remnant ecosystems by urbanization and intensive agriculture will present a challenge to animal and plant species with low-dispersal capabilities, particularly where valuable patches of habitat are small and spatially isolated from typical dispersal corridors features, such as

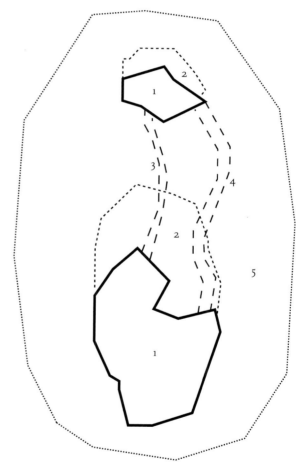

FIGURE 11.4
Five basic adaptation strategies for conservation reserves: 1) maintain existing reserves; 2) enlarge reserves northward and upward in elevation; 3) add high-elevation corridors; 4) add riparian corridors; and 5) reduce matrix hostility.

Illustration by Kristina Hill.

streams or ridges. Both corridors and new stepping-stone or enlarged patches are needed to reduce the distance species must travel between suitable patches of habitat. The maximum distance that can be crossed depends on the intrinsic mobility of the species that needs refuge. Species that fly or are wind-dispersed may be able to move without corridors, but species that move on land will probably benefit from vegetated corridors that provide cover from predators, food and water resources, and fewer at-grade intersections with roads.[21]

In addition to providing places of refuge for plant and animal species that are currently characteristic of a region's biological diversity, conservation strategies will need to address conservation for "new native" species that may arrive and be able to thrive under new climate conditions. Some of these new natives, or "neophytes," as they are known in European conservation, will eventually be accepted as part of a new regional flora and fauna. In Europe, the term is commonly used to denote species that were brought to Europe after AD 1500 during the European diaspora and subsequent era of global exploration. European biologists have long recognized that animals and plants were brought from region to region before AD 1500 as well, and thus the term "native" is not commonly used. Instead, "archaeophyte" is used to refer to species that existed in a landscape before the era of extensive global exploration.

This will be a more difficult conversation in North America, where the precolonial flora and fauna have provided a useful reference for the definition of characteristic regional diversity, and no neophyte species have yet been of conservation interest—except as invasives. The new need to pay positive attention to species that were not characteristic of regions before the colonial era will challenge long-standing conservation priorities. The issue of whether these neophyte species will be accepted as members of a new regional flora and fauna, rather than treated as unwanted invasive species, will probably center on whether these species are currently part of the characteristic biodiversity of regions in adjacent warmer latitudes, or in adjacent lands at lower elevations. If they are, they may be seen as shifting or expanding their range. If they are from nonadjacent global regions, they may continue to be

seen as undesirable invaders. The real test, however, should probably be whether they contribute to a sustainable increase in functional diversity—since that supports ecosystem function overall.

Cases of Application in Urban Design and Planning
Pacific Northwest Urban Conservation and Design

It may be that the best way for planning and design to increase support for biodiversity in urban areas is to learn from examples, and to consider those examples in light of predictions made using either models or the expert opinions of biologists. It's possible to identify certain strategic weaknesses in urban ecological design strategies using climate change predictions as a logical test. For example, the cities of Seattle, Washington, and Portland, Oregon, have made major strides in adapting their stormwater management and design to benefit salmon species. They have developed, implemented, and monitored designs that retrofit existing urban landscapes and street rights-of-way to reduce the impacts of paving on urban stream systems. They know the costs of these designs, and have opened the doors to broader implementation by monitoring their performance and promoting public acceptance; they have even succeeded in enlisting members of the public in maintaining the planted designs. But the planners and designers in this region have not yet publicly discussed their "Plan B," which will be needed if the fresh and marine waters in that region become too warm for these cold-water fish species (Figure 11.5).

The species-level approach taken by the Federal Endangered Species Act, which has pushed much of this innovative work in the Pacific Northwest, may not be effective in the coming century if the "taking" of individual organisms is not attributable to local human action, but rather to global climate disruption. If there is no local authority that can be held accountable with the threat of fines, then the pace of implementation may slow and even stop. A broader purpose is needed that goes beyond the presence of federally listed threatened species. The options include a new goal of conserving ecosystem functions, rather than individual species. In the case of the Pacific Northwest, that might involve

FIGURE 11.5
Green roof proposal for the Seahawks stadium, Seattle, with nest boxes for osprey (sea hawks).
Image courtesy of Emily Podolak.

efforts to support species that bring nutrients to terrestrial ecosystems from marine systems, as one example of the functional role played by anadromous salmon species. The movement of these salmon from streams in the foothills of mountains to the open ocean has given them a role as an "umbrella species," meaning that protecting their habitat needs can also serve to protect many other species' needs. If protecting functions was substituted as a new strategy in a warming climate that would preclude cold-water fish from that region, it is not clear whether the functions would protect as large a number of species. It is also not clear whether functional goals would have the same level of public support as the protection of a well-loved animal or plant that is seen as culturally iconic for a region, as the salmon are.

Jodhpur, India

In another case with strong cultural resonance, a monkey species that lives in and around the city of Jodhpur provides a useful example of the surprising role that cities may play in conserving biodiversity.

This monkey species, the Hanuman Langur (*Semnopithecus entellus*), is widely distributed in South Asia and regarded as sacred because of its legendary connection to a Hindu god, Hanuman (Figure 11.6). During a recent severe drought year related to an El Niño climate event (in this case, La Niña event of 1999), the langur population and other mammal species experienced a die-off in the Kumbhalgarh Wildlife Sanctuary in Rajasthan, India. The langur population inside the sanctuary dropped by 50 percent. A nearby urban population of langurs in the city of Jodhpur showed no drop in population size during the same drought, leading the authors of a 2007 study to suggest that the effects of the drought were reduced by a food subsidy provided to the monkeys by humans for religious reasons.[22] According to the study's authors, as much as one-third of the diet of the urban population of langurs may be provided by humans, along with a constant supply of drinking water from irrigation practices (Figure 11.7).

Although this species has an unusual commensal relationship with humans, the langur's ability

FIGURE 11.6
Hanuman Langur in Jaipur.

Photograph by Thomas Schoch. Wikimedia Commons; GNU Free Documentation License.

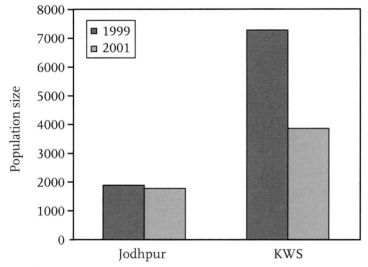

FIGURE 11.7
Langur population change in Jodhpur versus the Kumbhalgarh Wildlife Sanctuary (KWS).

Reprinted from Tom A. Waite et al., "Sanctuary in the City: Urban Monkeys Buffered against Catastrophic Die-off during ENSO-related Drought," *Ecohealth* 4, no. 3 (2007): 282.

to benefit from common processes such as irrigation points to the potential for this urban oasis effect to occur in other cities with other species, even in the absence of intentional food subsidies. All cities provide unintentional food subsidies to various species at everything from sidewalk cafes to dumpsters and landfills. It is also a common urban practice to irrigate parks, sports fields, and private landscapes. In addition, recent efforts to irrigate using recycled water may make this form of urban watering relatively sustainable if water prices increase during the drought trends that are predicted for many areas as a result of global climate change.

This case provides an example of the potential for cities to provide refugia in their own right, particularly in parks and other landscapes where human actions provide food and water resources to nonhuman species. Since cities are a relatively new feature of most landscapes, there are no Quaternary analogues for this ecosystem type, and it is not possible to use analogies to the era of repeated glaciations to predict how these refugia might affect species' populations and dispersal over time.

Antwerp, Belgium

At the port of Antwerp, an innovative strategy is in use to conserve habitat for the Natterjack Toad (*Bufo calamita*). The strategy is to use lands under public control as a "habitat backbone" for the toads, and to use parcels that are vacant on a temporary basis as components of a shifting mosaic of patches that extend the area available to the species. The backbone patches could function as a refuge for individual toads when temporary habitat is lost to occupation of formerly vacant sites by human uses.[23] This strategy is analogous to the use of core and buffer conservation areas in larger-scale biosphere reserve plans, except that the core areas are connected to the buffer areas by corridors, rather than by sharing an edge.

The location of commercial and industrial sites is often peripheral to core urban areas, the sites are typically large in area, and they are used only during office hours. These characteristics may be valuable to conservation of biological diversity. The challenges include barriers to dispersal, which can have significant effects on species with medium- to low-dispersal ability, such as the Natterjack Toad. In this case, a set of four permanent habitat areas were selected as backbone habitat, with continuous linear corridors of suitable habitat connecting them. An additional corridor was planned as a link to a parcel that is planned for use twenty years in the future, allowing it to be of value to the toads in the interim years. Mitigation measures were taken at points where corridors cross barriers, such as roads. Since the toads are an early successional species, the management of the parcels includes the intention to remove vegetation and topsoil periodically to simulate the disturbance effects of flood events.[24] Other early successional species that are of conservation interest because of reduced disturbance frequency in urban areas, where floods and fires are avoided or suppressed, may also benefit from this conservation strategy.

London, United Kingdom

The city of London and its metropolitan administrative area have been making sustained plans for biodiversity conservation over the last decade. The plans articulate the value of biodiversity for the city very clearly, based primarily on an ecosystem services framework for functional values. The initial plan in 2002 contained a greater emphasis on human enjoyment of biodiversity, while several plans published since then strike a more technical tone and emphasize tactics (Figure 11.8).[25] A partnership of organizations that include the metropolitan and city governments has been established to update a metropolitan biodiversity plan and to guide local boroughs in the development of their own plans. This partnership, which has produced a London Biodiversity Action Plan,[26] is focused on the species that have been identified as of conservation concern because their populations are declining. Not much discussion of the city as a refuge has occurred, although there are clear statements of ambition to maintain and enhance existing species richness in the city.

The basic strategy for conserving biodiversity in the metropolitan area is to conserve valuable patches of remnant ecosystems that have become rare and to connect them with corridors that facilitate movement by humans as well as nonhuman

FIGURE 11.8
Sites of importance for nature conservation in London.

Map based on data created by London boroughs and Greater London Authority; courtesy of Greenspace Information for Greater London.

Metropolitan Importance

Borough Importance Grade 1

Borough Importance Grade 2

Local Importance

The Sites of Importance for Nature Conservation have been identified since 1986 and the categorisation of sites is related to their protected status in the land-use planning system. The boundaries and site grades reflect the most recent consideration of each site, details of which are available from GiGL. Note that boundaries and grades may change as new information becomes available.

Scale 1:200000

Produced by Greenspace Information for Greater London
www.gigl.org.uk

Based upon the Ordnance Survey 1: 10 000 map with the permission of The Controller of Her Majesty's Stationery Office. © Crown Copyright. All rights reserved. Licence No. LA100032379 species. The East London Green Grid is cited in these plans as the initial version of the metropolitan corridor strategy. The East London Green Grid plan is proposed as a connected spatial network of "green infrastructure" components intended to produce a multifunctional landscape, one that supports biodiversity and ecosystem services as well as human quality of life and access to recreational resources. It is currently under development, relying on partnerships as well as publicly owned land to achieve the vision for its spatial pattern and management to support biodiversity.[27]

The plan documents for the East London Green Grid that has been made available to the public do not emphasize biodiversity, however. They are primarily focused on interventions that will improve public access to open space and provide additional flood storage capacity. There are planned interventions to conserve or improve wetland habitat areas, and improve "landscape structure"—presumably meaning to increase connectivity. But there are no innovative design or planning strategies cited that could benefit flora and fauna. Innovation would require a specific examination of the limits to reproductive success in a given region for specific species or functional groups. In order to plan for adaptation to climate change, these limits would need to be studied in the present as well as predicted over a twenty-five to one-hundred-year period, just as a starting point for hundreds of years of biological adaptation to new conditions. Interventions would then be tailored to remove or raise those limits. The only limits that are specifically identified in the East London Green Grid Plan are the availability of wetland habitat and the connectivity of wetlands and shrub/hedgerow features. These are important components of a plan, but it may be equally or more important to address limits generated by high levels of crow or cat predation on bird nests, for example, or trampling of nests and dens on the ground by humans who are using parks for recreation. While London may be planning to support biodiversity as the city's population grows and its climate changes, the specific strategies listed in the East London Green Grid Plan are not explicit enough yet to be credible from an ecological perspective.

It is interesting, however, to consider the language being used in the London plans about how to adapt to climate change in a city. In October 2009 and January 2010, plans were released on how to specifically address climate change and its predicted impacts on urban biodiversity. These plans have a more explicit ecological framework than the East London Green Grid Plan; they try to identify specific issues that may affect species' ability to persist and thrive in the city over the next hundred years.

Five specific ecological dimensions are noted in the most recent metropolitan London adaptation plans as processes that could be impacted by climate change:

(1) phenology (the seasonal timing of life history stages in plants and animals)
(2) species' distributions (spatial patterns of habitat use and population sizes)
(3) species' habitat preferences (associations between species and local conditions)
(4) composition of communities (relative dominance as well as presence/absence)
(5) ecosystem processes (e.g., rates of growth and decomposition, energy and nutrient cycles)[28]

Changes in several of these, such as changes in phenology and species' distributions, have already been documented. The ways in which these dynamic aspects of ecosystems interact with each other are often not well understood, even in contemporary landscapes—and are not clearly accounted for in predictive models, which must make assumptions about linkages and scenarios for climate, human behavior, and land use that may not be correct in twenty-five to fifty years.

The lessons from this case are several. First, the simple fact that metropolitan London has prioritized biodiversity not only in its planning processes, but also in its proposals for adaptation, is strikingly rare. The frameworks that are being established in London link biodiversity to issues that typically get more attention, such as flood protection and the attractiveness of cities to businesses. That may well be the most important idea to translate to other cities, putting biodiversity on a par—at least in the way documents are organized to juxtapose ideas—with infrastructure and economic considerations.

Second, the London case points out that the most obvious spatial strategy that increases flexibility in a fragmented landscape is to add many corridors. Connecting low-quality patches to high-quality patches has, however, been questioned in the ecological literature as a strategy that may cause loss of diversity in the high-quality patches as generalist predators and parasites are provided with easier access to better-quality habitat.[29] The mapping of London that has been made public to date does not identify the relative quality of the habitat patches, nor does it address this limitation for connectivity as a strategy for broad implementation. There can also be conflicts between human and nonhuman uses of the same vegetated corridors, if human use results in the importation of more invasive, exotic species (e.g., because of seeds on boots or bike tires), or paving of corridors that discourages small mammals from crossing, or leaves other signs behind that discourage sensitive species from dispersing along the corridors.

The strategy of minimizing the hostility of the matrix land uses that surround these patches in a fragmented, urban landscape is an alternative, and perhaps should be used in addition to corridors that link patches of similar habitat quality. It is possible that green roofs, green walls, and the development of mature trees with vertical habitat zonation (understory trees and shrubs) in private parcels could contribute to the capacity of the matrix itself to facilitate dispersal. In strategic terms, it would probably be best to pursue both strategies simultaneously—while limiting corridors to provide direct connections only among patches of similar quality.

Stockholm, Sweden

For the year 2010, Stockholm was designated the first Green Capital of the European Union. Spatial planning in the larger metropolitan region of Stockholm has created a city with a distinct radial geography, in which roads and rail networks were built in topographic low areas to serve new suburban developments, and the land between these radial arms was conserved as open space. The open spaces are narrower as they get closer to Stockholm, where developed areas spread out along other infrastructure pathways. This open space pattern is now referred to as Stockholm's "green wedges," and is described and defended as the primary strategy for regional biodiversity conservation. Some authors

believe the green wedge structure is in jeopardy and have noted that some species of conservation concern within these areas are in decline (Figure 11.9).[30]

With continued conservation, the green wedges are capable of functioning as corridors as well as source areas for some species. The goal is for animals and plants to be able to disperse east–west along the wedges from the Baltic Sea to Lake Mälaren and via a series of north–south routes along the marine shoreline and inland corridors composed of woodlands or meadows. This would allow animals and plants to disperse into the city of Stockholm as well. But instead of simply creating an urban corridor system, an effort has been made to establish a large patch of protected habitat within the city, with satellite patches around it. In 1995, the Swedish government gave a historic park (the Djurgården) a new designation as a "National Urban Park," including several nearby patches of undeveloped land (Figure 11.10).[31]

This large urban park is seen as having national significance in part because of the large number of ancient oak trees contained within it.[32] Oaks are currently in decline in much of Europe, and Sweden's oak forests are propagated primarily by the Eurasian

FIGURE 11.9
Stockholm's regional "green wedges" conservation plan.

Illustration courtesy of the Office of Regional Planning, Stockholm County Council.

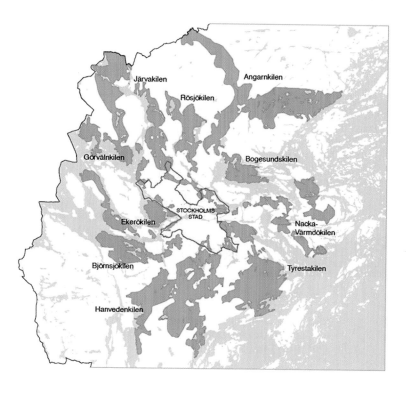

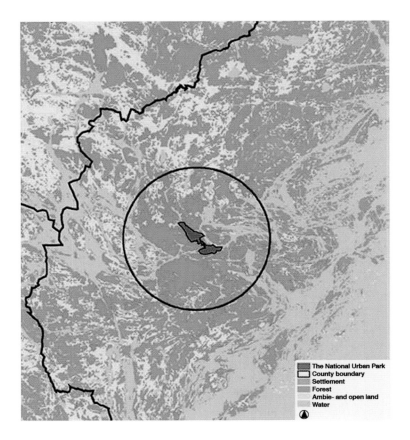

FIGURE 11.10
The National Urban Park in Stockholm.

Illustration courtesy of the Office of Regional Planning, Stockholm County Council.

The National Urban Park
County boundary
Settlement
Forest
Ambie- and open land
Water

Jay (Figure 11.11). This has turned some of the conservation focus onto jays as a "mobile link" species that performs a specific ecosystem service by burying acorns. Ecologists in Stockholm have valued the service provided by the jays at US$2,100–9,400 per hectare, based on an estimate of what it would cost to have humans do the job instead.[33] This kind of specific valuation has its uses, as cost-benefit analyses can take advantage of these numbers to support decisions to conserve open space and the species that are valued within it.[34]

The most interesting aspect of Stockholm's pattern of conserved land is that it creates a nested set of protected areas at three distinct scales: the metropolitan region, with its green wedges; the city, with a large urban conservation-oriented park; and the city's districts, which have biodiversity goals and specific habitat patches of their own. The use of this nested system of patches and corridor "wedges" is a strategy that is transferable to other metropolitan regions.

Stockholm's environmental agency has explored the significance of climate change for biodiversity within the city in a 2007 report. It identifies specific examples of biological processes, such as competition, timing of migrations by birds, and soil temperature as influential on future plant and animal species that will live in Stockholm, using examples of changes that have already been documented.[35]

At the smaller district scale, Stockholm's planning has explicitly addressed biological processes as well as human access to open space. The primary strategy to support biodiversity is by conserving existing remnant patches of nonurban habitat. In Hammarby-Sjöstad, a redeveloped district south of the city center that was an industrial brownfield, planners and designers paid specific attention to conserving key components of remnant patches, such as standing dead trees, which support both insect-eating birds and cavity-nesting birds. They also made significant investments in two "ecoducts," named after the functional notion of an aqueduct for biodiversity. These are large wildlife

FIGURE 11.11
The acorn-planting activities of this "mobile link" species, the Eurasian Jay, have been valued at US$4,900–22,500 per nesting pair (replacement cost).

Photograph by Luc Viatour / www.Lucnix.be.

crossing structures that allow animals to move over a regional highway to or from the marine shoreline of the district (Figure 11.12). At the shoreline itself, the development has either pleasure-boat docks or marsh plants—but separates these in space so that marsh plants can form a continuous corridor in the shallow water on one side of the urban waterfront.[36]

The lessons of this case include the observation that open space is subject to gradual attrition unless contemporary efforts vigorously reestablish the value of this planning legacy in each iteration of metropolitan planning. Permanent open spaces can provide a very important fixed structure around which smaller patches can vary in duration, ecological function, and human use. The Stockholm case also points to the need for large urban habitat patches, in the example of the National Urban Park, as a key part of the mosaic that allows animals and plants to be supported within the city itself. The example of the Hammarby-Sjöstad district provides a significant model for how planners and designers can reduce the hostility of matrix land uses that surround conserved habitat patches by retaining dead trees, allowing animals to access water, providing a water's edge for wildlife, and improving the quality of urban runoff.

FIGURE 11.12
"Ecoducts" (land bridges) over a highway connect terrestrial species to a regional protected area at Hammarby-Sjöstad. Internally, the stormwater park provides corridors to the water's edge. Standing dead trees are incorporated into the larger park areas.

Photograph courtesy of GlashusEtt.

Conclusions

The difficulty of adapting urban biodiversity conservation strategies to climate change is that the current state of the strategies is more conceptual than actual in most cities, even in the best examples. Cities like Stockholm, Munich, San Francisco, and Boston have significant legacy park systems from the nineteenth century, but Stockholm is the only one of these that has added a new, large inner-city park with conservation goals, thus creating new models for reducing the hostility of the urban matrix. Other cities, such as Portland, Oregon, are using newly purchased networks of habitat corridors to improve water quality and aquatic habitat that will also benefit the dispersal of other species, and provide flood storage in heavy rainfall events. London is pursuing a cohesive strategy of linked corridors but does not yet have metrics that can be used to determine their value to ecosystem processes (such as water filtration), or their benefits to wildlife dispersal. Their approach

is still heavily weighted toward creating spaces that humans will value. While this is critical to sustaining any landscape in an urban area, it is not sufficient for providing ecosystem services. Some kind of performance metrics must be included in planning efforts, beyond broad calls for ongoing monitoring, in order to improve the actual functioning of urban ecosystems over time.

The cities that are currently doing the most to address biodiversity are likely to have some interesting problems as a result of climate change. These problems are themselves instructive and may be generalizable as lessons are drawn from the cases for application elsewhere.

In the Pacific Northwest, where a species-level focus has been driven by the requirements of the federal Endangered Species Act, what happens if the species of concern (Chinook Salmon) is unsustainable in the region because of warming ocean waters and changing rainfall patterns? An entire program of stormwater retrofits and public right-of-way redesign, which has value for a large number of aquatic and terrestrial organisms, has been driven by an iconic regional species, the salmon. But salmon are a cold-water fish, and the oceans are warming; there may be a warming threshold past which the salmon do not return to the Pacific Northwest. The question will become whether the network strategy can be sustained and expanded for the sake of benefiting other species that may be far less iconic. Perhaps the street right-of-way redesigns could become a new norm based on their aesthetic appeal and their association with a healthier environment.[37]

Historically, Swedes and Norwegians have built strong biodiversity conservation programs around a few species that have cultural resonance, such as the oak or several flowering plants once associated with traditional agriculture. This cultural landscape strategy will have to accommodate an influx of new species from Europe, as Stockholm becomes a northern refuge for species that are temperature-limited in some way. Several Swedish plans note that the climate in Stockholm a century from now may be more similar to that of Berlin, Germany, today. It's possible that species will come from even farther south, and probable that familiar species—such as spruce—will recede further north. An oak decline across Europe has made Stockholm's oaks more valuable than ever for conservation, but if that decline is related to climate change, Stockholm's oaks may inevitably succumb as well. It's not clear how an urban conservation strategy that has been based on similarity to an iconic, preindustrial cultural landscape will fare, in terms of public support, when it becomes a strategy for supporting exotic species that are the "new natives" from the south.

The poignancy of lost species will be deeper in areas where culturally iconic species such as oaks or salmon are lost to an entire region. Will this poignancy promote apathy or engagement? Will conservation strategies be able to move to a model that is based on conserving species' traits as the more significant expression of biodiversity, rather than on conserving species themselves? While this may be a better strategy from a scientific perspective, there is much public education to be done for it to be widely supported or understood outside the small group of people who understand the relationship between traits and ecosystem functioning.

A functional approach to urban biodiversity planning and design that combines the traits of organisms with the physical and chemical functions of ecosystems would have the advantages of being easier to quantify in terms of monetary values—essentially using the cost of replacing those services with human or machine labor, in cases where it would be possible to do so. Swedish researchers have done this by putting a monetary value on the Eurasian Jay, as the "planter" of oaks. American researchers have done this by putting monetary values on the functional roles of urban trees[38] and decentralized urban stormwater detention designs.[39]

But the functional role of many species may be poorly understood and, therefore, very difficult to quantify. It would take much more research to understand these functions than it takes just to identify the presence of the species, and yet most jurisdictions do not even commit resources to basic monitoring. Streamlined methods are needed for assessing and monitoring the role of urban biodiversity in ecosystem functioning, or planners will be reduced to guessing based on similarity.[40] Efforts to predict regime shifts and manage systems to avoid them might be one example of streamlining, since these shifts are usually tracked using a small number of variables, such as river water temperature. But the effects of the shifts once they occur will be very complex to predict and manage, perhaps impossibly so.

Urban design and landscape architecture have recently shown exceptional interest in building dynamic landscapes that provide aesthetic and intellectual interest as well as functional values. Designers have been primarily interested in retrofitting the water systems in urban areas, from adding a pipe for recycled water in building plumbing systems to providing thousands of small, decentralized rainwater storage gardens, building flexible artificial shorelines along tidal waters, or designating "surge parks" to accommodate storm surges in areas subjected to flooding. Alterations of urban water systems are likely to be critical to creating potential for cities to act as refugia, as in the Jodhpur case. This physical planning trend is likely to include more climate adaptation goals in the future, as it has in London.

But contemporary design explorations are still very far from demonstrating an understanding of dynamics that go beyond physical structure in the biological world, such as addressing limits set by predators, competition, parasitism, or pathogens. Some of this complexity is not well understood by ecologists either, but when there are well-documented limits to reproductive success—such as nest predation by crows or cats on songbirds, or mortality caused by major roadways as large animals try to disperse across a region—designers need to actively incorporate and apply this knowledge in order to advocate for functional proposals that address significant aspects of the dynamism that is central to their recent theoretical interests.

Notes

1   Peter J. Mayhew, Gareth B. Jenkins, and Timothy G. Benton, "A Long-Term Association between Global Temperature and Biodiversity, Origination and Extinction in the Fossil Record," *Proceedings of the Royal Society B: Biological Sciences* 275 (2008): 47–53.

2   Arctic Monitoring and Assessment Programme, "Snow, Water, Ice, Permafrost in the Arctic (SWIPA)," accessed May 24, 2011, http://amap.no/swipa/.

3   For examples, see John G. Fleagle, *Primate Adaptation and Evolution* (San Diego: Academic Press, 1999), 283–308.

4   H. Allen Orr, "The Genetic Theory of Adaptation: A Brief History," *Nature Reviews Genetics* 6, no. 2 (February 2005): 119–27.

5   See Nun Amen-Ra, "How Dietary Restriction Catalyzed the Evolution of the Human Brain: An Exposition of the Nutritional Neurotrophic Neoteny Theory," *Medical Hypotheses* 69, no. 5 (2007): 1147–53; and Nun Amen-Ra, "Humans are Evolutionarily Adapted to Caloric Restriction Resulting from Ecologically Dictated Dietary Deprivation Imposed during the Plio-Pleistocene Period," *Medical Hypotheses* 66, no. 5 (2006): 978–84.

6   Other authors have questioned whether intelligence is correlated with anatomical changes in the brain. See, for example, Maciej Henneberg, "Evolution of the Human Brain: Is Bigger Better?," *Clinical and Experimental Pharmacology and Physiology* 25, no. 9 (September 1998): 745–49.

7   United Nations Population Fund, "State of World Population 2007: Unleashing the Potential of Urban Growth," accessed May 21, 2011, http://www.unfpa.org/swp/2007/english/introduction.html.

8   Richard T. T. Forman has influenced a generation or two of planners and designers by articulating the science behind these ideas and extending them to planning in his book *Land Mosaics: The Ecology of Landscapes and Regions* (Cambridge and New York: Cambridge University Press, 1995).

9   Philip H. Lewis, *Tomorrow by Design: A Regional Design Process for Sustainability* (New York: Wiley, 1996).

10   Simon A. Levin, "The Problem of Pattern and Scale in Ecology: The Robert H. MacArthur Award Lecture," *Ecology* 73, no. 6 (December 1992): 1943–67.

11   Jianguo Wu and Orie L. Loucks, "From Balance of Nature to Hierarchical Patch Dynamics: A Paradigm Shift in Ecology," *The Quarterly Review of Biology* 70, no. 4 (1995): 439–66.

12   Jeffrey Levinton et al., "Climate Change, Precipitation, and Impacts on an Estuarine Refuge from Disease," *PLoS ONE* 6, no. 4 (2011): e18849; John M. Marzluff et al., "Consequences of Habitat Utilization by Nest Predators and Breeding Songbirds across Multiple Scales in an Urbanizing Landscape," *The Condor* 109, no. 3 (2007): 516; and Jason F. Sandahl et al., "A Sensory System at the Interface between Urban Stormwater Runoff and Salmon Survival," *Environmental Science and Technology* 41, no. 8 (2007): 2998–3004.

13   Kristina Hill, "Shifting Sites," in *Site Matters: Design Concepts, Histories, and Strategies*, ed. Carol J. Burns and Andrea Kahn (New York and London: Routledge, 2004), 131–56. This is understandable in an applied professional discipline, where credibility and defensibility are typically seen as essential to mobilizing action in human society.

Processes that are described as random, or are unpredictable in other ways, are difficult to incorporate into planning in societies that consider risk in a very short-term context, such as the term of an elected official or the quarterly report of a business.

14   Gert Groening and Joachim Wolschke-Buhlman, "Some Notes on the Mania for Native Plants in Germany," *Landscape Journal* 11, no. 1 (1992): 116–26. Kim Sorvig followed with a response, "Natives and Nazis: An Imaginary Conspiracy in Ecological Design," *Landscape Journal* 13, no. 1 (1994): 58–61, and at least two more rounds of exchange followed via letters to the journal editors.

15   David Heath, "Warming Plant Zones," *Environment* 49, no. 2 (2007): 6.

16   See "New arborday.com Hardiness Zone Map Reflects Warmer Climate," Arbor Day Foundation, accessed May 20, 2011, http://www.arborday.org/media/zonechanges 2006.cfm. On the other hand, the use of temperature and drought predictions could effectively be used to help planners and designers avoid planting trees that are not likely to survive under future climate conditions based on those parameters alone. See Andreas Roloff, Sandra Korn, and Sten Gillner, "The Climate-Species-Matrix to Select Tree Species for Urban Habitats Considering Climate Change," *Urban Forestry and Urban Greening* 8, no. 4 (2009): 295–308. Other authors are including invasive species dynamics as well as land-use information to plan for new goals for vegetation management in urban areas, such as Jessica J. Hellmann, Knute J. Nadelhoffer, Louis R. Iverson, Lewis H. Ziska, Stephen N. Matthews, Philip Myers, Anantha M. Prasad, and Matthew P. Peters, "Climate Change Impacts on Terrestrial Ecosystems in Metropolitan Chicago and Its Surrounding, Multi-State Region," *Journal of Great Lakes Research* 36 (2010): 74–85.

17   See Margaret B. Davis, "Biology and Paleobiology of Global Climate Change: Introduction," *Trends in Ecology and Evolution* 5, no. 9 (September 1990): 269–70.

18   Nicole E. Heller and Erika S. Zavaleta, "Review: Biodiversity Management in the Face of Climate Change: A Review of 22 Years of Recommendations," *Biological Conservation* 142 (2009): 14–32.

19   Stuart L. Pimm, "Biodiversity: Climate Change or Habitat Loss—Which Will Kill More Species?," *Current Biology* 18, no. 3 (2007): 117–19.

20   See, for example, Robert S. Sommer and Frank E. Zachos, "Fossil Evidence and Phylogeography of Temperate Species: 'Glacial Refugia' and Post-Glacial Recolonization," *Journal of Biogeography* 36, no. 11 (November 2009): 2013–20; and for a review, see K. D. Bennett and J. Provan, "What Do We Mean by 'Refugia'?" *Quaternary Science Reviews* 27 (2008): 2449–55.

21   Richard T. T. Forman et al., *Road Ecology: Science and Solutions* (Washington, D.C.: Island Press, 2003), 120–22.

22   B. R. Manohar, "Jaipur Monkeys-Perspective of Ecology and Management," in *Indian Wildlife Resources*

Ecology and Development: A Study of Ecology, Conservation, Economic, and Applied Aspects of Indian Wildlife Resources, ed. B. D. Sharma (Delhi: Daya Pub House, 1999), 153–57; and Tom A. Waite et al., "Sanctuary in the City: Urban Monkeys Buffered against Catastrophic Die-off during ENSO-related Drought," *Ecohealth* 4, no. 3 (2007): 278–86.

23   Robbert P. H. Snep and Fabrice G. W. A. Ottburg, "The 'Habitat Backbone' as Strategy to Conserve Pioneer Species in Dynamic Port Habitats: Lessons from the Natterjack Toad (*Bufo calamita*) in the Port of Antwerp (Belgium)," *Landscape Ecology* 23 (2008): 1277–89.

24   Ibid.

25   Greater London Authority, Mayor of London, "Connecting with London's Nature: The Mayor's Biodiversity Strategy," July 2002, accessed May 21, 2011, http://legacy .london.gov.uk/mayor/strategies/biodiversity/docs/strat_ full.pdf.

26   "London's Action Plan," London Biodiversity Partnership, accessed May 20, 2011, http://www.lbp.org.uk/ londonap.html.

27   See the Greater London Authority, *East London Green Grid: Primer* (London: Greater London Authority, 2006). For specific sections of the grid, see East London Green Grid, Greater London Authority, "Lea Valley Area Framework: 1," accessed May 20, 2011, http://www.design forlondon.gov.uk/uploads/media/ELGGarea1.pdf.

28   London Climate Change Partnership, Greater London Authority, "Adapting to Climate Change: Creating Natural Resilience; Technical Report," October 2009, accessed May 20, 2011, http://www.london.gov.uk/lccp/publications/docs/londons-changing-climate-technical-report.pdf.

29   Chelsea Chisholm, Zoë Lindo, and Andrew Gonzalez, "Metacommunity Diversity Depends on Connectivity and Patch Arrangement in Heterogeneous Habitat Networks," *Ecography* 34, no. 3 (2011): 415–24.

30   Thomas Elmqvist et al., "The Dynamics of Social-Ecological Systems in Urban Landscapes: Stockholm and the National Urban Park, Sweden," *Annals of the New York Academy of Science* 1023 (June 2004): 308–22.

31   Stephan Barthel, Johan Colding, Thomas Elmqvist, and Carl Folke, "History and Local Management of a Biodiversity-Rich, Urban Cultural Landscape," *Ecology and Society* 10, no. 2 (2005), article 10.

32   Hendrik Ernstson and Sverker Sörlin, "Weaving Protective Stories: Connective Practices to Articulate Holistic Values in the Stockholm National Urban Park," *Environment and Planning A* 41, no. 6 (2009): 1460–79.

33   Cajsa Hougner, Johan Colding, and Tore Söderqvist, "Economic Valuation of a Seed Dispersal Service in the Stockholm National Urban Park, Sweden," *Ecological Economics* 59, no. 3 (September 2006): 354–64.

34   Ernstson and Sörlin, "Weaving Protective Stories," 1461.

35   Nina Ekelund, "Effekter på den biologiska mångfalden av ett förändrat klimat," Handlingsplan Motväxthusgaser, Stockholm Stad, accessed May 21, 2011, http://miljobarometern.stockholm.se/content/docs/gc/1/Effects%20from%20Climate%20Change%20on%20biodiversity.pdf.

36   *Hammarby-Sjostad: A Unique Environmental Project in Stockholm* (Stockholm: Glashusett, 2007), accessed October 15, 2012, http://www.hammarbysjostad.se/inenglish/pdf/HS_miljo_bok_eng_ny.pdf.

37   Melanie Mills, "Alternative Stormwater Design Within the Public Right-of-Way: A Residential Preferences Study" (master's thesis, University of Washington, Seattle, 2002).

38   Greg McPherson, James R. Simpson, Paula J. Peper, Scott E. Maco, and Qingfu Xiao, "Municipal Forest Benefits and Costs in Five US Cities," *Journal of Forestry* 103, no. 8 (December 2005): 411–16.

39   See The Trust for Public Land, Center for City Park Excellence, *The Economic Benefits of Seattle's Park and Recreation System*, March 2011, accessed May 21, 2011, http://www.seattleparksfoundation.org/TPL_EconomicBenefits.pdf.

40   Shahid Naeem, "Advancing Realism in Biodiversity Research," *Trends in Ecology and Evolution* 23, no. 8 (August 2008): 414–16.

CHAPTER 12

ARC Wildlife Crossing Competition: "hypar-nature"

HNTB Engineering and
Michael Van Valkenburgh Associates

hyper-nature: \hī-pər nā-chər\
a landscape of optimal ecological function at the point of scalar compression

hypar (hyperbolic parabaloid) vault: \hī-pär vȯlt\
a modular unit that pairs a doubly curved surface with a form that depends on a counter-resistance to the exertion of lateral thrust

THIS LANDSCAPE IS NOT FOR HUMANS. RATHER than allowing the primarily visual, aesthetic drivers of landscape design to determine form, the hypar-nature bridging system is driven by the demands of ecological engineering. Instead of attempting to re-create the surrounding nature, the design condenses and amplifies multiple landscape bands (Forest, Meadow, Shrub, Scree) into habitat corridors that provide connections for a larger cross section of species. The structure itself is a modular and cost-effective system of hypar forms that allows for minimal site disturbance and easy creation, assembly, and deployment, and can be expanded or adapted as migration pressures dictate. By combining a flexible structural solution with an adaptable approach to broad landscape

management, the hypar-nature bridging system offers a new hybrid vision for addressing habitat fragmentation.

Wide Span, Far Reach
The bridge landscape for West Vail Pass is designed to be a prototype for a regional network of wildlife overpasses that address larger-scale habitat fragmentation and represent the first phase of reconciling the mobility of humans and wildlife. The flexibility and efficiency of the bridge's structural component makes it extremely suitable for widespread use, and its minimally invasive construction allows it to be adapted to any location.

Thick Infrastructure
In order to address the complex conflict between roads and wilderness, three-dimensional solutions are required. Hypar-nature untangles the conflicting demands of human and animal transportation by bridging both under and over the road, by layering both driver experience and animal preferences, and by pursuing an adaptable framework for both vegetal and structural systems. In this

new prototype of landscape and structural collaboration, the performative ground can extend from a light-touch footing to a regional land management strategy.

Linking Public and Science

This design is meant not only to physically stitch together a fragmented habitat, but also to unite the various constituencies that will ultimately be responsible for the success of preserving the Rocky Mountain wildlife. Success lies in the connection with the general population that can be attained through outreach and education. Rather than relying on a single, physical observation point for any one bridge, the development of a digital observation platform would enable the public to observe a series of overpasses in real time, as well as access information on particular species, habitats, and changes in migration behavior. By allowing the public to engage with the science of ecosystem adaptive management, the design would work toward a shift in society's approach to operating in wildlands.

Complex Habitat Compression

Multiple habitat types from the surrounding landscape are selectively distilled and condensed into a series of parallel bands that act as crossing corridors for various animal species. The wide foraging bands provide an open field of view while narrow forest and shrub bands provide enclosed, covered corridors.

Structural Efficiency

Standard bridge construction requires the use of three individual structural components: abutment, beam, and deck slab. The efficiency of the precast hypar vault module is that it serves as a combination of all three. The hypar vault module is created through the use of very simple and easily constructed formwork. The concept anticipates precast elements similar to prestressed American Association of State Highway and Transportation Officials girders with type designations as a function of span length.

Implementable Construction

With a transport weight of less than eighty thousand pounds, the hypar vault is well within the limits for prestressed beam transport and trucking limits. The hypar vault modules are designed to be lifted and erected using a single rubber-tired mobile hydraulic crane. The hypar vault modules are set and temporarily supported at the median with temporary falsework. Erection activities would not require road closures. Construction could be undertaken one lane at a time during off-peak hours or at night, with crossovers maintaining two-directional traffic.

Landing Lightly

Placement at the West Vail Pass site intentionally minimizes mechanical disturbance of the existing grade by reducing the amount of cut-into grade. With the exception of the light trenching required for the precast footing, the grade change on-site is exclusively fill material. The selected positioning of the structure takes into consideration the existing tree line on both sides of Interstate 70 and the adjacent existing grades to minimize the amount of site intervention in the construction of the bridge and the landform.

Kit of Parts

The hypar module can be deployed in other capacities as various sites demand. In an expanded option, the bike lane could be routed through a bike-dedicated tunnel adjacent to but separated from the road traffic. The hypar vault accommodates the expanded width of Interstate 70 including the Advanced Guideway System rail, three lanes of traffic in each direction, and a bike lane.

Cultivating Complexity

Animal movement corridors can be induced by understory planting of browse grasses and sedges, selective thinning of forest canopy, and localized, controlled burns. Landscape management strategies can create enhanced browse corridors starting at the overpass and moving out into surrounding habitat patches along desired routes.

ARC Wildlife Crossing Competition: "hypar-nature"

01

White River
National Forest

Eastbound Traffic

10

2

3

7
6

4

5

8

9

10

I-70

1

Black Gore Creek

2

Ten Mile Vail Pass
National Recreation Trail

Westbound Traffic

1. Exclusionary Fencing
2. Bicycle Path
3. Stormwater Infrastructure Connections
4. Forest, Shrub, and Meadow Planting
5. Hypar Vault Structure Below

6. Jack-Tunnel Wildlife Underpass
7. Wet Meadow and Water Catchment
8. AGS Rail
9. Expanded Vehicular Traffic Lanes
10. Breakdown Lane and Snow Shoulder

N

0   50   100   200 Feet

Site Plan
Scale 1 : 1000

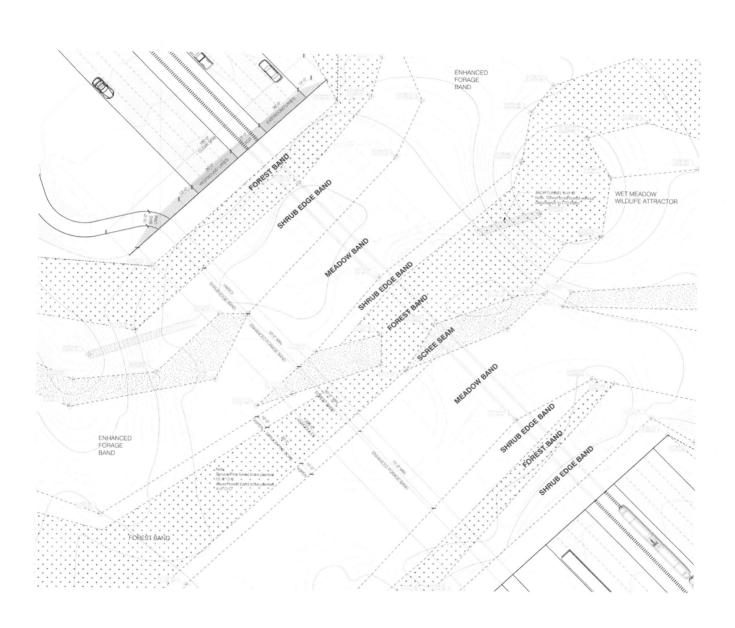

FOREST BAND

SHRUB EDGE BAND

MEADOW BAND

SHRUB EDGE BAND

FOREST BAND

SCREE SEAM

MEADOW BAND

SHRUB EDGE BAND

FOREST BAND

SHRUB EDGE BAND

ENHANCED
FORAGE
BAND

WET MEADOW
WILDLIFE ATTRACTOR

ENHANCED
FORAGE
BAND

FOREST BAND

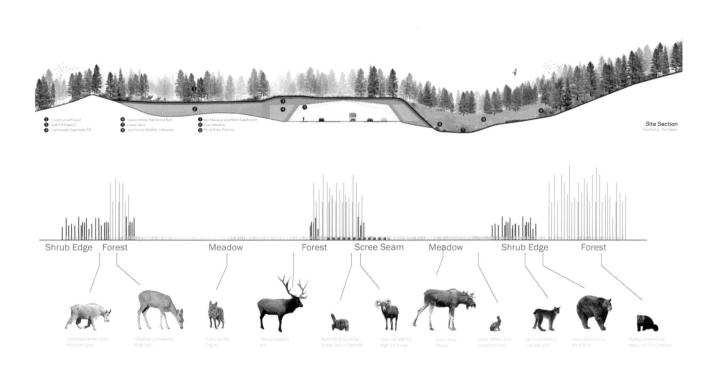

Site Section
Southwest - Northeast

1 Constructed Forest
2 Bulk Fill (Class 2)
3 Lightweight Aggregate Fill

4 Geosynthetic-Reinforced Soil
5 Hopper Vault
6 Jack-Tunnel Wildlife Underpass

7 Wet Meadow and Water Catchment
8 Open Meadow
9 Shrub Edge Planting

Shrub Edge   Forest   Meadow   Forest   Scree Seam   Meadow   Shrub Edge   Forest

Oreamnos americanus
Mountain Goat

Odocoileus hemionus
Mule Deer

Canis latrans
Coyote

Cervus elaphus
Elk

Marmota flaviventris
Yellow-bellied Marmot

Ovis canadensis
Bighorn Sheep

Alces alces
Moose

Lepus americanus
Snowshoe Hare

Lynx canadensis
Canada Lynx

Ursus americanus
Black Bear

Martes americana
American (Pine) Marten

Open Meadow

Tufted hairgrass (*Deschampsia cespitosa*)
Thurber's fescue (*Festuca thurberi*)
Alpine bluegrass (*Poa alpina*)
Geyer's sedge (*Carex geyeri*)
Idaho fescue (*Festuca idahoensis*)

Shrub Edge

Mountain mahogany (*Cercocarpus montanus*)
Yellow willow (*Salix lutea*)
Red elderberry (*Sambuca racemosa*)
Bearberry (*Arctostaphylos uva-ursi*)
Mountain snowberry (*Symphoricarpos oreophilus*)

Scree Seam

Common Juniper (*Juniperus communis*)
Blueberry (*Vaccinium spp*)
Wood's rose (*Rosa woodsii*)
Currant (*Ribes spp.*)

Forest

Subalpine fir (*Abies lasiocarpa*)
Engelmann spruce (*Picea engelmannii*)
Lodgepole pine (*Pinus contorta*)
Aspen (*Populus tremuloides*)

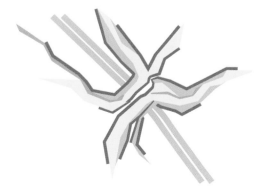

CHAPTER 13

The Role of Designers in Creating Wildlife Habitat in the Built Environment

ALEXANDER J. FELSON

WILDLIFE HABITAT DESIGN (WHD) IS AN idealized interpretation of a fragmented set of practices distributed across multiple disciplines. As we define it, WHD is the application of human ingenuity to the construction, reshaping, and enhancement of novel ecosystems. By focusing on the areas around human settlements, WHD seeks to construct new combinations of wildlife species and their habitats that can coexist with and even complement human society. Theoretical and applied ecologists, environmental practitioners, conservationists, land managers, and designers contribute to WHD from their respective fields rather than through collaboration. The concepts and methods they apply to promote wildlife populations include rapid assessments, introduction and removal of species, and habitat alterations.

In this essay, we advocate developing an overarching practical framework for creating and sustaining functional ecological communities designed to utilize resources available from coupled natural-human ecosystems and to enhance ecosystem services for local to regional communities.[1] These communities would be resilient after a biological invasion, responsive to design and management strategies, and adaptable to a variety of constraints from the built to the natural environment.

Different assumptions, methods, and goals inform the work of ecologists. Indeed, for ecologists, there are many theories that may apply to human impact on wildlife in an urban context. Furthermore, there is little consensus on the utility of applying these theories to constructed and managed novel ecosystems. Some ecologists argue that these theories may not apply to urban ecosystems, particularly in the uncertain course of climate change.[2] A growing number of ecologists recognize the need to adapt and modify biological systems and to generate theoretical frameworks around these modified ecosystems.[3]

In contrast to most ecologists, designers prioritize human needs and preferences, and focus on a subset of the ecological goals that ecologists seek to address.[4] Designers consider ecological factors such as urban microclimates, wind, and rainfall events into their design configuration and selection of plants. But other pertinent ecological applications are often not included. This is partly because designers must weigh ecological issues against financial, social, political, programmatic, and aesthetic concerns as well as practical issues such as safety, accessibility, and maintenance.[5] Part of this is also that ecological applications are knowledge intensive and difficult to apply. Designers' general training includes some ecological orientation, but mostly toward ecological site planning, sustainability frameworks, design details, and material science. But there is a gap between ecological applications by designers and those by ecologists.[6] Part of this is that ecological applications are knowledge intensive and difficult to apply. Many ecological applications are experimental and uncertain; therefore, they are difficult to incorporate into financially driven and time-sensitive client-based projects. Thus, many ecological components often do not inform design and therefore do not facilitate deep investigation into the latest ecological applications or sound science.[7] To date, designers have addressed this disparity by hiring environmental consultants including applied ecologists to participate on projects. Close collaborations with a broader range of theoretical and applied ecologists would permit designers to expand WHD beyond current strategies to overlap with ecological restoration, conservation techniques, experimentation, and other ecological methods.[8] Given the increased interest in constructed urban ecosystems and the expanding role for climate change mitigation strategies, the opportunities for designers to work on WHD are increasing.

Working together, designers and ecologists can seek novel approaches to constructing biologically productive habitats and integrating experimental research strategies into WHD, with new opportunities for assessment and adaptation. Teams can develop new methods of studying and constructing artificial yet adaptable and ecologically viable systems in urbanized landscapes.[9] As a step toward building these relationships, this essay reviews examples of designers and applied ecologists participating in WHD and chronicles the breakdowns in interdisciplinary dialogue. It identifies three improvements that could make WHD more efficient: (1) increasing the dialogue and collaboration between disciplines; (2) broadening the ecological application in design to include research, management, and monitoring practices; and (3) more accurately translating ecological knowledge into

applied practices.[10] In addition, we discuss other current collaborations between ecologists and designers that combine creativity, applied science, and technology, including "designer ecosystems,"[11] as well as WHD on compromised sites and under constrained conditions.

Involvement of Theoretical and Applied Ecologists in Wildlife Habitat Design

WHD involves theoretical ecologists located mainly in academia (who tend to focus on quantitative analysis and models) and applied ecologists, such as conservation biologists, environmental consultants, restoration ecologists, and wildlife managers (who work in nongovernmental organizations and public agencies as well as academia and who have more direct links to society at large). Ecologists have traditionally been more active in preserving existing high-value habitats than in designing new ones. Thus, they focus on habitats critical for specific wildlife and plant communities, habitats that support threatened and endangered species, or valuable nesting, breeding, and foraging habitats. Nevertheless, through diverse practices including species manipulation of wildlife populations and restoration ecology, ecologists contribute novel methods to WHD.[12]

Conservation biology seeks to balance ecological goals with political, economic, and cultural considerations in conservation areas and wildlife reserves, particularly those that overlap with indigenous human populations.[13] Their focus has expanded to include human-impacted sites, but their approach differs from that of WHD, since (for the most part) they seek to reduce human impacts and preserve natural areas, species, and ecosystems and only occasionally to restore degraded and disturbed sites.[14] For designers, such degraded sites are common. Human agency for conservation biologists is directed mainly toward minimizing or negating human impacts and maintaining high-value habitats, while in WHD it is directed toward enhancing wildlife populations and producing ecological benefits.[15]

Restoration ecologists regularly address ecosystems that have been degraded, damaged, or transformed by humans.[16] Conventional restoration ecologists investigate historic ecosystems and use them as the guide for construction. But they debate the adherence to historic reference sites in the context of climate change and human impacts, phenomena that would render such reversal efforts unrealistic.[17] In contrast, WHD focuses on the construction of novel ecosystems that combine ecological knowledge with creative design solutions and rely on technology, human management, constructed infrastructure, and long-term maintenance and monitoring to function in a changing environment.

Restoration ecologists are also starting to consider ecologically dynamic targets[18] where, in the absence of a single historical reference or target habitat, plant communities are designed to be adaptable and even responsive to climate change and human influences,[19] particularly in urbanized systems.[20] They tend to prioritize habitats, populations, and ecosystems over human engagement or recreation.[21] By contrast, WHD seeks compromises that establish viable wildlife habitat and include human uses while optimizing the potential ecological services within the context of a human-modified environment.[22] Within restoration ecology, few research scientists cross over into design; the restoration ecologist Steven N. Handel is a rare exception. Through his organization Center for Urban Restoration Ecology (CURE), a joint effort between Rutgers, The State University of New Jersey, and the New York Botanical Garden, he is working to restore and enhance the ecosystem performance of degraded public lands. Handel is contributing to the ecological function, layout, plant selection, maintenance, and monitoring strategies of several design projects.[23]

Applied ecologists including wildlife managers have been managing and manipulating ecosystems since the early twentieth century in order to foster wildlife habitats, rebuild or enhance ecosystem functions, and assess the long-term impacts of human interventions.[24] Many ecological practices (such as fisheries and wildlife management, habitat restoration, and species manipulations) can be viewed as a proactive "design" to optimize ecosystem functioning. Utilitarian conservation science has concentrated on manipulations that control ecosystems such that humans can harvest high yields of selected species of fish, timber, and game.[25] These applied utilitarian approaches tend to focus on one aspect of local systems that could be part of a larger and more complex system. Although it is easier to achieve rigorous monitoring, narrowing the focus to these subsystems can also lead to failures in design. These methods have shifted out of favor in exchange for increasingly ecosystem-oriented approaches. There is a growing demand to expand our scope and study the interaction between system complexity in temporal and spatial scales.[26] These opposing interpretations are debated in relation to forms of experimentation to interpret ecosystems.[27] Preservation of high-value ecosystems has been the priority due to the scarcity of resources for conservation, and because intact and functioning ecosystems are critical to maintaining our planet and our longevity.[28] A handful of ecologists have more recently begun to promote constructed nature and biodiversity in populated areas and to question the adequacy of nature reserves.[29] Ecologists have gone so far as to suggest re-wilding practices that introduce stand-in organisms such as camels, elephants, and other megafauna to compensate for lost diversity in North America. For example, as part of a design team for a 2012 exhibition at the Museum of Modern Art entitled *Foreclosed: Rehousing the American Dream*, the author proposed suburban housing that would employ the zoological park as an amenity. In a collaborative endeavor between the developer and the federal government, the government would finance habitat links to the suburb and, in return, the development would incorporate infrastructure with intensified habitat zones and productive ecosystems, providing jobs, public amenities, and regional habitat resources (Figure 13.1).[30] The concept builds on the knowledge that large predators are often instrumental in maintaining the structure, resilience, and diversity of ecosystems through initiating "top-down" ecological (trophic) interactions.

Other ecologists are working with existing and damaged systems and seeking ways of improving the function through manipulations. For example, ecologists in the limnology department at the University of Wisconsin manipulated Lake Mendota for decades through a series of "design" interventions aimed at (1) understanding the ecological implications and effectiveness of invasive species controls, (2) managing fish populations for recreational value, and (3) improving the aesthetics of the

A. PERIPHERAL HOUSE
Boundaries, walls and controlled apertures, nesting interface with habitat restoration, maintenance of habitats

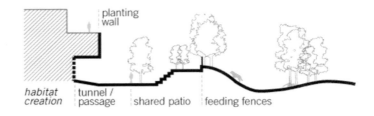

B. CORRIDOR HOUSE
Multilevel viewing, shared passages Vertical landscapes to increase corridor width in tight areas

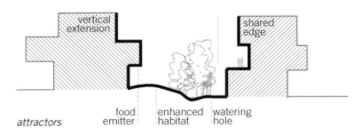

C. PRODUCTIVE BUILDING
Cultivation of nature to provide living materials to activate zoo enclosures

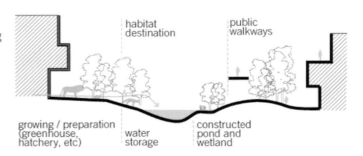

D. OBSERVATION HOUSE
Enclosure of constructed nature, Lookout and key part of suburban food web

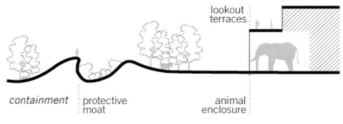

E. ZOO CIRCUIT
Public network through buildings and landscape, provides circuit view of wildlife

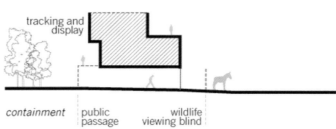

FIGURE 13.1

The Urban Ecology and Design Laboratory (UEDLAB), working as part of the Zago Architecture Team for the *Foreclosed: Rehousing the American Dream* exhibition at the Museum of Modern Art, proposed using suburbia along the exurban fringe as a site for testing re-wilding. Re-wilding asserts that large predators can be instrumental in maintaining the structure, resilience, and diversity of ecosystems by initiating top-down ecological interactions.

Illustration by Alexander J. Felson and Jacob Dugapolski.

lake by controlling algal blooms.[31] These interventions, alongside other anthropogenic effects such as non-point-source pollution and surrounding land-use changes, have disrupted the ecological function of organisms and habitats within the lake (Figure 13.2). The research and monitoring efforts at Lake Mendota successfully linked the impacts on the lake back to human uses and adjacent settlement patterns including non-point-source pollution.[32] The activities at Lake Mendota show that efforts to rehabilitate ecosystems are not always successful and can shift in unpredictable ways.

Interdisciplinary groups of ecologists outside of academia, environmental scientists, and activists in nonprofit organizations (NPOS) play important roles in WHD as well. Environmental scientists and applied biologists were hired by Washington

Department of Fish and Wildlife and the local NPO FISH to design solutions that would promote salmon survival and propagation within an urban context. The group headed efforts to reestablish populations of Chinook, Coho, and Steelhead Salmon in the Pacific Northwest through better habitat and land-use planning and management. Dilapidated creek beds are often found in densely populated urban areas such as the Issaquah Salmon Hatchery. In downtown Issaquah, Washington, large salmon populations return to their breeding grounds that are located in the midst of residences, shopping centers, and roadways. The reconstruction of breeding areas includes fish hatcheries that protect areas for eggs and sperm, raceways (an average of fifteen feet wide and eighty-five feet long), ponds for adult populations (twenty feet wide, ninety feet long, and

FIGURE 13.2
Timeline of major changes to Lake Mendota from 1850 to present. Abbreviations include: CWH, coarse woody habitat; LTER, long-term ecological research.

Diagram by Timothy Terway of the Urban Ecology and Design Lab based on Stephen R. Carpenter, "Understanding Regional Change: A Comparison of Two Lake Districts," *BioScience* 57, no. 4 (April 2007): 323–35.

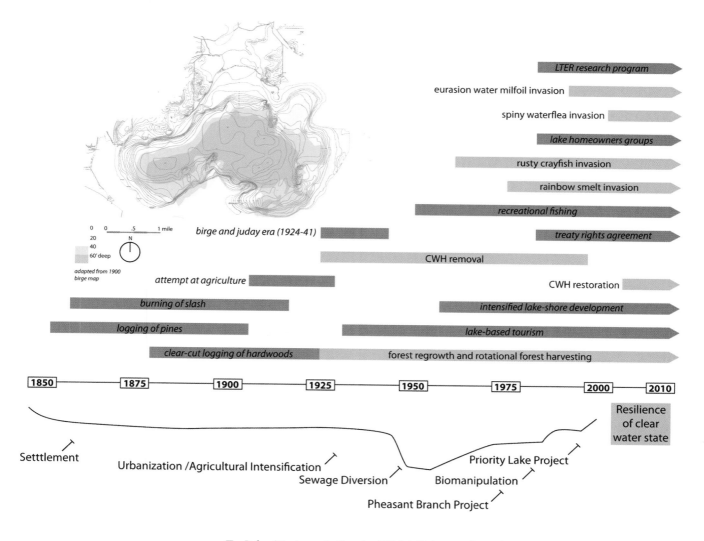

six feet deep), as well as hatching troughs, deep-tray troughs, hatchery baskets, egg trays, rearing ponds, water system, and racks and traps. Constructed as a Works Project Administration project from 1936 to 1937, the hatchery faced closure in 1992, but was ultimately maintained and now supports migrating Chinook and Coho Salmon populations of approximately twenty thousand since 2000. With three hundred thousand visitors a year, this is an eventful ecological and social venue.[33]

Although uncommon, a handful of ecologists have actively selected and prepared ecological information as templates to guide design strategies. The most influential and prolific contributor to design is the ecologist Richard T. T. Forman.[34] In his books on landscape ecology, urban regional ecology and planning, and road ecology, Forman effectively translates scientific findings and ecological understanding into applicable design considerations and specific management practices.[35] Forman's work builds on extensive references and discussions of ecological strategies (Figure 13.3).[36] Viewed as a founder of landscape ecology, his work has influenced generations of applied ecologists and many design practitioners.

Wenche E. Dramstad, James D. Olson, and Richard T. T. Forman translated ecological principles into guidelines for use in landscape architecture and land planning in *Landscape Ecology Principles in Landscape Architecture and Land-Use Planning* (1996). The book illustrates the compromises required to translate complex and often unresolved research-driven ecological understanding into applied design strategies. In "Hard and Soft

Boundaries," the argument that "a curvilinear 'tiny' patch boundary may provide a number of ecological benefits including greater wildlife usage," is based on the assumption that heterogeneity improves wildlife usage, but this would depend on the surrounding context and population densities. The "number of large patches" image relies on assumptions about which more effectively conserves biodiversity, "single large reserves or several small reserves" of overall equal size.[37] But these principles are generalized to simplify the message for educational purposes; however, this does not guarantee that the application of these practices in real-world solutions will be effective. Although they appear general and applicable to most sites, the actual application is highly dependent on the site context, which would have to be addressed with specific and in-depth research. Implementing experiments and monitoring programs to generate useful data requires tenacity in actual design projects.

Environmental consultants, who are often trained as biologists or environmental scientists, offer a critical link between scientific principles and design applications (Figure 13.4).[38] They are often hired as consultants to construct wildlife habitats as a mitigation strategy. For example, environmental consultants from the Louis Berger Group were hired for the Stewart International Airport Access Improvement Project in New York, which simultaneously improved access to the airport with new roadways, established nearly seven thousand acres of forest, preserved a historic site, preserved and established a seed bank for propagation of a large population of plants (e.g., purple milkweed), incorporated wildlife crossings into

FIGURE 13.3
In the process of conversion into illustrations and text, ecological principles, including the uncertainty and debates surrounding these principles, were simplified in order to translate complex and often unresolved research-driven ecological understanding into applied design strategies.

Illustration redrawn from Wenche E. Dramstad, James D. Olson, and Richard T. T. Forman, *Landscape Ecology Principles in Landscape Architecture and Land-Use Planning* (Cambridge, Mass.: Harvard University Graduate School of Design; Washington, D.C.: Island Press, 1996), 23 and 30.

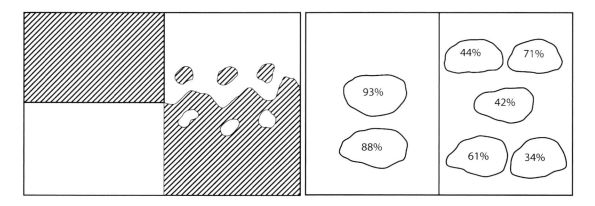

ALEXANDER J. FELSON

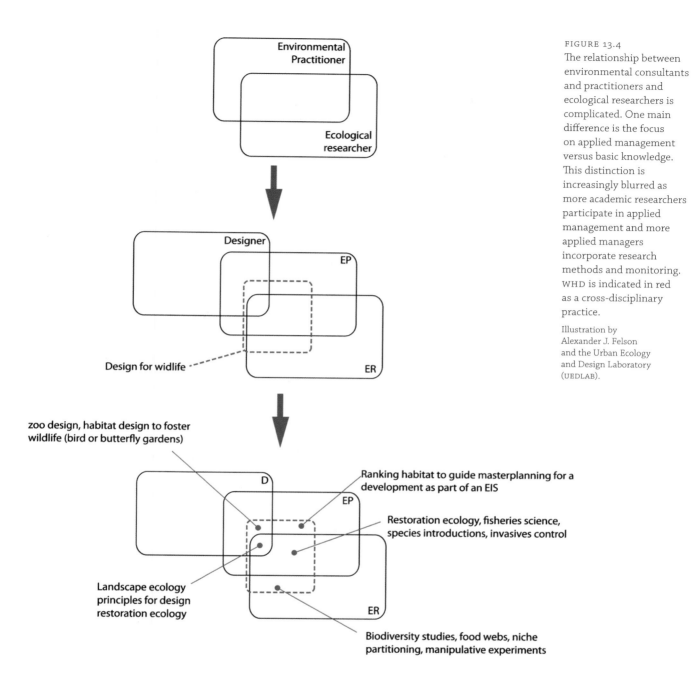

FIGURE 13.4
The relationship between environmental consultants and practitioners and ecological researchers is complicated. One main difference is the focus on applied management versus basic knowledge. This distinction is increasingly blurred as more academic researchers participate in applied management and more applied managers incorporate research methods and monitoring. WHD is indicated in red as a cross-disciplinary practice.

Illustration by Alexander J. Felson and the Urban Ecology and Design Laboratory (UEDLAB).

the highway design, conserved the roosting habitat of a federally endangered Indiana bat, and created twelve vernal pools and other wetlands across thirteen acres that will be monitored as breeding habitats (Figure 13.5).[39] Environmental consultants are hired to work on specific design projects for clients who typically prioritize financial goals and marketing over academic or conservation goals (Figure 13.3). In parallel, since consultants work under fast-paced timelines and perform site-specific research, they often use rapid-assessment approaches and observations and apply data gathered from unrelated sites rather than gathering site-specific data. The rapid assessments may be effective for establishing a basic understanding of the quality of habitats across the site but may be too coarse and general to inform site-specific design proposals. To date, the influence of environmental consultants on designers engaged

The Role of Designers in Creating Wildlife Habitat in the Built Environment

in WHD is rarely documented or described in peer-reviewed scientific literature.

Involvement of Designers in WHD

Design practice to promote wildlife includes zoological gardens and urban to rural park designs. A critical contributor is Ian L. McHarg, whose interdisciplinary program at the University of Pennsylvania sought to embed ecological science within the training process for designers.[40] McHarg proposed specific methodologies and decision-making processes, where ecological components and critical urban features are extracted into distinct and indexed layers. Participants combine layers to generate and compare different planning alternatives—in particular, the selection of conservation and development areas.[41] His methods were a precursor to geographic information systems, which is a technological application that has radically influenced conservation planning and practices, including WHD. His contributions have enhanced communication between ecologists and designers.[42]

McHarg's approach exemplifies the simplication of science when it is translated into design practice. He uses ecological information selectively, prioritizing its incorporation within the design framework. He distills scientific knowledge into a static scoring system, which is useful for determining where to avoid building and where to build. But this layering and mapping method often simplifies ecosystems and leaves out important ecosystem processes that may occur in reality.[43] Many designers view his methods as overly prescriptive with limited creativity. But his methods and education process directly and indirectly spurred a generation of knowledgeable and effective practitioners, including Carl Steinitz, Anne Spirn, Niall Kirkwood, and James Corner.[44]

Landscape architects (and other design firms) work on projects ranging from residential wildlife gardens to large waterfront parks or botanical gardens to regional and national park systems.[45] Certain firms specialize in WHD. For instance, the firm Jones and Jones in Seattle, Washington, focuses on zoological gardens, conservation-based design, and

FIGURE 13.6
Lurie Garden, illustrating the layering
of native and nonnative plantings to
assemble a prairie grassland community.

Photograph by Alexander J. Felson.

wildlife sanctuaries along with more traditional design projects. Jones and Jones has developed immersive zoo exhibits to replace the dismal gunite enclosures from the 1930s, adding more natural displays that include behavioral enhancements.[46] Other specialty firms, such as EDSA in Florida, concentrate on WHD as it relates to human experiences, such as ecotourism, resort planning, and planning for outdoor recreation. Environmental consulting firms such as the Bioengineering Group from Salem, Massachusetts, now include in-house landscape architects who work together with environmental scientists, biologists, and ecologists to address brownfield reclamation, habitat restoration, and urban infrastructure.[47]

In addition to projects that are directly tied to WHD, landscape architects and other designers commonly and casually incorporate habitat components into large parks projects, which may contain specialized habitat development.[48] Also, even without any specific manipulation for enhancing wildlife, landscapes that are designed for human needs and preferences often provide potential wildlife habitats. Consideration of biological responses as part of the built environment can inspire public ecological awareness and political fidelity to biodiversity, both of which can strongly influence contemporary urban landscape design. This approach assumes that if you build it, they will come—meaning that if designers incorporate habitat features intended to attract wildlife, then species will flock to the area. But the overall ecological values of both designed and remnant vegetative communities for wildlife are unknown.[49] A second assumption is that any generically defined habitat such as parcels of land including remnant forests or wetlands, which are often degraded in urban settings or are successional landscapes with invasive species, will be valuable as wildlife habitat.[50] These may or may not promote ecosystem performances.[51] The ecological expertise that goes into the configuration of wildlife habitat on design projects

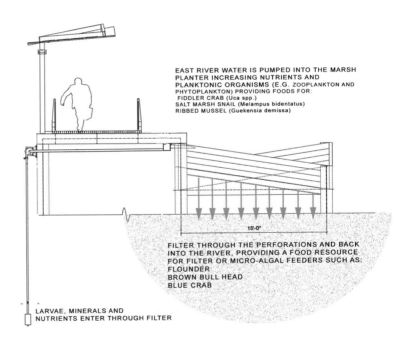

EAST RIVER WATER IS PUMPED INTO THE MARSH PLANTER INCREASING NUTRIENTS AND PLANKTONIC ORGANISMS (E.G. ZOOPLANKTON AND PHYTOPLANKTON) PROVIDING FOODS FOR:
FIDDLER CRAB (Uca spp.)
SALT MARSH SNAIL (Melampus bidentatus)
RIBBED MUSSEL (Guekensia demissa)

15'-0"

FILTER THROUGH THE PERFORATIONS AND BACK INTO THE RIVER, PROVIDING A FOOD RESOURCE FOR FILTER OR MICRO-ALGAL FEEDERS SUCH AS:
FLOUNDER
BROWN BULL HEAD
BLUE CRAB

LARVAE, MINERALS AND
NUTRIENTS ENTER THROUGH FILTER

FIGURE 13.7
The East River Marsh Planter is a project developed to function as a constructed food web catalyst along the bulkhead at 34th Street in New York City. A nutrient plume of macroinvertebrates catering to filter-feeding fish, including flounder and blue crab, is created using a pump to redirect water into salt-marsh planters.

Illustration courtesy of WORKSHOP © Ken Smith Landscape Architect, drawn by Alexander J. Felson.

FIGURE 13.8

The Orange County Great Park wildlife corridor, showing examples of constructed habitat enhancements for specific wildlife.

Illustration courtesy of WORKSHOP © Ken Smith Landscape Architect.

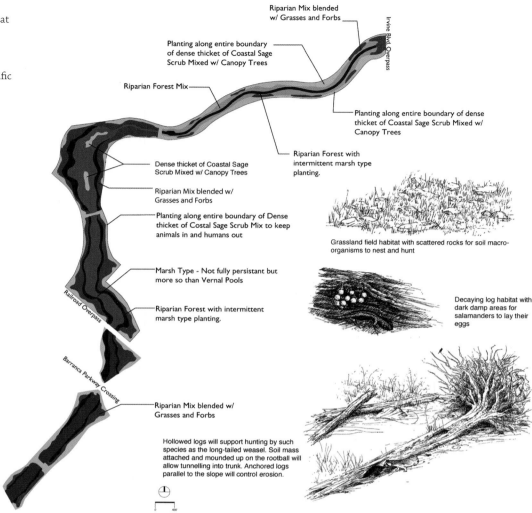

Riparian Mix blended w/ Grasses and Forbs

Planting along entire boundary of dense thicket of Coastal Sage Scrub Mixed w/ Canopy Trees

Riparian Forest Mix

Irvine Blvd. Overpass

Planting along entire boundary of dense thicket of Coastal Sage Scrub Mixed w/ Canopy Trees

Dense thicket of Coastal Sage Scrub Mixed w/ Canopy Trees

Riparian Forest with intermittent marsh type planting.

Riparian Mix blended w/ Grasses and Forbs

Planting along entire boundary of Dense thicket of Costal Sage Scrub Mix to keep animals in and humans out

Marsh Type - Not fully persistant but more so than Vernal Pools

Railroad Overpass

Riparian Forest with intermittent marsh type planting.

Barranca Parkway Crossing

Riparian Mix blended w/ Grasses and Forbs

Hollowed logs will support hunting by such species as the long-tailed weasel. Soil mass attached and mounded up on the rootball will allow tunnelling into trunk. Anchored logs parallel to the slope will control erosion.

Grassland field habitat with scattered rocks for soil macro-organisms to nest and hunt

Decaying log habitat with dark damp areas for salamanders to lay their eggs

can be limited, partly because environmental consultants and ecologists are often peripherally involved in the design process. Rarely considered are issues such as habitat structure, the type of food webs the vegetative community might promote, or the effects that remnant vegetation adjacent to the site have on dispersal and succession.[52]

The habitats designed as components of park projects are intended to serve both public and wildlife values, but human-centered design priorities can conflict with habitat values. This is attributed, in part, to wildlife territory constraints and to the impact of overlapping programmatic uses and human disturbances. Although many designers seek to create habitats that are aesthetically pleasing

and useful to humans while also promoting ecological functions,[53] it remains unclear how well these human and biological functions overlap. For example, the Lurie Garden in Chicago, Illinois, is loosely modeled after the prairie landscapes that were common to the Chicago area prior to industrialization. The garden is designed to engage people with the space and to encourage pedestrian traffic throughout the year. Plants were selected on the basis of flowering time, height, color, and texture, rather than seeking to reconstruct a historically referenced prairie ecosystem. From an ecological perspective, the combined use of natives and nonnatives and the creative selection of plants for aesthetic effect illustrates more contemporary practices of crafting novel ecosystems through a combination of ecological restoration and context (Figure 13.6).[54] Many of the species recently planted do attract insects and birds, and represent a compromise between ecological and human values.

Designers are beginning to recognize the value of controlled experiments on urban landscapes. Test plots and pilot studies are being used more often to monitor urban systems and to guide adaptive management.[55] For example, the design of a small-scale, experimental saltwater marsh planter along Manhattan's East River combines aesthetics with ecological research (Figure 13.7). Designed to merge aesthetics with function, the controlled experiment would provide an educational planter situated along the routes of thirty thousand daily commuters. The exposed salt-marsh pump will flood the planters with nutrient- and larvae-rich brackish East River water in the morning and evening, timed to coincide with the commute.[56] The promotion of small organisms and detritus will help catalyze a food web and nutrient plume in the East River. The planter will enable studies to evaluate the ecological value of a variety of habitat design and restoration strategies. Other efforts to merge science with design appear in projects ranging from backyard wildlife gardens to major city parks and wildlife-based recreation.

A range of other projects illustrates the increased attentiveness of designers to ecological applications. Designers are more frequently collaborating with ecologists to translate ecological understanding into design projects. Large park designs are a particular type of landscape commission that often includes wildlife habitat as a component of programmatic land uses. For example, Orange County Great Park is a decommissioned airport where the ecologist Steven N. Handel and landscape architect Ken Smith are developing a large-scale park with wildlife habitat. The project includes a wildlife corridor,

FIGURE 13.9
Presidio Fort Scott Creek and Historic Garden sections, illustrating alternative scenarios balancing wildlife habitat value with public access and use. The three options represent the results of a series of intensive stakeholder outreach and design session with an interdisciplinary group of designers, biologists, and restoration ecologists led by the author.

Illustration courtesy of AECOM.

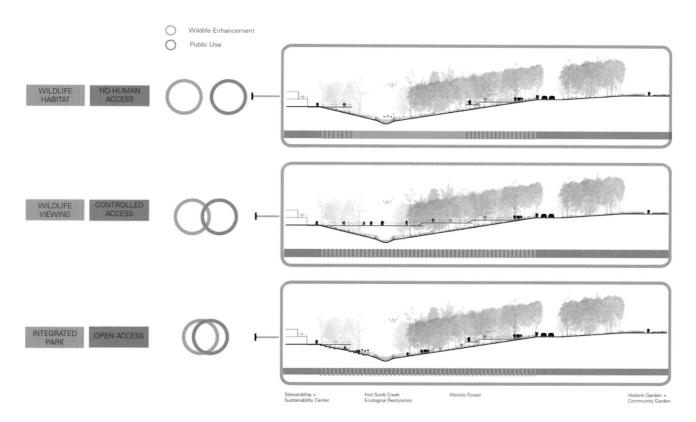

Presidio Fort Scott Creek + Historic Garden

Sections: These sections illustrate alternative scenarios balancing wildlife habitat value with public access and use.

a dynamic set of constructed ecological communities that overlap along a large ravine (Figure 13.8). Habitat for nesting, camouflage, and foraging are designed into the ravine, which is closed to the public. Tunnels allow crossing, and overlooks facilitate viewing of the plant and animal communities.[57] (For additional information on this project, see Steven N. Handel's essay, "Ecological Restoration Foundations in Designing Habitats in Urban Areas," this volume.)

Presidio of San Francisco, California, provides other examples of ecological design projects and illustrates the potentially controversial politics surrounding design and ecology. At Inspiration Point, as in most of the Presidio, landscapes of serpentine grasses, dune scrub, coastal prairie, and coastal scrub habitats were replaced with low diversity and ecologically limited monoculture forests of eucalyptus, Monterey Pine, and cypress groves. The proposal to remove the "historic forest" to reestablish the views from Inspiration Point was met with resistance. The Presidio Trust was able to bypass this resistance by soliciting community participation in an ecological restoration project in which trees were removed overnight and replaced with a restored ecosystem.[58] This project illustrates the compromises often required to accommodate ecology and public use (Figure 13.9).

Distinctions between Designers and Theoretical and Applied Ecologists

The Impact of Different Funding Sources on Ecologists and Designers

Whereas ecologists are often funded through grants and similar sources, designers are customarily hired by clients to work on projects. Clients typically establish the priorities of a project and heavily impact site selection, site boundaries, budget, and program.[59] Thus, the extent to which a designer incorporates conservation practices and habitat development into a project depends largely on the client and the knowledge and persuasiveness of the designer. The designer must balance the client's priorities with other factors such as programmatic uses of the site, cultural heritage, and adjacent land uses.[60] Applied ecologists, including conservation biologists and wildlife managers, also find employment with clients through private and public contracts.

By contrast, theoretical and many applied ecologists are supported primarily by grants that stipulate the use of funding. Grantees are required to specify their goals clearly and to identify their deliverables, labor, equipment, and other expenses.[61] For the most part, ecologists organize their sites around the value of conserving existing habitats and the life cycles of organisms being addressed. Thus, ecologists define the site and the research focus rather than being prescribed a site and a program. In addition to grants, environmental agencies and institutions also conduct fundraising to support scientific research and applied conservation projects. Organizations such as the Nature Conservancy raise funds to support land purchases and environmental agendas, and are a cross between clients and science-oriented funding of grants.[62]

Different Locations, Sizes, and Boundaries of Research Sites and Design Sites

Design sites tend to differ from sites on which ecologists focus. The locations, approach to delineating boundaries, and often the size of the land parcel differ between the fields of design and ecological research or applied ecology and conservation. Designers often work on highly contested sites close to human settlements, where habitat quality is not necessarily ideal for wildlife. For designers, degraded sites provide opportunities to reinvent nature.[63] Studying and restoring degraded sites is becoming increasingly popular with applied ecologists[64] and urban ecologists in the United States.[65]

Because ecologists approach sites from a scientific perspective, they typically identify boundaries in relation to the questions or hypotheses being investigated. Watersheds, ecosystem functions, species movements, and the types of regional and local habitat affect how ecologists interpret boundaries. By contrast, designers consider the broader site context and adjacent land uses, and often seek to expand their influence beyond the site boundaries; however, the actual boundaries, budget, and client's interest tend to control the ability to expand site boundaries. Thus, designers tend to develop design responses that work within the discretely bounded areas, responding less to the broader ecological region and adjacent land context and disregarding pressing ecological concerns of the time, such as invasive species.[66]

Theoretical and Applied Ecologists and Designers Work with Sites Differently

Designers evaluate sites using an approach different from that of ecologists.[67] Ecologists contribute substantial amounts of time and funding to site analysis. They concentrate on habitat evaluations, historical analysis, local outreach, and seasonal evaluations of different species, ecological processes, and ecosystem functions associated with the site.[68] For designers, site analysis tends to be a small component of the overall design process. Whereas ecologists learn as much about a particular site as possible, designers use rapid assessment to concentrate on factors that are most relevant to the design process.[69] Design occurs regardless of the quality of site information gathered. In this way, designers knowingly make decisions based on incomplete information. Theory that bridges design and ecology through an understanding of urban sites is taking place.[70]

Because time and funding are limited, both ecologists and designers must make concessions when evaluating sites. For biologists with limited resources, this means using sampling approaches that entail the use of transects, random sampling, or observation to evaluate the habitat of large sites. The rigor of these approaches varies, depending on the environmental consultants or ecologists involved in the assessment. Outside funding sources have been more effective in ensuring research quality on projects. But for many ecologists, scientific rigor is evaluated in the peer-review process. For designers, site analysis can be redirected to environmental consultants who typically apply rapid assessment practices rather than establishing research.

Where ecological concepts are central to the design concept, a common approach focuses on ecosystem services, including nitrogen absorption, carbon sequestration, and resilient vegetation. But evoking ecosystem services inevitably relies on complex ecological interactions that are poorly understood and that rapid assessments would likely overlook. Although rapid assessments can be rigorous, they may also be untested and only provide rough interpretations of the site conditions. Rapid assessments inform environmental impact statements (EIS), which provide a regulatory review of the environmental factors pertaining to designated projects. EIS receive limited peer review or circulation

to ensure that rigorous assessments are made.[71] Overall, deadlines that accommodate longer periods of site analysis would benefit both ecologists and designers. Thus, rapid assessment may not evaluate the ecological value of a site reliably.[72]

The Fresh Kills Project Illustrates the Challenges of Incorporating Ecological Science into Design

In 2001, an international design competition was initiated to convert the Fresh Kills Landfill on Staten Island into a large park. The six final entries proposed a range of ecologically driven design proposals. The winning proposal, by Field Operations, included the subconsultant firm Applied Ecological Services (AES). They were hired in part to inventory the local habitats of the site and to translate those habitat types into vegetative strategies for the project as a quasi-restoration ecology proposal. This included identifying initial reference sites and then generating novel ecosystems that prioritized site program, low maintenance, and rapid plant maturation (Figure 13.10). The findings and recommendations of AES inspired the project's aesthetic approach and suggested the design of vegetation planted on the site.[73] The design team proposed a vegetative matrix of lines, surfaces, and clusters intended to increase surface area for access and movement of seeds, biota, and people.[74] From an ecological perspective, the linear thickets of woody vegetation could serve as woodland corridors. The mats of freshwater swamps, swamp forest, and bogs replaced existing stormwater detention basins around the mounds. The clusters could serve as stepping stones or habitat patches. The team also consulted with Steven N. Handel and the earlier work he completed on Fresh Kills Landfill to understand seed-dispersal patterns by birds from adjacent remnant woodlots (for additional detail, see Steven N. Handel's essay, "Ecological Restoration Foundations in Designing Habitats in Urban Areas," this volume).

The Fresh Kills project shows how ecological knowledge derived from site inventories is translated and combined with design strategies that intend to restructure constructed land and balance ecological goals with the provision of space for human recreation. The results differ from those of restoration

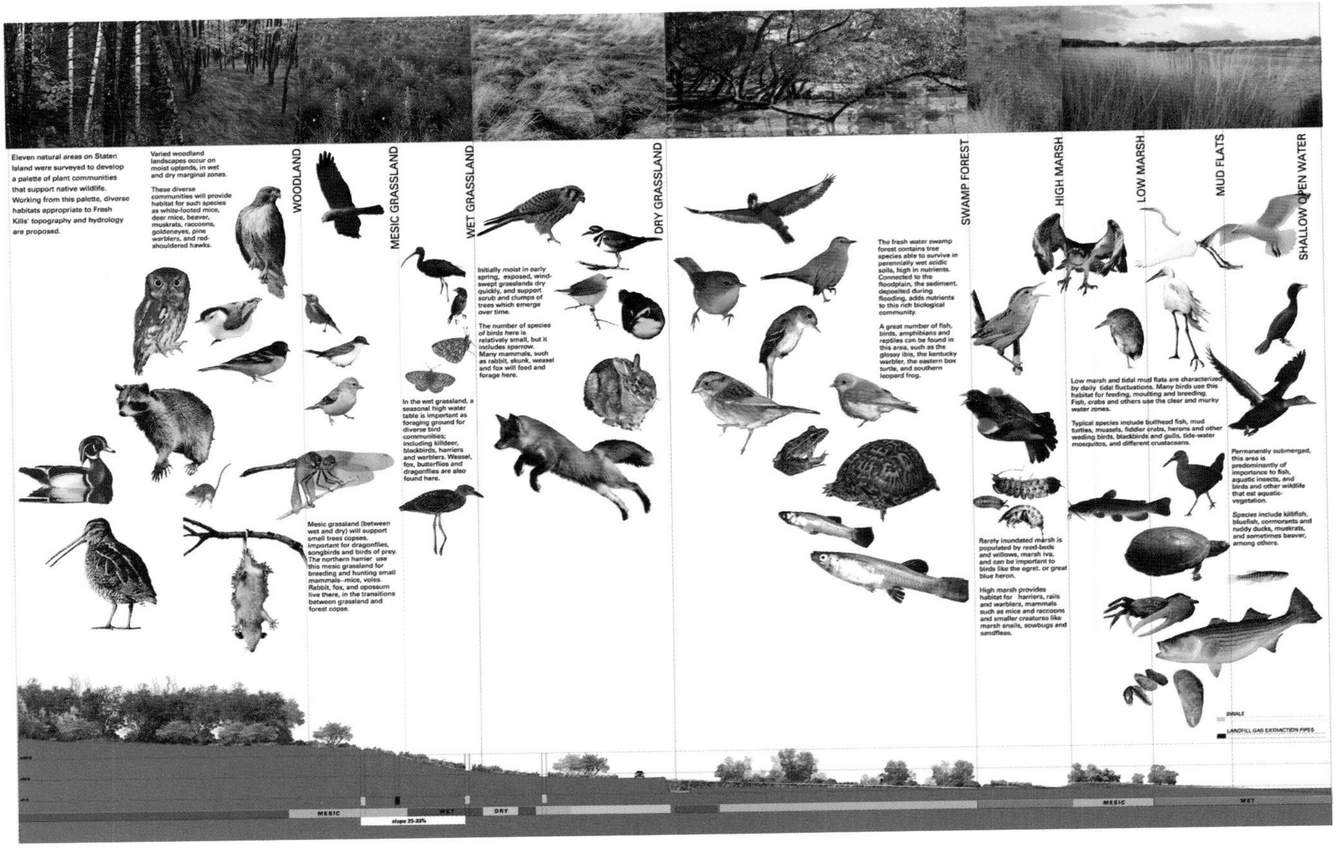

FIGURE 13.10
Fresh Kills Landfill illustrating several plant palettes selected to support native wildlife as suggested by, and based on, surveys of local habitats found on Staten Island.

Illustration courtesy of James Corner Field Operations.

ecologists who prioritize historical configuration of the ecosystem and site conditions to foster habitat. In this case, the constraints of the landfill site and the focus on design and aesthetics require compromises to the potential restoration agenda.

As the Fresh Kills project reiterates, designers often work on degraded sites that are not readily restorable as ecological communities. Human settlements and changes in land use clearly exert pressure upon wildlife habitat.[75] Scientific knowledge accumulates and dogma can shift with new discoveries.[76] Designers have not been engaged in these scientific debates, which fundamentally question the ecological value of applied habitat patches, corridors, and biodiversity. Even after years of scientific debate, the recommendations remain the same. Design professionals and regulators still follow an approach to minimize habitat fragmentation and to establish corridors when unavoidable to ensure that there are options for species dispersal and patch recolonization.[77] The distinct characteristics of many design projects make adhering to principles of restoration ecology difficult and warrant the use of creative design solutions. When human interventions have changed land uses substantially, it may not be possible to restore ecosystems to previous states that may no longer be the appropriate prototypes.[78] Thus, the approaches used by designers to construct habitats could influence the practices of restoration ecologists working on degraded sites.[79]

Landscape Urbanism Is a Process-Based Design Method that Seeks to Incorporate Ecological Principles

Designers are increasingly generating proposals that incorporate ecological, social, and cultural processes into their designs. This includes projects that shift from structured design methods to a more fluid process that is cognizant of nonlinear factors and heterogeneous environments.[80] Landscape urbanists seek to build on the common practice in landscape architecture of incorporating systems thinking and dynamic processes, such as succession, into their projects.[81] Dynamic ecological patterns, or in many cases, the patterns that result from dynamic processes, are used to generate design aesthetics rather than simply serving an ecological purpose. Such design serves as a catalyst and loose structure to guide a project through metamorphosis into a new aesthetic that combines successional landscapes and ecosystem function with programmed space. Process-based design contrasts with approaches in which social and ecological outcomes are controlled in a static and formal organization.[82] Landscape urbanists and other process-based designers adopt concepts such as resilience and adaptive management from ecological sciences.[83]

A major challenge of process-based design is how to represent landscape dynamics of interest to clients and the public in compelling ways. Given the stochastic nature of ecological systems, this process-oriented approach means either grappling with highly complex conditions or framing the design to ignore conditions such as nutrient fluxes and species interactions. Generating designs that capture processes in a meaningful way requires incorporating applicable ecological data and theories into the design plans.[84] Incorporating dynamic and stochastic processes into the organization of space, representing these processes in drawings and models, and modeling how these processes drive the design create new challenges for designers because predicting the resultant landscapes of process-based design approaches is likely impossible. The unpredictable outcomes of process-based design are particularly problematic for landscape architects who must generate innovative design solutions that fit the public perception of how parks and urban areas should look. The current expectations for parkland and picturesque- or naturalistic-style landscapes make selling process-based strategies, which are often unpredictable and unkempt, difficult. Public preferences for naturalistic design may allow some investigation of processes, however, and they have facilitated a variety of successional gardens and maintenance practices, such as the piling of woody debris in Central Park.

Process-based design can also be highly speculative. The competition proposal by Field Operations for Downsview Park in Toronto, for example, suggested an evolving and productive food web similar to Fresh Kills (Figure 13.10).[85] The proposal was speculative because of the inherent uncertainty in ecology and the unclear importance of immigration and emigration, both of which suggest that an evolving community of organisms is unpredictable and dependent on adjacent populations. Such an urbanized park is likely to become overrun with invasive and nuisance species. Planting a healthy and native vegetative community is not guaranteed to attract an ideal wildlife community. Furthermore, a wildlife habitat with a food web, as envisioned for Downsview Park, would benefit from the use of other ecological tools and a robust approach to wildlife management, possibly including species introductions, long-term management of invasive species, disease-control efforts, and controlled public access.[86] A fundamental challenge is renegotiating functioning wildlife habitat with substantial human and vehicular traffic. In a study at the Presidio—developed through intensive outreach with ecologists, designers, and park users—an interdisciplinary group from AECOM Design, working with the Presidio Trust, realized that compromises are required for the coexistence of wildlife habitat and human traffic in close proximity (Figure 13.9). Furthermore, the ecological value of habitat patches and corridors are debated even in the context of nonurban settings, where most of the research has occurred. In situ and site-specific research within urban systems that clarifies the value and functionality of wildlife corridors is limited.[87] Thus, predictions of the ecological value of wildlife habitats and food webs created in projects such as Downsview Park are riddled with uncertainties. Translating ecological assumptions based on nonurban settings to human settlements increases uncertainty because there are a variety of additional known and unknown factors that exist in fragmented and urbanized settings.[88]

Landscape urbanists are particularly skilled in exposing interdependencies between ecosystems and society. This skill could aid in the transformation of urban systems today, because it can turn pressing sustainability challenges into opportunities to reconnect humans and nature through major physical modification of urban land. But from an ecological perspective, the scope of landscape urbanists is constrained to specific ecosystem components. These tend to follow what are seemingly the most

FIGURE 13.11
The urban-rural
gradient studies
performed along
a transect from
New York City
into Connecticut
exposed a unique
ecosystem structure
and function of
urban forests in
relation to the
suburban and rural
forest stands.

Illustration by
Alexander J. Felson;
adapted from M. J.
McDonnell, S. T. A.
Pickett, R. V. Pouyat,
R. W. Parmelee,
M. M. Carreiro, P. M.
Groffman, P. Bohlen,
W. C. Zipperer, and
K. Medley, "Ecology
of an Urban-to-Rural
Gradient," *Urban
Ecosystems* 1
(1997): 21–36.

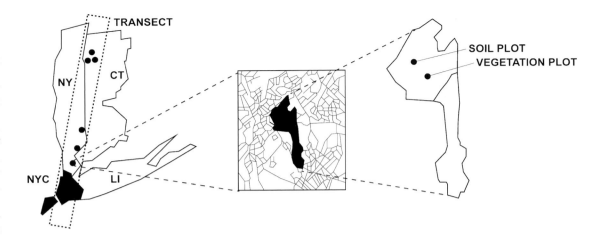

relevant to humans. In the field of ecology, a much wider array of critical theories, concepts, and methods exists that together reveal potential crises in cities, as well as possible solutions.[89] In process-based projects, many of the most critical ecological factors are invisible and are therefore difficult to represent. To understand and address ecological concerns better, designers must recognize that many important ecological variables may be hidden but can still have important implications (Figure 13.11). The relationship between representation and design of ecological systems is evolving from the tendency in landscape urbanism to acknowledge only ecological processes that spatially and temporally relate to human scales and therefore have client and public appeal to interpreting a broader range of critical ecological processes and patterns—even those that are not visible such as soil microbial communities and regional air pollution.

Challenges and Opportunities: Exchanges between Ecologists and Designers to Optimize Wildlife Habitat Design

Designers and ecologists commonly work within their respective fields with minimal cross-disciplinary collaboration. Although there are examples of successful collaborations between ecologists and designers, differences between the disciplines tend to constrain the dialogue. When designers and ecologists work together, ecologists usually provide input to designers who then filter scientific inputs and proceed without further aid from ecologists.[90] Although filtering of the ecologists' recommendations is often necessary, it creates a situation in which the designer translates scientific knowledge into practice without appropriate expertise.[91] It also significantly limits the designer's ability to apply relevant and reliable scientific data to policies and decision-making related to WHD. Because ecological data on urban systems is limited, assessing the values of different design proposals for wildlife habitats in these contexts is especially challenging.

These shortcomings in communication can be attributed to limitations in expertise, challenges of translating ecological information into design practice, and the constraints of a design process that does not lend itself to scientific investigation. These are not insurmountable obstacles and combining principles of WHD with the ecological sciences will enhance outcomes. Designers and ecologists can promote this agenda by (1) improving the dialogue across disciplines; (2) better translating science into practice; and (3) expanding design to incorporate ecological research, management, and monitoring practices.

Improving the Dialogue across Disciplines

Facilitating communication between ecologists and designers will enhance existing WHD practices. Ecologists should consider partnering with designers on conservation-based projects.[92] Designers should solicit the help of ecologists and proactively seek their expertise during key stages of the design process. To enhance the participation of ecologists, designers must expand the scope of work to allow for more rigorous site analysis and promote reviews from ecologists during the design process. Ecologists often need to study a site over several seasons to begin to understand the conditions of the existing ecosystems. With many design projects, however, the time frame for development is too brief to allow for research. Allotting sufficient time for rigorous site analysis and, whenever possible, for research and monitoring would encourage theoretical ecologists to participate in the design process. Through these measures, ecologists can assume greater responsibility for the project. Successful collaboration requires strategic compromises from both sides.

The dialogue between ecologists and designers tends to occur more from the direction of science to design than from design to science. An example of such exchange is Habitat Conservation Planning, which was introduced through the Endangered Species Act.[93] A Habitat Conservation Plan (HCP) is required for approval of incidental take of endangered and threatened species. A HCP allows development and subsequent incidental take of a subset of the overall area while preserving, monitoring, and adaptively managing the remaining habitat.[94] Habitat removal and the death or displacement of individuals of the focal species are allowed as a component of land-use development and economic gain. A HCP requires private developers to work toward preserving listed species by adopting responsible and scientific land-development practices. For a HCP to ensure long-term species survival effectively, land developers must rely on scientific data to guide their decisions at various stages of planning. These plans develop around the best existing scientific understanding, but also encourage dialogue between developers and environmental representatives. Furthermore, a HCP provides methods for coupling development and revenue generation with long-term monitoring and field assessments of the focus species and its habitat.[95]

Additionally, trends including sustainability, landscape urbanism, and ecological urbanism promote dialogue from the design perspective. In his book *Win-Win Ecology*, Michael L. Rosenzweig presents the concept of reconciliation ecology using examples of humans either intentionally or accidentally constructing ecological niches that replace degraded sites, and highlights projects in which multiple stakeholders including ecologists and designers are satisfied.[96] Designed experiments[97] provide an example in which voluntary exchange occurs between designers and ecologists in choosing and configuring the project site, and transforming ecological experiments established to scientifically test a question within a design project. The Tuxedo Reserve amphibian research project, developed through collaboration between AECOM Design, Rutgers, and the Related Company, is a designed experiment that builds on Rosenzweig's win-win theory.[98] The developer commissioned amphibian migration studies that were used to guide conservation and facilitated approval of the development by the planning board (Figure 13.12). The research proposal arose from a design team who proposed to construct permanent drift fences on the inside and outside perimeter of the houses and then to stitch them together with permanent corridors to corral and direct salamanders. It was framed to the developer as a management tool and to the academic ecologists as an experiment to assess the impact of development. The spatial data on migration patterns informed neighborhood and road layout and stormwater management. Houses were realigned to accommodate migration routes.

The project provides an example of situating ecological research with land-development practices at scales that are relevant to both the researcher and the developer. The results of the initial studies led to the removal of the upper road and associated housing and the rest of the houses were pushed to the outskirts of the vernal pool habitat to incorporate a fifteen- to fifty-meter buffer. The watershed impacts were reduced from 70 to 10 percent. The positive results from the first study, including low cost for high-value returns, and the potential for achieving similar solutions to address the wide buffer needs,

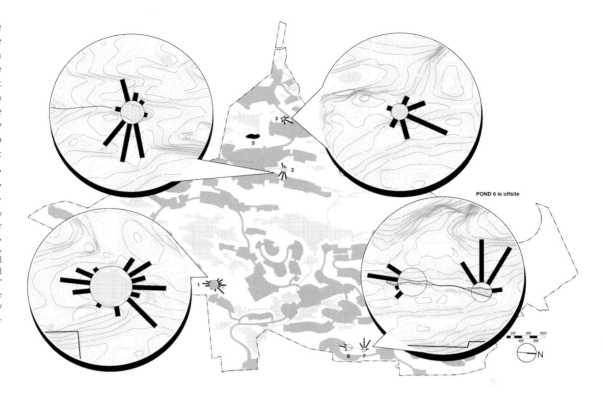

FIGURE 13.12
Tuxedo Reserve amphibian migration studies were performed as part of the master plan process with the Related Company during 2007–9 to guide the layout of neighborhoods, houses, roadways, and infrastructure.

Illustration by Timothy Terway and Alexander J. Felson of the UEDLAB, from Alexander J. Felson, "Suburbanization and Amphibians: Designed Ecological Solutions," (PhD diss., Rutgers, The State University of New Jersey, 2010), 143.

and in anticipation of the planning board requesting further similar information as part of its review of future subphases of the project, led the client to agree to support multiple vernal pool migration studies on five ponds across the five-hundred-hectare development site. Researchers benefited by obtaining more data and a new funding source, regulators can cite a progressive ecological planning standard, and the master planning team can include the project in their portfolio of environmental work.

Translating Ecological Science into Applications
There are substantive opportunities to improve the translation of ecological science into WHD. Many designers want tangible information that directs decision-making without having to grapple with issues of scientific uncertainty and complexity.[99] As a result, a series of popularized ecological concepts and practices of questionable scientific value have filtered into the design professions.[100] For example, habitat corridors are often proposed as solutions for the fragmentation caused by land development. But the sizing of corridors and their value in linking habitat patches is controversial.[101]

The uncertainty and the need for further investigation of such approaches are typically not part of the design framework. Designers and developers tend to include many assumptions, while shifting uncertainty and the lack of specific data or site context into the background. Improved scientific understanding of the conditions and species interactions would enable designers to make more informed design decisions. The broader challenge of translating ecological science into applied principles compounds this problem, however.[102] Topics such as the role of biodiversity in the performance of an ecosystem, and how we may be able to design such processes, or how those ecological function at different sites, are all underdeveloped for use in real-world applications and underutilized by managers and practitioners.[103] Thus, there are many concepts that should be considered in WHD, such as identifying ecosystem thresholds or establishing context-dependent ecological patterns, that all remain sidelined for lack of methods to apply them.

Ecologists are increasingly interested in investigating urban areas through design and design practitioners.[104] With the growing public ecological awareness, people are shifting from uninformed

BACK TO THE FUTURE

1: OYSTERS // MUSSELS // EEL GRASS

3. NEW GOWANUS

2. PALISADES REEF

FIGURE 13.13
Image of SCAPE's proposal for the *Rising Currents* exhibition at the Museum of Modern Art. The project is called "Oyster-tecture" and illustrates a strategy for expanding the oyster life cycle into the New York City harbor as a series of programmed activities and functions.

Illustration courtesy of SCAPE.

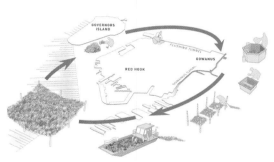

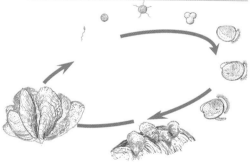

and unintentional human impacts on biological systems to more informed choices and intentional modifications of these systems that promote ecosystem services. Therefore, opportunities for designers to contribute to scientific endeavors are being recognized. Designer ecosystems focus on balancing the constraints of the site with human social and economic needs to create habitats that promote a high-functioning community of organisms and provide a series of ecosystems services.[105] Designer ecosystems blend technological innovations with scientific knowledge and design inventiveness to create novel ecosystems. They recognize that site conditions and pressures on organisms have changed, and seek to optimize the potential ecological services within a

human-modified environment.[106] Designer ecosystems differ from more traditional wildlife management practices by blending the social, political, and economic demands of humans with technology, creativity, and innovation to address ecosystem services and wildlife needs. They also seek greater flexibility in restructuring biological communities that may incorporate human interventions to facilitate the longevity of the system and to enhance the biological function of the system.[107]

For example, the landscape architecture firm SCAPE created a designer ecosystem for the recent exhibition *Rising Currents* at the Museum of Modern Art. The project proposed bioengineering solutions relying on the oyster life cycle to create a harbor nursery and to clean up excess nutrients in the Gowanus Canal post super-fund treatment. The proposal links the biological processes of an organism to the scales of remediation of the harbor ecosystem, using the oyster as an ecosystem engineer linked to urban planning and technology.[108] Configured as an infrastructural armature, the oysters serve to absorb nutrients, clean the Gowanus Canal, perform physical wave attenuation, and increase habitat around Governors Island. The appropriately scaled ecological oyster life cycle reprograms the harbor geographically and responds to anthropogenic impacts to the harbor (Figure 13.13).

Although designer ecosystems such as "Oystertecture" seek to capitalize on biological processes, they are distinct from conservation efforts. Designer ecosystems apply more to sites that are already disturbed and can afford ecological restoration combined with human ingenuity and creativity. Designer ecosystems build on the understanding that anthropogenic impacts across ecosystems worldwide are unequivocal and innovative solutions are therefore imperative.[109] With limited resources to address environmental dilemmas such as the loss of habitat and species extinctions, we need to broaden our methods to take advantage of where money is currently being spent and where populations are living to create new opportunities for increasing wildlife habitats and for educating the public. This should occur without losing sight of the fact that traditional strategies of wildlife preservation remain a critical and pragmatic approach to address species losses.[110]

Expanding Design to Include Ecological Research, Environmental Management, and Monitoring

Management strategies are another important area in need of refinement. Given the multiple ecological paradigms that relate directly to managing wildlife and the critical role that environmental management plays in the functionality of constructed ecosystems, designers should include management strategies to make the design a truly ecological endeavor. Park designers recognize that maintenance is an essential part of a successful park. Restoration ecologists also highlight the importance of maintenance and monitoring in adaptively managing and evaluating the long-term success of a system.[111] Although management and

monitoring are necessary components of designing a wildlife habitat, they are often neglected in the design plan. Many essential management factors, such as removal of invasive species or soil inoculations, have little or no tangible design expression. Given that management of designed sites such as park spaces has a long history of neglect, achieving this agenda will be challenging. Management and monitoring are critical, but often undervalued and underfunded. Solving these issues will require addressing the more widespread problem of undervaluing park maintenance.[112] Designers and ecologists face the same dilemma of how to make underappreciated practices mainstream. This is as much of a design problem as it is a management issue, and if addressed it could help to foster rich ecological design projects.

As part of MillionTreesNYC, the New York City Afforestation Project (NY-CAP) is converting city parkland into a combination of public parkland and ecological experiments to study the design, management, and natural processes that influence urban forest ecosystem performance and human interactions with these systems. NY-CAP redirected committed funds for planting and design to provide both the intended uses of the project (recreation, green infrastructure, carbon storage, and habitat) and an urban ecological experiment. The research experiment designed as public parkland aims to answer questions about the sustainability and resiliency of novel urban forest ecosystems. Park managers usually implement such landscape designs on the basis of experience and assumptions that are often debated in the primary literature. NY-CAP follows an emerging approach in urban ecology called "Designed Experiments."[113] As such, it uses a large-scale capital investment initiative to implement a scientific experiment as a designed urban landscape with basic and applied goals, the latter of which rely on the successful establishment and maintenance of native trees planted as saplings. The experimental treatments include organic amendment, low and high tree species richness, and low and high system complexity (i.e., without or with shrub and herbaceous plantings). The landscape design is synonymous with the experimental design, with the resources allocated to the landscape design redirected to meet the original

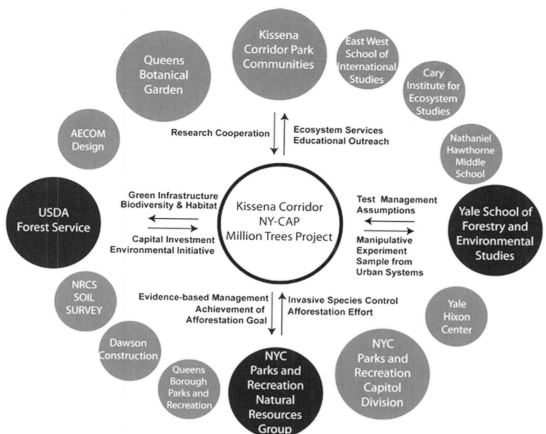

FIGURE 13.14
NY-CAP, a research
effort run through Yale
University as part of the
MillionTreesNYC project,
includes a wide variety of
stakeholders.

Illustration by Alexander J.
Felson and the Yale Urban
Ecology and Design Lab team.

intention of landscape restoration and also to generate an ecological experiment that tests underlying assumptions and theory. In this manner, "Designed Experiments" provide multiple values for urban ecology, namely: (1) they provide a means to situate manipulative experiments in urban areas—where there is often minimal space for such efforts—and to generate urban ecological data; (2) they establish research experiments embedded within the urban social and physical environment and therefore implicitly connect stakeholders such as city agencies, park users, and ecologists; and (3) they can provide robust scientific data to inform and adaptively manage urban ecosystems.[114] The team worked with multiple stakeholders in New York City to deploy the hypothesis-driven research with public park design (Figure 13.14). The research is providing a venue for students to participate in urban ecological research and teaches public users

about science as a tool for testing and evaluating critical aspects of the urban ecosystem.

Conclusions

WHD is still a small but vital area of expertise that is dispersed across multiple disciplines. Practices used to design wildlife habitats are widespread. Currently, although both ecologists and designers are involved in designing wildlife habitats, exchanges across disciplines are limited. Designers often serve as the leaders of a project and the synthesizers of information. Ecologists tend to provide input only during the early stages of a design project. Ecological considerations are filtered through the designer's experience and agenda. To improve the scientific merit of practices, novel approaches are needed. Combining the expertise of both fields to inventively optimize solutions is essential for addressing anthropogenic impacts on wildlife and countering the unprecedented rate of extinctions.

Moving forward with WHD requires careful dialogue between ecologists and designers. Both need to foster exchanges of knowledge and collaboration between disciplines, and both need to play central roles in bridging the gaps between science and WHD. Ecologists must proactively include designers in conservation-based projects and help designers translate science into practice. To promote collaboration, ecologists should become more active in translating research into policy and practice. Ecologists must compromise by accepting a large degree of uncertainty when applying ecological principles to WHD. At the same time, designers need to allow scientists to review and contribute ecological understanding to the design process. Expanding the scope of their projects would facilitate the participation of ecologists in site analysis. Designers should also seek ways to allow ecologists to establish research and monitoring as components of a design project. Through more collaborative exchanges of ideas between disciplines, designers and ecologists could discover areas of compromise, producing design outcomes that benefit humans and wildlife alike.

Notes

1 Margaret A. Palmer, Emily Bernhardt, Elizabeth Chornesky, Scott Collins, Andrew Dobson, and Clifford Duke et al., "Ecological Science and Sustainability for a Crowded Planet: 21st-Century Vision and Action Plan for the Ecological Society of America," Report from the Ecological Visions Committee to the Governing Board of the Ecological Society of America, April 2004, accessed March 10, 2010, http://esa.org/ecovisions/ppfiles/EcologicalVisionsReport.pdf. Also see Jianguo Liu, Thomas Dietz, Stephen R. Carpenter, Carl Folke, Marina Alberti, and Charles L. Redman et al., "Coupled Human and Natural Systems," *AMBIO: A Journal of the Human Environment* 36, no. 8 (2009): 639–49; and Margaret A. Palmer, Emily Bernhardt, Elizabeth Chornesky, Scott Collins, Andrew Dobson, and Clifford Duke et al., "Ecology for a Crowded Planet," *Science* 304 (2004): 1251–52.

2 Jeremy T. Lundholm and Paul J. Richardson, "Habitat Analogues for Reconciliation Ecology in Urban and Industrial Environments," *Journal of Applied Ecology* 47 (2010): 966–75.

3 Peter S. Kareiva, Sean Watts, Robert McDonald, and Tim Boucher, "Domesticated Nature: Shaping Landscapes and Ecosystems for Human Welfare," *Science* 316 (2007): 1866–69.

4 Julia Czerniak, "Looking Back at Landscape Urbanism: Speculations on Site," in *The Landscape Urbanism Reader*, ed. Charles Waldheim (New York: Princeton Architectural Press, 2006), 107–23.

5 Louise A. Mozingo, "The Aesthetics of Ecological Design: Seeing Science as Culture," *Landscape Journal* 16, no. 1 (Spring 1997): 46–59; and Laura R. Musacchio, "The Scientific Basis for the Design of Landscape Sustainability: A Conceptual Framework for Translational Landscape Research and Practice of Designed Landscapes and the Six E's of Landscape Sustainability," *Landscape Ecology* 24, no. 8 (2009): 993–1013.

6 Bart R. Johnson, Janet Silbernagel, Mark Hostetler, April Mills, Forster Ndubisi, Edward Fife, and Mary Carol Rossiter Hunter, "The Nature of Dialogue and the Dialogue of Nature: Designers and Ecologists in Collaboration," in *Ecology and Design: Frameworks for Learning*, ed. Bart R. Johnson and Kristina Hill (Washington D.C.: Island Press, 2002), 305–55. See also James Corner, "Eidetic Operations and New Landscapes," in *Recovering Landscape: Essays in Contemporary Landscape Architecture*, ed. James Corner (New York: Princeton Architectural Press, 1999), 153–70.

7 Richard T. T. Forman, "The Missing Catalyst: Design and Planning with Ecology Roots," in Johnson and Hill, *Ecology and Design*, 85–109.

8 Stephen R. Carpenter, E. Virginia Armbrust, Peter W. Arzberger, F. Stuart Chapin, James J. Elser, and Edward J. Hackett et al., "Accelerate Synthesis in Ecology and Environmental Sciences," *BioScience* 59, no. 8 (2009): 699–701. See also Ronald H. Pulliam and Bart R. Johnson, "Ecology's New Paradigm: What Does It Offer Designers and Planners," in Johnson and Hill, *Ecology and Design*, 51–84.

9   Sadahisa Kato and Jack Ahern, "'Learning by Doing': Adaptive Planning as a Strategy to Address Uncertainty in Planning," *Journal of Environmental Planning and Management* 51, no. 4 (2008): 543–59; and Eric Katz, "Another Look at Restoration: Technology and Artificial Nature," in *Restoring Nature: Perspectives from the Social Sciences and Humanities*, ed. Paul H. Gobster and R. Bruce Hull (Washington D.C.: Island Press, 2000), 49–70.

10   Alexander J. Felson and Steward T. A. Pickett, "Designed Experiments: New Approaches to Studying Urban Ecosystems," *Frontiers in Ecology and the Environment* 3, no. 10 (2005): 549–56.

11   Palmer et al., "Ecology for a Crowded Planet," 1251–52.

12   P. B. Bridgewater, "Biosphere Reserves: Special Places for People and Nature," *Environmental Science and Policy* 5, no. 1 (2002): 9–12; and Janis B. Alcorn, "Indigenous Peoples and Conservation," *Conservation Biology* 7, no. 2 (1993): 424–26.

13   Martha J. Groom, Gary K. Mefe, and C. Ronald Carroll, *Principles of Conservation Biology*, 3rd ed. (Sunderland, Mass.: Sinauer Associates, 2006), 173–212.

14   Groom, Mefe, and Carroll, *Principles of Conservation Biology*, 553–90; and Niall Kirkwood, introduction to *Manufactured Sites: Rethinking the Post-Industrial Landscape* (London and New York: Spon Press, 2001), 2–10.

15   Michael E. Soulé and John Terborgh, eds., *Continental Conservation: Scientific Foundations of Regional Reserve Networks* (Washington, D.C.: Island Press, 1999), 199–216.

16   Andy P. Dobson, A. D. Bradshaw, and A. J. M. Baker, "Hopes for the Future: Restoration Ecology and Conservation Biology," *Science* 277 (1997): 515–22.

17   Katharine A. Suding, Katherine L. Gross, and Gregory R. Houseman, "Alternative States and Positive Feedbacks in Restoration Ecology," *Trends in Ecology and Evolution* 19, no. 1 (January 2004): 46–53. See also James A. Harris, Richard J. Hobbs, Eric Higgs, and James Aronson, "Ecological Restoration and Global Climate Change," *Restoration Ecology* 14, no. 2 (2006): 170–76.

18   Katharine N. Suding and Katherine L. Gross, "The Dynamic Nature of Ecological Systems: Multiple States and Restoration Trajectories," in *Foundations of Restoration Ecology*, ed. Donald A. Falk, Margaret A. Palmer, and Joy B. Zedler (Washington, D.C.: Island Press, 2006), 190–208.

19   Margaret Palmer, E. S. Bernhardt, J. D. Allan, P. S. Lake, G. Alexander, and S. Brooks et al., "Standards for Ecologically Successful River Restoration," *Journal of Applied Ecology* 42 (2005): 208–17. See also Young D. Choi, "Theories for Ecological Restoration in Changing Environment: Toward 'Futuristic' Restoration," *Ecological Research* 19, no. 1 (2004): 75–81.

20   Lundholm, "Habitat Analogues for Reconciliation Ecology in Urban and Industrial Environments," 966–75; and Jelte van Andel and Ab P. Grootjans, "Concepts in Restoration Ecology," in *Restoration Ecology: The New Frontier*, ed. Jelte van Andel and James Aronson (Oxford: Blackwell, 2006), 16–30.

21   Truman P. Young, "Restoration Ecology and Conservation Biology," *Biological Conservation* 92 (2000): 73–83. See also Donald A. Falk, Margaret A. Palmer, and Joy B. Zedler, introduction to *Foundations of Restoration Ecology*, 1–10.

22   Kareiva, Watts, McDonald, and Boucher, "Domesticated Nature," 1866–69. See also Michael L. Rosenzweig, *Win-Win Ecology: How the Earth's Species Can Survive in the Midst of Human Enterprise* (Oxford and New York: Oxford University Press, 2003), 69–100.

23   See Leslie McGuire, "One Great Big Beautiful Buffet: The Ecological Restoration of Orange County's Great Park," LandscapeOnline.com, 2010, accessed April 16, 2011, http://www.landscapeonline.com/research/article/10427; and Ken Smith, *Ken Smith: Landscape Architect* (New York: Monacelli Press, 2009), 204–15.

24   Clark E. Adams and Kieran J. Lindsey, *Urban Wildlife Management* (Boca Raton, Fla.: CRC Press, 2010), 3–25; and David Lindenmayer, Richard J. Hobbs, Rebecca Montague-Drake, Jason Alexandra, Andrew Bennett, and Mark Burgman et al., "A Checklist for Ecological Management of Landscapes for Conservation," *Ecology Letters* 11 (2008): 78–91.

25   Groom, Mefe, and Carroll, *Principles of Conservation Biology*, 468–507.

26   Margaret A. Palmer, Richard F. Ambrose, and N. LeRoy Poff, "Ecological Theory and Community Restoration Ecology," *Restoration Ecology* 5, no. 4 (December 1997): 291–300.

27   Stephen R. Carpenter, "Microcosm Experiments Have Limited Relevance for Community and Ecosystem Ecology," *Ecology* 77, no. 3 (1996): 677–80; and David K. Skelly, "Experimental Venue and Estimation of Interaction Strength," *Ecology* 83, no. 8 (2001): 2097–101.

28   Groom, Mefe, and Carroll, *Principles of Conservation Biology*, 517–25.

29   Rosenzweig, *Win-Win Ecology*, 165–81.

30   Josh Donlan, Joel Berger, Carl E. Bock, Jane H. Bock, David A. Burney, and James A. Estes et al., "Pleistocene Rewilding: An Optimistic Agenda for Twenty-First Century Conservation," *The American Naturalist* 168, no. 5 (2006): 660–81.

31   Stephen R. Carpenter, Barbara J. Benson, Reinette Biggs, Jonathan W. Chipman, Jonathan A. Foley, and Shaun A. Golding et al., "Understanding Regional Change: Comparison of Two Lake Districts," *BioScience* 57, no. 4 (2007): 323–35.

32   Elena M. Bennett, Tara Reed-Andersen, Jeffrey N. Houser, John R. Gabriel, and Stephen R. Carpenter, "A

Phosphorus Budget for the Lake Mendota Watershed," *Ecosystems* 2 (1999): 69–75.

33 John Kugen, foreman at Issaquah Hatchery, personal communication, January 30, 2010. See also the Friends of Issaquah Hatchery website, accessed June 27, 2012, http://www.issaquahfish.org; and Lea Knutson and Virginia L. Naef, *Management Recommendations for Washington's Priority Habitats: Riparian* (Olympia: Washington Department of Fish and Wildlife, 1997), 78–115.

34 See Richard T. T. Forman, *Urban Regions: Ecology and Planning Beyond the City* (Cambridge: Cambridge University Press, 2008); and Richard T. T. Forman, *Land Mosaics: The Ecology of Landscapes and Regions* (Cambridge: Cambridge University Press, 1995).

35 Richard T. T. Forman, *Road Ecology: Science and Solutions* (Washington D.C.: Island Press, 2003), 297–314.

36 Wenche E. Dramstad, James D. Olson, and Richard T. T. Forman, *Landscape Ecology Principles in Landscape Architecture and Land-Use Planning* (Cambridge, Mass.: Harvard University Graduate School of Design; Washington, D.C.: Island Press, 1996), 20–45.

37 Ibid.

38 Judy L. Meyer, Peter C. Frumhoff, Steven P. Hamburg, and Carlos de la Rosa, "Above the Din but in the Fray: Environmental Scientists as Effective Advocates," *Frontiers in Ecology and the Environment* 8 (2010): 299–305. For the perspective of ecologists interested in increasing participation in policy and planning, see Stephen R. Carpenter, E. Virginia Armbrust, Peter W. Arzberger, F. Stuart Chapin, James J. Elser, and Edward J. Hackett et al., "Accelerate Synthesis in Ecology and Environmental Sciences," *BioScience* 59, no. 8 (2009): 699–701.

39 Debra Nelson and Lisa Weiss, "Stewart Airport Ecosystem: Taking Off with Innovative Approaches," *in Proceedings of the 2007 International Conference on Ecology and Transportation*, ed. C. Leroy Irwin, Debra Nelson, and K. P. McDermott (Raleigh, N.C.: Center for Transportation and the Environment, North Carolina State University, 2007), 32–37.

40 Anne Whiston Spirn, "Ian McHarg, Landscape Architecture, and Environmentalism: Ideas and Methods in Context," in *Environmentalism in Landscape Architecture*, ed. Michael Conan (Washington, D.C.: Dumbarton Oaks Research Library and Collection, 2000), 97–114.

41 Ian L. McHarg, *Design with Nature* (Garden City, N.Y.: Natural History Press, 1969), 31–41.

42 Ian L. McHarg, "Natural Factors in Planning," *Journal of Soil and Water Conservation* 52, no. 1 (1997): 13–17.

43 Forster Ndubisi, "Landscape Ecological Planning," in *Ecological Design and Planning*, ed. George F. Thompson and Frederick R. Steiner (New York: John Wiley, 1997), 9–43. See also S. T. A. Pickett, M. L. Cadenasso, and J. M. Grove, "Resilient Cities: Meaning, Models, and Metaphor for Integrating the Ecological, Socio-economic, and Planning Realms," *Landscape and Urban Planning* 69, no. 4 (2004): 369–84; and Elizabeth K. Meyer, "The Post-Earth Day Conundrum: Translating Environmental Values into Landscape Design," in Conan, *Environmentalism in Landscape Architecture*, 187–244.

44 Spirn, "Ian McHarg, Landscape Architecture, and Environmentalism," 97–114.

45 Julie Czerniak, *Case—Downsview Park Toronto* (Munich and New York: Prestel; Cambridge, Mass.: Harvard University Graduate School of Design, 2001), 58–65. See also Nina-Marie Lister, "Sustainable Large Parks: Ecological Design or Designer Ecology?," in *Large Parks*, ed. Julie Czerniak and George Hargreaves (New York: Princeton Architectural Press; Cambridge, Mass.: Harvard University Graduate School of Design, 2007), 35–57.

46 Elizabeth Hanson, *Animal Attractions: Nature on Display in American Zoos* (Princeton: Princeton University Press, 2002), 162–86.

47 Wendi Goldsmith, "Science, Engineering, and the Art of Restoration: Two Case Studies in Wetland Construction," in Kirkwood, *Manufactured Sites*, 165–76.

48 George Hargreaves, "Large Parks: A Designer's Perspective," in Czerniak and Hargreaves, *Large Parks*, 121–74.

49 Lister, "Sustainable Large Parks," 35–57.

50 Joan G. Ehrenfeld, "Exotic Invasive Species in Urban Wetlands: Environmental Correlates and Implications for Wetland Management," *Journal of Applied Ecology* 45, no. 4 (August 2008): 1160–69.

51 Piet Oudolf and Noël Kingsbury, *Planting Design: Gardens in Time and Space* (Portland, Ore.: Timber Press, 2005), 9–24.

52 Pulliam and Johnson, "Ecology's New Paradigm," 51–84.

53 Lister, "Sustainable Large Parks," 35–57.

54 Choi, "Theories for Ecological Restoration in Changing Environment," 75–81.

55 Felson and Pickett, "Designed Experiments," 549–56.

56 Liat Margolis and Alexander Robinson, *Living Systems: Innovative Materials and Technologies for Landscape Architecture* (Berlin: Birkhauser-Verlag, 2007), 181.

57 McGuire, "One Great Big Beautiful Buffet."

58 Alexander J. Felson, "The Design Process as a Framework for Collaboration between Ecologists and Designers," in *Resilience in Ecology and Urban Design: Synergies for Theory and Practice in the Urban Century*, ed. Steward T. A. Pickett, Mary Cadenasso, Brian McGrath, and Kristina Hill (New York: Springer-Verlag, forthcoming).

59 Czerniak, "Looking Back at Landscape Urbanism," 107–23.

60 Carol J. Burns and Andrea Kahn, "Why Site Matters," in *Site Matters: Design Concepts, Histories, and Strategies*, ed. Carol J. Burns and Andrea Kahn (New York: Routledge, 2005), vii–xxviii. See also Kevin Lynch and Gary Hack, *Site Planning*, 3rd ed. (Cambridge, Mass.: MIT Press, 1984), 67–105.

61 Richard A. Carpenter, "Ecology Should Apply to Ecosystem Management: A Comment," *Ecological Applications* 6, no. 4 (1996): 1373–77.

62 Reed F. Noss, "From Plant-Communities to Landscapes in Conservation Inventories—A Look at the Nature Conservancy (USA)," *Biological Conservation* 41, no. 1 (1987): 11–37.

63 Lucinda Jackson, "Beyond Clean-Up of Manufactured Sites: Remediation, Restoration, and Renewal of Habitat," in Kirkwood, *Manufactured Sites*, 32–38.

64 Suding, Gross, and Houseman, "Alternative States and Positive Feedbacks in Restoration Ecology," 46–53.

65 S. T. A. Pickett and Mary L. Cadenasso, "Altered Resources, Disturbance, and Heterogeneity: A Framework for Comparing Urban and Non-Urban Soils," *Restoration Ecology* 12 (2009): 23–44.

66 Forman, "Missing Catalyst," 85–109.

67 Nigel Cross, "From a Design Science to a Design Discipline: Understanding Designerly Ways of Knowing and Thinking," in *Design Research Now: Essays and Selected Projects*, ed. Ralf Michel (Basel, Switz.: Birkhauser, 2007), 41–54.

68 Lindenmayer et al., "Checklist for Ecological Management," 78–91; and Patrick S. Bourgeron, Hope C. Humphries, Mark E. Jensen, and Bennett A. Brown, "Integrated Ecological Assessments and Land-Use Planning," in *Applying Ecological Principles to Land Management*, ed. Virginia H. Dale and Richard A. Haeuber (New York: Springer, 2001), 276–314.

69 Lister, "Sustainable Large Parks," 35–57.

70 Mary L. Cadenasso and Steward T. A. Pickett, "Urban Principles for Ecological Landscape Design and Maintenance: Scientific Fundamentals," *Cities and the Environment* 1, no. 2 (2008): 1–16.

71 Laura H. Watchman, Martha Groom, and John D. Perrine, "Science and Uncertainty in Habitat Conservation Planning," *American Scientist* 89, no. 4 (July–August 2001): 351–59.

72 Elaine K. Harding, Elizabeth E. Crone, Bret D. Elderd, Jonathan M. Hoekstra, Alexa J. McKerrow, and John D. Perrine et al., "The Scientific Foundations of Habitat Conservation Plans: A Quantitative Assessment," *Conservation Biology* 15, no. 2 (April 2001): 488–500.

73 Linda Pollak, "Matrix Landscape: Construction of Identity in the Large Park," in Czerniak and Hargreaves, *Large Parks*, 87–120.

74 *Fresh Kills Park: Draft Master Plan* (New York: New York City Department of City Planning, 2006), 34–35.

75 Michael E. Soulé, "Land Use Planning and Wildlife Maintenance: Guidelines for Conserving Wildlife in an Urban Landscape," *American Planning Association* (Summer 1991): 313–23; and Forman, *Urban Regions*, 168–88.

76 Steward T. A. Pickett, Jurek Kolasa, and Clive G. Jones, *Ecological Understanding: The Nature of Theory and the Theory of Nature*, 2nd ed. (San Diego: Academic Press, 2007), 26–53.

77 Soulé, "Land Use Planning and Wildlife Maintenance," 313–23.

78 Harris, Hobbs, Higgs, and Aronson, "Ecological Restoration and Global Climate Change," 170–76.

79 Berit Junker and Matthias Buchecker, "Aesthetic Preferences versus Ecological Objectives in River Restorations," *Landscape and Urban Planning* 85, nos. 3–4 (2008): 141–54; and Mitchell A. Pavao-Zuckerman, "The Nature of Urban Soils and Their Role in Ecological Restoration in Cities," *Restoration Ecology* 16, no. 4 (December 2008): 642–49.

80 Charles Waldheim, "Landscape as Urbanism," in Waldheim, *The Landscape Urbanism Reader*, 35–54.

81 Anita Berrizbeitia, "Re-Placing Process," in Czerniak and Hargreaves, *Large Parks*, 175–98; and Waldheim, "Landscape as Urbanism," 35–54.

82 Meyer, "The Post-Earth Day Conundrum," 187–244.

83 Waldheim, "Landscape as Urbanism," 35–54.

84 Berrizbeitia, "Re-Placing Process," 175–98.

85 Czerniak, *Case—Downsview Park Toronto*, 12–23.

86 Ibid.

87 Scott L. Collins, Stephen R. Carpenter, Scott M. Swinton, Daniel E. Orenstein, Daniel L. Childers, and Ted L. Gragson et al., "An Integrated Conceptual Framework for Long-Term Social-Ecological Research," *Frontiers in Ecology and the Environment* 9, no. 6 (2010): 351–57.

88 Andrew F. Bennett, *Linkages in the Landscape: The Role of Corridors and Connectivity in Wildlife Conservation* (Gland, Switz.: IUCN–The World Conservation Union, 2003), 125–51.

89 Waldheim, "Landscape as Urbanism," 35–54.

90 Johnson et al., "Nature of Dialogue and the Dialogue of Nature," 305–55.

91 Forman, "Missing Catalyst," 85–109.

92 Sarah Taylor Lovell and Douglas M. Johnston, "Creating Multifunctional Landscapes: How Can the Field of Ecology Inform the Design of the Landscape?," *Frontiers in Ecology and the Environment* 7 (2009): 212–20.

93 Reed F. Noss, Michael A. O'Connell, and Dennis D. Murphy, *The Science of Conservation Planning: Habitat Conservation under the Endangered Species Act* (Washington D.C.: Island Press, 1997), 19–47.

94   Timothy Beatley, *Habitat Conservation Planning: Endangered Species and Urban Growth* (Austin: University of Texas Press, 1994), 23–39.

95   Ibid.

96   Rosenzweig, *Win-Win Ecology.*

97   Felson and Pickett, "Designed Experiments," 549–56.

98   Alexander J. Felson, "Ecological Experiments," *Urban Land* (2007): 90–94.

99   Forman, "Missing Catalyst," 85–109.

100   Kristina Hill, "Shifting Sites," in Burns and Kahn, *Site Matters*, 131–55.

101   David B. Lindenmayer and Joern Fischer, *Habitat Fragmentation and Landscape Change: An Ecological and Conservation Synthesis* (Washington D.C.: Island Press, 2006), 121–32.

102   Lindenmayer et al., "Checklist for Ecological Management," 78–91.

103   Margaret A. Palmer, "Reforming Watershed Restoration: Science in Need of Application and Applications in Need of Science," *Estuaries and Coasts* 32, no. 1 (2009): 1–17.

104   Steward T. A. Pickett, Mary L. Caldenasso, Mark J. McDonnell, and William R. Burch Jr., "Frameworks for Urban Ecosystem Studies: Gradients, Patch Dynamics, and the Human Ecosystem in the New York Metropolitan Area and Baltimore, USA," in *Ecology of Cities and Towns*, ed. Mark J. McDonnell, Amy K. Hahs, and Jürgen H. Breuste (Cambridge: Cambridge University Press, 2009), 25–50.

105   F. S. Chapin III, M. E. Power, S. T. A. Pickett, A. Freitag, J. A. Reynolds, R. B. Jackson, D. M. Lodge, C. Duke, S. L. Collins, A. G. Power, and A. Bartuska, "Earth Stewardship: Science for Action to Sustain the Human-Earth Syste," *Ecosphere* 2, no. 8 (2011): 1–20.

106   Palmer et al., "Ecological Science and Sustainability for a Crowded Planet," 1251–52; and Liu et al., "Coupled Human and Natural Systems," 639–49.

107   Carl Folke, Steve Carpenter, Thomas Elmqvist, Lance Gunderson, C. S. Holling, and Brian Walker, "Resilience and Sustainable Development: Building Adaptive Capacity in a World of Transformations," *AMBIO: A Journal of the Human Environment* 31, no. 5 (2002): 437–40.

108   James E. Byers, Kim Cuddington, Clive G. Jones, Theresa S. Talley, Alan Hastings, John G. Lambrinos, Jeffrey A. Crooks, and William G. Wilson, "Using Ecosystem Engineers to Restore Ecological Systems," *Trends in Ecology and Evolution* 21, no. 9 (2006): 493–500.

109   *Intergovernmental Panel on Climate Change*, accessed September 11, 2009, http://www.ipcc.ch/index.htm; and Peter M. Vitousek, Harold A. Mooney, Jane Lubchenco, and Jerry M. Melillo, "Human Domination of Earth's Ecosystems," *Science* 277 (1997): 494–99.

110   Craig L. Schaffer, *Nature Reserves: Island Theory and Conservation Practice* (Washington, D.C.: Smithsonian Institution Press, 1990), 35–74.

111   Joy B. Zedler and John C. Callaway, "Tracking Wetland Restoration: Do Mitigation Sites Follow Desired Trajectories?," *Restoration Ecology* 7, no. 1 (1999): 69–73.

112   Michael Murray, "Private Management of Public Spaces: Nonprofit Organizations and Urban Parks," *Harvard Environmental Law Review* 34 (2010): 179–256.

113   Felson and Pickett, "Designed Experiments," 549–56.

114   Felson, "Ecological Experiments," 91–94.

CHAPTER 14

Integration across Scales

Landscape as Infrastructure for the Protection of Biodiversity

Kongjian Yu

THE ISSUE OF BIODIVERSITY CONSERVATION IS not about individual species; it is about how to save the earth as a life-support system and as a living system itself. A holistic understanding and protection of a species's wide range of habitats, instead of protecting isolated natural areas, will ensure long-term environmental sustainability. The rapidly expanding human demand for agricultural and urban land requires the protection of a vast network of integrated natural habitats. How can we minimize land consumption and enhance spatial pattern planning and design so that urbanization can coexist with natural processes and biologically diverse habitats? The solution is identifying and planning for what I term "security patterns," defined as safeguards for individual natural processes that can be combined in an integrated landscape pattern called "ecological infrastructure." Such infrastructure is strategically important in sustaining ecosystem services, including the provision of life-support systems for biodiversity.

Ecological infrastructure is a recovered notion that is part of a larger effort to describe critical landscape infrastructure: the many overlapping human and natural systems that compose the built environment, from climate and hydrology to agriculture and transportation. In China, the concept can be traced to the prescientific model of feng shui—the sacred landscape setting for human settlement. In the West, precedents include the nineteenth-century notion of greenways as urban recreational spaces, the early twentieth-century idea of greenbelts to limit sprawl, and the late twentieth-century strategy of connecting ecological networks to preserve biodiversity, all of which strove to balance human habitation with natural processes. Ecological infrastructure is designed to integrate critical landscape elements and structures to safeguard natural and cultural assets such as biodiversity, species flow, hydrologic and geologic processes, and heritage corridors. The strategy of ecological infrastructure is to plan and develop land more effectively with the goal of preserving valuable ecosystem services.

From broadscale biodiversity planning for all of China, to regional-scale planning of Beijing, to the fine-scale urban park, my design firm, Turenscape, uses the powerful tool of ecological infrastructure to safeguard nature's processes and to protect and re-create biologically diverse habitats.

The Challenges: The Earth as an Endangered Species

In China as in other countries, several forces threaten biodiversity, including climate change, expanding urbanization, agriculture, and pollution. Habitat loss caused by desertification is especially severe in China. Each year, 3,436 square kilometers of land is turned into desert, and this figure is increasing annually. At present, the total area of desertification amounts to about 20 percent of the whole country, and each year about five billion tons of soil erodes into the ocean.[1] In the past fifty years in China, 50 percent of the nation's wetlands have disappeared, and 40 percent of the surviving wetlands have been polluted.[2] China also suffers from fragmentation of natural systems. National and regional highways have cut the national landscape into discontinuous pieces. At the end of 2009, China had sixty-five thousand kilometers of highways, second only to the United States, which has more than eighty thousand kilometers.[3] River systems are similarly fragmented. China now has about twenty-five thousand high dams, with 5,340 of them above thirty meters—more than 50 percent of the total number in the world.[4] These dams have proved to be one of the major causes of biodiversity loss in the country.[5] Pollution also threatens biodiversity. In China alone, it was officially announced by the government that 75 percent of the surface water is polluted. According to official statistics, about 150 million *mu* (ten million hectares) of arable land in China has also been polluted. The real problem is usually much more serious than the incomplete official data reveals.

Facing the evidence of our degrading environment, two questions and corresponding strategies arise. Should we bother to save individual species if the whole national and global living system is degrading and dying? The wiser solution is to preserve and conserve the landscape and the globe as a living system, with biodiversity conservation as a corollary benefit. While development and urbanization are inevitable, the key question is how can we minimize their impact so that urbanization and development can coexist with natural processes and biologically diverse habitats?

The Integrated Solution across Scales: Ecological Infrastructure for Ecosystems Services

In light of these considerations, planning and design of ecological infrastructure becomes the practical and wise solution. As a planning strategy, ecological infrastructure is similar to what some scholars sought over one decade ago: "The spatial solution is a pattern of ecosystems or land uses that will conserve the bulk of, and the most important attributes of, biodiversity and natural processes in any region, landscape or major portion thereof."[6] Ecological infrastructure can be considered as the structural landscape network that is composed of the critical landscape elements and spatial patterns that are of strategic significance in preserving the integrity of the landscape and securing sustainable ecosystem services.

The cognition of landscape in terms of structural frameworks has deep roots, both in China and the West. Among the prescientific models is the ancient Chinese art of geomancy, or feng shui, which always gave priority to the natural patterns and processes of Qi (or breath).[7] Orderly from large to small, the entire national landscape, including mountains and water courses, is considered as an interconnected dragon vein and a network of Qi movement, a sacred landscape infrastructure that any human actions have to come to terms with.[8] This model has been applied to the establishment and construction of villages and cities, roads, bridges, and even tombs, all of which are understood as connected in hierarchical patterns. In China, as in many other cultures, remnant sacred landscapes, especially forests, contain many of the threatened species of both flora and fauna.[9] From the model of feng shui, or geomancy, there are three points to be learned: (1) the protection of landscapes of a minimum critical size that are strategic for multiple processes; (2) the integration of natural, biological, and cultural processes; and (3) the understanding of landscape in terms of hierarchical form and across scales (Figure 14.1).

In the United States, the understanding of landscape in terms of structural frameworks has numerous precedents. Since the late nineteenth century, parks and green spaces have served as fundamental infrastructures to solve urban problems and to protect the natural landscape. Familiar examples include projects by Frederick Law Olmsted, such as Boston's Emerald Necklace Conservancy and the Minneapolis parkway system.[10] At the regional scale, green spaces are systematically planned as a metropolitan infrastructure, as shown by Charles Eliot's 1890s plan for the Metropolitan Park System for greater Boston. A similar idea of natural system protection was even attempted at the national scale in *Warren Manning's "National Plan."* Published in part in 1923, it combined data about many kinds of resources, including climates, forests, rivers, railroads, and highway systems, and made recommendations for land use and conservation. These traditions have been continued by the greenway movement in the United States, enriched and integrated with more comprehensive functions including the protection of natural processes, cultural heritage, and recreational purposes.[11]

The idea of ecological infrastructure is also rooted in conservation biology. As the biologist E. O. Wilson commented: "In the expanding enterprise, landscape design will play a decisive role. Where environments have been mostly humanized, biological diversity can still be sustained at high levels by the ingenious placement of woodlots, hedgerows, watersheds, reservoirs, and artificial ponds and lakes. Master plans will meld not just economic efficiency and beauty but also the preservation of species and races."[12] A variety of planning and design strategies have been developed for the preservation of biodiversity, especially in the context of stressed landscapes, including concepts such as ecological frameworks,[13] ecological networks,[14] extensive open-space systems,[15] and multiple-use modules, habitat networks, and wildlife corridors.[16] These concepts, although varying slightly, all indicate that the philosophy of nature conservation is changing from species-centered and site-protective approaches in its early phases into ecosystem-oriented ones, emphasizing the significance of deeply integrated conservation infrastructure.

From these many roots, the science of landscape ecology has become the single most important basis for the planning and design of landscapes. As an aspect of landscape ecology, ecological infrastructure is an important tool for moving built landscapes, metropolitan regions, and cities toward more sustainable conditions. But what makes the concept of ecological infrastructure such a powerful tool today is its marriage with the understanding of ecosystem services. Four categories of services have been identified: provisioning, related to production of food, water, and energy; regulating, related to the control of climate and disease and the mediation of flood and drought (i.e., the purification of water, carbon sequestration and climate regulation, waste decomposition and detoxification, pest and disease control); supporting, related to nutrient dispersal and cycling, seed dispersal, and habitat for wild plant and animal species; and cultural—intellectual and spiritual inspiration, recreational experiences, ecotourism and scientific discovery.[17] With respect to ecosystem services, ecological infrastructure can be understood as the necessary structures of sustainable landscapes or ecosystems in which the output of the goods and services is maintained, and the capacity of those systems to deliver same goods and services for future generations is not undermined. The many traditions of landscape ecology and more contemporary ideas about landscape as infrastructure finally come together in the understanding of natural capital and ecosystem services, and merge into the concept of ecological infrastructure. Although largely based in natural systems, other landscape elements such as cultural heritage corridors can also be integrated into plans for ecological infrastructure.

Ecological Infrastructure and Landscape Security Patterns

Here, ecological infrastructure is defined as the structural landscape network in which essential landscape elements are configured hierarchically. Both existing and potential spatial patterns are of strategic significance in preserving natural, biological, and cultural processes, which in turn are critical in securing the integrity and identity of the natural and cultural landscapes, as well as in securing the natural capital that supports sustainable ecosystem services.

It is important to note that ecological infrastructure is process-oriented, not just a visible

FIGURE 14.1

Ecological infrastructure can be designed in large, medium, and small scales. a) Large scale: The regional ecological infrastructure was planned, through the identification of critical landscape patterns (security patterns), for the following processes: (1) abiotic processes (flood control and storm and water management), (2) biotic processes (biodiversity conservation), and (3) cultural processes (cultural heritage protection and recreation).

Alternatives of ecological infrastructure are developed at various security levels (high, medium, and low); they are used as structural frameworks in guiding and framing urban development patterns. b) Medium scale: Guidelines were developed for green corridors that function as critical ecological infrastructure elements in water management and biodiversity conservation, recreation, and heritage protection. c) Small scale: At a selected site, alternative urban development models are designed to test the possibility of building an ecological infrastructure–based city, in which ecosystem services safeguarded by ecological infrastructure are delivered into the urban fabric.

Image courtesy of Kongjian Yu.

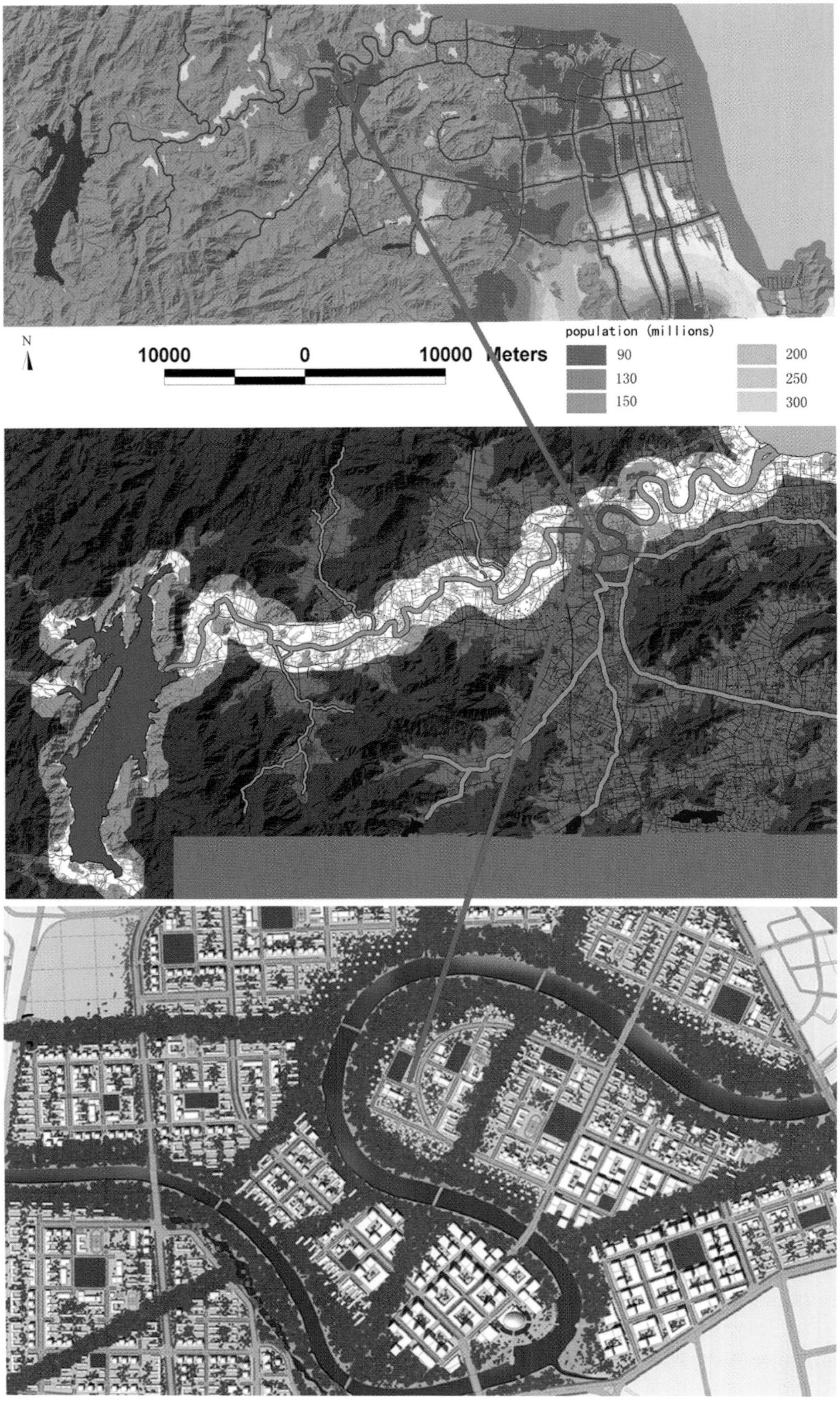

spatial pattern. With respect to the identification and planning of ecological infrastructure, a process-oriented model of spatial analysis, what I term a security pattern approach, might be useful.[18] A brief review of this approach will reveal the conceptual underpinnings of the case studies I present subsequently in this essay. Security patterns are composed of strategic geographic elements and spatial patterns that are critically important in safeguarding and controlling ecological processes and landscape change. Security patterns can be identified according to the properties on a general surface model of flows and processes. Potential surfaces are developed using landscape resistance to represent the dynamics of horizontal ecological processes (e.g., species movement, the spread of urban development, and water flow).

Four strategic landscape components are commonly identified on the potential surfaces: buffer zones, intersource linkages, radiating routes, and strategic points. These components, specified by certain quantitative and qualitative parameters, together with the identified sources (e.g., native habitats), compose the ecological security patterns and can be maintained at various security levels depending on their critical significance. These security patterns can be integrated into an overall ecological infrastructure and used by defenders of ecological processes as defensive frontiers and strategies of spatial bartering in landscape changes.

With these objectives in mind, the planning of ecological infrastructure is composed of the following steps:

(1) Process analysis. Processes associated with critical ecosystem functions or services are targeted to be safeguarded by ecological infrastructure, so systematic analysis is carried out using Geographical Information Systems (GIS), an efficient tool to simulate natural and cultural processes across the landscape. These processes include: a) abiotic processes, associated with the regulation and life-supporting services of ecosystems; b) biotic processes, associated with providing habitat for wild plant and animal species, safeguarding native species and biodiversity conservation; and c) cultural processes associated with information functions

including visual perception, heritage protection, and recreational activities.

(2) Defining landscape security patterns. Landscape security patterns are identified for the individual targeted processes. Models including suitability analysis, minimum cost distance, and surface analysis are used in the identification of security patterns for the individual processes.[19] Alternative security levels—low, medium, and high—are used to define the attributes of the security patterns in safeguarding each of the targeted processes.

(3) Defining ecological infrastructure across scales. An overlay technique is used to integrate the security patterns for individual processes. Alternatives are developed at various quality levels: high, medium, and low. Green lines are drawn to define and protect the ecological infrastructure. The ecological infrastructure is planned across scales.

a)   National scale (extra-large): The overall ecologically protected land.

b)   Regional scale (hundreds to thousands of square kilometers, large): At the regional scale, green lines are drawn to define the structural elements as corridors and restricted areas for construction.

c)   Intermediate scale (tens of square kilometers, medium): At this scale, the overall design and management guidelines are developed for ecological infrastructure, and especially for the green corridors that work as critical elements in water management, biodiversity conservation, heritage protection, and recreation.

d)   Small scale (less than ten square kilometers, small): At a specific site, a green network is designed to allow ecosystem services to be delivered into the urban fabric.

Building Ecological Infrastructure for Biodiversity Protection across Scales

Based on the theories of security patterns, a research framework for ecological infrastructure at various scales can be proposed. To address specific needs and problems at different scales, security patterns can be devised for various aspects of landscape, such as floodwater and stormwater, geological disaster, biodiversity, cultural heritage, and recreation. Then, these individual security patterns are integrated into comprehensive ecological security patterns, namely the overall ecological infrastructure.

The balance of this essay presents three case studies of ecological infrastructure. They range from extra-large and large scale (the national scale), to medium scale (the metropolitan-area scale), and then to the small scale (the site scale). Ecological infrastructure in the extra-large and large scale forms a strategic framework for landscape protection, and ecological infrastructure in the medium scale focuses on local, key regions and corridors. Finally, ecological infrastructure in the small scale applies a wide range of techniques to solve specific problems of the site. All three form an integrated hierarchical system to maintain ecological functions and protect biodiversity.

Ecological Infrastructure at the Extra-Large Scale: The Chinese National Ecological Security Pattern Program

Sustainable development is crucial for China today and in the future. The population of China has grown from 541.67 million in 1949 to 1.34 billion in 2008, making it one of the most densely populated countries in the world. By 2050, the total population is expected to reach 1.41 billion, and 70 percent will reside in urban areas.[20] Given this magnitude of development, the environment will continue to be under relentless pressure. Ecological security in China has, therefore, become a key area of scientific research for a strategy of sustainable development.

In spring of 2007, at the request of the National Bureau (now Ministry) of Environmental Protection,[21] Peking University Graduate School of Landscape Architecture initiated a pilot project that aims to establish an ecological security pattern at the national scale to protect the most sensitive ecological landscapes and to guide wise conservation and development.[22] Critical natural processes were analyzed systematically at the national scale, including headwater conservation, prevention of soil erosion, stormwater management and flood control, combating desertification, and promoting biodiversity conservation. Individual security patterns

for safeguarding each of these natural processes were identified and then integrated into an overall ecological security pattern. Three levels of National Ecological Security Pattern were defined: the lower-security level, the moderate-security level, and the higher-security level, which encompass 35.7, 65.1, and 84.9 percent of the national land, respectively. This study is expected to provide a scientific basis for ongoing national function zoning, incorporating ecological security patterns into land-use planning at the national scale (Figure 14.2).

Ecological Infrastructure at the Large Scale: The Ecological Baseline of Urban Development for Beijing

Strategic landscape elements and patterns for stormwater management and flood control, biodiversity conservation, cultural heritage protection, and recreational use are integrated using GIS models into a comprehensive ecological infrastructure, which is then used to determine future urban growth patterns. This project demonstrates how landscape planning can play a leading role in urban development through applying ecological infrastructure as a tool for smart growth and conservation.[23]

Beijing, the capital of China, is situated in the North China Plain, with a total area of 16,410 square kilometers. Due to rapid urbanization during the last thirty years, its population has doubled from 8.7 million in 1978 to about 17 million in 2009; its built-up area has expanded sevenfold and is still growing. The notorious "scrambled egg" pattern of Beijing today is the evidence of the speed and magnitude of urban sprawl and the failure of conventional planning, which tries to control urban growth using arbitrarily located greenbelts. A consequence of the uncontrolled spread of the growing

FIGURE 14.2
a) The topographic map of China; b) security patterns for national water; c) vegetation coverage of China; d) key regions for flora protection; e) key regions for fauna protection; and f) national ecological infrastructure: integrated national ecological security patterns of China.

Illustrations courtesy of Peking University Graduate School of Landscape Architecture.

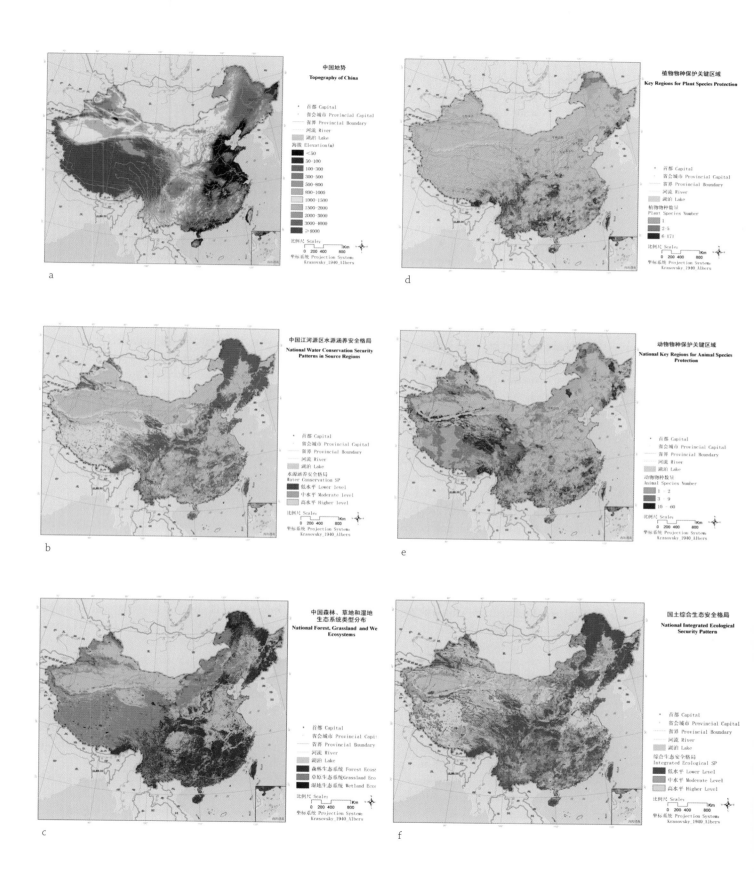

中国地势
Topography of China

· 首都 Capital
· 省会城市 Provincial Capital
— 省界 Provincial Boundary
河流 River
湖泊 Lake
海拔 Elevation (m)
<50
50-100
100-300
300-500
500-800
800-1000
1000-1500
1500-2000
2000-3000
3000-4000
≥4000

比例尺 Scale:
0 200 400 800 Km
坐标系统 Projection System:
Krasovsky_1940_Albers

a

植物物种保护关键区域
Key Regions for Plant Species Protection

· 首都 Capital
· 省会城市 Provincial Capital
— 省界 Provincial Boundary
河流 River
湖泊 Lake
植物物种数量
Plant Species Number
1
2-5
6-171

比例尺 Scale:
0 200 400 800 Km
坐标系统 Projection System:
Krasovsky_1940_Albers

d

中国江河源区水源涵养安全格局
National Water Conservation Security Patterns in Source Regions

· 首都 Capital
· 省会城市 Provincial Capital
— 省界 Provincial Boundary
河流 River
湖泊 Lake
水源涵养安全格局
Water Conservation SP
低水平 Lower level
中水平 Moderate level
高水平 Higher level

比例尺 Scale:
0 200 400 800 Km
坐标系统 Projection System:
Krasovsky_1940_Albers

b

动物物种保护关键区域
National Key Regions for Animal Species Protection

· 首都 Capital
· 省会城市 Provincial Capital
— 省界 Provincial Boundary
河流 River
湖泊 Lake
动物物种数量
Animal Species Number
1-2
3-9
10-60

比例尺 Scale:
0 200 400 800 Km
坐标系统 Projection System:
Krasovsky_1940_Albers

e

中国森林、草地和湿地
生态系统类型分布
**National Forest, Grassland and We
Ecosystems**

· 首都 Capital
· 省会城市 Provincial Capi:
— 省界 Provincial Boundary
河流 River
湖泊 Lake
森林生态系统 Forest Ecos
草原生态系统 Grassland Eco
湿地生态系统 Wetland Eco:

比例尺 Scale:
0 200 400 800 Km
坐标系统 Projection System:
Krasovsky_1940_Albers

c

国土综合生态安全格局
National Integrated Ecological Security Pattern

· 首都 Capital
· 省会城市 Provincial Capital
— 省界 Provincial Boundary
河流 River
湖泊 Lake
综合生态安全格局
Integrated Ecological SP
低水平 Lower Level
中水平 Moderate Level
高水平 Higher Level

比例尺 Scale:
0 200 400 800 Km
坐标系统 Projection System:
Krasovsky_1940_Albers

f

Integration across Scales

city is that local and regional natural systems and cultural heritage have all been damaged significantly. The city is now facing multiple challenges, including water shortages, increased vulnerability to geological disasters, habitat and biodiversity loss, diminished integrity and authenticity of cultural landscapes, decreased access to landscape for recreational uses, and dramatic loss of agricultural land and soil fertility.

Although greenbelts and green wedges have been planned to stop urban sprawl and maintain good landscape structure, they have largely failed. Greenbelts encircling Beijing were planned artificially and lack an intrinsic relationship with topography and ecological systems. They also lack integration with ecosystem services, and are vulnerable to land-use change—they have already been fragmented by large settlement areas. New and more effective tools have to be developed to address a wiser and sustainable development of the limited land.

Using minimum space, an ecological infrastructure for Beijing would safeguard critical ecosystem services. It would retain stormwater as much as possible to recharge the aquifer, while protecting the city from the threat of floods; minimize the risk of geological disasters; protect critical native habitats, and build an effective biological framework to maximally safeguard biodiversity; protect and regain the integrity and authenticity of cultural landscapes; increase the accessibility of the landscape for recreational uses; and maximally protect fertile land from being swallowed by urban development while not impeding urban growth. The overall objective is smart protection with smart growth (Figure 14.3).

THE CRITICAL PROCESSES

Critical processes in three categories are targeted to be safeguarded:

a) Abiotic processes: flood control, stormwater management, surface resource protection, and geological disaster prevention
b) Biotic processes: native species and biodiversity conservation
c) Cultural processes: cultural heritage protection and recreational needs

DEFINING LANDSCAPE SECURITY PATTERNS FOR BEIJING

a) Security patterns for abiotic processes: Strategies for water management include analysis of existing surface water features and buffer zones around them, and definition of areas most suitable for retaining rainwater and recharging the aquifer. Both historical flood data and simulated flood risk rating are used to calculate the floodable area. Security patterns to minimize geological disasters are created by identifying source elements (such as debris flow, landslide, mining subsidence, land subsidence, ground fissure, and soil erosion) and by establishing buffer zones around them.

b) Security patterns for biodiversity conservation: These security patterns are developed following the focal species approach. Three focal species are selected to represent biodiversity in the Beijing area: the Great Egret, Mallard, and Ring-necked Pheasant. These birds are selected because they are listed as protected species, yet each displays comparatively wide adaptive capability to diverse habitats. They might thus be considered as indicators of overall improvement of the landscape in terms of biodiversity protection. While all three are listed as national protected species, the Great Egret is designated as a first-grade species by the Beijing municipal government, and both the Mallard and Ring-necked Pheasant as the national second-grade. For the past several decades, these birds have rarely been seen due to illegal hunting and loss of habitat, not only in Beijing but also in much of China. Security patterns for each of the focal species are defined by integrating both suitability analysis and spatial pattern analysis. The overall patterns for biodiversity conservation are developed by combining the security patterns for individual focal species. The combined security patterns are composed of habitat patches, corridors, and strategic points that are crucial for maintaining the integrity of the biological network.

c) Security patterns for cultural heritage preservation: These security patterns are composed of both existing and potential heritage sites and the linear features between them. Both designated heritage sites and vernacular landscapes that are

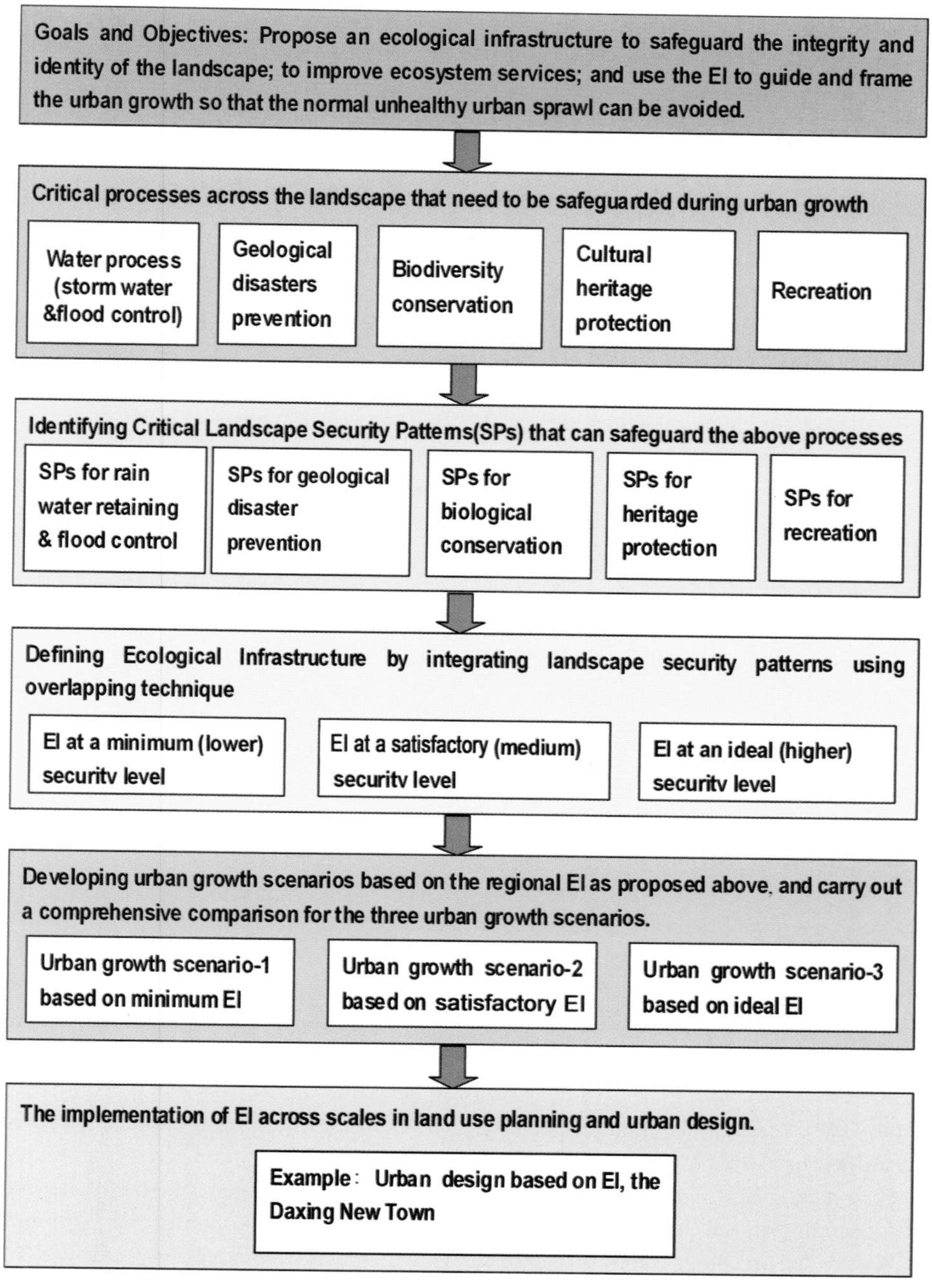

Goals and Objectives: Propose an ecological infrastructure to safeguard the integrity and identity of the landscape; to improve ecosystem services; and use the EI to guide and frame the urban growth so that the normal unhealthy urban sprawl can be avoided.

Critical processes across the landscape that need to be safeguarded during urban growth

| Water process (storm water & flood control) | Geological disasters prevention | Biodiversity conservation | Cultural heritage protection | Recreation |

Identifying Critical Landscape Security Patterns(SPs) that can safeguard the above processes

| SPs for rain water retaining & flood control | SPs for geological disaster prevention | SPs for biological conservation | SPs for heritage protection | SPs for recreation |

Defining Ecological Infrastructure by integrating landscape security patterns using overlapping technique

| EI at a minimum (lower) security level | EI at a satisfactory (medium) security level | EI at an ideal (higher) security level |

Developing urban growth scenarios based on the regional EI as proposed above, and carry out a comprehensive comparison for the three urban growth scenarios.

| Urban growth scenario-1 based on minimum EI | Urban growth scenario-2 based on satisfactory EI | Urban growth scenario-3 based on ideal EI |

The implementation of EI across scales in land use planning and urban design.

Example: Urban design based on EI, the Daxing New Town

FIGURE 14.3
The framework for an ecological infrastructure approach to urban growth planning.

Image courtesy of Kongjian Yu.

part of Beijing's identity are listed for protection. Historical linkages are identified based on written and graphic data. Suitability for building heritage corridors is calculated based on land cover and distances from the heritage sites and linear features. A network of heritage corridors is then planned for preservation, education, and recreation purposes.

Security patterns for recreation are defined according to both existing and potential recreational resources of natural and cultural landscapes, as well as their accessibility and potential linkages. Urban parks, national and regional parks, cultural heritage sites, vernacular landscapes, and potential natural and cultural sites are assessed in terms of recreation use. Suitability for building recreation corridors is calculated based on land cover and distances from the recreation resources and linear features. Sites are classified according to recreational values, accessibility, and potential linkages. A regional network for recreation is planned based on the identified security patterns.

Defining Comprehensive Ecological Infrastructure by Integrating the Security Patterns of Individual Processes

Landscape security patterns that safeguard individual processes are integrated into the overall comprehensive ecological infrastructure. Using an overlay technique to integrate the security patterns for individual processes, alternatives of regional ecological infrastructure are developed at three quality levels:

a) Ecological infrastructure at low (minimum) quality: 47 percent of the total land, including 24 percent of the most fertile land, is protected. The integrity of the critical ecological processes will be protected at a minimum level, providing basic ecosystems services. The regional environment will be stable for the time being.

b) Ecological infrastructure at medium (satisfactory) quality: 70 percent of the total land, including 45 percent of the most fertile land, is protected. The integrity of the critical ecological processes will be protected at a satisfactory level, providing adequate and sustainable ecosystem services. The regional environment will be regenerated gradually.

c) Ecological infrastructure at high (ideal) quality: 85 percent of the total land, including 100 percent of the most fertile land, is protected—the latter for organic agriculture. The integrity of critical ecological processes will be protected at an ideal level, providing the best possible ecosystem services. The regional environment will be regenerated dramatically.

Detailed guidelines have been developed for the protection and management of ecological infrastructure components at various scales. Using the three alternative quality levels as a guide, multiple scenarios of regional urban growth patterns were simulated using GIS:

Scenario 1, the "scrambled egg": urban growth without ecological infrastructure
Scenario 2, green infrastructure within the city: urban growth based on minimal ecological infrastructure
Scenario 3, city as green infrastructure: urban growth based on satisfactory ecological infrastructure
Scenario 4, suburban garden: urban growth based on ideal ecological infrastructure

Comparative evaluations are made for all four urban growth scenarios based on their impacts on ecological, cultural, and economic processes, and their capacity to address the national and regional challenges identified at the introduction of this essay. Scenario 3, city as green infrastructure, might best fulfill the goals of both conservation and development, and meet the requirement of all competing land-use requirements. This is a smarter scenario, in which the limited land can be used more efficiently, through a better configuration for both conservation and urban development (Figure 14.4).

Ecological Infrastructure as a Design Strategy: Ecosystem Services in an Urban Park in Shanghai: Houtan Park

Green space has historically been an asset because of the psychological and physical benefits to the surrounding community. The reality of many traditional urban parks, however, particularly those built within the last twenty years in China, is the economic and environmental burden they present to the city through maintenance, repairs, and water and energy consumption. While the beauty of traditional ornamental parks has been appreciated, the more authentic and vigorous "beauty of wild grasses" apparent in vernacular landscapes is undervalued, especially in terms of the sustainable services they provide.[24] Stormwater management, including minor flooding, is often seen as a threat to urban progress. Slow-moving streams and rivers have been straightened and channelized to move water efficiently, resulting in the loss of groundwater supplies and the diminished availability of potable water. Native plants have been replaced with massive swaths of ornamentals that lack biodiversity. Taming nature's messy ecosystems into more

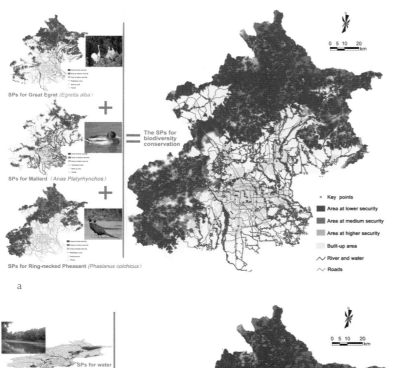

a

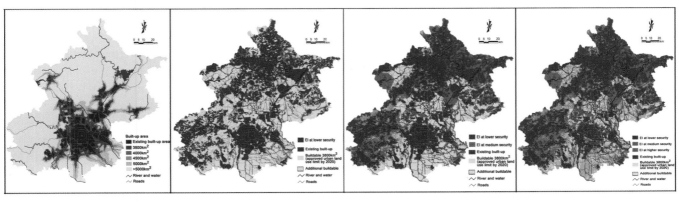

b

c

FIGURE 14.4
a) Beijing landscape security pattern for biodiversity protection based on focal species. The overall security patterns for biodiversity conservation is developed by combining security patterns for each of the focal species; the combined security patterns are composed of habitat patches, corridors, and key points that are strategic for keeping the integrity of the biological network. b) Beijing regional ecological infrastructure. Landscape security patterns that safeguard the individual processes are integrated into the overall comprehensive ecological infrastructure. Using overlaying techniques to integrate the security patterns for individual processes, alternatives of regional ecological infrastructure are developed at various quality levels: low (minimum), medium (satisfactory), and high (ideal); they will be used to guide and frame regional urban growth. c) Beijing urban growth scenarios, with or without ecological infrastructure.

Illustrations courtesy of Peking University Graduate School of Landscape Architecture.

"sophisticated" and ornamental urban parks has all but removed nature's ecological benefits.

As engineering and mechanized services have been standardized throughout the urban world, natural systems have been severely degraded or completely destroyed. When an ecosystem is no longer sustainable, the environment becomes sterile, blighted, and/or contaminated, and requires human intervention to repair it. We often find ourselves approaching the problem with nearly the same solution that caused it. We create new public spaces with neatly placed shrubs and treat contaminated water and soils using mechanical methods, then celebrate a restored environment. The contamination is addressed but at a significant expense to the government or people, and the environment is still incapable of sustaining itself.

It is therefore critical to recover landscape as a living ecosystem that has the ability to adapt, change, and provide ecosystem services. As mentioned previously, these include provisioning, regulating, supporting, and cultural services. Houtan Park, in Shanghai, became an experimental showcase of regenerative design in the middle of a densely populated urban setting. Created in conjunction with the 2010 Shanghai Expo, the park integrated site topography, flood control, and native habitat to rejuvenate ecosystem services. It reactivated valuable open space and rebuilt biodiversity while managing stormwater, cleaning contaminated river water and soil, and educating the community about the beauty of diverse native landscapes.

The Challenges of the Site
The fourteen-hectare (34.6-acre) site is located on the southern boundary of the Expo grounds, locked between the east bank of the Huangpu River and Puming Road, a main thoroughfare. This thin band of land challenged the ability of the landscape architects at Turenscape to effectively organize public spaces over a long distance; it features a water frontage over 1,700 meters (1 mile) in length, while averaging only 50–80 meters (164–260 feet) in width, with the narrowest area approximately 30 meters (100 feet) wide. The degraded riverfront presented other design challenges. A brownfield site previously occupied by a steel factory and a shipyard, it was largely used as a landfill and a storage

yard for industrial materials. The Huangpu River is severely polluted and currently designated as a Grade V water body, which is considered unsafe for swimming and recreation and devoid of aquatic life. The foremost design challenge was to remediate the site to create a safe and healthy public space in a limited time frame. The design was initiated in early 2007, construction was completed in October 2009, and the park opened to the public in May 2010.

The major infrastructural challenge was to address flood control; the goal was to create an ecologically sensitive waterfront and provide direct public access to the river, while protecting the city from flooding. The site is relatively flat with an elevation of 4–7 meters (13–23 feet); the existing floodwall, designed to protect against a one-thousand-year flood event, had a top elevation of 6.7 meters (22 feet). The average tide fluctuation of the Huangpu River is 2.24 meters (7.3 feet), with an average high-tide elevation of 3.29 meters (11 feet) and an average low-tide elevation of 1.19 meters (3.9 feet). The disparity between the water elevation and levee height restricted public access to the waterfront. A sloped riverfront design would require more space than available and possibly erode, while maintaining the existing floodwall would continue to prevent accessibility and remain devoid of aquatic life and habitat. An alternative had to be found.

The park also had to address the challenge of heavy usage. The Expo's west entrance is located on the southern boundary of Houtan Park; it was the sole access point for the waterfront and the central green space for the Expo. Eighty million visitors were expected to attend the 2010 Shanghai Expo, so pedestrian circulation, safety, and evacuation routes were critical to address during the design phase. Creating organized, well-developed routes and gathering spaces was crucial to create a comfortable and safe pedestrian environment.

Design Concept and Strategy:
A Living System for Ecosystem Services
A layered approach was used to organize the space, to integrate multiple functions and ecosystem services into the design, to interpret the site's history and future potential, to express the unique character of the park, and to address access and circulation

Huangpu River

FIGURE 14.5
Shanghai's
Houtan Park,
the existing
landscape, a
brownfield site.

Image courtesy of
Kongjian Yu.

challenges. The layering of ecological services, combined with references to regional agriculture and the industrial heritage of the site, created an environmentally sensitive, postindustrial landscape that speaks specifically about the past, present, and future of Shanghai. Weaving these layers of landscape into an integrated system is a network of paths and places that create aesthetically pleasing experiences for visitors during the Expo and afterward.

The design preserves a remnant four-hectare (ten-acre) riparian habitat located along the Huangpu riverfront immediately adjacent to the park site, the only such patch on the Huangpu in Shanghai. An existing concrete levee was reconfigured as a tidal wetland planted with native species and reinforced with permeable riprap. Two levees run the length of the park, one along the riverbank that provides protection from twenty-year floods, and a second, higher one on the inland edge of the site meant to protect against one-thousand-year floods. The valley between forms the spine of the park; it is occupied by a series of ponds surrounded by native trees and forbs, forming a quiet refuge for both wildlife and people within a bustling metropolis. Boardwalks, stairways, and platforms meander through large swaths of native plants and wildflowers that form a lush and biologically productive wetland: a carbon

sink, a flood-resilient buffer, and a pleasing experience of biodiversity.

Houtan Park avoids both the engineered and the ornamental. Wetlands are created with impermeable clay liners rather than concrete. Vigorous native plants, instrumental both in water purification and biomass production, require less maintenance than ornamentals. Recycled materials reduced construction costs and energy expenditures: a skeletal steel mill was painted red and reused for small pavilions intended to serve as restaurants and teahouses, an old dock was redesigned as a fishing pier and shade structure, and salvaged and recycled brick and stone were used for paths in the park.

The park's main features might be summarized as follows:

a) Landscape for flood regulation: The constructed terraces and linear wetlands act as a buffer between the Huangpu River and the city, absorbing and retaining flood water between the twenty-year and one-thousand-year flood event levees. The terraced design reduces the relative elevation change between the city and the river and subsequently the strength requirements for the levee. The existing concrete retaining wall replaced by a more ecologically sensitive riprap

01. Water Intake
02. Terraced Fields
03. Waterfront Reed Scenery
04. Vegetation Bubble
05. Transformed industrial relic: "sky garden square"
06. Original Wetland
07. Reed Platforms
08. Inner River Wetland
09. Red Ribbon Elements
10. Watergate Square
11. Watergate Docklands
12. Houtan Rain Water Pumping Station
13. Waste Water Pumping Station
14. Original Architecture (air shaft)

0   50   100   200m

FIGURE 14.6
Site plan for Shanghai Houtan Park.

Image courtesy of Kongjian Yu.

FIGURE 14.7
Shanghai's
Houtan
Park; design
strategy for
the landscape
as a living
system that
provides
multiple
ecosystem
services.

Image courtesy
of Kongjian Yu.

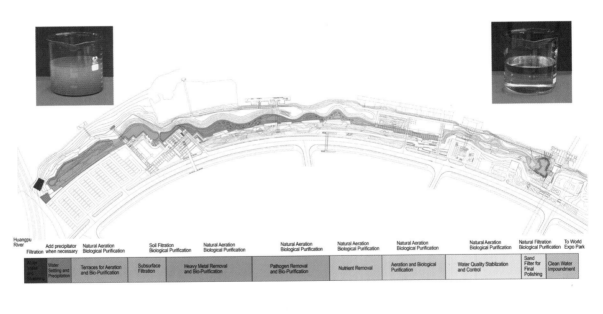

Huangpu
River
Filtration   Add precipitator   Natural Aeration   Soil Filtration   Natural Aeration   Natural Aeration   Natural Aeration   Natural Aeration   Natural Aeration   Natural Filtration   To World
             when necessary   Biological Purification   Biological Purification   Biological Purification   Biological Purification   Biological Purification   Biological Purification   Biological Purification   Biological Purification   Expo Park

| Water Intake and Screening | Water Settling and Precipitation | Terraces for Aeration and Bio-Purification | Subsurface Filtration | Heavy Metal Removal and Bio-Purification | Pathogen Removal and Bio-Purification | Nutrient Removal | Aeration and Biological Purification | Water Quality Stabilization and Control | Sand Filter for Final Polishing | Clean Water Impoundment |

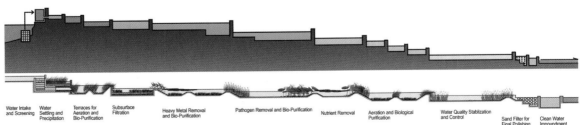

Water Intake
and Screening   Water Settling and   Terraces for   Subsurface   Heavy Metal Removal   Pathogen Removal and Bio-Purification   Nutrient Removal   Aeration and Biological   Water Quality Stabilization   Sand Filter for   Clean Water
                 Precipitation   Aeration and   Filtration   and Bio-Purification   Purification   and Control   Final Polishing   Impoundment
                                       Bio-Purification

254   KONGJIAN YU

system will encourage native vegetation and new habitats to emerge.

b) Landscape that cleans water: Currently the Huangpu River water is designated as Lower Grade V, the poorest quality on a scale of I–V. Water from the Huangpu River is diverted to the constructed wetland where it is biologically treated to an improved Grade III designation via a series of wetland cells that facilitate settling, aeration, and vegetative and microbial processes. The treated river water can then be used safely for landscape irrigation and other nonpotable uses in adjacent parks. Full-scale, pilot-testing results indicated that the Houtan Park treatment wetland has the ability to treat over 2,400 cubic meters (630,000 gallons) of water per day.

c) Landscape that produces food: The terraced belt that forms a transition between the constructed wetland and the one-thousand-year levee and road is inspired by China's famous terraced fields. Agricultural crops from Shanghai's past and wetland plants with water-purification capacities were selected to create an urban agricultural garden rich with seasonal changes. Memories of agrarian culture are evoked through the scene of the golden rapeseed blossoms *(Brassica capestris)* in spring, splendid sunflowers in summer, the fragrance of rice in fall, and green clover (Chinese Milkvetch, *Astragalus sinicus*) in winter. The design showcases the image of the productive earth, reconnects the urban dweller to the land, and provides an educational venue for the children of Shanghai to learn about agriculture and ecosystems. In addition, the crops produce abundant food for wildlife.

d) Landscape as infrastructure for biodiversity: The park has proven to be a great success, and one

a

b

c

FIGURE 14.8a–c
Landscape that cleans water: dirty river water spills down a rock face, then is aerated and filtered through a series of ponds at Shanghai's Houtan Park, delivering clean water at the downstream end of the site.

Image courtesy of Kongjian Yu.

unusual aspect of this success is that the park has become a refuge for diverse native species. Just one year after completion, some twenty species of birds have found a home in this small park (see the list of fauna and flora in Table 14.1). In addition to the designed plantings, many species have immigrated from the adjacent remnant riparian patch and taken root along the river corridor. It is important to note that the protection of this habitat immediately adjacent the park played an important role as one of the key sources of biodiversity, and the Huangpu River has actually played a role as a species-transporting and migratory corridor. Although it is but a node and a small-scale place, Houtan Park acts as part of landscape infrastructure at the regional and even national scale (Figures 14.5–14.8).

Conclusion

In the context of rapid development and global climate change, the most effective solution for biodiversity conservation is through planning and design of new security patterns for critical habitats at every scale. Rigorous security pattern analysis for rural, suburban, and urban environments will lead to the creation of ecological infrastructure, safeguarding biodiversity while helping to preserve and restore critical ecological services. The protection of individual species is secured within larger efforts to protect the earth itself as a living system.

d

FIGURE 14.8d
Landscape for biodiversity: Houtan Park supports a wide array of plant, bird, fish, and insect species, along with some amphibians, reptiles, and mammals.

Image courtesy of Kongjian Yu.

e

f

FIGURE 14.8e–f

Landscape that produces food: rice, rapeseed, and sunflowers are among the food crops produced in the park for human and animal consumption.

Image courtesy of Kongjian Yu.

g

h

i

FIGURE 14.8g–i
Landscape for flood control: a twenty-year flood event levee runs along the river; a thousand-year levee is farther inland. Pathways and benches parallel the levee system.

Image courtesy of Kongjian Yu.

j

k

l

m

FIGURE 14.8j–n
Ecological infrastructure as design: boardwalks, stairs, and docks
connect visitors with upland and aquatic vegetation, underlining
park narratives about biodiversity and water purification.

Image courtesy of Kongjian Yu.

n

TABLE 14.1

PLANTS HYDROPHYTE RESOURCES	TYPE		COMMON NAME	LATIN NAME	FUNCTION IN SHANGHAI HOUTAN PARK
	Emergent plants		Common reed	*Phragmites communis Trin.*	Removing organic pollutants; Transporting oxygen to the soil around roots; Increasing penetration of soil mediator
			Southern cattail	*Typha angustata Bory et chaub*	
			Manchurian wild rice	*Zizania latifolia (Griseb.) Stapf*	Transporting oxygen to the soil around roots
			Purple loosestrife	*Lythrum salicaria Linn*	
			Roof iris/wall iris	*Iris tectorum*	Removing organic and inorganic contaminants; Increasing penetration of soil mediator
			Foxnut	*Euryale ferox Salisb. ex DC*	
			River club-rush	*Scirpus validus Vahl*	
			Sweet flag	*Acorus calamus L.*	
			Small reed mace	*Typha angustifolia*	
			Sacred water lotus	*Nelumbo nucifera*	
			Polygonum hydropiper	*Polygonum viscosum Polygonum hydropiper L.*	
			Great water plantain	*Rhizoma Alismatis Alisma plantago-aquatica*	
			Dasheen	*Colocasia tonoimo Nakai*	
			Pennywort	*Hydrocotyle vulgaris*	
			Club-rush	*Scirpus triqueter L.*	
			Pickerel weed	*Pontederia cordata*	
			Purple loosestrife	*Lythrum salicaria L.*	
			Arrow head	*Sagittaria sagittifolia*	
			Pickerel weed	*Monochoriamorsakowii Pontederia cordata*	
			Thalia	*Thalia dealbata*	
	Floating plants		White water lily	*Nyphaea tetragona Georgi*	Removing organic and inorganic contaminants; Decreasing chemical oxygen demand; Increasing dissolved oxygen; Providing aquatic animals with shelter
			Foxnut	*Euryale ferox Salisb. ex DC*	
			Duckweed	*Lemna minor L*	
			bit	*Hydrocharis dubia (Bl.) Backer*	
			Water fringe	*Nymphoides peltatum(Gmel.)O.Kuntze*	
	Submerged Plants	Spermatophyte	Curly pondweed	*Potamogeton crispus*	Removing organic and inorganic contaminants; Decreasing chemical oxygen demand; Increasing dissolved oxygen; Providing aquatic animals with habitat and nutrition; Removing pathogenic microorganisms
			Pondweed	*Potamogeton*	
			Pondweed	*Potamogeton*	

PLANTS	TYPE		COMMON NAME	LATIN NAME	FUNCTION IN SHANGHAI HOUTAN PARK
HYDROPHYTE RESOURCES (*continued*)	Submerged plants	Spermatophyte	Water milfoil	*Myriophyllum spicatum*	Removing organic and inorganic contaminants; Decreasing chemical oxygen demand; Increasing dissolved oxygen; Providing aquatic animals with habitat and nutrition; Removing pathogenic microorganisms
			Eel grass	*Vallisneria spiralis L.*	
			Fennel-leaved pondweed	*Potamogeton pectinatus L.*	
		Phycophyta	Hydrilla	*Hydrilla verticillata*	
			Hornwort	*Ceratophyllum demersum L.*	
			Waterweed	*ceratophyllum demersum*	
			Spirogyra/ Green algae	*Spirogyra intorta Jao*	
			California barberry	*Dactylococcopsis fascicularis*	They are the primary producers in an aquatic ecosystem that synthesizes organic matter through photosynthesis with solar energy and carbon dioxide
			Freshwater algae	*D. rhaphidioides*	
			Gloeocapsa	*Gloeocapsa punctata*	
			P.tenus	*Phorimidium tenus*	
			Dinoflagellate	*Gymnodinium aeruginosum*	
			Dinoflagellate	*Peridinium gatunense*	
			Cyclotella/Diatoms	*Cyclotella sp.*	
			Cyclotella/Diatoms	*Cyclotella comta*	
			Synedra acus	*Synedra acus*	
			Synedra ulna	*Synedra ulna*	
			Synedra tabulata	*Synedra tabulata*	
			Synedra amphicephala	*Synedra amphicephala*	
			Navicula/Diatom	*Navicula sp.*	
			Navicula/Diatom	*N. exigua*	
			Navicula/Diatom	*N. rhynchocephala*	
			Navicula/Diatom	*N. cincta var.leptocephala*	
			Cocconeis/Diatom	*Cocconeis placentula*	
			Cymbella/Diatom	*Cymbella affinis*	
			Gomphonema/ Diatom	*Gomphonema olivaceum*	
			Gomphonema/ Diatom	*G. constrictum*	
			Chlorella/Green algae	*Chlorella vulgaris*	
			Gloeoactinium	*Gloeoactinium limneticum*	
			Micractinium	*Micractinium pusillum*	

PLANTS **HYDROPHYTE** **RESOURCES** (*continued*)	TYPE		COMMON NAME	LATIN NAME	FUNCTION IN SHANGHAI HOUTAN PARK
	Submerged plants	Phycophyta	Scenedesmus/Green algae	*Scenedesmus quadricauda*	They are the primary producers in an aquatic ecosystem that synthesizes organic matter through photosynthesis with solar energy and carbon dioxide
			Westella botryoides	*Westella botryoides*	
			Pandorina/Green algae	*Pandorina morum*	
			Chodatella quadriseta	*Chodatella quadriseta*	
			Ulothrix/Green algae	*Ulothrix sp*	
			Ulothrix/Green algae	*U.variabilis*	
			Ulothrix/Green algae	*U. zonata*	
			Crucigenia/Green algae	*Crucigenia quadrata*	
			Crucigenia/Green algae	*C.tetrapedia*	

PLANTS **HYGROPHYTE** **RESOURCES**	TYPE	COMMON NAME	LATIN NAME	FUNCTION IN SHANGHAI HOUTAN PARK
	Hygrophytes	Hardy Sugar Cane	*Saccharum arundinaceum*	Intercepting floating litter; Soil and water conservation; Providing animals with habitat
		Reed Sweetgrass	*Glyceria maxima*	Soil and water conservation; Providing animals with habitat; Creating biodiversity
		Giant reed	*Arundo donax*	
		Umbrella papyrus	*Cyperus alternifolius*	

PLANTS **TERRESTRIAL** **PLANT** **RESOURCES**	TYPE		COMMON NAME	LATIN NAME	FUNCTION IN SHANGHAI HOUTAN PARK
	Woody plants	Arbor	Pond Cypress	*Taxodium ascendens Brongn*	Providing animals with habitat; Creating biodiversity
			Dawn redwood	*Metasequoia glyptostroboides Hu et Cheng*	
			Pterocarya stenoptera	*Pterocarya stenoptera C. DC*	
			Weeping willow	*Salix babylonica*	
			Chinese elm	*Ulmus parvifolia Jacq*	
			Campho	*Cinnamomum camphora (L.) Presl*	
			Woodland Elaeocarpus	*Elaeocarpus sylvestris (Lour) Poir*	
			London Plane	*Platanus acerifolia*	
			Vegetable tallow	*Sapium sebiferum (L.) Roxb*	
			Paper mulberry	*Broussonetia papyrifera*	
			Chinese Bishopwood	*Bischofia polycarpa*	
			Tulip tree	*Liriodendron chinense (Hemsl.) Sarg.*	
			Happy tree	*Camptotheca acuminata*	

	TYPE		COMMON NAME	LATIN NAME	FUNCTION IN SHANGHAI HOUTAN PARK
TERRESTRIAL PLANT RESOURCES (*continued*)	Woody plants	Arbor	Japanese zelkova	*Zelkova serrata (Thunb.) Makino*	Providing animals with habitat; Creating biodiversity
			Lapsi/Candy tree	*Choerospondias axillaris (Roxb.)Burtt et Hill*	
			Fragrant olive	*Osmanthus fragrans*	
			Maidenhair tree	*Ginkgo biloba*	
			Persimmon	*Diospyros kaki Linn.f.)*	
			Jujube	*Zizyphus jujuba*	
			Swamp cypress	*Taxodium mucronatum*	
			Chinese privet	*Ligustrum lucidum*	
			White mulberry	*Morus alba L.*	
		Shrub	Oleander	*Nerium oleander*	Soil and water conservation; Providing animals with habitat; Creating biodiversity
			Cotton rose	*Hibiscus mutabilis*	
			Rhododendron	*Rhododendron simsii&R.spp.*	
			Rhododendron	*Rhododendron simsii*	
			Cape Jasmine	*Gardenia jasminoides Ellis*	
			Primrose jasmine	*Jasminum mesnyi Hance*	
			Camellia	*Camellia sasanqua*	
			Chinese tamarisk	*Tamarix chinensis*	
			Hedge bamboo	*Bambusa multiplex (Lour.) Raeusch.*	
			Viburnum odoratissimum	*Viburnum odoratissimum Ker-Gawl.*	
			Ilex purpurea	*Ilex purpurea Hassk.*	
			Japanese aralia	*Fatsia japonica*	
	Liana		Japanese honeysuckle	*Lonicera Japonica*	Providing animals with habitat; Creating biodiversity
	Herbaceous plants	Gramineae	Mucunasempervirens Hemsl	*Mucunasempervirens Hemsl*	
			Pampas grass	*Cortaderia selloana*	
			Lyme Grass	*Leymus arenarius*	
			Esparto grass	*Nassella tenuissima*	
			Maiden Grass	*Maiden Grass*	
			Eulalia	*Miscanthus sinensis var. purpururascens*	
			Chinese fountain grass	*Pennisetum alopecuroides (L.) Spreng.*	
			Chinese fountain grass	*Pennisetum alopecuroides (L.) Spreng.*	
			Chinese fountain grass	*Pennisetum alopecuroides (L.) Spreng.*	
			Kou-chiku	*Phyllostachys viridis (Young) Mc Clure.*	
			Cogongrass	*Imperata cylindrica 'Red Baron'*	
			Black-eyed Susan vine	*Thunbergia alata*	

PLANTS	TYPE		COMMON NAME	LATIN NAME	FUNCTION IN SHANGHAI HOUTAN PARK
TERRESTRIAL PLANT RESOURCES (continued)	Herbaceous plants	Gramineae	Evening primrose	Oenothera biennis Linn.	Providing animals with habitat; Creating biodiversity
			Tortoiseshell Bamboo	Phyllostachys heterocycla (Carr.)	
			Triarrherca sacchariflora	Nakai Triarrherca sacchariflora	
			Green bristle grass	Setaria viridis (L.) Beauv.	
			Coix Seed	Coix lacroyma-jobi L. var. ma-yuen (Roman.) Stapf	
		Wildflowers	Farewell to Spring/ Godetia	Godetia amoena G. Don	
			Red flax/scarlet flax/ crimson flax	Linum grandiflora	
			Corn poppy	Papaver rhoeas L	
			Violet orychophragmus	Orychophragmus violaceus	
			African mustard	Malcolmia africana (Linn.) R. Br	
			Silene pendula	Silene pendula L.	
			Globe Amaranth/ Bachelor Button	Gomphrena globosa	
			Mealy sag	Salvia farinacea	
			Marvel of Peru	Mirabilis jalapa Linn	
			Oxeye daisy	Chrysanthemun leucanthemum	
			Dandelion	Herba Taraxaci	
			Blue Butterfly Larkspur	Delphinium grandiflorum	
			Californian poppy	Eschscholtzia Californica	
			Sweet rocket	Hesperis matronalis	
			Verbena hybrida Voss	Verbena hybrida Voss	
			Chinese Astilbe	Astilbe chinensis (Maxim.) Franch.etSav.	
			Pink	Dianthus plumarius	
			Six Hills Giant	Giant Catmint	
			Moss Phlox	Phlox subulata	
			Shasta daisy	Chrysanthemum maximum	
			Persian Buttercup	Ranunculus asiaticus	
			Cosmos	Cosmos bipinnatus Cav.	
		Groundcover plants	Hymenocallis americana	Hymenocallis americana	Soil and water conservation; Providing animals with habitat; Creating biodiversity
			Liriope	Liriope palatyphylla Ophiopogon japonicus (L.F.)Ker.- Gawl	
			White clover	Trifolium repens Linn.	
			Shrubberry rhodiola	Kalanchoe blossfeldiana	
			Fulva/Tawny Daylily	Hemerocallis fulva (L.) L.	

PLANTS TERRESTRIAL PLANT RESOURCES (*continued*)	TYPE		COMMON NAME	LATIN NAME	FUNCTION IN SHANGHAI HOUTAN PARK
	Herbaceous plants	Groundcover plants	Caper spurge	*Euphorbia lathyris L.*	Soil and water conservation; Providing animals with habitat; Creating biodiversity
			Bermuda grass	*Cynodon Dactylon (Linn.) Pers.*	
			Cleistogenes squrrosa	*Cleistogenes squrrosa*	
			Chop-suey greens	*Chrysanthemum Coronarium Linn*	
			Korean lawn grass	*Zoysia japonica*	
			Herba violae	*Viola philippica Car*	
			Canadian goldenrod	*Solidago canadensis L*	Invading the living space of other species

PLANTS CROP RESOURCES		COMMON NAME	LATIN NAME	FUNCTION IN SHANGHAI HOUTAN PARK
	Crops	Sweet corn	*Zea mays L*	Providing animals with habitat; Creating biodiversity
		Bread wheat	*Triticum aestivum Linn.*	
		Sorghum	*Sorghum Sorghum bicolor*	
		Buckwheat	*Fagopyrum esculentum*	
		Sweet potato	*Ipomoea batatas*	
		Sunflower	*Helianthus annuus*	
		Rapeseed	*Brassica campestris L.*	

ANIMALS AQUATIC ANIMAL RESOURCES	TYPE	COMMON NAME	LATIN NAME	FUNCTION IN SHANGHAI HOUTAN PARK
	Zooplankton	Rotifer/B.calyciflorus	*B.calyciflorus*	They are small zooplankton or have weak swimming abilities, composing plankton together with phytoplankton. Zooplankton contains a large number of species, from unicellular radiolarian to larvae of crab and lobster. They are divided into two groups: lifelong plankton, which spend all their lifes floating in water, and temporary/seasonal plankton, which float in water before maturity.
		Rotifer/Rotaria neptunia	*Rotaria neptunia*	
		Rotifer/B.angularis	*B.angularis*	
		Rotifer/B.crceus	*B.crceus*	
		Rotifer/B. budapestiensis	*B. budapestiensis*	
		Rotifer/Keratella cochlearis	*Keratella cochlearis*	
		Rotifer/Filinia longiseta	*Filinia longiseta*	
		Rotifer/F.major	*F.major*	
		Rotifer/Trichocerca weberi	*Trichocerca weberi*	

ANIMALS	TYPE	COMMON NAME	LATIN NAME	FUNCTION IN SHANGHAI HOUTAN PARK
AQUATIC ANIMAL RESOURCES *(continued)*	Zooplankton	Rotifer/Lecane luna	*Lecane luna*	They are small zooplankton or have weak swimming abilities, composing plankton together with phytoplankton. Zooplankton contains a large number of species, from unicellular radiolarian to larvae of crab and lobster. They are divided into two groups: lifelong plankton, which spend all their lifes floating in water, and temporary/seasonal plankton, which float in water before maturity.
		Rotifer/Cephalodella exigua	*Cephalodella exigua*	
		Rotifer/Monostyla closterocerca	*Monostyla closterocerca*	
		Rotifer/Asplanchna priodonta	*Asplanchna priodonta*	
		Nauplius	*nauplius larva*	
		Copepodid larva	*copepodid larva*	
		Daphnia/water fleas/ Diaphanosoma leuchtenbergianum	*Diaphanosoma leuchtenbergianum*	
		Daphnia/water fleas/D.hyalina	*D.hyalina*	
		Daphnia/water fleas/ Daphnia longispina	*Daphnia longispina*	
		Daphnia/water fleas/D.carinata	*D.carinata*	
		Daphnia/water fleas/D.pulex	*D.pulex*	
		Daphnia/water fleas/ Moina macrocopa	*Moina macrocopa*	
		Daphnia/water fleas/ Alona rectangula	*Alona rectangula*	
		Daphnia/water fleas/A.diaphana	*A.diaphana*	
		Daphnia/water fleas/A.pulchella	*A.pulchella*	
		Daphnia/ water fleas/A. quadrangularis	*A.quadrangularis*	
		Daphnia/water fleas/ Leptodora kindti	*Leptodora kindti*	
		Daphnia/water fleas/ Sinocalanus sinensis	*Sinocalanus sinensis*	
		Daphnia/water fleas/S.dorrii	*S.dorrii*	
		Daphnia/water fleas/ Eucyclops serrulatus	*Eucyclops serrulatus*	
		Daphnia/water fleas/E.macruroides	*E.macruroides*	
		Daphnia/water fleas/ Microcyclops varicans	*Microcyclops varicans*	
		Daphnia/water fleas/M.mictura	*M.mictura*	
		Daphnia/water fleas/ Simocephalus vetulus	*Simocephalus vetulus*	
		Daphnia/water fleas/S.vetuloides	*S.vetuloides*	
	Benthos	River Prawn	*Marcrobrachium nipponense*	Most of these kinds of animals fix themselves on the rock surface or bury themselves in sand; some attach themselves to plants or other benthos. By consuming organic matter, they make the water body clean and promote material cycle.
		Triangle shell mussel	*Hyriopsis cumingii (Lea)*	
		Dugong	*Dugong dugon*	

ANIMALS	TYPE	COMMON NAME	LATIN NAME	FUNCTION IN SHANGHAI HOUTAN PARK
AQUATIC ANIMAL RESOURCES (continued)	Benthos	Asian clam	*Corbicula fluminea*	Most of these kinds of animals fix themselves on the rock surface or bury themselves in sand; some attach themselves to plants or other benthos. By consuming organic matter, they make the water body clean and promote material cycle.
		Caridina	*Caridinanilotica-gracilipesDeMan*	
		Big-ear radix	*Radix auricularia*	
		Tubificid worm	*Branchiura sowerbyi Beddard*	
		Oligochaetes	*Limnodrilus hoffmeisteri Claparède*	
		Limnodilus claparedianu	*Limnodilus claparedianu*	
		Sludge worm/sewage worm	*Tubifex tubifex*	
		Limnodrilus grandisetosus Nomura	*Limnodrilus grandisetosus Nomura*	
		Nais communis	*Nais communis Piguet*	
		Aulodrilus Bretscher	*Aulodrilus Bretscher*	
		Chinese mitten crab	*Eriocheir sinensis H.Milne-Edwards*	
		Chironomids/ non-biting midges	*Chironomidae*	
		Chironomids	*Propsilocerus akamusi*	
		Bellamya aeruginosa Reeve	*Bellamya aeruginosa Reeve*	
		Stenothyra glabra	*Stenothyra glabra*	
		Purufossarulu striatulu	*Purufossarulu striatulu.*	
		Alocinma longicornis	*Alocinma longicornis*	
		Radix swinhoei	*Radix swinhoei (H. Adams)*	
		Trumpet snail	*Planorbidae;trumpet snail*	
	Fishes	Tilver carp	*Hypophthalmichthys molitrix*	Most of these are primary consumers in the aquatic ecosystem. By consuming organic debris of plants and animals, they keep an ecological balance and promote biodiversity.
		Bighead carp	*Aristichthys nobilis*	
		Mandarin Fish	*Siniperca spp*	
		Culter alburnus	*Culter alburnus*	
		Black carp	*Mylopharyngodon Peters Mylopharyngodon Piceus*	
		Grass carp	*Ctenopharyngodon idellus*	
		Suckermouth catfish	*Hypostomus plecostomus*	
		Spotted steed	*Hemibarbus maculatus Bleeker*	
		Smallscale yellowfin	*Plagiognathops microlepis*	
		Megalobrama skolkovii	*Megalobrama skolkovii*	
		Chinese high fin banded shark	*Myxocyprinus asiaticus*	
		Yellowhead catfish	*Pelteobagrus fulvidraco*	
		Dojo Loach	*Oriental weatherfish*	
		Mosquitofish	*Gambusia affinis*	

ANIMALS AQUATIC ANIMAL RESOURCES (continued)	TYPE		COMMON NAME	LATIN NAME	FUNCTION IN SHANGHAI HOUTAN PARK
	Fishes		Common carp	*Cyprinus carpio*	Most of these are primary consumers in the aquatic eco-system. By consuming organic debris of plants and animals, they keep an ecological balance and promote biodiversity.
			Koi Carp/gold fish	*Carassius auratus*	
			Ophicephalus argus	*Ophicephalus argus*	

ANIMALS BIRD RESOURCES	TYPE		COMMON NAME	LATIN NAME	FUNCTION IN SHANGHAI HOUTAN PARK
	Birds	Waterfowl	Little Grebe	*Trachybaptus ruficollis*	By consuming organic debris of plants and animals, they keep an ecological balance and promote biodiversity.
			Mallard	*Anas platyrhynchos*	
			Common Gallinule	*Gallinula chloropus*	
			Bar-tailed Godwit	*Limosa lapponica*	
		Wading birds	Striated Heron	*Butorides striatus*	
			Great Blue Heron	*Ardea herodias*	
			Grey Heron	*Ardea cinerea*	
			Great Knot	*Calidris tenuirostris*	
			White-breasted Waterhen	*Amaurornis phoenicurus*	
			Black-crowned Night Heron	*Nycticorax nycticorax*	
			Water Rail	*Rallus aquaticus*	
		Others	Hill pigeon	*Columba rupestris*	
			Great Tit	*Parus major*	
			Kingfishers	*Alcedo ; kingfishers*	
			Zitting Cisticola	*Cisticola juncidis*	
			Shrike	*shrike*	
			Long-tailed Shrike	*Lanius schach*	
			White Wagtail	*Motacilla alba*	
			Passer montanus	*Passer montanus*	

ANIMALS INSECT RESOURCES	TYPE		COMMON NAME	LATIN NAME	FUNCTION IN SHANGHAI HOUTAN PARK
	Insect		Longhorn beetle	*Cerambycidae*	They help form a complete food chain. By consuming organic debris of plants and animals, they keep an ecological balance and promote biodiversity.
			Cryptotympana atrata	*Cryptotympana atrata*	
			Aspongopus chinensis Dallas	*Aspongopus chinensis Dallas.*	
			Mantis	*Mantidea Mantodea*	
			Scarabaeidae	*Scarabeidae*	
			Campsosternus gemma	*Campsosternus gemma Candeze*	
			Migratory locust	*Locusta migratoria manilensis (Meyen)*	
			Katydid/bush-crickets	*Tettigoniidae*	
			Cricket	*Gryllidae*	

ANIMALS	TYPE	COMMON NAME	LATIN NAME	FUNCTION IN SHANGHAI HOUTAN PARK
INSECT RESOURCES *(continued)*	Insect	Locust	*locust , grasshopper*	They help form a complete food chain. By consuming organic debris of plants and animals, they keep an ecological balance and promote biodiversity.
		Atractomorpha sinensis	*Atractomorpha sinensis*	
		Gesonula punctifrons	*Gesonula punctifrons*	
		Oxya chinesis	*Oxya chinesis*	
		Oxya chinensis	*Oxya chinensis*	
		Sogatella furcifera	*Sogatella furcifera*	
		European corn borer	*Pyrausta nubilalis (Hubern)*	
		Trichogrammatidae	*trichogrammatid*	
		Beet armyworm	*Spodoptera exigua Hübner*	
		Western honey bee	*Apis mellifera*	
		Drosophila melanogaster	*Drosophila melanogaster*	
		Culex	*Culex*	
		Asian tiger mosquito	*Aedes albopictus*	
		Dark Sword-grass	*Agrotis ypsilon*	
		Anopheles sinensis	*Anopheles sinensis*	
		Tryporyza incertulas	*Tryporyza incertulas (walker)*	
		Aeschna melanictera	*Aeschna melanictera*	
		Scarlet Skimmer	*Crocothemis servilia*	
		Lilacbush	*delgoidea*	
		Greenhouse whitefly	*Trialeurodes vaporariorum (Westwood)*	

ANIMALS	TYPE		COMMON NAME	LATIN NAME	FUNCTION IN SHANGHAI HOUTAN PARK
OTHER ANIMAL RESOURCES	Amphibians		Eastern golden frog	*Rana plancyi*	By consuming organic debris of plants and animals, they keep an ecological balance and promote biodiversity.
			Common toad	*Bufo bufo*	
	Reptiles	Water and land	Chinese Pond Turtle	*C. reevesii*	
			Asiatic Soft Shelled Turtle	*Trionyx Sinensis*	
			Chinese Stripe-necked Turtle	*Ocadia sinensis*	
		Land	Formosan Chinese skink	*Eumeces chinensis*	They help form a complete food chain. By consuming organic debris of plants and animals, they keep an ecological balance and promote biodiversity.
			Japonicus	*Japonicus*	
			Hokouensis	*Hokouensis*	
			Indian Forest Skink	*Sphenomorphus indicus*	
			Ground skinks	*Scincella modesta*	
	Mammalian		Reed Vole	*Microtus fortis*	By consuming organic debris of plants and animals, they keep an ecological balance and promote biodiversity.
			Vesper bats	*Vespertilionidae*	
	Arthropod		Wolf spiders	*Lycosidae*	
			Water spider/Diving bell spider	*Argyroneta aquatica*	
			Tetranychus cinnabarinus	*Tetranychus cinnabarinus*	

Notes

1   Jiang Gaoming and Liu Meizhen, "Sand Storm," *China Environment and Development Review* 2 (2004): 310–22; and Zhao Jingxing, Huang Ping, Yang Chaofei, and Guo Xiaomin, "Situation of China's Environment and Development," *China Environment and Development Review* 2 (2004): 23–50.

2   Chen Kelin, Lu Yong, and Zhang Xiaohong, "No Water Without Wetland," *China Environment and Development Review* 2 (2004): 296–309.

3   "China's Total Mileage of Expressways Open to Traffic Reached 65,000 Kilometers," *SourceJuice*, January 15, 2010, http://www.sourcejuice.com/1295980/2010/01/15/China-total-mileage-expressways-open-traffic-reached-65-000.

4   Zhou Jianping, Yang Zeyan, and Chen Guanfu, "Discussion on Construction and Type Selection of China High Dams," *Engineering Sciences* 7, no. 2 (2009): 35–40, 71.

5   Young-Seuk Park, Jianbo Chang, Sovan Lek, Wenxuan Cao, and Sebastien Brosse, "Conservation Strategies for Endemic Fish Species Threatened by the Three Gorges Dam," *Conservation Biology* 17, no. 6 (December 2003): 1748–58.

6   Richard T. T. Forman and Sharon K. Collinge, "Nature Conserved in Changing Landscapes with and without Spatial Planning," *Landscape and Urban Planning* 37, nos. 1–2 (June 1997): 129–35.

7   Evelyn Lip, *Chinese Geomancy* (Singapore: Times Books International, 1979); Stephen Skinner, *The Living Earth Manual of Feng-Shui: Chinese Geomancy* (London and Boston: Routledge and Kegan Paul, 1982); and Kongjian Yu, "Landscape into Places: Feng-Shui Model of Place Making and Some Cross-Cultural Comparisons," in *CELA 94: History and Culture; Conference Proceedings, Council of Educators in Landscape Architecture Annual Conference*, ed. J. D. Clark (Washington, D.C.: Landscape Architecture Foundation/Council of Educators in Landscape Architecture, 1994), 320–40.

8   Yu, "Landscape into Places," 322.

9   Jan Decher and Luri Kanton Bahian, "Diversity and Structure of Terrestrial Small Mammal Communities in Different Vegetation Types on the Accra Plains of Ghana," *Journal of Zoology* 247, no. 3 (March 1999): 395–408; S. Alemmeren Jamir and H. N. Pandey, "Vascular Plant Diversity in the Sacred Groves of Jaintia Hills in Northeast India," *Biodiversity and Conservation* 12, no. 7 (July 2003): 1497–510; Michael O'Neal Campbell, "Sacred Groves for Forest Conservation in Ghana's Coastal Savannas: Assessing Ecological and Social Dimensions," *Singapore Journal of Tropical Geography* 26, no. 2 (July 2005): 151–69; M. L. Khan and R. S. Tripathi, "Sacred Groves of Manipur, Northeast India: Biodiversity Value, Status, and Strategies for Their Conservation," *Biodiversity and Conservation* 14, no. 7 (June 2005): 1541–82; Jan Salick, Anthony Amend, Danica Anderson, Kurt Hoffmeister, Bee Gunn, and Fang Zhendong, "Tibetan Sacred Sites Conserve Old Growth Trees and Cover in the Eastern Himalayas," *Biodiversity and Conservation* 16, no. 3 (March 2007): 693–706; Shrinidhi Ambinakudige and B. N. Sathish, "Comparing Tree Diversity and Composition in Coffee Farms and Sacred Forests in the Western Ghats of India," *Biodiversity and Conservation* 18, no. 4 (April 2009): 987–1000; and Kristian Metcalfe, Richard Ffrench-Constant, and Ian Gordon, "Sacred Sites as Hotspots for Biodiversity: The Three Sisters Cave Complex in Coastal Kenya," *Oryx* 44, no. 1 (2010): 118–23.

10   Ervin H. Zube, "The Advance of Ecology," *Landscape Architecture* 76, no. 2 (1986): 58–67; Ervin H. Zube, "Greenways and the US National Park System," *Landscape and Urban Planning* 33, nos. 1–3 (October 1995): 17–25; Charles E. Little, *Greenways for America* (Baltimore: Johns Hopkins University Press, 1990); Jack Ahern, "Greenways as Strategic Landscape Planning: Theory and Application" (PhD diss., Wageningen Universiteit, 2002); and Julius G. Fabos, "Greenway Planning in the United States: Its Origins and Recent Case Studies," *Landscape and Urban Planning* 68, nos. 2–3 (2004): 321–42.

11   Ahern, "Greenways as Strategic Landscape Planning," 131–55; and Fabos, "Greenway Planning in the United States," 321–42.

12   Edward O. Wilson, *The Diversity of Life* (Cambridge, Mass.: Belknap Press of Harvard University Press, 1992), 317.

13   Klas Kerkstra and Peter Vrijlandt, "Landscape Planning for Industrial Agriculture: A Proposed Framework for Rural Areas," *Landscape and Urban Planning* 18, nos. 3–4 (February 1990): 275–87.

14   N. T. Bischoff and R. H. Jongman, *Development of Rural Areas in Europe: The Claim for Nature* (The Hague: Netherlands Scientific Council for Government Policy, 1993).

15   Jack Ahern, "Planning for an Extensive Open Space System: Linking Landscape Structure and Function," *Landscape and Urban Planning* 21, nos. 1–2 (September 1991): 131–45.

16   Reed F. Noss and Larry D. Harris, "Nodes, Networks, and MUMs: Preserving Diversity at All Scales," *Environmental Management* 10, no. 3 (May 1986): 299–309.

17   Robert Costanza and Herman E. Daly, "Natural Capital and Sustainable Development," *Conservation Biology* 6, no. 1 (March 1992): 37–46; Robert Costanza, Ralph d'Arge, Rudolf de Groot, Stephen Farber, Monica Grasso, and Bruce Hannon et al., "The Value of the World's Ecosystem Services and Natural Capital," *Nature* 387 (1997): 253–60; Gretchen C. Daily, *Nature's Services: Societal Dependence on Natural Ecosystems* (Washington, D.C.: Island Press, 1997); and Carlos Corvalan, Simon Hales, and Anthony McMichael, *Ecosystems and Human Well-Being: Health Synthesis* (Geneva: World Health Organization, 2005).

18   Kongjian Yu, "Security Patterns in Landscape Planning: With a Case in South China" (DDes diss., Harvard University, 1995); and Kongjian Yu, "Security Patterns and Surface Model in Landscape Ecological Planning," *Landscape and Urban Planning* 36, no. 1 (October 1996): 1–17.

19   Yu, "Security Patterns and Surface Model in Landscape Ecological Planning," 1–17.

20   *State of World Population 2011* (New York: United Nations Fund for Population Activities, 2011), 5.

21   Kongjian Yu, Li Hai-Long, Li Di-Hua, Qiao Qing, and Xi Xue-Song, "Primary Study of National Scale Ecological Security Pattern," *Acta Ecologica Sinica* 29, no. 10 (2009): 5163–75.

22   Ibid.

23   Kongjian Yu, Wang Si-Si, Li Di-Hua, and Li Chun-Bo, "The Function of Ecological Security Patterns as an Urban Growth Framework in Beijing," *Acta Ecologica Sinica* 29, no. 3 (2009): 1189–204; and Kongjian Yu, Wang Si-Si, Qiao Qing, and Li Di-Hua, "The Minimum Ecological Security Pattern for Beijing's Urban Sprawl: Basic Ecosystems Services and Their Security Patterns," *City Planning Review* 2 (2010): 19–24.

24   Kongjian Yu and Mary G. Padua, "China's Cosmetic Cities: Urban Fever and Superficiality," *Landscape Research* 32, no. 2 (April 2007): 255–72.

Contributors

John Beardsley

John Beardsley is director of Garden and Landscape Studies at Dumbarton Oaks and adjunct professor in the Department of Landscape Architecture at the Harvard University Graduate School of Design (GSD). He has written extensively on public and environmental art, including the books *Earthworks and Beyond: Contemporary Art in the Landscape* (4th ed., 2006) and *Gardens of Revelation: Environments by Visionary Artists* (1995). Most recently, he edited *Landscape Body Dwelling: Charles Simonds at Dumbarton Oaks* (2011), for which he also contributed the essay, "Charles Simonds: The Dumbarton Oaks Project." He has organized exhibitions for numerous museums, including the Hirshhorn Museum and Sculpture Garden and the Corcoran Gallery of Art in Washington, D.C., and the Museum of Fine Arts in Houston. In 1997, he was curator of the visual arts project "Human/Nature: Art and Landscape in Charleston and the Low Country" at the Spoleto Festival USA in Charleston, South Carolina. Over the past decade, he has worked on a series of exhibitions and publications on southern African American folk and vernacular art, including *The Quilts of Gee's Bend* (2002), and on the recent work of the self-taught painter and sculptor Thornton Dial (2005). In 2008, he co-organized the GSD exhibition *Dirty Work: Transforming the Landscape of Nonformal Cities in the Americas.*

B. Deniz Çalış

B. Deniz Çalış is an architect and historian of Ottoman architecture and landscape culture, practicing and teaching in Istanbul, Turkey. She received her architectural diploma from Middle East Technical University (METU) in Ankara in 1995; she completed a master's degree in architecture at the Pratt Institute in Brooklyn, New York, in 1996, and a PhD in architecture at METU in 2004. Çalış has received a fellowship from the Scientific and Technological Research Council of Turkey (1996–98) and grants from the Turkish Academy of Sciences (2008) and the Hamad bin Khalifa Symposium on Islamic Art (2007). She was also a junior fellow at Dumbarton Oaks in Garden and Landscape Studies in 2003–4. She is one of the editors of the website *Middle East Garden Traditions* (www.middleeastgarden.com); her work has also been published in *Topos* and Dumbarton Oaks publications, among others. She is currently writing a book on the deviant landscape culture of Ottoman Sufis from the sixteenth to the eighteenth century. Çalış teaches at Istanbul Bilgi University in the Faculty of Architecture.

Jane Carruthers

Jane Carruthers is a research professor in the Department of History at the University of South Africa and a fellow of the Royal Society of South Africa and Clare Hall, Cambridge. She has held visiting fellowships in Australia and is chair of the academic advisory board of the Rachel Carson Center for Environment and Society at the Ludwig Maximilian

University in Munich. Currently, she is the president of the International Consortium of Environmental History Organizations; she has been president of the Southern African Historical Society. She serves on the editorial boards of numerous academic journals and book series. Carruthers has written a number of books and book chapters as well as more than thirty articles in scholarly journals. Her doctoral thesis, *The Kruger National Park: A Social and Political History* (1995), is a standard reference work. She is engaged in research around the history of biology and national parks, colonial art, and heritage and cartography in southern Africa and Australia, and she has been involved in land restitution claims and land reform.

Alexander J. Felson

Alexander J. Felson is an assistant professor with a joint appointment in the School of Forestry and Environmental Studies and the School of Architecture at Yale University. He is a landscape architect, ecologist, and teacher, with a focus on marketable, research-based design and adaptive management solutions for land systems. His scholarly research and practice bring together ecological research with the built environment and socio-ecological components of the city and countryside. His design practice focuses on urban design, land planning, and infrastructure projects. Through his work, he integrates ecosystem services and applied ecological research with public space and urban design. He has been a principal investigator working with the New York City Department of Parks and Recreation to implement research on the MillionTreesNYC project, specifically a large-scale urban forestry study of carbon accumulation, sustainable management, and biodiversity.

Joshua R. Ginsberg

Joshua R. Ginsberg is senior vice president and deputy chief conservation officer at the Wildlife Conservation Society (WCS) in New York. He spent fifteen years working as a field biologist across east and southern Africa, leading a variety of mammal ecology and conservation projects. As director of the Asia and Pacific program at WCS from 1996 until September 2004, he oversaw one hundred projects in sixteen countries. Ginsberg was also acting director of the WCS Africa program for ten months in 2002 and vice president for conservation operations from 2003 to 2009. He received a BSc from Yale University and an MA and PhD in ecology and evolution from Princeton University. He served as the chairman of the National Oceanic and Atmospheric Administration/National Marine Fisheries Service Hawaiian Monk Seal Recovery Team from 2001 to 2007. Ginsberg has held faculty positions at Oxford University and University College London, and is an adjunct professor at Columbia University, where he teaches conservation biology and international relations of the environment. He is an author of more than fifty reviewed papers and has edited three books on wildlife conservation, ecology, and evolution.

Stuart Green

Stuart Green is a landscape architect and principal of Green & Dale Associates in Melbourne, Australia. He studied biogeography at the University of Manchester, then worked as a landscape planner specializing in urban redevelopment and landscape planning. He completed a postgraduate diploma in landscape architecture at the University of Edinburgh and worked in Ireland, Canada, and Singapore before settling in Australia and forming a practice that has provided specialist skills in the planning and design of parks and zoos for the past twenty years. Green has become a leading design specialist in Australia and Southeast Asia on zoological planning and design, initially in the natural habitat of the Australian bush with the Alice Springs Desert Park, and later in animal conservation in Cambodia with the Cambodia Wildlife Sanctuary. Other projects, such as the Trail of the Elephants and the Orangutan Sanctuary at Melbourne Zoo, are linked to education and conservation programs in Southeast Asia and Indonesia and concentrate on the preservation of natural habitat and wildlife. His work has involved trips to study the habitats of these species and to gain an understanding of the conflicts regarding wildlife management and the increased pressures of population growth.

Steven N. Handel

Steven N. Handel is professor of ecology in the Department of Ecology, Evolution, and Natural Resources at Rutgers, The State University of New Jersey. He studies the potential to restore native communities to many habitats, adding sustainable ecological services, biodiversity, and amenities to the landscape. He has explored pollination, seed dispersal, growth patterns, and most recently, problems of urban and heavily degraded lands. He works with both biologists and landscape designers, trying to improve our understanding of restoration protocols and applying this knowledge to public projects. Handel was an undergraduate at Columbia College and received his MS and PhD in ecology and evolution at Cornell University. Prior to his appointment to Rutgers in 1985, he was a biology professor and director of the Marsh Botanic Gardens at Yale University. Also, since 2006, he has been selected as an adjunct professor of ecology at the University of California at Irvine. In 2012, he was visiting professor at Harvard's Graduate School of Design. He serves as director of the Center for Urban Restoration Ecology at Rutgers, which is dedicated to rebuilding native habitats throughout the region. Handel is an Aldo Leopold Leadership Fellow of the Ecological Society of America; he has been an editor of the journals *Restoration Ecology*, *Evolution*, and *Urban Habitats*. For his scientific achievements, he has been named as a fellow of the American Association for the Advancement of Science, the Australian Institute of Biology, and the Explorers Club. He was elected an honorary member of the American Society of Landscape Architects (ASLA) in 2007 for "achievements of national or international significance or influence." In 2009, he received ASLA Honor Awards for research and for analysis and planning. He has worked on the planning of ecological restoration in major urban areas, including the Fresh Kills Landfill and new Brooklyn Bridge Park in New York City, the Duke Farms 2,700-acre holdings in New Jersey, the landscape for the 2008 Olympic Games in Beijing, and new public parks in Dublin, Ireland, and Orange County, California.

Kristina Hill

Kristina Hill is a scholar, teacher, and consultant who specializes in understanding the ecology of urban regions and developing design strategies to improve urban performance. She is primarily interested in altering water systems in coastal cities to support biodiversity and to address social justice concerns. Her recent work has focused on the influence of climate-change trends on the selection of strategies for urban adaptation. She has consulted and engaged in research on urban water systems internationally, as well as in Seattle, New Orleans, and New York City. She was an editor and author of *Ecology and Design: Frameworks for Learning* (with Bart Johnson, 2002) and has authored numerous articles and book chapters on urban design and ecology. Her current writing project is a book on adaptation of urban water systems. Hill holds a PhD from Harvard University in landscape architecture and ecology, a master's degree in landscape architecture from Harvard's Graduate School of Design, and an undergraduate degree in geology. She has taught as a member of the faculty at the Massachusetts Institute of Technology, the University of Washington, Iowa State University, and the University of Virginia, where she was an associate professor and chair of the Department of Landscape Architecture. She is currently associate professor in the Department of Landscape Architecture and Environmental Planning at the University of California, Berkeley, and a member of the National Academy for Environmental Design Research Committee.

Shepard Krech III

Shepard Krech III was trained as an anthropologist and has conducted ethnography in the North American Arctic among the Gwich'in as well as historical and material cultural research in archives and museums on several continents. In recent years, he has written on the intersections of indigenous people, ecology, and conservation; his publications include *Indigenous Knowledge and the Environment in Africa and North America* (with David Gordon, 2012), *Spirits of the Air: Birds and American Indians in the*

South (2009), *Encyclopedia of World Environmental History* (with Carolyn Merchant and John McNeill, 2004), and *The Ecological Indian: Myth and History* (1999). He is currently emeritus professor of anthropology at Brown University, research associate in anthropology at the National Museum of Natural History, Smithsonian Institution, and trustee of the National Humanities Center.

Shahid Naeem

Shahid Naeem is professor of ecology and chair of the Department of Ecology, Evolution, and Environmental Biology at Columbia University. He is also a fellow of the American Association for the Advancement of Science and an Aldo Leopold Leadership Fellow. His area of expertise is in the ecological consequences of biodiversity loss, and his work has demonstrated how the loss of species affects the functioning and stability of ecosystems. Naeem earned his master's and doctoral degrees from the University of California at Berkeley. He has authored numerous scientific articles, research papers, and textbook chapters on issues in conservation, ecosystem functioning, restoration, and biodiversity. He is also a recent recipient of Columbia University's prestigious Lenfest Prize and a recipient of the Ecological Society of America's George Mercer Award.

Harriet Ritvo

Harriet Ritvo is the Arthur J. Conner Professor of History at the Massachusetts Institute of Technology, where she teaches courses in environmental history, British history, and the history of human-animal relations. She is the past president of the American Society for Environmental History. Her books include *Noble Cows and Hybrid Zebras: Essays on Animals and History* (2010); *The Dawn of Green: Manchester, Thirlmere, and Modern Environmentalism* (2009); *The Platypus and the Mermaid, and Other Figments of the Classifying Imagination* (1997); and *The Animal Estate: The English and Other Creatures in the Victorian Age* (1987).

Michael Van Valkenburgh

Michael Van Valkenburgh is the Charles Eliot Professor in Practice of Landscape Architecture at the Harvard University Graduate School of Design (GSD). He has taught at GSD since 1982; he served as program director from 1987 to 1989 and as department chair from 1991 to 1996. As founding principal of Michael Van Valkenburgh Associates, Inc. (MVVA), with offices in New York City and Cambridge, Massachusetts, Van Valkenburgh has designed a wide range of project types ranging from intimate gardens to full-scale urban design undertakings. Some of his recent projects include Brooklyn Bridge Park in New York City, the Lower Don Lands in Toronto, and the Jefferson National Expansion Memorial (Gateway Arch) in Saint Louis. MVVA has received numerous American Society of Landscape Architects design awards, including the Design Award of Excellence for the Alumnae Valley Restoration in 2006. Van Valkenburgh was the 2003 recipient of the Smithsonian Institution's Cooper-Hewitt National Design Award for Environmental Design, and, in 2010, he became the second landscape architect in history to receive the Arnold W. Brunner Memorial Prize from the American Academy of Arts and Letters for contributions to architecture as an art. Van Valkenburgh received a BS in landscape architecture from Cornell University and an MLA from the University of Illinois at Urbana-Champaign. In 2009, Yale University Press published a book on his work titled *Michael Van Valkenburgh Associates: Reconstructing Urban Landscapes*.

Thomas L. Woltz

Thomas L. Woltz is a principal and co-owner of Nelson Byrd Woltz Landscape Architects (NBW), a thirty-person design practice in Charlottesville, Virginia, and New York City. Woltz holds master's degrees in architecture and landscape architecture from the University of Virginia, where he has taught part-time for fourteen years. NBW has designed a broad array of public and private projects, including botanic gardens and zoos, academic and corporate campuses, and town planning. Woltz recently developed the Conservation Agriculture Studio around a family of projects that employs the sensibilities of contemporary landscape architecture to integrate sustainable agriculture with best management practices for the conservation of wildlife and natural resources.

Kongjian Yu

Kongjian Yu is professor of urban and regional planning and founder and dean of the Graduate School of Landscape Architecture and College of Architecture and Landscape Architecture at Peking University. He received his doctor of design degree at the Harvard University Graduate School of Design in 1995. Yu is the founder and president of Turenscape, one of the first and largest private architecture and landscape architecture firms in China. His practice includes the planning and design of landscapes and urban developments in major cities, including Beijing, Shanghai, and Tianjin. Yu's projects have received numerous awards, including two American Society of Landscape Architects (ASLA) Excellence awards and seven Honor, Design,

and Planning awards as well as many international design competition prizes. His projects have been featured in leading journals, such as *The Architectural Review, Journal of Landscape Architecture*, and *Topos*. Professor Yu has been the keynote speaker for four International Federation of Landscape Architects world congresses and two ASLA annual conferences, has been invited to lecture and design critique at more than thirty universities worldwide, and has seved as visiting professor of landscape architecture and urban planning and design at the Graduate School of Design. His recent titles include *Back to the Land* (2009), *The Art of Survival: Recovering Landscape Architecture* (2006), and *Negative Planning* (2005). He is the chief editor of *Landscape Architecture China* (published in Chinese and English), and a member of the editorial board for the *Journal of Landscape Architecture* and *Landscape and Urban Planning*. He serves as a member of several expert committees for the ministries of Housing, Rural and Urban Construction, Culture and Land Resources of China, and for the city of Beijing.

Index

Page numbers in *italics* indicate illustrative materials.

buffalo, African, 119

Buglé people, 97

Busbecq, Ogier Ghislain de, 36, 38, 41, 42, 43, 44–45n20

bushmeat. *See* birds and indigenous people in neotropical forests

Byron, George Gordon, Lord, 17

Çalış, B. Deniz, 6, 29–46, 273

Cambodia Wildlife Sanctuary (cws), 7, 142–51; agriculture and agroforestry issues, 143, 143–44, 144, 152n28; background and design objectives, 131, 142–43; deforestation and reforestation, 143, 143–44, 144, 146, 146–47, 147; design challenges, 143, 148–51; design process, 145, 146–48; economic and social opportunities at, 149; educational programs, 148, 150; funding, 145–46, 149; government involvement at, 145–46, 149; habitat identification at, 144, 146, 146–47, 147; indigenous and local communities and, 143, 144, 148–49, 150; Kulen Promtep Wildlife Sanctuary (kpws) and, 142, 147, 149, 150; location, geology, and natural history, 142; personal safety issues in, 143, 144; scientific research, access to, 150

captivity-scale conservation interventions, 49, 53–54, 54

caribou, 48

Carruthers, Jane, 6, 7, 107–30, 273–74

cats, domestic, 20, 21, 68

cattle, 16, 21–23, 22, 147

Çelebi, Evliya, 41

Center for Urban Restoration Ecology (cure), 217

Central Park, New York City, 115, 229

Central Rock Rat, 142

chachalacas, 96

Chailert, Sangduen "Lek," 146

Chan Chich, Belize, 89–91, 90

cheetahs, 119

Chesneau, Jean, 32

Chillingham herd of white cattle, United Kingdom, 22, 22–23

China, ecological infrastructure in. *See* infrastructure for biodiversity protection, landscape as

Chinese Milkvetch (green clover, *Astragalus sinicus*), 255

Chinook Salmon, 201–2, 219, 220

Church, Thomas, 128n27

cites (Convention on International Trade in Endangered Species of Wild Fauna and Flora), 99

cities. *See* urban areas

classification of species. *See* species

claypans, 135, 137, 137–38

climate change: Anthropocene and, 70, 71; avian habitats adversely affected by, 95; challenge of, 5; human evolution and, 188–89

climate change in cities, 7, 187–205; Antwerp, Natterjack Toad conservation in, 196–97; conservation strategies and, 189–90; dynamic systems, landscape design allowing for, 190–94, 193, 203–4n13; Jodhpur, India, Hanuman Langur conservation in, 195–96, 196; links between climate, cities, and biodiversity, 187–91, 188; London, Biodiversity Action Plan for, 190, 197, 197–99; Pacific Northwest, urban conservation and design in, 194–95, 195, 201–2; spatial pattern and, 189–90, 191–94, 193; species adaptations, 191, 194–95, 202, 204n16; Stockholm, "green wedges" in, 199, 199–201, 200, 201, 202; wildlife corridors and *refugia*, 189–90, 192–94, 193, 196

Clouded Leopard, 148

Clutton-Brock, Juliet, 26

Coho Salmon, 219, 220

Collinson, Roger, 119, 122–23, 124–25

Common Piping Guans, 100

Conan, Michael, 1

concepts of wildness and wilderness, 6, 15–27; aesthetic sensibility, changes in, 19; classification and species concept, 25, 25–26; definition of terms, 20–21; degrees of wildness and domestication in animals, 20–25, 21–24; ecosystems, recognition of, 19–20; garden and landscape design, "wilderness" in, 8–9; hybrid species, 25, 26; large predators, changing human views on, 17–19, 17–20, 21; natural and artificial selection, Darwin's comparison of, 15–17, 16; "natural," "wild," or "pristine" landscapes, lack of, 20, 76, 77–78

Conservation Action Planning process, 51

conservation ecologists and conservation biology, 169, 217, 243

Conservation Wildlife Society Cambodia, 147

Convention on International Trade in Endangered Species of Wild Fauna and Flora (cites), 99

Cook, James, 153

Cook, Robert, 1

coolabah, 137

Coppolillo, Peter B., 59

corkwood (*Hakea suberea*), 133

Corner, James, 222

corridors. *See* fragmented landscapes; wildlife corridors

Costa Rica: Amistad Biosphere Reserve montane forest, 92; neotropical forest in, 92, 94

Cowles, Henry C., 4

coyotes, 188

cracids. *See* birds and indigenous people in neotropical forests

Crested Guan, 92, 95, 97

critical reserve size, 52

Cronon, William, 3, 11n7, 20, 21

Crutzen, Paul, 2

culture and nature, relationship between, 3

curassows. *See* birds and indigenous people in neotropical forests

CURE (Center for Urban Restoration Ecology), 217

cws. *See* Cambodia Wildlife Sanctuary

cypress, 226

Dances with Wolves (film; 1990), 95

Daniel, Samuel, *111*

Darwin, Charles, 6, 16, *16*, 20, 25, 26, 77

Dasmann, Raymond Frederic, 113, 115, 128n31

De Quincey, Thomas, 19, 24

deer, 35, 147

Defoe, Daniel, 19, 24

deforestation and reforestation: Atlantic Forest (Brazil, Paraguay, and Argentina), 92–94, 99; at Cambodia Wildlife Sanctuary (cws), *143*, 143–44, *144*, *146*, 146–47, *147*; of neotropics, 92–94; New York City Afforestation Project (ny-cap), 234–35, *235*; at Orongo Station, New Zealand, 154, *164*; Reduced Emissions from Deforestation and Forest Degradation (redd), 51. *See also* agriculture and agroforestry

degraded landscapes, 75, *76*, 78, 170, 172–77, 216–17

Derby, Earl of, 23

Dernschwam, Hans, 32

Desert Bulldog Ant, 138

Deshayes de Cormenin, Louis, 36

design and ecology. *See* ecology and design, interplay of

Design with Nature (McHarg, 1969), 190–91

"Designed Experiments," 234–35

designer ecosystems, 233–34, *234*

designing wildlife habitats. *See* wildlife habitat design

"The Destruction of Sennacherib" (Byron, 1815), 17

Dickens, Charles, 81

Didier, Karl A., 59

Dingo, 140, 141

Dipterocarpus species, 143

dispersal mutualisms, 173–76, *175*, *176*, 199–200, *200*, 202

dogs, domestic, *16*, 21, 23

dogs, wild, 19, 55–57, *56*, 58, 59, 134

dolphins, 41

domesticated animals: classification and species concept, 26; degrees of wildness and tameness, 20–25, *21–24*; in Edenic landscape or Peaceable Kingdom, 68, *68–69*; hybrid wild/domestic animals, 26; natural and artificial selection, Darwin's comparison of, 15–17, *16*

Downing, John A., 81

Downsview Park, Toronto, 229

Dramstad, Wenche E., 220

du Toit, Johan T., 51

Dumbarton Oaks: aquatic habitat, Ellipse Fountain, *9–10*, *10*; bird survey (2009–2012), 9–10, 12–13; Garden and Landscape Studies at, 1, 9, 10, 65; pool terrace, Beatrix Farrand's drawing for, *10*; "wild garden," *viii*, 8; "wilderness walk," 7–9, *8*; wildlife habitat design at, *viii*, 7–10, *8–10*, 12–13

Dunnart, 139, 140, 141

dynamic systems, landscape design allowing for, 190–94, *193*, 203–4n13, 229

earth, as living system, 241, 242, 256

East London Green Grid, 198

East River Marsh Planter, New York City, *223*

ecological infrastructure. *See* infrastructure for biodiversity protection, landscape as

ecological poverty, 79–83, *80*

ecology and design, interplay of, 7, 215–40; collaboration and dialogue between designers and ecologists, 230–32; conservation ecologists, 217; designer ecosystems, 233–34, *234*; environmental consultants, 220–22, *221*, *223*; expanding design with research, management, and monitoring, 234–35, *235*; at Fresh Kills project, 227–28, *228*, 229; funding sources, 226; landscape designers, role of, 222–26, *223–25*; landscape urbanism, concept of, 228–30, *230*; process-based design, 229; research sites versus design sites, 226; restoration ecologists, 216–17; site evaluation processes of designers versus ecologists, 227; theoretical and applied ecologists, role of, 216–22, *218–22*; translating ecological science into design applications, 232–34, *233*

Ecuador: cracid hunting in, 97, 102; San Isidro forest, *91*; Yasuni National Forest, 97

Edenic landscape, concept of, 67–70, *68*, *69*, 71, 78, 82, 107–8

Edirne, Turkey, 29, 35, 38, 41–43

edsa, *223*

educational programs: Alice Springs Desert Park (asdp), Australia, 140–42, *141*, 149–50; Cambodia Wildlife Sanctuary (cws), 148, 150; as factor in success of design project, 149–50; Pilanesberg National Park, South Africa, 117, 122

eis (environmental impact statements), 227

El Niño, 82, 195

eland, 119

Elephant Nature Park, Thailand, 145–46

elephants, *32*, 35, 36, 37, 51, 119, 120, *123*, 129n58, 147, 148

Eliot, Charles, 243

Ellipse Fountain, Dumbarton Oaks, *9–10*, 10

Emu, 137, 140, 141

endangered and threatened species, 216, 221, *222*, 242; Alice Springs Desert Park (asdp),

Australia, 137, 140, 141, 142; breeding facilities for, 6, 53, 142; at Cambodia Wildlife Sanctuary (CWS), 148; captivity-scale interventions for, 54; Convention on International Trade in Endangered Species of Wild Fauna and Flora (CITES), 99; establishment of first national parks to protect, *19*; Federal Endangered Species Act, 194, 201, 231; indigenous peoples consuming (*See* birds and indigenous people in neotropical forests); IUCN Red List, 48, 91; in metapopulations, 54; in neotropical forests, 91, 96, 99, 103; at Orongo Station, New Zealand, 154; wildness and wilderness, concepts of, *19, 26*

England. *See* United Kingdom

environmental consultants, 220–22, *221, 223*

environmental impact statements (EIS), 227

eucalyptus, 93, 121, 133, 139, 226

Eurasian Jay, 199–200, *200, 202*

extensive breeding facilities, 54, 55

exurban development, scale, and conservation interventions, 49–50, *50*

falcons, 21, 36

farming. *See* agriculture and agroforestry

Farrand, Beatrix, 7–9, *10*

Farrell & Van Riet, 114, 115, 117

Felson, Alexander J., 2, 7, 215–40, 274

feng shui or geomancy, 241, 242

ferrets, 21

Field, Erastus Salisbury, *68*

Field Operations, 227, 229

finances. *See* funding

Firdevsi, Uzun, 44n10

Fishing Cat, 148

Fluttering Shearwaters, 154, *159*

foot-and-mouth disease outbreak, Britain (2001), 24–25

Foreclosed: Rehousing the American Dream (Museum of Modern Art exhibition; 2012), 217, *218*

forestry. *See* agriculture and agroforestry; deforestation and reforestation

Forman, Richard T. T., 190, 203n8, 220

Fossil Rim Wildlife Center, 54

fragmented landscapes: hypar-nature bridging system, 207–8, *209–13*; neotropical forest fragments, landscape design to link, 93, *94*; scale issues in conservation efforts, 49, 54–55. *See also* urban areas; wildlife corridors

Fresh Kills project, Staten Island, New York, 173–76, *174, 175*, 227–28, *228, 229*

Fresne-Canaye, Philip du, 32

From Bauhaus to Ecohouse (Anker, 2010), 116

funding: Alice Springs Desert Park (ASDP), Australia, 134, 149; Cambodia Wildlife Sanctuary (CWS), 145–46, 149; ecology and design, interplay of, 226

Fusco Engineering, 180

Galdikas, Birute M. F., 82

Gallon Jug estate, Belize, 89–91

Garden and Landscape Studies at Dumbarton Oaks, 1, 9, 10, 65

The Garden of Earthly Delights (painting; Bosch, ca. 1480–1505), 68

The Garden of Eden (painting; Field, ca. 1860), *68*

The Gardens of Eden (Graham, 1973), 108

gaur, 147, 148

gazelles, *33, 35*

gemsbok, 119

geomancy or feng shui, 241, 242

George III (king of England), 23

Gerlach, Stephan, 41

ghost gum *(Eucalyptus papuana)*, 133, *136, 137*

giant gaur, 147, 148

Ginsberg, Joshua R., 6–7, 47–64, 274

giraffes, 19, 32, 119

global warming. *See* climate change; climate change in cities

Gold Fields Foundation, 122

golden rapeseed *(Brassica capestris)*, 255

Goodman, Peter, 119

Gorongosa National Park, Mozambique, 115

Gowanus Canal "Oyster-tecture" project, New York City harbor, *233*, 233–34

Graham, Alistair, 108

Gran Chaco, Bolivia, 102

gray wolf, 26

great apes, 19

Great Britain. *See* United Kingdom

Great Curassow, 91, 92, 95, 97, 100, *101*

Great Park, Irvine, California, 179–83, *180–82*, 224

Great Tinamou, 89, *90*, 91, 95, 97

green clover (Chinese Milkvetch, *Astragalus sinicus*), 255

Green & Dale Associates, 132, 142, 151n24

Green Shield Ecology, 180

Green, Stuart, 7, 131–52, 274

greenways and greenbelts, 241, 242–43

Grevillea species, 139

Grey-faced Petrel, 154, *159*

Grey-winged Trumpeter, 102

guans, *92*, 95, 96, 97, 99, 100, 102

Gussett, Markus, 57

gypsum pans, 137–38

Habitat Conservation Planning (HCP), 231

habitat design. *See* wildlife habitat design

Hall, Marcus, 4

Halprin, Lawrence, 2

Hammarby-Sjöstad, Stockholm, redevelopment of, 200–1, *201*

Hancock, Peter, 122

Handel, Steven N., 7, 55, 169–86, 217, 225–26, 227, 275

Hanuman Langur, 195–96, *196*

Hargreaves, George, 2

hartebeest, 119, 121

hawks, 36, 141

HCP (Habitat Conservation Planning), 231

Heller, Nicole E., 192

Herdwick sheep, *24*, 24–25

herons, 179

Hicks, Edward, *69*

highways. *See* roads and highways

Hill, Kristina, 7, 187–205, 275

Hippodrome, Istanbul, 32, 33, *37, 38*

hippopotamuses, 20, 119

Hluhluwe-Umfolozi Park, KwaZulu Natal, South Africa, 56

HNTB Engineering, 207–13

Hoberdanacz, Johann, 35

Horouta Canoue, 153

horseshoe crabs, 95

Hoti people, 96

Houck, Oliver A., 82

Houtan Park, Shanghai, 250–56; animal species, 256, *265–69*; challenges of site, 252, *253*; design concept and strategy, 252–56, *254*; maps of existing site and site plan, *253, 254*; pictures of recovered landscape, *255–59*; plant species, 255, 256, *260–65*

Howell, Steve N. G., *91*

Huaoroni people, 97, 102

Humboldt, Alexander von, 78

Hunt, John Dixon, 1

hunting: of birds by indigenous peoples (*See* birds and indigenous people in neotropical forests); Ottoman hunting preserves and expeditions, *35*, 36, *39, 40,* 41–43, *42,* 45n32; in Pilanesberg National Park, South Africa, 117, 122, *123*; threats and scale in conservation interventions, *50*

Huntley, Brian, 115

Hyacinth Macaw, *98, 99*

hybrid species, *25*, 26

hybrid wild/domestic animals, 26

hyenas, 33

hypar-nature bridging system, 207–8, *209–13*

ibis, 147

Ibn 'Arabî, 40–41, 45n38

impala, 119

India: Jodhpur, Hanuman Langur conservation in, 195–96, *196*; Kumbhalgarh Wildlife Sanctuary, Rajasthan, 195, *196*; Malenad-Mysore Tiger Landscape, Karnataka, 57, *58*; Nagarahole-Bandipur National Parks, 57–58; tigers in Western Ghats of, 57–59, *59*

indigenous people: Alice Springs Desert Park (ASDP), Australia, and, 133, *134, 135,* 140, 142, 148, 149, 150; Cambodia Wildlife Sanctuary (CWS) and, 143, *144,* 148–49, 150; as factor in design success, 131, 148–49, 150, 151; Orongo Station, New Zealand, historical and cultural significance of, 153, 154. *See also* birds and indigenous people in neotropical forests; Pilanesberg National Park, South Africa; *specific peoples*

infrastructure for biodiversity protection, landscape as, 7, 241–71; Chinese National Ecological Security Pattern Program, 246, *247*; definition of ecological infrastructure, 243; earth viewed as living system and, 241, 242, 256; historical models of, 241, 242–43; integrating security patterns of individual processes, 250, *251*; landscape security patterns, *244,* 245, 248–50, *251*; process-oriented nature of, 243–45; scale in, *244,* 245–46; urban development planning for Beijing, 246–50, *249, 251. See also* Houtan Park, Shanghai

Inner Mongolian grasslands, 81

International Union for Conservation of Nature (IUCN): Red List, 48, 91; World Conservation Strategy of 1980, 124

invasive species, 183–84, 191, 194, 204n16, 217

ironwood *(Acacia estrophiolata),* 132–33, 136

Issaquah Salmon Hatchery, Washington State, 218–19

Istanbul. *See* Ottoman gardens and landscapes

IUCN. *See* International Union for Conservation of Nature

Ivory-billed Woodpecker, 79

Izoceño-Guarani people, 102

Jacutinga, 99

Jefferson, Thomas, 9

Jensen, Jens, 4

Jodhpur, India, Hanuman Langur conservation in, 195–96, *196*

jointed cactus *(Opuntia* species), 121

Jones and Jones, 222–23

Jordan, William, III, 3

The Jungle Book (Kipling, 1894), 19

Kaxinawá people, 102

Mexico: Palenque, neotropical forest birds of, 92; Sian Ka'an Biosphere Reserve, 91, 92

Meyer, Stephenie, 81

Mia Lehrer + Associates, 180

Michael Van Valkenburgh Associates, 2, 7, 177, 207, 276

microhabitats, *182, 183*

Migge, Leberecht, 2

Millennium Ecosystem Assessment, 74, 83–84, *84*

MillionTreesNYC, 234

Minneapolis parkway system, 243

Miquelle, Dale G., 59

Mlilwane nature reserve, Mbabane, Swaziland, 120

Moll, Eugene, 115

monkeys, 147, 195–96, *196*

Monterey Pine, 226

Monticello, 9

Mossman, Archie S., 113, 119

mouflons, 24, 26

Mount Vernon, 9

mugwort *(Artemisia vulgaris)*, 172

mulga *(Acacia aneura)*, *133*, 136, 141

Mulga Parrot, 140

Mulgara, 140

muntjacs, 148

Murad III (Ottoman sultan), 36, 37, 42

Museum of Modern Art exhibitions, 217, *218*, 233, 233–34

mutualisms, 173–76, *175*, *176*, 199–200, *200*, 202

The Myth of Wild Africa (Adams and McShane, 1996), 108

Mzilikazi, 111

Naeem, Shahid, 6, 7, 65–87, 276

Nagarahole-Bandipur National Parks, India, 57–58

Nail-tail Wallaby, 138

Nakkaşhane, 33

National Audubon Society, 4

National Park Service, 8

National Parks Board of Trustees, South Africa, 113, 115, 116, 120, 124, 128n30

National Wildlife Federation, 4

native people. *See* indigenous people

native species, concept of, 191

Natterjack Toad, 196–97

natural fragments. *See* fragmented landscapes

natural selection, 15–17, 25, 26, 176

Nature Conservancy, 51, 226

NBW (Nelson Byrd Woltz Landscape Architects), 7, 153

Nekola, Jeffrey C., 80

Nelson Byrd Woltz Landscape Architects (NBW), 7, 153–67

neotropical forests. *See* birds and indigenous people in neotropical forests

nestedness, concept of, 51–52

"new native" species or neophytes, 194, 202

New York City: Botanical Gardens, 55; Bronx Park, 55; Bronx Zoo, 53, *54*, 55; Brooklyn Bridge Park, *177*, 177–79, *178*, 181; Central Park, 115, 229; East River Marsh Planter, *223*; Fresh Kills project, Staten Island, 173–76, *174*, *175*, 227–28, *228*, 229; MillionTreesNYC, 234; "Oyster-tecture" project, Gowanus Canal, *233*, 233–34; urban-rural gradient studies, New York City–Connecticut, *230*

New York City Afforestation Project (NY-CAP), 234–35, *235*

New Zealand: Maori people, 95, 153, 154. *See also* Orongo Station, New Zealand

Ngai Tamanuhiri people, 154

Ngöbe people, 97

Nigari, *30, 31*

Nolen, John, 4

nonplanted species in restored spaces, proliferation of, 172, 174, *175*, 256, *260–69*

Northern Helmeted Curassow, 96, 97

oak decline in Europe, 199–200, *200*, 202

"observer intrusion," 47, *48*

Ocellated Turkey, 91, 96, 100, *101*

oil palm plantations, 93

Olmsted, Frederick Law, 2, 3, 115, 128n27, 190, 243

Olson, James D., *220*

On the Origin of Species (Darwin, 1859), 15, 20

Orange County Great Park, Irvine, California, 179–83, *180–82*, *224*, 225–26

Orongo Station, New Zealand, 7, 153–67; agriculture and reforestation, 154–55, *158*, *164*; historic house and gardens, 155, *167*; historical and cultural significance, 153, 154, *164*; Maraetaha River and floodplain, 154, *165*, *166*; master plan, 153–55, *155–59*, *161*, *164*, *165*; pest control and excluder fence at, 153–54, *160*, *161*; roads, realignment of, 154, *161*, *164*; tuatara and Tuatara Preserve, 154, *159*; wetlands, 154, *158*, *159*, *161–63*

Osman II (Ottoman sultan), 36

osprey (sea hawks), *195*

ostriches, 35

Ottoman gardens and landscapes, 6, 29–46; concepts of wildness and wilderness, 29–30, *30*; flora, cultivated and wild, 35; hunting preserves and expeditions, *35*, *36*, *39*, *40*, 41–43, *42*, 45n32; menageries, 29, *31–35*, 31–36, 46n55; parades and processions, 37, 37–38, 42–43; Paradise Gardens, 30, *31*, 43; sultan, body of, 29–30, *30*, *31*, 39–41, 43, 44n2; *tashbîh* and *tanzîh*, 40–41; Topkapı Palace and gardens, Istanbul, 31, 33–35, 41, 42; urban culture, wild animals as part of, *31*, 36, 37, 37–38; wildlife observations, 41 owls, 36, 141

"Oyster-tecture" project, Gowanus Canal, New York City harbor, *233*, 233–34

Pacaya-Samiria National Reserve, Peru, 100

Pacific Northwest, salmon conservation and urban design in, 194–95, *195*, 201–2, 219–20

Pale-billed Woodpecker, 89, *90*

Palenque, Mexico, neotropical forest birds of, 92

Panama, cracid hunting in, 97–98, 100

Paradise Gardens, Ottoman, 30, *31*, 43. *See also* Ottoman gardens and landscapes

Paraguay: Atlantic Forest, 92–94, 99; cracids and cracid hunting in, 92, 98; Mbaracayú Reserve, 98

parakeets, 99

"Pardisan," 128n29

Pareto, Vilfredo, and Pareto law, 80

parrots, 97, 99, 140

PAWS (Performing Animal Welfare Society), 146

Peaceable Kingdom (painting; Hicks, 1834), *69*, 70

Peaceable Kingdom, concept of, *69*, 70, 71, 82

Peking University Graduate School of Landscape Architecture, 246

Pemon people, 96

Perentie, 138

Performing Animal Welfare Society (PAWS), 146

Peru: cracid hunting in, 100, 101, 102; Pacaya-Samiria National Reserve, 100; Reserva Comunal Tamshiyacu-Tahuayo, 102

pest control at Orongo Station, New Zealand, 153–54, *160*, *161*

Phillips, John, 115, 116–17

philosophical issues of wildlife habitat design, 5–6

pigs, 22

Pilane, Tidimane, 112, 118, 119, 124, 125

Pilanesberg National Park, South Africa, 6, 7, 107–30; Agricor (Agricultural Development Corporation of Bophuthatswana), 113–14, 119, 121, 122; biodiversity at, 124; Bophuthatswana and, 107, 112–13, 115, 119–20, 122, 124, 125, 127n13; current management philosophy, objectives, and style (since 1994), 125; development and landscape design plans (1970s), 113–18, *114*, *117*; displacement or discounting of indigenous and local peoples by parks, 107–8, 115, 118; educational programs, 117, 122; first five years (1978–1983), 118–23, *120–23*; hunting in, 117, 122, 123; location, geology, and natural history, 108–10, *109–10*; "Operation Genesis" (movement of animals into park), 119–23, *120*; political history of area, 110–13, *111*, *112*; precolonial abundance of wildlife in area, 110; revision of original plans (1983–1984), 123–25; role of indigenous and

local people in, 7, 115–16, 118, 119, 123, 124–25; Sun City complex, 113, *114*, 116, 119, 122; zoning of, 116, *117*, 124

Pim, Joane, 114

Pinchot, Gifford, 3

Pocahontas (film; 1995), 95

Poiani, Karen A., 51

political economy of wildlife habitat design, 6, 110–13

pollination mutualisms, 176

pollution, scale, and conservation interventions, 49, *50*

population persistence and scale, 53–54

Portland, Oregon, urban conservation and design in, 190, 194–95

Prairie Club, 4

prairies, restored versus unrestored, 79–80

Presidio Fort Scott Creek and Historic Garden, San Francisco, 225, 226, 229

Preston, Frank W., 80

Priestly, Joseph, 72, *73*

process-based design, 229

psittacines, 99

Pygmy Goanna, 138

Qi, 242

Quichua people, 97

Rahbek, Carsten, 47

Rahmî, 30

rainbowfish, 138

Rálamb, Claes Brorson, 42, 46n50

Rálamb paintings, 46n50

rarity of most species (ecological poverty), 79–81, *80*

Razor-billed Curassows, 100

red gum, 137

red hartebeest, 121

Red Kangaroo, 137, *139*, 140, 141

Red Knots, 95

Red-tailed Phascogale, 142

red wolf, 26

REDD (Reduced Emissions from Deforestation and Forest Degradation), 51

Redford, Kent H., 50

Reduced Emissions from Deforestation and Forest Degradation (REDD), 51

Reflections of Eden: My Years with the Orangutans of Borneo (Galdikas, 1996), 82

reforestation. *See* deforestation and reforestation

refugia, 192–94, *193*, 196

regional-scale conservation interventions, 49, 59

Rehmann, Elsa, 4

23; national parks and land management in, 115; Zoological Society of London, 23

United States: national parks and land management in, 115; repatriation of African elephants from, 119, 129n58. *See also specific sites*

University of Wisconsin Arboretum, 4

unmanaged or "natural" landscapes, *75, 76, 77–78, 82*

urban areas: constraints of, 183–84; ecological infrastructure and urban development planning for Beijing, 246–50, *249, 251*; landscape urbanism, concept of, 228–30, *230*; Ottoman empire, wildlife as part of urban culture in, *31, 36, 37, 37–38*; translating ecological science into design applications in, 232–34. *See also* climate change in cities; restoration ecology in urban areas

Urban Ecology and Design Laboratory (UEDLAB), Yale University, *218, 221, 222, 232*

urban-rural gradient studies, New York City–Connecticut, *230*

Van Riet, Willem, 114–16, 118, 124, 128n35

Van Valkenburgh, Michael, and Michael Van Valkenburgh Associates, 2, 7, 177, 207, 276

Vanderbilt, George, 3

The Variation of Animals and Plants under Domestication (Darwin, 1868), 15

Vasquez, Gilberto, 89–91, *90*, 95, 96

Vassar College, arboretum and botanical garden at, 4

Veltre, Thomas, 38

Venezuela, cracid hunting in, 96–97

vernal pools, 221, *222*

Walker, Pete, 2

wallabies, 138, 141

Wallace, Alfred, 77

Washington, George, 9

waterbuck, 119

Wattled Guan, 98

Wedge-tailed Eagle, 140, 141

West Vail Pass, hypar-nature bridging system for, 207–8, *209–13*

Western Ghats, India, tigers in, 57–59, *59*

Western Quoll, 142

wetlands: Boston Fens, 3; Brooklyn Bridge Park, New York City, 177, *178, 179*; East London Green Grid, 198; Houtan Park, Shanghai, 253, 255; at Orongo Station, New Zealand, 154, *158, 159, 161–63*; restored versus original, 76; Stewart International Airport Access Improvement Project, New York, 220–21, *222*

WHD. *See* wildlife habitat design

Whistling Kite, 140, 141

white cattle, alleged wildness of, *22, 22–23*

White Oak Plantation, 54

White-plumed Honey-eater, 138

whitewood *(Atalaya hemiglauca)*, 133

"Why Look at Animals?" (Berger, 1977), 6

wild dogs, 19, 55–57, *56*, 58, 59, 134, 140, 141, 147

"wild garden," Dumbarton Oaks, *viii, 8*

wildebeest, 51, 119

Wilderness Society, 9

"wilderness walk," Dumbarton Oaks, 7–9, *8*

wildflowers and domestic cats, 20

Wildlife Conservation Society, 53

wildlife corridors: climate change in cities and, 189–90, *193*, 193–94, 199; as ecological infrastructure, 231; hypar-nature bridging system, 7, 207–8, *209–13*; living fences, 93, *94*; Orange County Great Park, Irvine, California, 179–83, *180–82*, 224, 225–26; Stewart International Airport Access Improvement Project, New York, 220–21; translating ecological science into design applications, 232. *See also* fragmented landscapes

wildlife habitat design (WHD), 1–13; biodiversity issues, 7, 65–87 (*See also* biodiversity and ecosystem function); birds and indigenous people, 7, 89–106 (*See also* birds and indigenous people in neotropical forests); climate change (*See* climate change; climate change in cities); complexities of integrating functional ecologies into design, 4–6; concept of wild and, 6, 15–27 (*See also* concepts of wildness and wilderness); conservation, restoration, and preservation, 2–4; culture and nature, relationship between, 3; defined, 215; at Dumbarton Oaks, *viii*, 7–10, *8–10*, 12–13; ecology and design, interplay of, 7, 215–40 (*See also* ecology and design, interplay of); factors affecting successful design projects, 148–51; highway crossings, 7, 207–8, *209–13*; as infrastructure, 7, 241–71 (*See also* infrastructure for biodiversity protection, landscape as); interplay of ecology and landscape design in, 7, 215–40 (*See also* ecology and design, interplay of); in Ottoman landscapes, 6, 29–46 (*See also* Ottoman gardens and landscapes); political economy of, 6, 100–13; restoration ecology in urban areas, 7, 169–86 (*See also* restoration ecology in urban areas); scale affecting, 6–7, 47–64 (*See also* scale in conservation interventions); science and design, collaboration between, 1–4, 65; site studies, 7 (*See also* Alice Springs Desert Park [ASDP], Australia; Cambodia Wildlife Sanctuary [CWS]; Orongo Station, New Zealand; Pilanesberg National Park, South Africa; *other specific sites*)

The Wilds, 54

Williams, Raymond, 20

Wilson, Edward O., *6*, 243

Win-Win Ecology (Rosenzweig, 2003), 231

Dumbarton Oaks Colloquium
on the History of Landscape Architecture

PUBLISHED BY DUMBARTON OAKS RESEARCH LIBRARY AND COLLECTION, WASHINGTON, D.C.

The Dumbarton Oaks Colloquium on the History of Landscape Architecture series volumes are based on papers presented at scholarly meetings sponsored by the Garden and Landscape Studies program at Dumbarton Oaks. These meetings provide a forum for the presentation of advanced research on garden history and landscape architecture; they support a deepened understanding of landscape as a field of knowledge and as a practice carried out by landscape architects, landscape artists, and gardeners.

Further information on Garden and Landscape Studies publications can be found at www.doaks. org/publications.

1. *The Italian Garden*, edited by David R. Coffin

2. *The Picturesque Garden and Its Influence Outside the British Isles*, edited by Nikolaus Pevsner

3. *The French Formal Garden*, edited by Elisabeth B. MacDougall and F. Hamilton Hazlehurst

4. *The Islamic Garden*, edited by Elisabeth B. MacDougall and Richard Ettinghausen

5. *Fons sapientiae: Renaissance Garden Fountains*, edited by Elisabeth B. MacDougall

6. *John Claudius Loudon and the Early Nineteenth Century in Great Britain*, edited by Elisabeth B. MacDougall

7. *Ancient Roman Gardens*, edited by Elisabeth B. MacDougall and Wilhelmina F. Jashemski

8. *Beatrix Jones Farrand (1872–1959): Fifty Years of American Landscape Architecture*, edited by Diane Kostial McGuire and Lois Fern

9. *Medieval Gardens*, edited by Elisabeth B. MacDougall

10. *Ancient Roman Villa Gardens*, edited by Elisabeth B. MacDougall

11. *Prophet with Honor: The Career of Andrew Jackson Downing, 1815–1852*, edited by George B. Tatum and Elisabeth B. MacDougall

12. *The Dutch Garden in the Seventeenth Century*, edited by John Dixon Hunt

13. *Garden History: Issues, Approaches, Methods*, edited by John Dixon Hunt

14. *The Vernacular Garden*, edited by John Dixon Hunt and Joachim Wolschke-Bulmahn

15. *Regional Garden Design in the United States*, edited by Therese O'Malley and Marc Treib

16. *Mughal Gardens: Sources, Places, Representations, and Prospects*, edited by James L. Wescoat, Jr., and Joachim Wolschke-Bulmahn

17. *John Evelyn's "Elysium Britannicum" and European Gardening*, edited by Therese O'Malley and Joachim Wolschke-Bulmahn

18. *Nature and Ideology: Natural Garden Design in the Twentieth Century*, edited by Joachim Wolschke-Bulmahn

19. *Places of Commemoration: Search for Identity and Landscape Design*, edited by Joachim Wolschke-Bulmahn